Financial Regulation in the European Union

This collection offers a comparative overview of how financial regulations have evolved in various European countries since the introduction of the single European market in 1986. It includes a number of country studies which provide a narrative of the domestic financial regulatory structure at the beginning of the period, as well as the means by which the EU Directives have been introduced into domestic legislation and the impact on the financial structure of the economy.

In particular, studies highlight how the discretion allowed by the Directives has been used to meet domestic conditions and financial structure as well as how countries have modified that structure. Countries covered are France, Germany, Italy, Spain, Estonia, Hungary and Slovenia. The book also contains an overview of regulatory changes in the UK and Nordic countries, and of the more recent developments in international financial standards and their inclusion in the European framework. This comparative approach raises questions about whether past and more recent regulatory changes have in fact contributed to financial stability in the EU and/or to the efficiency of individual banks and national financial systems.

The crisis has demonstrated the drawbacks of formulating the regulatory framework on standards borrowed from the best industry practices of large developed countries, originally designed exclusively for large global banks, but now applied to all financial institutions.

Rainer Kattel is Program Head and Professor of Innovation Policy and Technology Governance at Tallinn University of Technology, Estonia.

Jan Kregel is a senior scholar at the Levy Economics Institute of Bard College, USA, and Director of its Monetary Policy and Financial Structure program.

Mario Tonveronachi is Professor of Financial Systems at the University of Siena, Italy.

Routledge Critical Studies in Finance and Stability

Edited by Jan Toporowski
School of Oriental and African Studies, University of London, UK

The 2007–2008 Banking Crash has induced a major and wide-ranging discussion on the subject of financial (in)stability and a need to revaluate theory and policy. The response of policymakers to the crisis has been to refocus fiscal and monetary policy on financial stabilisation and reconstruction. However, this has been done with only vague ideas of bank recapitalisation and 'Keynesian' reflation aroused by the exigencies of the crisis, rather than the application of any systematic theory or theories of financial instability.

Routledge Critical Studies in Finance and Stability covers a range of issues in the area of finance including instability, systemic failure, financial macroeconomics in the vein of Hyman P. Minsky, Ben Bernanke and Mark Gertler, central bank operations, financial regulation, developing countries and financial crises, new portfolio theory and new international monetary and financial architecture.

1. Banking Systems in the Crisis
The faces of liberal capitalism
Edited by Sue Konzelmann and Marc Fovargue-Davies

2. Post-Keynesian Views of the Crisis and its Remedies
Edited by Óscar Dejuán Asenjo, Eladio Febrero Paños and Jorge Uxo Gonzalez

3. The Rise and Fall of Money Manager Capitalism
Minsky's half-century from World War Two to the Great Recession
Eric Tymoigne and L. Randall Wray

4. Cycles, Growth and the Great Recession
Edited by Annalisa Cristini, Steven M. Fazzari, Edward Greenberg and Riccardo Leoni

5. Liquidity Preference and Monetary Economies
Fernando J. Cardim de Carvalho

6. Civil Society and the Reform of Finance
Taming capital, reclaiming virtue
Charles McDaniel, Jr.

7. Financial Regulation in the European Union
Edited by Rainer Kattel, Jan Kregel and Mario Tonveronachi

Financial Regulation in the European Union

Edited by Rainer Kattel, Jan Kregel and Mario Tonveronachi

Routledge
Taylor & Francis Group
LONDON AND NEW YORK

First published 2016
by Routledge
2 Park Square, Milton Park, Abingdon, Oxon OX14 4RN

and by Routledge
711 Third Avenue, New York, NY 10017

Routledge is an imprint of the Taylor & Francis Group, an informa business

British Library Cataloguing in Publication Data
A catalogue record for this book is available from the British Library

Library of Congress Cataloging in Publication Data
Financial regulation in the European Union / edited by Rainer Kattel, Jan Kregel and Mario Tonveronachi. -- First Edition.
Includes bibliographical references and index.
1. Financial services industry--State supervision--European Union countries.
2. Banks and banking--State supervision--European Union countries. 3. Monetary
policy--European Union countries. I. Kattel, Rainer, 1974- editor. II. Kregel, J. A., editor. III. Tonveronachi, Mario, editor.
HG186.A2F5726 2015
332.1094--dc23
2015016579

ISBN: 978-1-138-91404-9 (hbk)
ISBN: 978-1-315-69101-5 (ebk)

Typeset in Times New Roman
by GreenGate Publishing Services, Tonbridge, Kent

MIX
Paper from responsible sources
FSC® C013604

Printed and bound by CPI Group (UK) Ltd, Croydon, CR0 4YY

Contents

Figures

Tables

Contributors

Judit Badics, University of Pannonia

Christophe Blot, Observatoire français des conjonctures économiques, Sciences Po

Santiago Carbo-Valverde, Bangor Business School

Jérôme Creel, Observatoire français des conjonctures économiques, Sciences Po and ESCP Europe

Anne-Laure Delatte, Le Centre national de la recherche scientifique and Observatoire français des conjonctures économiques, Sciences Po

Daniel Detzer, Hochschule für Wirtschaft und Recht Berlin

Giampaolo Gabbi, University of Siena

Hansjörg Herr, Hochschule für Wirtschaft und Recht Berlin

Alfred Janc, Poznań University of Economics

Egert Juuse, Tallinn University of Technology

Rainer Kattel, Tallinn University of Technology

Jan Kregel, Levy Economics Institute of Bard College and Tallinn University of Technology

Fabien Labondance, Observatoire français des conjonctures économiques, Sciences Po

Sandrine Levasseur, Observatoire français des conjonctures économiques, Sciences Po

Paweł Marszałek, Poznań University of Economics

Massimo Matthias, University of Siena

Jože Mencinger, EIPF and University of Ljubljana

Károly Miklós Kiss, University of Pannonia

Elisabetta Montanaro, University of Siena and Tallinn University of Technology

Francisco Rodriguez-Fernandez, University of Granada

Zsolt Stenger, University of Pannonia

Szabolcs Szikszai, University of Pannonia

Mario Tonveronachi, University of Siena and Tallinn University of Technology

Pietro Vozzella, University of Siena

1 Introduction[1]

Jan Kregel, Mario Tonveronachi and Rainer Kattel

1 The evolution of the general regulatory framework in the European Union

The intention of the 1986 Single European Act was to provide renewed stimulus to the process of European integration initiated in the 1957 Treaty of Rome creating the European Economic Community or European 'common market'. By the early 1970s, the expansion in intra-EEC trade driven by the erection of a common external tariff and elimination of internal tariff barriers had slowed. It became clear that if economic integration were to progress beyond the limits set by the simple application of a common external tariff, more radical steps would have to be taken to implement full integration of internal markets. Although there were diverse proposals and expert commission reports on how this fuller financial integration would be achieved through the creation of unified money and financial markets, the decision was eventually taken to proceed via the creation of a common European currency. This path had several clear implications for the institutional structure of the EU. In particular, it required a single issuing authority for the common currency, the euro, which took the form of a European Central Bank (ECB), independent of the control of the government of any member state, but without a Federal EU governance structure.

Following the example of the post-war Bank Deutscher Länder (itself modelled on the United States Federal Reserve's system of geographically dispersed 'District' banks), the European System of Central Banks was supported by a similar system comprised of the European Central Bank supported by the existing national central banks who became the operative agents of monetary policy determined by the central institution. Following the German example, and the dominant economic theory of the period, the ECB was given by statute a single objective, price stability, that was to be implemented by a single monetary policy effectuated through a uniform interest rate. For a common interest rate policy to be effective in implementing the policy objective, and have similar impact on the member states adopting the common currency, all member states would have to have similar financial performance and similar financial architecture to ensure the efficient transmission of the single monetary policy actions implemented by the central bank into national financial conditions.[2]

In order to ensure the required uniformity in economic performance a number of conditions of entry into the single currency were imposed in the form of a maximum rate of inflation, similarity of interest rates, compliance with the existing exchange rate mechanism (ERM), a maximum fiscal and debt position and a sustainable current account balance of payments. Because monetary policy is primarily transmitted through the impact of interest rates on the performance of the lending behaviour of the private financial system, the decision to adopt a single currency also meant the creation of a common organizational structure for the financial systems of the member states. Indeed, the divergences in the institutional financial structure and monetary policy instruments and operating procedures used in the national banks of the component member states were as large, and in some cases even larger, than the differences in inflation performance or government fiscal policy stance. Most governments of the initial member states had made extensive use of direct controls over lending or interest rates, active management of exchange rates and direct ownership of domestic financial institutions, to implement monetary policy in the 1950s and 1960s in support of post-war recovery programs. Opening such diverse, managed domestic financial systems to a uniform, open European financial market made untenable the existing apparatus of controls and subsidies. In particular, the widespread use of directed and concessionary interest rates became increasingly difficult in the face of market determination of interest rates in other countries and their defence required both capital controls, which were in contrast with the objective of a single financial market, and exchange rate management, which was in contrast with the move to a single currency unit within a unified European financial market.

As a result, after the decision to implement monetary integration via limitations on exchange rate volatility via the 'snake' procedures instituted after the breakdown of the Bretton Woods System in the early 1970s and the more formal Exchange Rate Mechanism of the European Monetary System as part of the move to Economic and Monetary Union at the end of the 1970s, the European Commission initiated a series of measures starting in the 1980s to widen the scope of the single market to include measures to ensure the necessary uniformity in the structure of financial markets to ensure full integration of the markets in financial services. In particular, the controls on cross-border investments that had been a major part of domestic policies of directed lending, interest rate limits and exchange rate management were eliminated. With the decision to move toward open financial borders, the adoption of common rules and homogeneous supervisory practices became an integral part of the objective of integration of the European internal markets.

While this process of convergence of financial structure was implicit in the movement to the integration into a single market via a common currency, it also took place within a global framework leading toward greater deregulation of financial institutions and the liberalization of financial markets in the major financial centres of the developed world that commenced after the US suspended the Bretton Woods gold parity of the dollar in 1971. This approach implied an increasing emphasis on the role of market forces in the global distribution of financial assets and the regulation of financial institutions. Increased market competition was seen as a more effective means than government controls to improve efficiency, the allocation of financial resources, and the freedom of cross-border operations of financial institutions. These measures were presumed to be a prerequisite for support of long-term economic growth, since markets would be more efficient in providing the innovation of financial practices, products and institutions in support of financial and economic stability. Thus, relaxation of the constraints on international financial flows and the activities of international financial service providers accompanied the reduction of controls on capital flows and institutions within the European Community. The enduring regulatory dispute between strict application of prudential rules versus discretionary interpretation of financial regulations by national supervisors was won by the latter and the new common European regulatory structure was influenced by and largely reflected this approach to place greater reliance on market self-discipline and what came to be known as 'light touch' regulation.

Given the particular requirements of the European integration process, the process of the creation of a common financial market as reflected in the details of its legal agenda became more far reaching than the similar movement on the international level. The single European passport for financial institutions incorporated in, and regulated by, the home regulatory authority provides one example. The extension of the Basel I regulations to all banks, rather than only to those operating at the international level, as was the clear intention of the first Basel Accord, is another.

However, given the preservation of national regulatory jurisprudence and supervisory jurisdictions, based on diverse national legal codes and practices, substantial discretion was left to individual member countries in the practical implementation of the common EU rules and principles. As a result, the implementation of the common European Union financial marketplace was effectuated via the issuance of European Directives that, in difference from EU Regulations, are not introduced directly into member country jurisprudence, but have to be adapted and adopted with the agreement of national legislative bodies. The result was a substantial amount of national differentiation in financial market regulation.

Another important source of national differentiation within the introduction of common principles is the use of subsidiarity and proportionality in the national application of EU legislation. In practice, this means that the minimum degree, rather than the maximum, of harmonization would be the standard achieved in national legislation. In addition, the failure to introduce a common EU regulatory agency, which was implicit in the Maastricht Treaty, meant that national authorities retained full discretionary powers in the interpretation and application of EU Directives once formally adopted and incorporated in national legislation.

2 The structure of the country studies

Chapters 2–9 of the book present eight country studies on the implementation of the European Directives on banking and finance in the period from the introduction of the Single European Act to the 2007/2008 global financial crisis and the additional national measures that have been taken in response to the crisis.[3] Each of the country studies provides a narrative of the domestic financial regulatory structure at the beginning of the period, defined as the date of the Single European Act, as well the means by which the EU Directives have been introduced into domestic legislation and the impact on the financial structure of the economy. In particular, the studies highlight how the Directives have been modified to meet then-existing domestic conditions and financial structure as incorporated into national legislation, as well as how they have modified that structure.[4]

The topics of regulatory and supervisory activity chosen for presentation by the country studies may be divided into three notional categories: those that were fully incorporated into EU regulation; those lightly or partially regulated; and those left outside the scope of formal regulation. As stated, the recent trend appears to be towards the elevation of the elements of the latter two categories to the higher category, increasing harmonization and reducing the space for national diversity.

The liberalization of cross-border capital movements and the single European passport for banks and providers of financial services were the first relevant measures in laying the foundation for the implementation of a single financial market. In general, the implementation of capital requirements was driven by the Basel Committee on Bank Supervision process of formulating uniform global standards of good practice and corresponded to those recommendations. Common principles on consolidation in reporting and consolidated supervision were necessary appendixes to what essentially remained cross-border activities rather than EU-wide establishment and operation of financial institutions through branches or subsidiaries. Given this framework, it was necessary to avoid unfair competition due to divergent national implementation by imbedding the various regulations in the various versions of the Basel Accords and in the specific legislation that national governments applied to different market institutions via the Markets in Financial Instruments Directive. The introduction of more binding EU rules on large exposures introduced more precision into the necessarily vague Basel principles and reduced the tendency toward discretionary application.

These are the major areas in which the EU Directives concentrated attention and in which the country studies show the largest degree of regulatory convergence, although this has not necessarily been accompanied by convergence in supervisory practice. The continued presence of national regulatory and supervisory agencies, which exercised the option of incorporating national exception into national legislation and then discretion in the interpretation of these principles, meant that strong initial differences have made the de facto convergence much more limited than is exhibited by the changes in national legislation and financial structure.

In addition, the country studies cover a second range of issues in which greater national discretion allowed for increased divergence in those lightly or partially regulated financial operations, including deposit guarantee schemes, recovery and resolution procedures and accounting standards. Although the creation of deposit guarantee schemes and participation became compulsory for all banks, the differences for the funding and coverage of the various national systems have until recently remained substantially unchanged. The conditions covering bank recovery and resolution were mainly directed at specifying the responsible authority for cross-border crises, rather than imposing homogeneous procedures on the liquidation or recapitalization of insolvent institutions.

The homogenization of accounting standards towards IFRS international standards was only compulsory for listed or large banks; moreover, the determination of this standard is outside the direct control of the EU and thus leaves banks and national authorities with a wide set of options and discretion. This issue is of crucial importance in interpreting the actual application of regulations since accounting practices are central to a system of core bank regulation that relies on the balance sheet calculation of regulatory capital as a risk-weighted minimum. This second category of measures also includes topics that have taken on additional relevance due to their aleatory application and implementation in the evolution of the recent financial crisis.

The third category of regulatory issues includes topics such as rules on liquidity, bank resolution, competition policy, usury and taxes. The provision of liquidity was a topic of the Basel Core Principles that was left to the implementation of local supervisory authorities. It was only subsequently included in the second pillar of Basel II on the basis of discretionary interpretation of principles more than strict rules and, in any case, only implemented in Europe since 2007. Before the crisis, few countries had in place specific legislation for dealing with bank crises, especially dealing with the failure of large banks. There is no specific competition policy for the banking sector for the EU, leaving large variations in the degree of bank concentration. Usury laws are present in only a few European countries. Finally, tax treatments are widely different across European member countries, although being crucial under several profiles, as for the provisioning policy of impaired assets.

The regulation process promoted by the Single European Act has undoubtedly produced a convergence on rules, supervisory practices and, above all, on institutional and structural features for the countries analysed in the previous chapters. As might have been expected, the changes were more marked for the formerly centrally planned economies. Since the Directives introduced were in large part consonant with a convergence towards international standards in all developed financial systems, the general framework, if not specific national features, would have been followed in many cases even in absence of the push towards unification of the financial systems in EU member states. However, the level playing field created by the introduction of the system of a single European passport has produced a greater harmonization than might have been reached otherwise, despite the limited degree of convergence that has resulted by the acceptance of a minimum level of harmonization and the discrepancy between formal rules and supervisory practices.

The recent global financial and European Sovereign debt crisis has made evident the relevant limits inherent in the application of the three categories of regulations presented above. Remedies have been adopted to expand and augment the regulations surveyed in the first category via Basel II.5 and then with Basel III, which was designed to remedy some deficiencies of the previous versions, notably incorporating the formal treatment of liquidity.

The crisis has also led support for tighter interpretation and application of existing regulation, as well as widening its application to encompass a higher level of harmonization. The result is a reversal of the initial approach and an increased reliance on Regulations rather than on Directives, and the creation of the European Supervisory Authorities (ESAs), whose technical standards are statutorily directed at producing a single rulebook and single supervisory handbook for banks, insurance companies and markets.[5] Similarly to the Dodd-Frank Act in the US, the ESAs are mandated to draft hundreds of technical standards to fully implement the new legislation. A Directive on minimum harmonization at the EU level of bank recovery and resolution has recently been finalized. The need for maximum harmonization for countries inside the currency union has led to the Banking Union with its two pillars, the Single Supervisory Mechanism and the Single Resolution Mechanism.[6]

The crisis has thus produced a shift of some of those items that were previously subject to weak or national discretion in coverage into the group of items to be covered by obligatory EU harmonization.

To better understand the regulatory dynamics, Chapter 10 offer a narrative on how, before the recent crisis, the interplay between financial innovations, bank crises and regulatory reforms, significantly influenced the British institutional framework, and became a reference model for light-touch regulation and supervision. Its role on weakening financial resilience only became apparent in the evolution of the recent crisis. As a result, the British regulatory reaction to the recent crisis has been more marked than in Continental Europe, partly due to being host to a leading international financial centre.

Chapter 11 shows how the prompt and efficient way in which the Nordic countries managed their early 1990s systemic crises continues to offer important indications of the appropriate response measures to deal with managing bank recovery and resolution after major insolvency in the financial system.

Finally, Chapter 12 outlines the efforts by the G20, the Financial Stability Board and international standard setters to reach a new regulatory balance for the banking industry, where a reaffirmation of the benefits of the internationalization of finance is mitigated by a recognition of particular national or regional interests. This is also due to the fact that the post-crisis deepening and widening of the regulatory and supervisory scope could not avoid allowing a much larger role for idiosyncratic features of national financial structures. As a consequence, the concept of the regulatory level playing field is *de facto* evolving, especially for wholesale banking, from being based on rules to the discretionary recognition of equivalent results. This evolution has been felt unevenly in the European Union, where the original concept of the level playing field and creation of a common financial market has generated a search for greater uniformity of rules and supervisory practices inside the newly created Banking Union, while the other EU countries seem reluctant to surrender national discretions in exchange for as yet unproven benefits of increased harmonization.

3 Open problems and perspectives

The international reaction to the crises of the last decades, not just to the most recent, has fallen short of measures to deal with the structural roots of the increasingly virulent nature of systemic collapse. A small number of large international or multinational intermediaries remain the fragile backbone benefiting from the misery of the international monetary (dis)order. At the international, regional and domestic level, the way in which the crisis has been managed has produced larger banks and more concentrated banking systems, while systemic interconnections have not been abated. The trend towards larger cross-border banks will be reinforced in Europe by reforms aimed at increasing harmonization in rules and supervisory practices, particularly inside the euro area.

Since the start of the reform process, the international mandate has been to mend the weaknesses of the previous regulatory and supervisory system without limiting the freedom of private operators to innovate. The reality has been even more limited because systemic threats have not been dealt with by means of structural measures aimed at reinforcing international and national financial systems' provision of stable financial support for the economy. Where structural interventions have been introduced for banks, as for example in the USA, the UK, France and Germany, their scope is so restricted to raise serious doubts on their efficacy.[7]

The result is that prudential regulation and supervision remain the main pillar for ex ante resilience. The complacency of the authorities on adopted reforms might fall short of meeting the desired objective because the improvements that have been introduced, although substantial, come on top of a previous distressingly low standard. However, the authorities appear conscious that, having excluded a profound reconfiguration of the financial system, the prudential approach will not impede 'It' from happening again. Their regulatory activity has therefore focused on the ex post action to resolve banking crises, especially cross-border ones, aimed at limiting systemic disruptions and, above all, safeguarding public finances. To a certain extent, governments, still burdened by the costs of the last crisis, are asking that in the next one private investors repay the favours that they have currently received.

The European Union is following this general approach. However, as the country studies included in the next chapters show, the EU's 'unconventional' architecture and composition poses and exposes further problems.

The international standards incorporated into EU regulations were based on 'best industry' practices applied in developed countries and were meant to apply to large banks operating on the global level. Thus, in the EU these standards are applied to all financial institutions irrespective of size and national level of economic and financial development. In addition, the complexity of supervisory tasks surpasses the ability and resources of even large, high-income countries. The narratives for Estonia and Slovenia show different aspects of the unnecessary costs linked to the common regulation, as is also the case for smaller local banks in other countries of the EU. If the regulation and supervision of large and small banks requires a differential regulatory and supervisory regime, as recognized by efforts initiated in the USA, Europe presents the further problem since inherent national differences in financial structure are being treated homogeneously in the absence of automatic fiscal compensations implemented by a federal agency.

The rejection of effective structural measures in favour of prudential regulation, based on market-based risk hedging, has been the result of the deregulation of financial systems and the isolation of financial policy from government fiscal policies driven by the presumed importance of central bank independence in implementing monetary policy with the sole objective of managing inflation. This has deprived single countries of tools capable of managing specific problems, particularly serious for economies undergoing structural adjustments in their political and economic systems. Especially for the members of the Eurozone, the disappearance of these degrees of freedom has come on top of losing control of monetary and fiscal policy to the ECB and the recent reforms of the Stability and Growth pact. The current push for EU-peripheral countries to undertake more extensive structural changes within the given fiscal limits make them more cumbersome. With significant structural differences still characterizing the EU economies, the benefits of a higher level of financial harmonization and centralization appears questionable, given that the main power of economic intervention to deal with specific problems remains at national level.

For different reasons, and with different influence, resistance by some EU countries against the push toward increased centralization and harmonization is mounting. If the recent crisis has shown the necessity for higher levels of harmonization meant as higher standards, it has also shown the limits of the one-rule-fits-all paradigm in a Union that remains an association of sovereign countries, each one with its idiosyncratic legal codes, fiscal powers and national priorities. In the European Union, sectorial interests often become national interests to be met with compromises in the EU legislation. Specific features of the French and German bank governance had to be included in the Regulation adopting Basel III, weakening the quality of the capital base and thus causing a first negative reaction by the Basel Committee. Different capabilities to accept higher capital requirements in different EU countries induced the adoption of a minimum level lower than advocated by some country regulatory authorities, but due to the pressing request from the UK the regulation departed from the Basel standard adding a further discretionary capital buffer.

In addition, the rethinking on the role of regulation and the appropriate EU regulatory system imposed by the recent crisis has not followed a common path. For instance, the UK, France and Germany have introduced different legislation on structural measures (ring fencing) well in advance and independently from the EU. When the EU will finally legislate on the matter it will have to insert criteria of equivalence for the recognition of different schemes inside what is supposed to be a single financial market. In some areas the UK is returning to a more interpretative and judgemental approach to supervision. In such conditions it will be difficult for the European Banking Authority to meet its goal of enforcing a truly single rulebook and supervisory handbook across the euro area.

The maximum harmonization to be reached inside the area covered by the Banking Union area could also discourage some non-euro countries from joining the scheme, adding a further element to the increased opposition to more uniform regulations leading to losses of national sovereignty. The potential advantages coming from the single resolution authority and fund may be lost if doubts exist that it can effectively shield taxpayers of member states, while single supervision reduces the domestic freedom of action. Despite the fact that the EU treaties oblige all countries, except the UK and Denmark, to swiftly adopt convergence policies for joining the euro, the recent imposition of the requirement to join the Banking Union seems to have produced a hard core of countries that have no intention to comply with them. The way in which the recent crisis has been managed inside the euro area has thus raised additional doubts on the net benefits coming from adopting the common currency.

This makes it even more compelling to proceed with a revision of the approach to EU financial regulation, for instance implementing harmonization across homogeneous financial actors, rather than across national borders, allowing more recognition of relevant differences in national financial structures and domestic policy requirements. Beyond specific regulatory revisions, a more general overhaul of the architecture and practices of the euro construction is necessary to dispel doubts on the efficacy of its monetary, fiscal and regulatory safety nets.

Notes

1 The research leading to these results has received funding from the European Union Seventh Framework Programme (FP7/2007–2013) under grant agreement No 266800.
2 Article B of the Maastricht Treaty makes it clear that among the goals of the newly rebranded European Union there is 'the establishment of economic and monetary union, ultimately including a single currency' for all member countries. The only possible exceptions are the indefinite opt-out permitted to UK and Denmark.
3 The countries are Estonia, France, Germany, Hungary, Italy, Poland, Slovenia and Spain.
4 To aid in cross-country comparison, a grid presenting the legislation for each country for the major Directives is also available at www.dropbox.com/s/lsi3k7823nirzd2/D4.03%20grids%20new%201.04.214.xlsx.
5 However, the Regulations on the European Supervisory Authorities temper the push towards maximum harmonization by mandating the Authorities to allow for national specificities.
6 Membership of the Banking Union is compulsory for countries of the euro area and it is open to voluntary adhesion from the other EU countries. The Single Resolution Mechanism will have to follow the general framework dictated by the Bank Recovery and Resolution Directive that fixes the minimum harmonization for all EU countries.
7 In any case, it is not easy to configure radical interventions without a concomitant and profound revision of the international monetary order.

2 Financial regulation in France

Christophe Blot, Jérôme Creel, Anne-Laure Delatte, Fabien Labondance and Sandrine Levasseur

1 Introduction

The objective of this contribution is to present the structural and regulatory evolutions and reforms of the French banking and financial system. Since the 1980s, structures have changed and reforms have been manifold, influenced not only by the European integration process but also by the historical worldwide context of deregulation and, more recently, by the crisis (see e.g. Blot et al., 2012, for an extensive presentation).

From the 1980s onward, three main periods can be distinguished in terms of regulations. First, the Banking Act of 1984 paved the way for a substantial regulatory overhaul of the French banking system. The Banking Act aimed at 'unifying, renovating and streamlining the laws and regulations governing the banking industry, promoting competition within the banking sector and making banking a more widespread activity'. Credit controls were eliminated, and all financial institutions were subject to the same regulatory and supervisory authorities (Commission Bancaire, Comité de Réglementation Bancaire and Comité des Établissements de Crédit). The banking act entailed the adoption of the model of universal banking in France. A gradual removal of exchange controls started in 1985. This national regulation anticipated the implementation of the Single European Act (SEA) in 1986. The SEA, and more broadly all the European legislations since that, has constituted the second wave of legislation that frames the European banking and financial structures until the crisis. Finally, the recent crisis forced the regulators to modify the regulation since 2008. In this respect the project of a banking union emerged as a consequence of both European integration and the crisis. On this subject, the structure of the French banking system, based on universal and powerful banks reluctant to change their model, is crucial (see for example Gaffard and Pollin, 2013).

In the following, we present these three waves of regulation. Section 2 presents the situation during the 1980s. Section 3 shows how European integration influenced French regulation. Section 4 details the impact of the crisis on banking and financial regulation. In section 5, we present the French regulatory framework and we finally conclude.

2 Historical, political economic and international background

2.1 Changes in the French banking and financial system up to the 1980s

The French banking regulations prompted by the crisis of the 1930s were not radical. The original legislation that set up the structure of the banking network in 1885 with the establishment of savings banks was further strengthened in 1941 with the adoption of the first banking law. In 1945, the banks were separated into three categories (i.e. deposit banks, investment banks and medium and long-term lending banks) with each category being specialized into specific activities. In the post-war period, the organization of the banking system was driven by the need to finance reconstruction. Alongside the nationalization process of banks, the French authorities multiplied the incentives for non-financial agents (households in particular) to increase their savings and tried to steer these, through the specialization and supervision of financial intermediaries, towards certain areas – e.g. housing and the productive investment of resident companies. In addition, from the 1970s, regulated interest rates and monetary controls were overseen by government supervisors. The extent of financial regulation by the State until the 1980s in France is interesting with respect to early-bird legislation about financial liberalization. The free movement of capital was included in Law no 66-1008 (known as Debré law) of 28 December 1966. It stated that 'financial relations with foreign countries were free in due respect of international commitments signed by France'. Nevertheless, article 3 authorized 'temporary exceptions' to free movements of capital. 'Temporary' measures, like exchange controls, continued until 1989!

To summarize, at the very beginning of the 1980s, the French financial system was relatively closed, highly regulated and compartmentalized. The State played a significant role in the organization and functioning of the system.

In the early 1980s, two phenomena posed a challenge to the French financial and banking system. First, the need for international openness pushed the French authorities to make fundamental changes to the structure of the country's financial system. In the 1970s, global interest rates rose more than the French rates, meaning that exchange controls became increasingly necessary to maintain low interest rates in France. This intensified the contradiction between the tighter controls needed to maintain the financial system and the openness required by European and global economic integration. Second, the French banking system was facing a serious crisis in this period. This crisis was due to international developments (with the US disinflation policy leading to higher real interest rates, along with the international debt crisis of developing countries and the first Mexican crisis) and to the inconsistent structure and poor profitability of the banking system. The model of universal banking (recommended by the Mayoux report in 1979) had not yet been fully incorporated into French banking practice, and remained so until the Banking Act of 1984; deregulation then finally allowed the French banking and financial sectors to undergo a major transformation.

2.2 The 1980s: a period of banking reform and of profound changes in the French financial system

The French financial system went through a profound transformation in the 1980s, following a wave of deregulation that, having originated in the United States in the mid-1970s, modified both its structure and its operating conditions. Two types of deregulation can be distinguished: the organization of the system ('structural deregulation') and the way they operated ('conduct deregulation').

2.2.1 Legal and regulatory changes introduced by the left-wing government

The nationalizations of 1982 represented the first step in the State's effort to radically overhaul the French banking system in order to deal with financial globalization. These nationalizations as part of a more sweeping reform by the Socialist government of the financial and banking systems, were intended (i) to finance priority investments, (ii) to improve the control of credit and (iii) to reduce the cost of bank loans. The French State thus nationalized 36 deposit banks and two investment banks (or *compagnies financières*). This gave the State control of virtually the entire banking sector, meaning that it could now steer investment and reform the financial system.

In seeming contrast with the process of nationalization, the cornerstone of the French financial (de)regulation since 1980 has undoubtedly been the Banking Act of 1984, relative to the activity and control of the credit organizations, which has to be linked to the liberalization context of the international financial system. The reforms introduced by Finance Minister Pierre Bérégovoy starting in 1984 aimed at establishing a unified monetary and financial market where interest rates were set freely (subject to the intervention of the Banque de France). This Banking Act, proposed by the government of Pierre Mauroy (PS), aimed at strengthening competition and improving efficiency of the entire banking system. It put a halt to the bank specialization by creating the 'universal bank': every organization that received an agreement could carry out every type of operation peculiar to credit organizations and could choose its customers without restrictions. These 'credit organizations' encompassed the AFB banks such as BNP-Paribas or Société Générale, the 'mutualist' or cooperative banks (Crédit Agricole), the savings banks, the local credit banks, the financial societies (CETELEM, COFINOGA) and the specialized financial institutions. The Banking Act also created three collegial authorities, whose functioning is tightly linked to the functioning of Bank of France, to provide control for the banking sector's activities: the Banking Regulation Committee (CRB), the Credit Organisations Committee (CEC) and the Banking Commission (CB). The CB had to control whether the credit organizations respected the several enforceable legislative and regulatory clauses and to punish them if necessary. Last, the Banking Act introduced a liquidity and solvability constraint for the credit organizations. The latter had to abide by accounting norms and by a balanced financial structure in order to guarantee their liquidity and solvability, under the supervision of the CRB. This liberalization had some quick effects on the securitization movement through which France lived from 1986 to 1990. This market-oriented policy was pursued through several measures like the lifting of the credit framework in 1987, the lifting of control on assets movements or the dismantling of the exchange control in 1989.

Additional important changes in the financial and banking landscape were as follows. In 1983, the creation of the monthly settlement market unified the stock exchange trading while the creation of a second market (*second marché*) gave smaller companies, mainly family firms, access to the stock market. In 1985, certificates of deposits were created, i.e. debt securities primarily intended for professional investors as very short-term investments (between one day and one year), and the money market was opened to non-banks. The MATIF futures market was created to allow trading in futures instruments, and then the MONEP market for (financial) options.

To summarize, the Banking Act of 1984 has had a long-lasting influence on the French banking and financial system. Also noticeable is its seniority as regards many European directives. Such was the case in a wide array of legislative reforms that the Banking Act generated (see Blot et al., 2013, for details): liberalization of capital movements (EU directive in 1988), cross-border competition and definition of permitted activities (EU directive in 1989 and 1993), capital requirements (EU directive in 1989), definition of investment services (EU directive in 1993), deposit guarantee (EU directive in 1994), and crisis management schemes (EU directive in 2001).

2.2.2 The partial reversal of nationalizations

The process of nationalization was partially reversed in 1986, with the arrival of a right-wing government. Société Générale, Compagnie Paribas, Compagnie Suez and Crédit commercial de France were privatized. However, despite these privatizations, the French State retained control of nearly 69 per cent of the commercial banks and 42 per cent of the banking sector in 1988. After the return to power of a left-wing government in 1988, the process of privatization was pursued (partial opening of the capital of Crédit local de France in 1991) due to the pressures of European Union's competition policy and to the needs of finding fiscal revenues (the proceeds from privatization helped reducing immediately public debt). In addition, the left-wing government was precocious in foreseeing how to take advantage of the benefits of the market economy, confirming their determination to make Paris an important financial centre. However, the Socialists' willingness to privatize must be nuanced by the fact that most of these operations were partial: the State continued to be the major shareholder of the formerly fully State-owned banks.

2.2.3 Concentration in the French banking sector

To generate productivity gains, to streamline activities and, ultimately, to be able to compete internationally, French banks had to intensify their process of concentration at the end of the 1980s, giving rise to a sector dominated by a handful of institutions. Restructuring gained momentum in the mutual and cooperative networks (e.g. Crédit Agricole) but also among financial firms, as 104 establishments disappeared between 1991 and 1992. Restructuring was accompanied by the grouping of a large portion of banks into several powerful credit institutions: at the start of 1992, out of the 462 licensed banks, 106 belonged to one of the seven major non-mutualist groups (i.e. Banque Nationale de Paris (BNP), Crédit Lyonnais, Société Générale, Compagnie de Paribas, Compagnie de Suez, Compagnie Financière de CIC et de l'Union Européenne, Crédit Commercial de France). Suez and Paribas were very important players in the field of mergers and acquisitions (M&A), acting as strong private financial centres. Restructuring favoured the concentration of overall activity of credit institutions, including specific activities like deposits and loans.

2.2.4 The 'bancassurance'

The growing interlinkages between banking and insurance activities constitute another important development of the French financial sector. *Bancassurance*, a banking diversification strategy that consists of a credit institution engaging in insurance activities, has developed in France since the early 1980s either through the simple distribution of insurance products or through a more aggressive approach involving the acquisition or creation of insurance subsidiaries. In the first case, the bank simply provides its network with insurance services. In the second case, the bank conducts a more autonomous but riskier policy by engaging in activities that are not traditionally its own province, such as life insurance and capitalization, or property and casualty insurance. By the late 1980s, credit institutions had a 40 per cent share of the market for insurance products, up from virtually zero at the beginning of the decade. Numerous mergers also took place between banks and insurance companies (Crédit Agricole and Prédica, Société Générale and Sogécap, etc.). These were different, however, from cross-shareholdings between banks and insurance companies (e.g. direct holdings between BNP and UAP, or between CIC and GAN).

2.2.5 The internationalization of the French financial system

Gradually, the French financial system opened up internationally. In 1989, the Commission des Operations de Bourse (COB – France's stock exchange watchdog) saw its power and independence strengthened, which enhanced its credibility and therefore the attractiveness of Paris to international investors.

The dismantling of foreign exchange controls took place between 1985 and 1989, allowing the full integration of the French financial market into the world market.

Regulations governing the entry of foreign banks onto the domestic financial markets were considerably relaxed (lifting controls on capital movements in 1989). However, candidates for entry were required to have a minimum amount of capital and a thorough investigation had to be conducted in advance by the host country. Concerning other key variables for the banking and financial markets, the regulatory changes in the 1980s (described above) led to profound transformations in the competitive conditions on the banking and financial markets. Opening of the domestic markets to foreign banks, of the money markets to non-banks and of the financial markets to all non-financial agents increased the number of participants in these markets. To quote a few: Barclays created its life insurance subsidiary in France in 1992; the Crédit Suisse Group bought the French operations of the Hottinguer bank in 1997; and Deutsche Bank, which has operated on French territory since 1977, began its investment activities in Paris in 1992. In 1996, investments by foreign banks in France expressed in terms of flows represented 14.9 per cent of all foreign direct investment in the country. In terms of stocks, their assets represented 9.2 per cent of FDI in France, according to data from 1995.

2.2.6 The emergence of Paris as a financial centre

The structural changes in the French banking and financial landscape had a relatively rapid impact on the trend towards securitization and on capital inflow into France. Driven by the wave of privatizations, the stock market rose sharply between 1986 and 1987. The crash of 1987 was quickly followed by a recovery, and prices hit record highs in 1989, as the CAC 40 exceeded 2000 points for the first time in its history. The issue of new securities also picked up pace, in particular equities Trading volumes increased more rapidly than prices and new issues, at around 30 per cent per year on average, reflecting the emergence of a market-based financial management. The MONEP options market alone had transactions involving 9 million contracts in 1995, and the number of individual holders of securities also rose massively, to about 14 million in the early 1990s.

2.2.7 The consequences of the new system of financing

Banking disintermediation took place in the 1980s and the role of the market was growing. Companies were financing themselves increasingly through financial instruments and less and less through intermediated bank loans. However, in a context of low investment and high profits (the share of profits in value added increased from 22 per cent in the early 1980s to over 30 per cent in the early 1990s), the French corporates favoured business self-financing, which rose sharply during the 1980s (from 59 per cent in 1982 to 92 per cent in 1987; Hautcoeur, 1999).

The strengthening of equity capital through equity issues (which enabled companies to shed significant debt) was a new assessment of firms' stability and investment capacity. French companies were in effect able to increase their equity capital by ten percentage points, from 26 per cent in 1987 to 37 per cent in 1995 (Sauve and Sheuer, 1999).

The changes in the system of corporate financing described above were accompanied by a more contrasting situation for SMEs, which suffered from the end of the subsidized loans and government guarantees that protected them from rising interest rates on loans. The banking system itself suffered from the direct recourse by corporations to the money and bond markets, with some large industrial groups taking advantage of the absence of regulations to engage in sophisticated financial transactions in order to deal with considerable losses. The development of SICAVs (Sociétés d'Investissement à Capital Variable, similar to US mutual funds) reduced the free resources of financial institutions (deposits in banks, deposits in savings banks), which meant an increase in the cost of resources. The banks were therefore obliged to convert partially from the lending business to financial services, an obligation that was even more difficult to handle in a situation marked by both the debt crisis of the developing countries, in which French banks were heavily involved, and stiffer competition from the older specialized networks created by the State and previously intended to segment the market (Crédit Agricole, La Poste, savings banks), but whose privileges were still maintained. For example, La Poste, which retained exclusive rights on livret d'épargne (i.e. savings accounts very popular among French households), had broadly diversified its financial activities, including *bancassurance*, thereby competing directly with the business of banks. These financial difficulties led French banks to take risks in activities in which they had insufficient experience (e.g. real estate) during periods of speculation (including the late 1980s), leading some into bankruptcy or requiring State bail-outs (e.g. Crédit Lyonnais).

The long-term consequences of this new system of financing are more difficult to determine. On the one hand, the operating costs of the financial system per se fell sharply, the allocation of capital was facilitated and businesses were no longer constrained in their quantitative funding requirements, since integration with the international capital markets now enabled them to seek outside funding. On the other hand, economic fluctuations originating abroad were no longer cushioned in the way they had been, which was reflected in particular in the greater intensity of financial and economic crises. The French financial system thus became more vulnerable to the changing international environment, to the multiplicity of international investors and to interactions with subsidiaries in order to provide itself self-financing. Cross-shareholdings among large corporations and the subsistence of family-style capitalism did not give the system a strong enough foundation to deal with this vulnerability.

3 The impact of European integration on the French financial system

In this section we briefly review the impact of European integration on the French financial system, with respect to the financialization of the French economy, the organization of banking and financial services, the development of financial markets and the payment system. Needless to say, France has gone through an extended process of globalization and has conformed to the process of European integration. The French financial system is no exception to these trends, though the State has long tried to limit the incidence of globalization on the nature of French capitalism.

3.1 The structural crisis of the 1990s

The 1990s were marked by the continuing internationalization of financial markets and actors. In concrete terms, that meant (i) an acceleration in the cross-border activities of financial institutions, (ii) many financial innovations like complex financial instruments that cannot be classified in a specific financial sector (were they banks, investing societies or insurance societies?) and (iii) the setup of financial conglomerates. These evolutions have led to reflections on the needs for new regulations which would tackle prudential rules and the organization of supervisory authorities. The 1996 Act about the 'modernisation of the financial activities' has translated in French law 1993's European directive relative to the investment services in real estate. These investment services were able to be proposed by some new providers which are the 'investment firms'. The latter are now able to establish a subsidiary in every European country they want to and to supply services from a distance (what is called 'free service'). The 1996 Act about investment services has created a European financial go-between status. The 1999 Act relative to savings and financial security has instituted a guarantee fund for banks. It has been the first blanket system which covers every credit organization for their essential activities (bank deposits, equity deposits, guarantees), even if insurance on bank deposits was already provided. Preventive interventions have now a legal foundation with the Deposits Guarantee Fund (FGD) which brings all of the banking organizations together. The cooperation between the FGD, the CB and the CEC is reinforced to carry out a better regulation.

During the 1990s, fears that had emerged in the late 1980s were materialized: the system plunged into a deep and unprecedented crisis. In 1993, provisions and losses on bad debts reached 127 billion francs. In 1994, net banking income decreased in volume for the first time in history. Although the position of French banks improved in 1996, they were less profitable (in terms of financial profitability, i.e. the ratio between net income and equity) than their international competitors. This relative weakness had three major consequences: a handicap for growth; a downgrade in ratings by international agencies, which translated into higher refinancing costs.

The roots of the crisis were structural and not the result of competitive distortions. Indeed, the structural reforms implemented during the 1980s (market deregulation, expanded range of intermediaries, internationalization) resulted in a significant increase in competitive pressures. But the adjustments needed to deal with these pressures, especially within the banks' structures and operations, but also from the regulatory point of view, failed to take place (see Lambert, Le Cacheux and Mahuet, 1997). Facing competitive pressures and unable to adjust, the banks made both tactical errors (collective blindness on real estate bubbles) and strategic errors, including blind faith in the universal banking model. Three exogenous factors, however, acted as a catalyst, transforming what had been difficulties into a crisis: the downturn in the housing market; the inversion of the interest yield curve between 1989 and 1994 (which prevented the banks from realizing gains on conversion, i.e. using interest rates to make a profit on the conversion of a portion of their assets into shorter-term maturities); and the overtaxation of the banking sector (in particular the payroll tax in lieu of VAT, which represented 9 billion francs in 1994).

The role of the State, perceived as an ambivalent shareholder and poor manager, was roundly condemned: the 1996 Senate report on the health of the French banking system called into question both its handling of the banking crises by a systematic recapitalization of unviable lending institutions and the system for the prevention of banking risks. This led to debate about reforms to pull the State out of the banking sector.

3.2 The impact of the transition to the single currency

Starting in 1997, French banks benefited from the economic recovery and a renewed dynamism in the financial markets. They built up their international activities by expanding their presence abroad, especially in expectation of the larger market in 1998 (see the reports of the Commission Bancaire, 1997 and 1998). Moreover, their cost-control policies allowed them to deal with the transition to the euro in relatively good conditions.

These developments set the framework for restructuring the banking sector at the turn of the Millennium. First, the advent of the euro accelerated the trend towards concentration, in particular in the field of investment banking. This took the form of either national acquisitions (acquisition of Crédit du Nord by Société Générale, acquisition of about 25 per cent of Natixis by Caisse Centrale des Banques Populaires) or foreign acquisitions (acquisition by Société Générale of the English bank Hambros and of the American investment bank Cowen Securities).The increase in the size of potential market caused a search for an optimal size as well as for economies of scale to generate higher levels of profitability. Moreover, the modernization and liberalization of capital movements associated with the deregulation of financial and banking activities resulted in widening the institutions' field of action in a context of more harmonized regulatory and prudential standards. The result was an intensification of international competition on the French market, leading the country's banks to diversify into other regions and into the major foreign financial centres.

After the transition to the euro, French banks showed some resilience in the face of a harsh international economic and financial environment. Despite geopolitical factors and sectorial problems in the early 2000s (impact of the burst of the Internet bubble; persistent difficulties in telecommunications, transport and energy; risks in Latin America; increased international tensions in the Middle East), a high level of business failures and a slowdown in the demand for financing from credit institutions, the annual results of French credit institutions highlighted their ability to face up to the deteriorating economic situation. How can this be explained? With the active encouragement of French, European and international prudential supervisors, not only had the credit institutions diversified and chosen their risks more carefully but they had also improved their operating profitability, which helped to reduce their overall exposure to cyclical risks. Indeed, the major French banking groups had tier one capital ratios (a measure of a bank's ability to pay its debts, or the gross operating surplus) that were well above the regulatory minima. Moreover, the overall immediate credit risk facing French credit institutions fell by 4.8 per cent in 2005 and, the market risks as calculated by France's Commission bancaire declined by 11 per cent in the same year (see Report of the Commission Bancaire, 2006).

3.3 The overall situation today

Up to 2008, French banks saw a steady increase in business that was related to a period of sustained global economic growth and a good situation on the financial markets. At end 2004, 50 French banks were operating in 85 countries or regions, and the foreign subsidiaries of the three main groups accounted for between 17 per cent and 25 per cent of their total assets (see Bulletin of the Bank of France, 2012).

The 2000s saw the large corporates relying on abundant, cheap funding. In this respect, French banks played a role in the development of a strong syndicated loan market, especially in Europe, and the share of leveraged loans (LBO) experienced unprecedented growth. In a context of high competition, French banks were forced to accept lower margins on their most important activities, highlighting how syndicated loans were increasingly resembling tendered products. LBO funds were themselves accompanied by an increase in leverage and a reduction in debt quality, posing a medium-term threat of a possible downturn in the credit cycle. In addition, the 2000s saw the emergence of a strong recovery in commercial property and sustained growth in the housing business. Foreign markets served as a source of growth for the major French banking groups, which were often engaged in increasingly diversifying their risks. Similarly, in order to counteract fluctuations in consumer credit, the banks increased their investments in local government. Finally, the

Table 2.1 Simplified description of the French banking system income situation

	2004	*2005*	*2006*	*2007*	*2008*	*2009*	*2010*	*2011*	*2012*
Net banking income (% of total assets)	2.08	2.00	1.84	1.50	1.08	1.49	1.39	1.33	1.38
Cost-to-income ratio (%)	63.9	6.43	62.4	68.4	84.4	60.2	64.4	65.4	61.5
Gross non-performing loans (€ billions)	62.3	59.3	56.3	58.9	67	90.7	97.4	100.3	101.7
Gross non-performing loans (% of total loans)	5.1	4.5	3.8	3.5	3.7	4.9	5.1	5.0	5.1

Source: ACPR (2013).

2000s saw a renewed interest from major French banking groups in emerging economies like Russia. The Russian market became the second-largest market after the French market for the Société Générale Group. Société Générale, which acquired Rosbank in 2008, has nearly 25,000 employees and three million individual customers, 6000 SMEs and 2000 large corporations over the world.

Since 2008, the deterioration of the financial environment and its resulting impact on the real economy has severely tested the strength of the French financial system. The financial turmoil arising from the subprime crisis and from its spread to all segments of the financial market created a more difficult operating environment for the banks, which also faced a generalized crisis of confidence. The French banking system has been strongly hit by the financial crisis. Table 1 illustrates that the net banking income (NBI) ratio dropped to a mere 1.08 per cent in 2008 while the cost-to-income ratio increased sharply to 84.4 per cent. Since then, both indicators have improved. However, these positive outcomes cannot hide unfortunate developments. In particular, non-performing loans are on an upward trend since the beginning of the financial crisis.

3.4 Disentangling the European influence

According to Coriat (2008), the financialization of the French economy came both from the US, as a driving example for the privatization process, and from the EU, as a reform catalyst. The ongoing change in the capital accumulation mode dominated by finance was introduced by the EU in 1986, under the implicit influence of the US capital accumulation mode. Indeed, following the phase of disintegration in Europe in the 1970s, with a slowdown in trade flows within the European Economic Community (EEC), the Delors Commission in 1984 decided to boost European economic integration with the Single European Act of 1986 (ratified in 1987) in order to establish a single market in 1993. European liberalization was a by-product of globalization.

The Single European Act allowed the establishment of a European integrated financial and monetary market under the aegis of the four fundamental freedoms of movement (i.e. people, goods, services and capital). Competition was fostered and, because harmonization of national standards remained a tricky issue, the principle of mutual recognition was imposed. For all EU countries, it meant trust in the standards of other European partners, recognition of the validity of their technical and social standards; hence, it led to minimum standards all over Europe. A higher level of competition has had strong implications on monopolies and utilities, as well as on public procurement. The privatization processes and the change in cross-holdings of French companies are a consequence of globalization and European integration processes.

In addition, the implementation of the single market, joint with EU directives of 1979 and 1989, fostered French banking reforms of the 1980s and 1990s. These reforms were meant to open French banking industry to international competition and to ensure equal and competitive access to banking services. Financial integration stated by the Single European Act was deepened with various treaties, directives and regulations that have succeeded in promoting a large unified market for European currencies and finance. The integration of the European financial sector accelerated in 1999 with the Financial Services Action Plan (FSAP), launched by the European Commission and the White Paper of the European Commission published in December 2005.

Coriat (2008) also recalls that there has been intense haggling and lobbying to enable Europe to provide financial services on a 'broader' basis, with the introduction of the single passport which allows extra-European banks and financial institutions to exercise automatically in the European Economic Area insofar as they have a subsidiary in at least one EU country. For example, in France,

> under the principle of mutual recognition of authorizations, credit institutions, investment firms and authorized payment institutions in the form of a French company are empowered to offer banking services and/or financial and payment services in another Member State when they have completed the required formalities and the ACP (Control and Prudential Authority) has informed the competent authority of the host state.
>
> (Coriat, 2008)

3.4.1 Development of financial markets

As shown by Goyeau and Tarazi (2006), France has witnessed increased competition and a radical change in financial markets, along with a movement of technological cooperation and concentration that established a competitive European market.

With regard to technological and market organization, we have to mention the movement of mergers and clustering of European stock markets, leading notably to Euronext. It was meant to increase economies of scale by attracting a larger number of issuers, on the one hand, and investors and financial intermediaries, on the other hand. The Law of 22 January 1988 cancelled the monopoly of brokers, hence allowing to open their capital to financial intermediaries. It gave rise to the development of trading companies which were authorized to perform operations for their own account as well as for third parties. Founded in 1990, the 'Société des Bourses Françaises' (French SBF-Bourse de Paris) was first transformed into a limited company: Euronext NV, before merging in September 2000 with the stock markets of Amsterdam and Brussels to become a listed company in 2001. Then, in 2002, the Lisbon Stock Exchange and the international derivatives market based in London, Liffe, joined Euronext. The group existed independently from 2000 to 2006 before combining with the New York Stock Exchange (NYSE) in 2007. In 2012, NYSE–Euronext merged with another US network: IntercontinentalExchange (ICE).

Meanwhile, the ongoing revolution of information and communication technology spread to France: the stock market adopted the CAQ system (continuous assisted quotation) in 1986 to enhance the competitiveness of the Paris stock exchange against other markets, especially London's. Since then, financial transmissions of orders, executions, payments and stocks and bonds deliveries have been automated.

3.4.2 Payment systems

As far as payment systems are concerned, there are two interbank payment systems in France, stemming from European-wide initiatives: a high-amount payment system ('wholesale') and a retail one.

The 'wholesale' payment system is TARGET2-Banque de France, a component of the European system TARGET2 (Trans-European Automated Real-time Gross settlement Express Transfer) of the Eurosystem. It relies on a single technical platform that is shared between European financial institutions and national central banks to smooth the establishment of business relationships between the TARGET2 participants (the involved financial institutions have an open account vis-à-vis their central bank) and national central bank. The relationships between the national central banks and the banking community are completely decentralized. At the end of 2011, the ECB reported a total number of almost 60,000 participants in TARGET2, i.e. credit institutions which had access to the payment system.

As for the retail payment system, the SEPA (Single Euro Payments Area) system is managed by the ECB, enabling customers to make cashless euro payments to anyone located anywhere in Europe, by credit transfer, direct debit or debit card. SEPA hence creates a single market for retail payments in euros, not only in the euro area, but also in the EU and beyond. As a country using euros in its retail payments, France is obviously an active participant in this system.

3.4.3 Competition policy

As part of European influence on the French banking and financial system, it is also worth mentioning competition policy. However, two important features need to be kept in mind: first, despite European impetus in favour of competition, it has to be recalled that the French banking system remains highly concentrated; second, France has long had its own legislation favouring competition to a broader set of economic activities, including banking and financial ones.

As a matter of fact, the 1 December 1986 Order, codified in the Code of Commerce, established a Competition Council (*Conseil de la Concurrence*), which replaced the Competition Commission established in 1977, and affirmed the principle of self-determination of prices by competition. Economic operators were free to set their own pricing policies according to their business strategy; the goal was to let the market itself regulate the level of prices of goods and services through the interplay of supply and demand. However, competition can be expressed only if the operators do not engage in conducts designed to distort, restrict or prevent competition; since then, the Code of Commerce prohibited anti-competitive practices. The practices in question stem from collusion between operators, abusive practices from companies in a dominant position, or excessively low prices. The Order extended the possibilities of referral, transferred the power of sanction from the Minister to the Council and implemented a procedure that guarantees the rights of the concerned party.

The 15 May 2001 'New Economic Regulations' law amended competition law in order to strengthen the effectiveness of the fight against anti-competitive practices (introduction of leniency and transaction procedures, rise in punishment ceiling), to ensure compliance to the principle of equality of arms (between firms), to improve international cooperation and to control concentrations in a more systematic and transparent way.

Under Community impulse, French competition law underwent a profound modernization movement: regulation EC/1/2003 which entered into force on 1 May 2004 in France organized the decentralization of Community law and the 'networking' of national competition authorities; it also increased the Council's powers. In this movement, the 4 November 2004 order completed the decision-making powers of the Council by bringing them into line with those of other European competition authorities.

The 4 August 2008 'Modernization of the Economy' law created the Competition Authority, transferred to it the powers of the former Competition Council and granted it a new one: the Competition Council controls M&A operations to ensure that they will not produce anti-competitive consequences and distortions. The Authority took over from the Minister of Economy in the control of concentrations. In addition, it is now able to conduct its own investigations and has the opportunity to make recommendations to the Minister in charge of the sector in order to improve the functioning of competitive markets.

The 13 November 2008 Order on modernization of competition regulation gave the Competition Authority increased resources. The General Directorate for Competition, Consumer Affairs and Fraud Control (DGCCRF) contributes to the detection of anti-competitive practices through the spatial distribution of its investigators. Micro-anti-competitive practices do not justify a treatment by the Authority but may be subject to an administrative process by the minister's services; this jurisdiction is limited to practices affecting local markets and companies whose individual turnover is less than €50 million.

4 Financial crisis and reform of financial regulation

4.1 Banking regulation

The financial crisis revealed fundamental weaknesses in the operation and regulation of the banking system. The contraction of world economy has pulled the French economy into a severe recession and put its financial sector under stress. Government recapitalization and liquidity measures were required to support the sector. By publishing Basel III in 2010, the Basel Committee on banking supervision has set new international standards on capital adequacy and liquidity of banks. Most of these standards constitute a revision of existing rules, but some others are completely new and are about areas not previously covered. In France particularly, further actions are required to fully uncover and address underlying vulnerabilities in the banking sector (French banks' net earnings have dropped sharply and their leverage remains relatively high) (van Rixtel and Gasperini, 2013).

First, the financial crisis has revealed that the setup of (international) standards has encouraged credit institutions to disguise risk they take. In particular, solvency requirements and risk management have led them to transfer a large share of the risks they generate through securitization transactions, which have increased in France since 1980. Moreover, the 2000s gave birth to a rising type of asset: credit derivatives and financial structured products. It is worth noting that securitization has reduced the risk from an accounting perspective. It modifies the treatment of asset risk: after securitization, the risk generated by the asset is no longer considered as a credit risk but as a market risk. The asset is no longer counted in a bank holding (or 'banking book') but in a trading portfolio (or 'trading book'). The problem remains that capital requirements to cover market risk are lower than those required to cover the risks of the assets before securitization. From a regulatory perspective, securitization helps to reduce the risk although it has no incidence in macroeconomic terms. Then, securitization transfers risk off the balance sheet or to other players that are not facing the same regulatory requirements as banks (pension funds or investment funds for instance).

Second, the (international) standards have neglected the existence of a liquidity risk. The financial crisis has indeed shown that credit standards were insufficient to prevent bank failures because of the possibility of a liquidity crisis. In France, the latest regulation applicable to liquidity dated back to 1988 and subjected banks to a liquidity ratio of at least 100 per cent between their short-term assets and liabilities. Institutions were also required to calculate three 'observation ratios' reflecting their forecast liquidity status (quarterly, biannually and annually). The requirements, defined in terms of liquidity of stock, do not sufficiently address the developments in banking and markets, particularly with regard to the growing impact of market liquidity. Banks have indeed ceased being mere suppliers of liquidity and have become dependent on market liquidity, which has a major impact on their balance sheets. However, market liquidity has a direct impact on solvency through the valuation of securitized assets. The effect of uncertainty (the inability to assign probabilities to different situations) on markets development are increased by information asymmetries between issuers and buyers of securities. Moreover, with the valuation at market value, any uncertainty about asset values turns into uncertainty about the solvency of financial institutions. This results in some tensions at the heart of the system, i.e. the interbank markets.

Finally, (international) standards themselves have generated a systemic risk because of their procyclicality. Solvency ratios are indeed criticized for their procyclicality: in times of economic downturn, the weights applied to commitments in light of the risks are increasing, which increases capital requirements. To continue to meet the existing standards, banks are then forced to reduce their credit supply which induces a credit crunch. Conversely, in periods of high growth, lower risk encourages banks to lend more, which can have the effect of feeding speculative bubbles. Prudential standards are then suspected to exacerbate the economic cycle. Moreover, as the principle of 'fair value' accounting means taking into account the unrealized gains and losses, it increases the variability in the value of capital and hence the capital adequacy ratio of banks. This procyclicality is particularly damaging as the measure of fair value is not completely reliable when estimated from models at the discretion of individual institutions.

The French authorities (following the 'Pauget recommendations' in the 2012 report ordered by the Minister of Economy and Finance Christine Lagarde) have been active in supporting the European regulatory reform and have proposed a series of steps, namely (i) to strength the supervision of EU-wide financial groups, (ii) to harmonize the regulatory frameworks, (iii) to undertake a joint supervision of cross-border banks and insurance companies, and (iv) to enhance the transparency and surveillance of non-regulated markets, credit-rating agencies and compensation.

Nevertheless, the closeness between political power and the French banking industry is worth noticing. Numerous banks' CEOs previously worked in the administration. It gives them an easy access to political and regulatory power, allowing the banking industry to exercise strong lobbying strategies. These actions undermine the effectiveness of new regulations when the latter intend to minimize the size of this specific and systemic industry. The controversy in France about the Barnier proposal on banking regulation is a good example. While this initiative only tried to separate the banking activities, in accordance with many reports on the question like the Liikanen report, the French banking lobby quickly bashed this proposition to get rid of it (see e.g. Gaffard and Pollin, 2014).

4.2 Financial markets regulation

As for the European regulation of financial markets, a post-crisis emblematic action has undoubtedly been the regulation of Credit Default Swaps (CDS) market, which takes part of a more global regulation process, the EMIR (European Market Infrastructures Regulation).

Similarly to most financial derivative products, transactions in the CDS market are traded 'over-the-counter' (OTC). A new regulation on short selling and naked CDS came into effect across the European Union in November 2012. First, the regulation sets out a temporary restriction in uncovered short selling of bonds and shares in the case of a significant fall in price (the European text actually expands to the European Union a German restriction on sovereign bonds and major financial shares in effect since 2010 and it catches up on a regulation already existing in the US). Second, to increase market transparency, investors are required to disclose major net short positions to regulators and the general market (a goal that will be difficult to reach as this regulation does not cover corporate CDS, which introduces regulatory arbitrage). Last but not least, the European specificity concerns the ban of naked sovereign CDS (a ban proposal that was debated in the US in 2009 but finally abandoned). From November 2012 on, investors willing to trade sovereign CDS in an EU country must hold the underlying bond or hold a portfolio of assets correlated to the value of the sovereign debt.

In total, this regulation has the advantage to harmonize the regulation about short selling across the EU. Beyond that, its relevance is questionable in the context of the EMIR, the new European regulation on over-the-counter derivatives currently implemented. Indeed, EMIR aims at increasing transparency in the opaque OTC market along similar moves in the US through the Dodd-Franck act, whereas this CDS regulation cannot reach this goal.

Beyond this EU regulatory move, France has had its own two post-crisis emblematic regulations on financial markets: the tax on financial transactions (which came into force on 1 August 2012) and the bill on bonuses controls and prohibition of stock options.

The tax on financial transactions provides for a 0.1 per cent tax on shares exchanges of companies whose market capitalization exceeds €1 billion and which are headquartered in France. With a rate ten times lower (at 0.01 per cent), it also targets certain products or transactions charged to foster speculation: the 'naked' CDS on EU sovereign bonds and 'high-frequency trading' based on an automated processing system any nanosecond. This French tax aims to cause a ripple effect on its European neighbours.

The bill on bonuses controls and prohibition of stock options is one of the strong measures directly affecting the remuneration of traders. The first step in this direction was made in April 2009 when the French right-wing government (under Sarkozy's presidency) decided to ban stock options and free shares for enterprises having received State support (through loans and/or guarantees). Then, the successive governments battled to either cap bonuses (e.g. Nicolas Sarkozy in November 2009 at G20 in Pittsburgh) or to ban bonuses and stock options (e.g. François Hollande, who included a commitment to legislate on this issue in his presidential programme). In each case, the goal of French initiatives was to launch a European impetus even if it did not always fully succeed. In Pittsburgh, Nicolas Sarkozy (together with Angela Merkel) failed to cap bonuses. Instead, the G20 countries opted for measures requiring banks to defer many bonuses for at least three years and to distribute the bulk of top executives' remuneration in shares. That was transmitted into the French legislation as early as end-December 2009 through an 'Arrêté', then going ahead as the European Directive amending the Capital Requirement Directive ('CRD') in several directions, including the remuneration policies within banks. However, the legislation was unable to curb bank bonuses. In 2012, in his presidential programme, François Hollande then stated he will suppress stock options (except for start-ups) and will control bonuses. To date, the government under Hollande's presidency has capped the full remuneration of CEOs in public companies: their remuneration should no longer be more than 20 times the smallest (full-time) wage of the company. Moreover, since July 2012, taxes on stock options and free shares have been increased. By constrast, the idea of suppressing the stock options seems to have been abandoned by the left-wing government: probably, it would be politically unsustainable.

5 The present regulatory framework and authorities in France

The international and European contexts have deeply modified the French regulatory framework since the 1980s: the reading grid of the actual French regulation is both international (in light of the proposals of the Basel committee for instance) and European (in light of a requirement for a Community regulation). Since the crisis, it is crutial to reach European and international harmonization, in order to avoid the regulatory costs due to fragmentation and potentially leading to regulatory arbitrage (traders go where regulation is more lax). Thus, if the supervision and coercive authorities are national, the applied rules and regulation result from international norms and practices.

The French regulation is based on two major authorities, the ACPR (Autorité de Contrôle Prudentiel et de Résolution) for the supervision of the banking and insurance sectors and the AMF for the supervision of financial markets. They coordinate their policies via the 'Pôle Commun'. With a view to harmonization, the AMF is part of the ESMA, a European organisation that brings together all the European authorities in charge of financial markets. Its role is primarily dedicated to data collection or supervision of the European financial market.

5.1 The ACPR's role

The ACPR delivers banking licences; it has a supervision power as it orders stress tests, controls for the compliance to regulatory constraints, etc. It has also the power to sanction if necessary. This authority was created in 2010 by the merger of four banking and insurance authorities (CB, ACAM, CEA and CECEI). The fact that the ACPR leans back on the Banque de France could have been a drawback because it raises the issue of a target conflict at the central bank that has to pursue monetary policy. However, this situation is an important advantage to guarantee the stability of the entire financial sector because ACPR consequently receives the economic and financial expertise from the central bank. Furthermore, this situation favours coordination and thus strengthens French regulatory policy. The issues relative to different sub-sectors are tackled by sectoral sub-colleges. The Authority looks after the quality of the financial situation to guarantee the financial sector stability and customers' protection and includes an enforcement committee (CS) in case of breach of those principles. In legal terms, the Authority's College 'examines every general question common to banking and insurance sectors and analyzes the risks of those sectors under the economic situation. It deliberates on control priorities'. This prudential control can take the form of permanent control or in-place inspection and is run on both banking and insurance sectors.

As for the banking sector, the ACPR ensures that credit organisations, investment firms and financial companies respect the legal and regulatory clauses. For this purpose, it runs on a quarterly basis an inquiry about the accounting and prudential states of the credit organisations and analyses precisely their governance operations. All the information collected by the ACPR during its permanent and in-place inspections leads it to express some recommendations with a view to improving management operations and risk profiles of the organisations. This information is also useful for possible additional requirements of prudential equity (e.g. second mainstay of Basel II). Thus, the ACPR has imposed equity requirements above the regulatory minimum for 82 institutions that represent 97 per cent of the national banking system risks. Finally, the ACPR has contributed to the 'stress tests' coordinated by the European Banking Supervisors Committee (CECB) and pays attention to the liquidity risk.

The ACPR conducts the same supervision and regulation for the insurance sector, which encompasses insurance societies and mutual companies. It pays an additional attention to sovereign risks facing French insurance organisations and their beneficiaries. Insurance societies indeed generally invest a great part of their assets in sovereign bonds.

Finally, the ACPR attaches great importance to the protection of customers. Until its inception, the mission of consumer protection in the banking and insurance sector was exercised mainly by regulating the solvency of financial institutions. It thus allowed having the certainty that insurers had means to fulfil their commitments and that bank deposits were not jeopardized by any excessive risk taking. Henceforth, ACPR's customers' protection includes the control of business practices.

5.2 The AMF's role

The AMF is 'committed to ensuring the promotion of effective financial regulation to ensure safety and market integrity' (AMF Annual Report, 2010). From this perspective, the AMF has to protect investors, regulate and control the investment services, regulate the market infrastructure and the market discipline.

First, the issue of investor protection is a central concern for the Authority. In this context, the Directorate for relations with investors (DRE) has been created: its objective is to inform investors, to analyse their behaviour and their marketing practices and assist them in resolving disputes. For instance, the marketing of financial products to retail investors is part of mediation cases: some subscribers complained that they had been pressured to invest without having received clear and complete information or being alerted about potential risks. In some cases, the wrongdoers may compensate the subscribers. Similarly, the devaluation of shares acquired at the time of their placing on the market raises many claims and takes part in the AMF mission of investor protection.

Second, the AMF authorizes, regulates and controls the OPCVM and other collective savings products, management companies, investment services providers, and market infrastructures while ensuring the development and innovation in the financial services industry. It supervises the functioning of the market, the quality of financial reporting and the compliance by financial intermediaries of their professional obligations. To this end, the AMF is in close collaboration with other national and foreign authorities responsible for supervision of banking and financial professions (Banque de France, ACPR, H3C and ANC).

The AMF is one of the few European regulators that exercise direct supervision of the order book on its national regulated market. It then develops automated alerts on suspicious behaviour and it devotes a part of its monitoring workforce to process that data.

When the AMF observes that some behaviour may fall within the jurisdiction of other authorities (judicial, administrative or professional), it transmits to them information in its possession and reports it has established. Finally, it has a penalty procedure for non-compliance with the regulation.

The AMF is part of the ESMA that brings together all European financial markets authorities. Its role is essential through data collection. An example of such a role emerges from the Greek debt crisis: during debt restructuring, creditors and negotiators had to know precisely the amounts of Greek debt that European banks had in their balance sheets and to what extent they could be affected by debt restructuring. These data were present in banks' balance sheets but were of course non-public; they have been made available through these authorities and were pooled by a supervisor.

5.3 Articulation of supervisory authorities

The Prudential Control Authority (ACPR) takes individual decisions for approval of credit institutions, mutual, insurance, market and investment firms after an authorization of the Financial Markets Authority (AMF), except for decisions referring to portfolio management companies that depend only on the AMF. It also has a double function of control and punishment: it supervises compliance with legislation or regulations and penalizes infractions. The ACPR has a look on the quality of the financial situation of credit and investment institutions, especially in terms of solvency and liquidity. Finally, the ACPR is responsible for the protection of customers of mutual insurance and credit institution.

The Financial Markets Authority (AMF) is an independent administrative authority which regulates and supervises all financial transactions that involve listed companies. It delivers the approvals for portfolio management companies and controls the exercise of activities of investment services and market structures.

Besides these authorities, there are advisory bodies like the Advisory Committee of the legislation and financial regulation (CCLRF), the Advisory Committee of the Financial Sector (CCSF) and the Higher Council of Mutuality (CSM).

The Minister of Economy and Finance appeals to the Advisory Committee of Financial Legislation and Regulation in order to deliver an opinion about projects on normative acts with a general purpose in the banking, financial and insurance sector. There can be some exceptions for some normative acts that depend solely on the Financial Markets Authority.

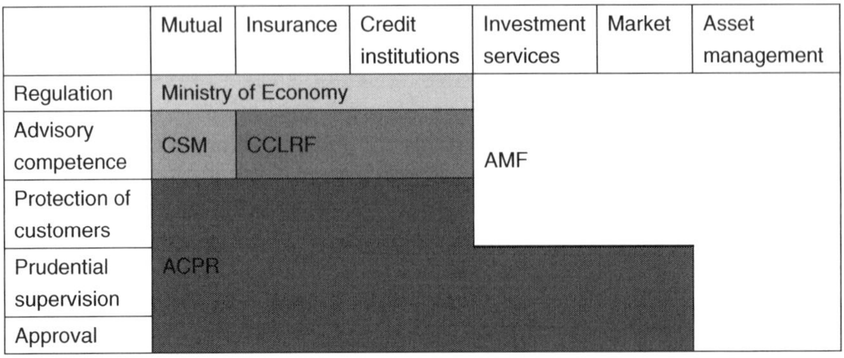

Figure 2.1 The expertise fields of supervisory authorities

The Advisory Committee of the Financial Sector is responsible for studying issues referring to relations between financial institutions and their customers. It has full discretion on submitting an issue or it can be referred to by the Ministry of Economy and Finance or representative organizations for professionals and consumers.

The Higher Council of Mutuality is in charge of Mutual Insurance Company. The Prudential Control Authority, the Advisory Committee of Financial Legislation and Regulation and the Advisory Committee of the Financial Sector are all affiliated to the Banque de France. The chart below helps to summarize the extent of the role of these different institutions.

At the European level, the European System of Financial Supervisors (ESFS) was created in 2010 in response to the crisis (see figure below). First, the strengthening of macro-prudential supervision throughout the European financial system comes through the implementation of the European Systemic Risk Board (ESRB). The latter is responsible for monitoring and analysing risks which could occur in the financial system in its entirety. To achieve this mission, the ESRB has to warn early against systemic risk, and if necessary makes recommendations for corrective actions and warnings to member states, national and European supervisory authorities, which in turn must comply with recommendations or explain why they did/could not. The President and vice-president of the European Central Bank (ECB), governors of national central banks, a member of the Commission and the heads of the European regulatory authorities and national supervisory authorities take part in the ESRB. Second, the strengthening of micro-prudential supervision comes through the establishment of European Supervisory Authorities (ESA). These authorities are supposed to intervene rapidly with national supervisors. They enact technical standards for the implementation of the European legislation. The European Supervisory Authorities are made up of:

- The European Banking Authority (EBA), which is responsible for harmonizing the prudential rules, for ensuring coordination between national supervisory authorities and for playing a mediating role.
- The European Insurance and Occupational Pensions Authority (EIOPA), which is an independent advisory body for the European Parliament and the European Union Council. The EIOPA's mission is to support the financial system stability, the markets and financial products transparency and the protection of those who benefit from insurance and pension schemes.
- The European Securities and Markets Authority (ESMA) which is an independent authority from the European Union; it ensures the smooth functioning of markets (in terms of integrity, transparency and efficiency) as well as the investor protection.

This reform aims to implement the report of de Larosière (2009), a former governor of Bank de France.

With respect to supervision at the European level, in France, the Committee on Financial Regulation and Systemic Risk (COREFRIS) aims to ensure the coordination of the various institutions concerned with financial stability.

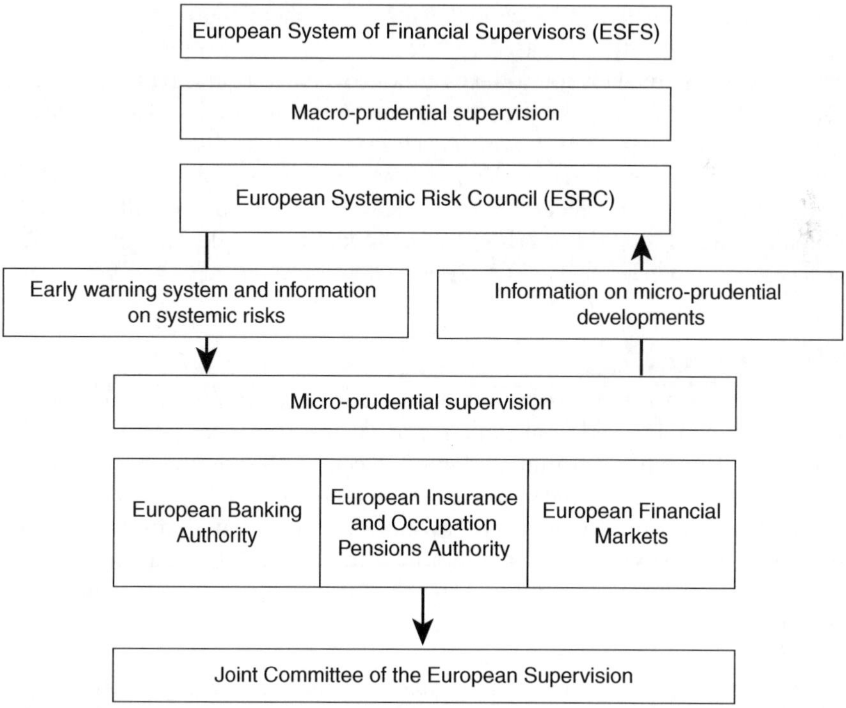

Figure 2.2 Supervision at the European level

It is made up of the Banque de France (BDF), the General Committee of the Treasury, the Accounting Standards Authority (ANC), the Financial Markets Authority (AMF) and the Prudential Control Authority (ACPR).

5.4 Prudential and accounting norms

Prudential rules and control methods are similar in major industrialized countries because of a movement of international harmonization driven by the Basel Committee. The EU has taken over the movement of harmonization but created its own legislation that French authorities have translated in national terms.

As for the prudential norms, the Basel regulation aims at preventing bank failures by imposing a minimum level of capital to cover risks. In this perspective, Basel I (1988) has specified a solvability ratio (ratio Cooke) and Basel II (2004) has led to a new set of regulation aiming at taking better in account the diversity of risks (credit versus market risks). Basel III, signed in 2010, will impose a higher capital ratio in banks' balance sheets, a minimum 'leverage ratio' and two liquidity ratios. Initially scheduled to be introduced from 2013 until 2015, the implementation of Basel III's ratios is extended until March 31, 2018.

Accounting norms are essential since the implementation of Basel II's ratio (the estimation of available capital depends on accounting rules). Capital requirements regulation is based on the idea that a bankruptcy will occur if cash that assets are likely to produce cannot cover all disbursements associated to liabilities. For this reason, the prevention of bank failures is based on a measure of their 'economic' equity, which corresponds to the difference between the current value of assets and the current value of liabilities. This approach, which evaluates the balance sheet at market prices, is the one favoured by the international accounting standards (IFRS). It is opposed to a valuation at historical costs as recommended by traditional French accounting.

6 Conclusion

The objective of this contribution is to present the structural evolutions of the French banking and financial system. The historical context of deregulation, the European integration and, more recently, the crisis have all together shaped the structures of the banking system (Blot et al., 2012). Schematically, we can break down the regulations' evolutions since the 1980s into three periods: the changes of national regulation with the Banking Act of 1984; the impetus caused by the European integration process (in particular, the Single European Act and the single currency); and, finally, the influence of the crisis on financial and banking regulations.

Since the 1980s, both the international and European contexts have deeply modified the French regulatory framework. Consequently, the reading grid of the actual French regulation is international (in light of the proposals of the Basel committee for instance) but also European (in light of a call for a Community regulation). Since the crisis, there has been more effort to reach European and international harmonization, in order to avoid financial and banking actors having to engage in regulatory arbitrage.

Nevertheless, one has to keep in mind that the French financial actors are also part of the political and institutional process and try to deeply influence the future regulations. The closeness between political power and the French banking industry is worth noticing. Numerous banks' CEOs previously worked in the administration. It gives them an easy access to political and regulatory power, allowing the banking industry to exercise strong lobbying strategies. These actions undermine the effectiveness of new regulations when the latter intend to minimize the size of this specific and systemic industry. Two examples are worth recalling. First, on 19 February 2013, the French Parliament passed a law on the separation of banking activities, making a distinction between speculative activities for own accounts and other bank activities. The former are limited to a subsidiary and not mixed with bank customers' accounts. The 'nuisance' of this law for banks will be limited though: indeed, it is difficult to make a clear and practical distinction between hedging risk (which should not be mixed with 'speculative' activities) and 'pure speculation', or between activities to foster market liquidity and proprietary speculative activities. Legal vacuums in the clear definition of 'speculative activities for own accounts' will help banks circumvent the law. Second, the controversy in France about the former European Commissioner M. Barnier's proposal on banking regulation is a good example. While his initiative only tries to separate banking activities (loans versus market activities), in accordance with many recent reports on the question like the Liikanen report, the French banking lobby quickly bashed this proposition to get rid of it.

Note

1 The authors are grateful to Mathilde Viennot for her participation in a companion paper (Blot et al., 2013).

References

AUTORITE DE CONTROLE PRUDENTIEL ET DE REGULATION (2013) The French Banking Market in Figures. Banque de France's Publications.

AUTORITE DES MARCHES FINANCIERS (2010) Annual Report.

BLOT, C., CREEL, J., DELATTE, A.-L., DURAND, K., GALLOIS, A., HUBERT, P., LE CACHEUX, J., LEVASSEUR, S. and VIENNOT, M. (2012) The French Financial System from Past to Present. FESSUD Studies in Financial Systems No. 2.

BLOT, C., CREEL, J., DELATTE, LABONDANCE, L., LEVASSEUR, S. and VIENNOT, M. (2013) Country regulation study: the case of France. FESSUD Deliverable No. 4.03.

COMMISSION BANCAIRE, Annual Reports, various years.

CORIAT, B. (2008) L'installation de la finance en France. Genèse, formes spécifiques et impacts sur l'industrie. Revue de la régulation, No. 3/4.

GOYEAU, D. and TARAZI, A. (2006) Panorama du système financier: Concurrence et mutations des marchés financiers en Europe. *Cahiers Français*, 331.

GAFFARD J.-L., and J-P. POLLIN J.-P. (2013) Pourquoi faut-il séparer les activités bancaires? Les notes de l'OFCE, no 36, November.

GAFFARD J.-L., and J-P. POLLIN J.-P. (2014) The Barnier proposal on banking regulation: Whence the wrath? OFCE Blog, 10 February.

HAUTCOEUR P.-C., (1999) L'autofinancement: Théories, questions de méthode et tentative de cadrage macroéconomique pour la France (1914–1990). *Entreprises Et Histoire*, 22, 55–77.

LAMBERT T., J. LE CACHEUX and A. MAHUET (1997) L'épidémie de crises bancaire dans les pays de l'OCDE. *Revue De L'OFCE*, 61, 93–138.

(DE) LAROSIÈRE J. (2009) The High-Level group on financial supervision in the EU. European Commission Report.

PAUGET G. and E. CONSTANS (2012) L'avenir des moyens de paiement en France. Rapport de la Banque de France, March.

SAUVE A. and M. SCHEUER (1999) Modes de financement des entreprises allemandes et françaises. Projet de Recherche Commun de la Deutsche Bundesbank et de la Banque de France.

VAN RIXTEL A. and G. GASPERINI (2013) Financial crises and bank funding: Recent experience in the euro area. BIS Working paper, No. 406.

Appendix 1 Summary of the key events in the development of the French financial system, including political events

1885	Establishment of the Caisses d'Epargne (savings banks)
1945	Separation of banks into deposit banks, investment banks and lending banks
1981	Election of François Mitterrand (PS) as President of the Republic, first Socialist president of the Fifth Republic
1982	Wave of nationalizations in the banking sector
1984	Banking Act
1985	Creation of certificates of deposit, of the MATIF and the MONEP
1986	First cohabitation of François Mitterrand with an RPR government led by Jacques Chirac Development of mergers and acquisitions in the banking sector, wave of privatizations
1987	Privatization of Société Générale, Compagnie Suez, Compagnie Paribas Lifting of the credit framework
1988	Re-election of François Mitterrand, Socialist government Setup of an international solvability ration (ratio Cooke)
1989	Creation of the Commission des Opérations de Bourse (COB) Dismantling of exchange controls Lifting of controls on capital movements
1990	Opening of the domestic market to foreign banks
1991	Restructuring and regrouping of the banking sector Collapse of the property market
1993	Crisis in the European monetary system Setup of the banking European single market Directive about the investment services Second cohabitation of François Mitterrand with an RPR government led by Edouard Balladur Second wave of privatizations
1995	Election of Jacques Chirac (RPR) as President of the Republic
1996	Law on the modernization of financial activities
1997	Dissolution of the Assemblée Nationale and cohabitation of Jacques Chirac with a Socialist government led by Lionel Jospin
1999	Transition to the euro on the financial markets Introduction of the euro
2002	Re-election of Jacques Chirac as President of the Republic
2003	Law for financial security Creation of the Financial Market Authority (AMF)
2005	Setting up of the international accounting rules in the European Union
2006	Implementation in the European Union of the Basel II international standards on 31 December

2007	Election of Nicolas Sarkozy (UMP) as President of the Republic François Fillon (UMP) as the Prime Minister. Onset of the subprime crisis Tax rebates under the 'tax shield' (*bouclier fiscal*)
2008	Collapse of Lehman Brothers Bail-out plan for the French banks (through guarantees on loans and loans at interest rates granted by the State to the banks) Implementation of Basel II standards in France
2009	Reimbursement by a majority of French banks of State loans granted as part of the bail-out plan
2010	Publication of the Basel III recommendations Creation of the Prudential Control Authority (ACPR)
2011	Suppression of the 'tax shield'
2012	Election of François Hollande (PS) as President of the Republic Jean-Marc Ayrault (PS) as the Prime Minister
2013	Phased implementation into the European Union of the Basel III standards, from 1 January 2013 to 1 January 2018

Appendix 2 Abbreviations of political parties

EELV: Europe-Ecologie-Les Verts (the Greens)
MDC: Mouvement Des Citoyens
MDR: Mouvement Des Réformateurs
MRG: Mouvement des Radicaux de Gauche
NC: Nouveau Centre
PCF: Parti Communiste Français
PRG: Parti Radical de Gauche
PS: Parti Socialiste
RPR: Rassemblement Pour la République
UDF: Union pour la Démocratie Française
UMP: Union pour un Mouvement Populaire

Appendix 3 – Summary of successive French governments since 1980

1981	Election of François Mitterrand (PS) as President of the Republic Government (PS-PCF-MRG) of Pierre Mauroy
1984	Government (PS-PCF-MRG) of Laurent Fabius
1986	Government (RPR-UDF) of Jacques Chirac, 'First cohabitation'
1988	Re-election of François Mitterrand (PS) as President of the Republic Government (PS-MRG) of Michel Rocard
1991	Government (PS-MRG-MDR) of Edith Cresson
1992	Government (PS-MRG-MDR) of Pierre Bérégovoy
1993	Government (RPR-UDF) of Edouard Balladur, 'Second cohabitation'
1995	Election of Jacques Chirac (RPR) as President of the Republic Government (RPR-UDF) of Alain Juppé
1997	Government (PS-PCF-PRG-Verts-MDC) of Lionel Jospin, 'Third cohabitation'
2002	Re-election of Jacques Chirac (UMP) as President of the Republic Government (UMP) of Jean-Pierre Raffarin
2005	Government (UMP) of Dominique de Villepin
2007	Election of Nicolas Sarkozy (UMP) as President of the Republic Government (UMP-NC) of François Fillon
2012	Election of François Hollande (PS) as President of the Republic Government (PS-PRG-EELV) of Jean-Marc Ayrault

Appendix 4 – Set of acronyms used

ACAM	Autorité de Contrôle des Assurances et Mutuelles
ACPR	Autorité de Contrôle Prudentiel et de Résolution
AFB	Association Française des Banques
AMF	Autorité des Marchés Financiers
ANC	Autorité des Normes Comptables
CB	Commission Bancaire
CCA	Commission de Contrôle des Assurances
CCLRF	Comité Consultatif de Législation et de Réglementation Financières
CCSF	Comité Consultatif du Secteur Financier
CDS	Credit Default Swaps
CEA	Comité des Entreprises d'Assurances
CEC	Comité des Etablissements de Crédit
CECB	Comité des Contrôleurs Bancaires Européen
CECEI	Comité des Etablissements de Crédit et des Entreprises d'Investissement
CMF	Conseil des Marchés Financiers
COB	Commission des Opérations de Bourse
CRB	Comité de Régulation Bancaire
CS	Commission des Sanctions
DRE	Direction des Relations avec les Épargnants
DSP	Directive sur les Services de Paiement
EMIR	European Market Infrastructure Regulation
ESMA	European Securities and Markets Authority
FESCO	Forum of European Securities Commissions
FGD	Fonds de Garantie de Dépôts
H3C	Haut Conseil du Commissariat aux Comptes
IFRS	International Financial Reporting Standards
LSF	Loi de Sécurité Financière
OPCVM	Organisme de Placement Collectif en Valeurs Mobilières
PS	Parti Socialiste

3 Financial regulation in Germany

Daniel Detzer and Hansjörg Herr

1 Introduction[1]

This chapter attempts to give the reader an overview of the regulations and supervisory institutions governing the financial sector in Germany. First, a general overview of the structure of the financial system in Germany, its main peculiar features, and some key trends of the last decades will be given. This will be followed by an overview of the supervisory system and its developments. Thereafter, the key characteristics of the regulation of the financial system, which was put in place after World War II and remained relatively unchanged until around the mid-1980s, will be outlined. This then enables the description of the main drivers of change of the system until the outbreak of the financial crisis in 2007. The discussed drivers include the domestic initiatives to vitalize German financial markets, the changing role of the German central bank, and later also the role of international and European attempts to harmonize regulation. Eventually, a brief look at the financial crisis and its effect on regulation will be taken. While the regulatory changes are quite numerous, we only outline the broad changes. Capital requirements and deposit insurance, two particularly relevant types of regulation due to their importance in the public debate, will be discussed in more detail. This section may be skipped by the reader who is only interested in the general picture.

2 Overview of the main features of the German financial system

The German financial system has been classified as a prime example of a bank-based financial system. Despite attempts to promote security markets and certain regulatory changes conducive to their development in the 1990s, banks have remained the main actors in Germany's financial system (Detzer et al., 2013). Additionally, Germany has always followed the principle of universal banking; hence, there are only few restrictions on the types of financial service activities banks can pursue. Therefore, most German banks are in principle universal banks. A peculiar feature of the German banking system is that, in contrast to most other developed capitalist countries, it contains many publicly owned and cooperative banks. In 2014 private banks held 38.7 per cent of the banking sector's assets, while publicly owned banks and cooperative banks held 27.9 per cent and 13.6 per cent, respectively. Additionally, there are some special purpose banks, which account for 19.8 per cent of total assets.

Another defining characteristic is that the banking sector is divided into a layer of large banks, which are often active nationwide and to differing degrees internationally as well, and a layer of smaller locally oriented banks. The first group contains the big private banks and the head organizations of the cooperative and the public banks. The latter consists of the large number of primary savings (446) and cooperative banks (1234) as well as some regionally oriented private banks (159). While in terms of assets the first group of large banks is more relevant, the larger share of loans to the non-financial sector is provided by the group of smaller locally oriented banks (see Table 3.1).

Among the private banks the four biggest banks account for 24.7 per cent of total bank assets. Those are the Deutsche Bank, Commerzbank and Unicredit. The fourth private big bank is the Postbank. However, Deutsche Bank holds 93.7 per cent of its shares, and thus it cannot really be regarded as a separate institution. These big banks have traditionally acted as house banks to Germany's big industrial firms. They were connected through cross-shareholdings and supervisory board seats and formed the core of what was known as *Deutschland AG* (German Inc.). However, due to a variety of reasons, from the 1980s onwards the big banks increasingly retreated from this role and started focusing on investment banking activities (Deeg, 2002).

The savings bank sector consists of the primary savings banks, the regional Landesbanken and Deka Bank. The savings banks are normally owned by local city or county governments. Each savings bank is independent and managed locally and its business activities are restricted to customers within its locality. The main distinguishing feature from private banks is that savings banks main purpose is not profit making, but to serve the public interest of their local community. According to Deeg (2002) savings banks have focused on the provision of low-cost long-term financing based on sustainable long term relations and use this to compete with other banking groups. Despite their not-profit maximizing behaviour, their engagement for the promotion of the local economy and community, and possible influences due to their state ownership, they are not less competitive than their private counterparts. This is confirmed by their ability to maintain their market share in commercial lending. Furthermore, regarding profitability or efficiency, savings banks are not inferior to private banks.[2] The regional Landesbanken are on a second, higher, level in the savings bank sector. Their original purpose was to function as bankers to regional state governments and as the central institutions of the savings banks. Additionally, they developed a wide range of commercial and investment banking activities, in which they compete with the big private banks. A third level of the savings bank sector consists of the Deka Bank, which serves as the central asset manager of the savings bank

Table 3.1 Structure of the German Banking Sector, 1980–2014

Number of banks	*1980*		*1990*		*2000*		*2007*		*2014*	
	No.	*%*	*No.*	*%*	*No.*	*%*	*No.*	*%*	*No.*	*%*
Total	3,334	100	4,638	100	2,740	100	2,015	100	1,807	100
Private banks	243	7.3	365	7.9	294	10.7	260	12.9	276	15.3
Big banks	6	0.2	10	0.2	4	0.1	5	0.2	4	0.2
Regional banks	100	3.0	207	4.5	200	7.3	159	7.9	163	9.0
Branches of foreign banks	56	1.7	60	1.3	90	3.3	96	4.8	109	6.0
Savings bank sector	611	18.3	784	16.9	575	21.0	458	22.7	425	23.5
Landesbanken	12	0.4	12	0.3	13	0.5	12	0.6	9	0.5
Primary savings banks	599	18.0	772	16.6	562	20.5	446	22.1	416	23.0
Cooperative banks	2,289	68.7	3,416	73.7	1,796	65.5	1,234	61.2	1,049	58.1
Regional institutions	10	0.3	6	0.1	4	0.1	2	0.1	2	0.1
Primary cooperative banks	2,279	68.4	3,410	73.5	1,792	65.4	1,232	61.1	1,047	57.9
Others	191	5.7	73	1.6	75	2.7	63	3.1	57	3.2

Table 3.1 Structure of the German Banking Sector, 1980–2014 *continued*

Total assets	*1980*		*1990*		*2000*		*2007*		*2014*	
	Bil. €	*%*	*Bil. €*	*%*	*Bil. €*	*%*	*Bil. €*	*%*	*Bil. €*	*%*
Total	1,202	100	2,681	100	6,148	100	7,626	100	7,844	100
Private banks	283	23.6	720	26.9	1,704	27.7	2,258	29.6	3,034	38.7
Big banks	115	9.6	240	8.9	970	15.8	1,404	18.4	1,936	24.7
Regional banks	128	10.6	410	15.3	613	10.0	690	9.1	846	10.8
Branches of foreign banks	23	1.9	39	1.5	121	2.0	163	2.1	252	3.2
Savings bank sector	461	38.3	942	35.1	2,177	35.4	2,632	34.5	2,187	27.9
Landesbanken	196	16.3	389	14.5	1,223	19.9	1,587	20.8	1,061	13.5
Primary aavings banks	265	22.1	553	20.6	954	15.5	1,045	13.7	1,127	14.4
Cooperative banks	183	15.2	413	15.4	761	12.4	895	11.7	1,068	13.6
Regional institutions	52	4.3	111	4.1	227	3.7	263	3.4	281	3.6
Primary cooperative banks	131	10.9	303	11.3	534	8.7	632	8.3	787	10.0
Others	275	22.9	605.2	22.6	1506	24.5	1840	24.1	1555	19.8

Loans to non-banks	*1980*		*1990*		*2000*		*2007*		*2014*	
	Bil. €	*%*	*Bil. €*	*%*	*Bil. €*	*%*	*Bil. €*	*%*	*Bil. €*	*%*
Total	789	100	1,556	100	3,479	100	3,884	100	3,902	100
Private banks	176	22.3	463	29.8	920	26.4	1,046	26.9	1,093	28.0
Big banks	75	9.5	156	10.0	517	14.8	595	15.3	460	11.8
Regional banks	84	10.6	276	17.7	353	10.2	389	10.0	567	14.5
Branches of foreign banks	8	1.0	13	0.8	50	1.4	63	1.6	66	1.7
Savings bank sector	310	39.3	530	34.0	1,207	34.7	1,358	35.0	1,406	36.0
Landesbanken	129	16.3	197	12.6	541	15.6	636	16.4	547	14.0
Primary savings banks	181	23.0	333	21.4	666	19.1	722	18.6	858	22.0
Cooperative banks	102	12.9	220	14.2	434	12.5	490	12.6	632	16.2
Regional institutions	13	1.6	37	2.4	68	1.9	73	1.9	63	1.6
Primary cooperative banks	89	11.3	183	11.8	366	10.5	417	10.7	569	14.6
Others	201	25.4	343	22	919	26.4	990	25.5	772	19.8

Source: Deutsche Bundesbank (2015), our calculations.

group. Within the group many functions have been centralized, so that the local savings banks can profit from the economies of scale and scope of a big bank, without giving up their local focus.

The cooperative banking sector consists of the primary cooperative banks and two regional institutions. Similar to the savings banks, the primary cooperative banks are limited to local markets and focus mainly on traditional bank lending. They are owned by their members and are required to serve the interests of their members. The two regional institutions act as central organisation for the primary cooperative banks. They also compete with the big private banks and Landesbanken for commercial and investment banking business (Detzer et al., 2013).

As mentioned above, bank loans are the main source of external finance for non-financial firms, with shares and bonds playing a negligible role. German private domestic bond markets are largely used by banks for raising finance and recently also by other financial institutions. The stock markets are also relatively undeveloped. Trading value, stock market capitalization, and turnover ratios did increase with the stock market boom at the end of the 1990s. However, figures are still low compared to the US or the UK.

German private investors mostly hold their financial wealth in the form of bank deposits and insurance policies. The share held directly in the form of shares and bonds is relatively low and restricted to a relatively small group of individuals (Detzer et al., 2013). In the past, foreign investors were not particularly active in the German market. This was in part due to the regulatory framework, which was opaque for outsiders. Stock markets were largely self-regulated and rules regarding insider trading were lax. Other reasons for the reservations of foreign investors towards the German financial markets were the lack of attractive product innovations and relatively high trading fees. According to Lütz (2002) this system was beneficial for the big German banks but also depended on their support. At the same time the Bundesbank (the German central bank) played a moderating role regarding the spread of new financial instruments and actors in Germany, mainly because of concerns about the effectiveness of monetary policy.

Attempts to push this system more towards an Anglo-Saxon system were made by the big banks since the 1980s. These efforts were supported by political parties, the Bundesbank, but also big corporations, all of which had changed their attitudes. We will examine these changes in more detail below. All in all, substantial regulatory amendments were made and Germany experienced a short period of heightened interest for stock markets by the general public during the new economy boom in the 1990s, but the aim of establishing an 'equity culture' failed, and the German financial system remains largely bank based.

3 Supervisory institutions in Germany

In Germany financial supervision was split among different institutions until 2002. There were supervisory offices for each of the three main fields of finance – insurance, securities trading, and banking. A single supervisory authority was founded in 2002 to oversee all three fields. In banking supervision, besides the supervisory authority, the Bundesbank has always had an important role. In 2013, the Financial Stability Committee was established to cover macro-prudential supervision. Besides those bodies on a federal level, there are state-level and special purposes supervisors. The following section will give a short overview of the developments of the actors and the institutional structure of financial supervision in Germany.

Out of the three fields, the supervision of the insurance sector has the longest history in Germany. Already in 1902 the Imperial Supervisory Office for Private Insurance[3] was established. After a couple of changes during the Weimar Republic and the seizing of control by the Nazis in 1939, insurance supervision broke down at the end of World War II. Only in 1951 a Federal Supervisory Office for Insurance and Home Loans (*BAV*) was established again. In 1973 the supervision of building and loan association was transferred to the Federal Supervisory Office for Banking, so that the *BAV* was only responsible for insurance business.

Comprehensive banking supervision was only established after the banking crisis in 1931. Before, only individual groups of institutions (e.g. public savings banks or mortgage banks) or certain types of business (e.g. stock exchanges) had been supervised. An observing banking authority was first established in 1931 by emergency decree. More encompassing supervision was established in 1934, with the Banking Act of the German Reich,[4] which marked the starting point for a general codified banking supervision.

After the end of World War II, banking supervision was decentralized in the Western occupation zones. However, with the Banking Act of 1962 it was centralized again in the Federal Supervisory Office for Banking[5] (*BAKred*) (BaFin, 2014).

This office was entrusted with the supervision of banks, and was tasked with counteracting abuses in the banking system, which endangered the safety of the assets entrusted to credit institutions, interfered with the orderly conduct of banking business, or would have substantial disadvantages for the economy as a whole. For this goal it was allowed to enact regulatory standards for the conduct of banking business. The Banking Act also gave the Bundesbank an important role in the supervision of banks. This included certain participation rights when new laws or regulations were established (Deutsche Bundesbank, 1961). In practice, the Bundesbank was always highly involved in all areas of banking supervision. With its network of state central bank branches[6] and its substantial information it took over most of the day-to-day supervision and reporting (Krupp, 2001). In the following decades the powers and rights of the *BAKred* were extended. This included the extension to the types of institutions falling under its supervision as well as the strengthening of its powers of investigation and intervention (BaFin, 2014).

New rules were established under close cooperation between the concerned ministries, committees and market participants (often represented by the head organisations of banks). After the establishment of standards and rules, it was often left to market participants to ensure compliance to the rules through their respective associations. This practice of delegating, on the one hand allowed the *BAKred* to fulfil its tasks with relatively limited financial resources and manpower, while on the other hand led to a relatively high distance between the *BAKred* and the regulated institutions. Since the end of the 1970s, when international and especially European influence on German banking regulation increased, there was a trend towards more differentiated supervision, which the banking associations were less able to perform. Therefore, the *BAKred* assumed an increasing range of supervisory tasks. At the same time, *BAKred* became a representative in international and European bodies. Therefore, the banking associations lost their importance, while governmental supervision became more relevant (Frach, 2008).

Supervision of the securities sector was only established on a federal level in 1995 with the Second Financial Market Promotion Act[7]. It, for the first time, assigned supervisory powers of German securities markets to a Federal Agency – the Federal Securities Supervisory Office[8] (*BAWe*). It was supposed to ensure the integrity and transparency of capital markets. This included combating and preventing insider trading, monitoring ad-hoc disclosure, and other disclosure duties. Later on, it also became responsible for the supervision of takeovers, market manipulations, and director's dealing (BaFin, 2014).[9]

Reform of the supervisory structure came under discussion at the end of the 1990s, since the current framework was regarded as weak. This was partially due to the agencies being badly equipped in terms of financial and human resources, but also due to the lack of cooperation between the agencies. After lengthy disputes between the Bundesbank, the existing supervisory agencies, and the concerned ministries, a single supervisory authority was established in 2002: the Federal Agency for Financial Market Supervision[10] (*BaFin*). This new authority was structured along the three former fields of supervision. Cross-departments were supposed to ensure cooperation and coordination between the different fields. The Bundesbank's important position within the supervisory process was kept, and enhanced, by codifying it into law (Frach, 2008).

In response to the financial crisis, additional bodies were added to the institutional structure. The Federal Agency for Financial Market Stabilisation (*FMSA*)[11] was established in October 2008 to organize the bailout of problematic banks, and to restore trust in financial markets. It was established under the supervision of the Ministry of Finance and has been responsible for the Financial Markets Stabilisation Fund,[12] for the later established Restructuring Fund,[13] and for the establishment and supervision of Bad Banks (Becker and Peppmeier, 2011). Additionally, the Committee for Financial Stability[14] was established at the Ministry of Finance in 2013, to provide national macro-prudential regulation and serve as a link to the European Systemic Risk Board (Deutsche Bundesbank, 2013).

All over, the supervisory structure in Germany has changed from a system that depended more on self-regulation to one that puts more emphasis on state regulation. Additionally, Germany followed the general trend towards an integrated single supervisory authority. Finally, the strong involvement of the central bank in the supervision of banks is an important characteristic of the German supervisory system.

4 The development of the German system of financial regulation until 2007

4.1 The regulatory framework after World War II

In Germany, banking regulation was established relatively late during the banking crisis in 1931 when Chancellor Heinrich Brüning established it by emergency decree. In 1934 the Law of the German Reich on Banking[15] was implemented, whereby all credit institutions were put under supervision. The Banking Act[16] established in 1961, which is still the central law governing banking today, was based on this law (Lütz, 2002, pp. 116–33). A central tenet of German banking regulation was that it was restricted to set certain standards, like liquidity or capital requirements, but that direct intervention into banks' business decisions remained limited. Limits on banking activities, rules about portfolio composition, interest rate regulations, or branching restrictions were not important in Germany or were abolished much earlier than in other countries (Detzer et al., 2013, pp. 115–36).

The Banking Act used a very broad definition of banking, so that many financial service activities that are not regarded as banking in many other countries can only be conducted by banks. This limits the development of non-bank financial actors to certain restricted areas (such as mortgages, insurance, securities industries) that are governed by special laws. Due to their restrictions on assets and liabilities, those actors do not compete with the main business areas of banks. This encompassing regulatory framework of banking activities limited regulatory arbitrage and the development of a parallel banking system in Germany (Vitols, 1995).

After World War II, security exchanges were organized regionally and were largely self-regulating. While the German federal state governments were the formal supervisory authority of their respective stock exchanges, they pursued a policy of non-interference in capital markets. The regulatory framework was characterized by a lack of transparency and accountability, low protection of minority shareholders and no binding rules against insider trading. Additionally, German accounting rules were geared towards creditor protection (Detzer et al., 2013). Capital markets were dominated by the few big private banks, which had a strong position in most of the self-regulatory bodies of the German exchanges. (Lütz, 2002, pp. 79–89).

Prior to the 1990s, the regulatory framework for securities and securities markets remained relatively stable, which was supported by the big banks and the Bundesbank. The other sectors of the German financial system, public banks (*Sparkassen*) and cooperative banks, also had no incentive to push for changes. Each banking group had its field of business (see above, Lambsdorff, 1989). Until the mid-1980s German banks also did not show much interest in financial innovation. However, one has to distinguish between technology-driven innovation (payment systems, ATMs) and modality-driven innovation (derivatives, securitization, etc.) where the former are mostly useful, while the latter at least when used wrongly and with wrong incentives can be harmful or benefit the financial institutions at the expense of other societal groups (see Shirakawa, 2011). Germany was rather lagging behind on the latter type of innovation, while one of the strengths of the German system was its ability to offer cost-efficient, safe and fast payment and security transaction services (Franke, 1998). The prevailing universal banking principle could be one of the reasons why banks were reluctant towards modality driven innovation. In dual banking systems investment banks try to take over business of commercial banks by issuing new products such as securitized loans. Such a pressure for financial innovation does not exist in universal banking systems. Furthermore, the Bundesbank, as mentioned, resisted liberalization and destabilizing innovations.

4.2 Adaptions of the regulatory framework due to banking crises

While there were continuous small changes in the Banking Act, substantial revisions only occurred after banking crises unveiled serious weaknesses. Here in particular one should mention the bank failure of the Bankhaus Herstatt due to foreign exchange speculation in 1974, and the near default of the Bankhaus Schröder, Münchmeyer & Hengst due to large loan losses in 1983 (Detzer et al., 2013, pp. 115–136). After the breakdown of Bretton Woods and the accompanying currency fluctuations, the Herstatt bank was increasingly active in currency speculation, an area which was barely regulated at the time. After large losses the bank had to declare insolvency and its banking licence was withdrawn. As a regulatory response to this, currency positions were limited and the intervention rights of the supervisory authorities were bolstered. In addition, the crisis increased the pressure on private banks to improve their privately organized deposit insurance scheme. The crisis also had an international dimension – the counterparties in the currency trades, mostly other international banks, had to bear heavy losses. This, together with problems at the Franklin National Bank of New York, led to the setup of a committee, which later became the Basel Committee.

The near default of Bankhaus Schröder, Münchmeyer & Hengst was related to enormous loans, exceeding 800 per cent of the banks own equity, to the Esch-group, which dealt mainly in construction machines. The bank circumvented the large loan regulations, which were in place at that time, by extending loans through its Luxembourg subsidiary (*Der Spiegel*, 1983) and by extending them to different, only indirectly connected firms within the Esch-group. The collapse of the bank was only prevented by concerted action of the private banks, the *BaKred*, the private deposit insurance scheme and the Bundesbank (*Die Zeit*, 1986). As a consequence the Banking Act was amended in 1985, reforming, among other changes, the consolidation rules for borrower units.

4.3 Facilitators of changes from the 1980s on

4.3.1 The push for a bigger role of financial markets

In the 1990s and the early 2000s the German corporate governance system and with it the regulation of securities markets, underwent major changes, which did not result from outside pressure but were largely the product of 'deliberate governmental policy and [...] sustained party and interest groups politics' (Cioffi, 2006, p. 549). This substantial transformation, according to Cioffi (2006), reflects a shift of policy preferences in favour of financial markets that dates back to the years of the CDU/FDP[17] governments of the 1980s.

As mentioned above, traditionally the big German banks had tight relations with the big German industrial firms. The banks provided the firms with long-term loans, held large amounts of their shares, and were represented on their supervisory boards. This way, the banks formed the core of what is commonly referred to as *Deutschland AG*. This favourable position secured the banks a profitable field of business. However, the firms' need for external finance declined in the 1970s, and they increasingly used international markets to raise external finance. Additionally, international banks as well as the *Landesbanken* started competing for business with the big banks. With this, the big banks' business in this area declined. Initially they tried to compensate by increasing business with small and medium-sized companies. However, after this strategy failed, due to the strong position of the savings and cooperative banks in this area, they started to extend their investment-banking activities, mainly through acquisitions of existing international investment banks. With this strategic reorientation the banks loosened their ties with non-financial firms, and at the same time pushed the idea of establishing Germany as an international financial centre (Detzer et al., 2013). Their efforts took the form of the initiative '*Finanzplatz Deutschland*' (Germany as a financial centre) which was founded in 2003. This initiative was active until 2011, and was supported by the lobby organisation of the financial system, the German Ministry of Finance, and the German Bundesbank. Large German firms also supported the strengthening of financial markets, since they saw it as a welcoming opportunity to increase their financial flexibility. Besides these private initiatives, politicians and political parties were also pushing for a change of the system. The Kohl government (in particular the FDP and the pro-EU parts of the CDU) was willing to reform financial markets as the price to be paid for European unity and the single market programme.

But there was also support from parts of the trade unions and the regional governments. However, the Social Democratic Party in particular put the restructuring of financial markets and corporate governance reforms on its agenda. In the 1990s this put pressure on the conservative-liberal government, which was displayed as the defender of managerial elites and an increasingly dysfunctional economic order. Whilst in opposition, the SPD[18] was able to pressure the Kohl government to adopt relatively far-reaching reforms, which were also demanded by the European Commission. However, reforms gained speed when the coalition of the SPD and the Greens[19] came to power under Chancellor Gerhard Schröder in 1998 (see Cioffi, 2006). The most important changes will now be outlined.

Starting already in 1984, the Bundesbank, and later the government, passed a variety of deregulatory measures, which abolished hurdles for foreign engagements in the German financial system (e.g. certain tax laws), and allowed for more financial innovation (Domanski, 2003). However, the more substantial reforms were passed in the 1990s and early 2000s. Three areas of reform were seen as necessary for establishing a – what was regarded at the time – modern (i.e. market based) financial system: (1) regulation of securities and the securities market, (2) company law and corporate governance, and (3) taxation and the *Deutschland AG* Four Financial Market Promotion Acts were passed. The first two in particular aimed at improving accountability and transparency at the level of markets. The third act aimed to do the same at the level of the firm. Lastly, changes in taxation made in 2000 aimed at unwinding the *Deutschland AG* (Cioffi 2006).

Starting with the First Financial Market Promotion Act[20] in 1990, a range of legislative steps was taken to modernize financial markets to become more similar to their US and UK counterparts. The core was formed by the Prospectus Act,[21] which governed requirements for the prospectus of securities' initial public offerings. It was the first legislative act that had as its primary goal the protection of investors in German capital markets, but it also abolished a range of tax hindrances to securities trading, such as the Stock Market Transaction Tax (Deeg, 2005).

According to Vitols (2005), the Second Financial Market Promotion Act, which came into effect in 1995, introduced the most significant changes in regards to securities markets. With it, a range of US practices in financial market regulation were adopted and some EU directives were implemented. It established, for the first time, a federal agency (see above) responsible for the regulation of securities markets, similar to the US Securities and Exchange Commission. This moved the German system away from its focus on self-regulation of the securities markets and exchanges. Other main issues were the banning of insider trading, and more stringent information requirements for issuers of securities and traders, in particular ad-hoc news announcements. The anti-insider trading legislation met severe opposition prior to 1994. After Germany failed to comply with the European Commission Directive by the original deadline, the European Commission initiated infringement proceedings against Germany in October 1992. It was only in 1994 that Germany finally passed the required insider trading law, thereby becoming the last European Community member state to prohibit insider trading. Before the 1994 Act, insider trading was regulated by gentleman's agreements and moral codes, which were binding only in the case of voluntary submission by private contracts. Various insider-trading scandals in the four years prior to the passage of the Act were harmful for foreign investors' confidence in Germany's securities markets. Hence, according to the European Commission, the enactment of anti-insider trading legislation was key to fostering international competitiveness of German financial markets, and to opening those markets further for international investors (Pfeil, 1996). Besides this, a major change was the allowance of money market funds in Germany in 1994, which had for a long time been resisted by the Bundesbank (Fischer and Pfeil, 2004).

The Third Financial Market Promotion Act, including the Control and Transparency in Business Law[22] was passed in 1998. These acts can be seen as complementing the prior reforms of securities market regulations with changes in corporate governance regulation and a weakening of the *Deutschland AG* (Deeg, 2005; Cioffi, 2006). The reforms aimed at far-reaching reductions of banks' power and their role in corporate governance. The original SPD proposal mandated the reduction of banks' equity holdings in corporations, limited board seats, and totally prohibited bank's proxy voting. However, many of these changes were quickly abandoned after intensive pressure from the financial industry (Cioffi, 2002). For example, banks demanded far-reaching tax exemptions if they had to divest their equity shares and announced that they would retreat from providing proxy voting services. Eventually, these issues were dropped from the reform agenda.[23] Regarding banks' power, the final law included only some limitations on proxy voting and board seats.[24] More importantly, the law strengthened the position of the supervisory board against the management board, and introduced additional requirements for transparency and auditing. A third important area in which the law made changes was in the protection and empowerment of minority shareholders. These changes served to weaken insider control and to increase liquidity in securities markets, by abandoning voting caps and instituting a one-share-one-vote rule. The law also prohibited the voting of cross-shareholding stakes in board elections. These were seen as a defence against hostile takeovers, and their abandonment as a way of furthering the development of a market for corporate control. Finally, the new law allowed stock repurchases and the use of stock options as management compensation – practices typically found in Anglo-Saxon countries and associated with the concept of shareholder value.

In 2000 the Tax Reduction Act[25] eliminated the corporate capital gains tax, which up until then had been 50 per cent. This tax was seen as an important barrier to firms and financial institutions being able to liquidate their interlocking cross-shareholdings. Therefore, on the one hand, the Act aimed to increase the threat of hostile takeovers and create a more effective market for corporate control, and on the other hand to increase the liquidity and free float in German stock markets. Shortly after it came into effect in 2002 it set off a wave of corporate restructuring, and a further reduction of the interlocking cross-shareholdings in *Deutschland AG*. With this, for the first time hostile takeovers became a realistic threat for many German firms (Cioffi, 2002; Deeg, 2005).

A further important change was the Securities Acquisition and Takeover Act,[26] which came into force in 2001, and formally regulated mergers and acquisitions. This act limited the defence capabilities of firms against hostile takeover attempts (Bradley and Sundaram, 2003), a particularly controversial issue. Just a week before its passing, an EU directive on this topic was blocked due to German resistance. This has to be seen in the light of the previous pro-takeover reforms, and the hostile Vodafone Mannesmann takeover, which happened in 2000 and revealed the newly created vulnerability of German firms to hostile takeovers. This highly debated takeover was an eye-opener for many former reform supporters, as Mannesmann was one of the traditional big German firms, and had had no economic problems when it was taken over and split apart by Vodafone. In the light of this takeover support for further liberalization measures decreased.

One particular issue was that with the reduction of cross-shareholdings and the abandonment of golden shares, voting caps etc. German firms had given up a range of barriers to takeovers, which were still in place in most other EU countries. German companies feared that when the directive would be passed, they would be asymmetrically exposed to foreign takeovers. The mobilization against the takeover directive at the EU level was paralleled by mobilization against the national law. Due to this resistance, a range of measures that provided defence against hostile takeovers remained. Still, the German takeover rules today are among the most liberal ones (Cioffi, 2006).

The Fourth Financial Market Promotion Act, which also came into force in 2002, enlarged the investment opportunities for institutional investors, and allowed new financial investors to become active in Germany, such as hedge funds in 2004. In addition it aimed to implement the 1997 Basel Core Principles for Effective Banking Supervision. The Act further enhanced investor protection, increased market integrity and transparency, and had a profound effect on rules governing prudential supervisory legislation. Lastly, another major change that took place in 2002 was the establishment of the Federal Financial Supervisory Authority (see above).

4.3.2 The role of the Deutsche Bundesbank

As mentioned earlier, for a long time Germany was regarded as a laggard with regards to modality-driven financial innovation. In parts, this was due to the Bundesbank, which resisted liberalization and the introduction of many financial innovations due to concerns about the effectiveness of monetary policy, minimum reserve requirements, and a spread of short-termism. For example, for a long time and with the partial help of gentlemen's agreements, the Bundesbank limited the use of foreign DM[27]-bonds, certificates of deposits, zero-coupon bonds, and variable interest rate loans, and resisted the introduction of new financial actors such as money market funds. However, starting in the 1980s, the Bundesbank partially lost its capacity and willingness to slow down financial innovations, and secure high standards in banking regulation. Many of the transactions the Bundesbank wanted to inhibit in Germany were conducted abroad by subsidiaries and daughters of German banks, and restrictions in Germany led investors to pursue their business in financial centres like London or Luxembourg. In addition, restrictions inhibited foreign banks entering the German market, and allowed German banks to secure lucrative business for themselves at home. The Bundesbank was aware of these problems, but prioritized its target of monetary stability. It only changed its stance around the mid-1980s. The first signs of a change can be found in 1984, when the Bundesbank supported the abolishment of the coupon tax. After a 1985 Bundesbank internal paper stated that German banks were sheltered from the 'draught' of international competition by prevailing regulation, a major change took place. The paper criticized the Bundesbank for supporting monopoly rents for the banking industry and argued that the prevention of financial innovations in Germany drove residents to use foreign financial markets. Thereafter, the Bundesbank supported the strengthening of foreign banks in Germany, the abolishment of the stock exchange tax, and the liberalization of bond issues. Overall, the Bundesbank came to the conclusion that new financial innovations, such as derivatives and securitizations, did not inhibit its monetary policy to a large degree.

The Bundesbank was rather conservative in the area of banking supervision, where it advocated stricter rules. However, in the 1990s its influence on legislation in this area diminished, in favour of the EU and other international committees. Since then it could thus pursue its agenda, aimed at rather strict regulation, less often (Franke, 1998).

4.3.3 The increasing influence of EU and international regulations

Starting in 1977, directives at the community level were introduced to gradually harmonize regulatory frameworks among EEC member states and to create a single market for financial services. The First Banking Co-ordination Directive (77/780/EEC) set minimum licensing requirements and established the principle of home country control. In the following years further advances were undermined by the inability to agree on a common set of regulations, and only minor changes in the areas of consolidation and accounting followed. A major leap in the harmonization of financial regulation followed the publication of the 'Completing the Internal Market' white paper in 1985. The white paper based the further integration of banking on three premises: single banking licence, home country control, and mutual recognition. These premises were transformed into European law by the Second Banking Directive of 1989. This directive introduced the European Passport for banks. It allowed a bank licensed in one member state to conduct business in any of the other member states, while supervision remained the responsibility of the home country. This required further harmonization in other areas, and therefore, in parallel capital requirements were harmonized on the basis of Basel I.

A further major step in the establishment of the internal market was the full liberalization of capital movements, which was enacted by a directive in 1988 and had to be introduced by the member states by 1990. With the passage of a directive on deposit insurance another important and controversial area of regulation was addressed in 1994.

In 1999 the 'Financial Sector Action Plan' (FSAP), similar to the white paper, listed a range of measures which were seen as essential to accomplishing the full integration of the EU capital and banking markets: a single EU wholesale market, open and secure retail banking and insurance markets, the development of state-of-the-art prudential rules and supervision, and conducive broader conditions (essentially fiscal rules) for an optimal single financial market (Dermine, 2003).

The last step so far was taken by the white paper on financial services policy (2005–2010) published by the European Commission in 2005. The most important measures in this paper are the implementation and enforcing of existing rules stemming from the FSAP, and the fostering of competition between financial service providers, in particular in retail markets (Paul and Uhde, 2010). During the integration of EU-financial service markets many directives were passed in a range of areas, such as large exposure rules, investment services, deposit insurance, financial conglomerates, and crisis management, and only a few fields in banking and financial market regulation remained purely national (Heinrich and Hirte, 2009).

Looking at the impact of EU regulation on the German regulatory framework one has to distinguish different areas of regulation. In some areas EU legislation had no impact at all, since Germany already conformed to the demanded regulations. This was true for the directive on freedom of international capital movement, where Germany had already removed controls before the directive was passed. Similarly, when the first Banking Directive on minimum licensing requirements was passed, German regulation was already in line with it. In the areas of consolidation, financial conglomerates, and crisis management schemes, international regulation determined many of the introduced national rules, since there was no established system of regulation in place in Germany. In the area of consolidation legislative steps were only taken in Germany after an EC-directive was enacted. Before, there were only agreements between supervisors and banks to voluntarily submit information. Consolidation requirements for financial conglomerates were also only established in Germany after a directive was passed at the EC-level. The picture is different in the area of crisis management schemes. While at the EU-level a directive was prepared, Germany passed a national law before the directive was completed. However, the national law was already oriented along the expected directive. According to the current Minister of Finance, this new approach, to pass national regulation before international agreement is reached, is used to speed up the international processes and to set standards that trigger international regulations (Schäuble, 2013a).

The effect of international and especially EU level regulations in areas where long-standing national rules and regulations existed in Germany also differed by the area of regulation. For example, in the area of deposit insurance, Germany had specific schemes for different groups of banks in place, and was reluctant to change those. Eventually it adapted the schemes to conform to the directive without making any substantial changes (see section 5.1 for details).

In the area of capital requirements there was also an established system of regulation in Germany. Here the influence of directives was quite substantial. This can be seen in particular in the issue of eligibility criteria for capital. Despite pressure from some groups of the finance industry on the national level to soften those criteria, the legislator was reluctant to do so, and the Bundesbank was strictly against it. However, a major change took place with the implementation of the Solvency and the Own Funds directives from 1992. Despite concerns of some national actors, a possible topping up[28] on international rules was largely prevented due to concerns about the international competitiveness of German banks (see section 5.2 for details). While for many countries those new rules were stricter than what prevailed originally, harmonization in this field meant a softening of standards for Germany. That the trend to soften equity criteria was misleading became clear when during the financial crisis in 2008 and the following years the problematically low level of capital in many banks was a major problem. With the new Capital Requirements Regulation from 2013 the directive has been reversed and only capital of higher quality can fulfil regulatory requirements. However, this lesson came at high cost to the public purse, and economic development in general.

To sum up, the effect of EU legislation on the German regulatory framework was quite diverse. Sometimes there were no effects, and sometimes the EU legislation added important elements to the national regulatory framework. However, sometimes the EU legislation led to a misguided softening of the national standards. In the last case, Germany reduced its initial resistance gradually and used national freedom for stricter rules less often (Detzer and Herr, 2014; Detzer, 2015).

4.4 The effects of the financial crisis on German financial regulation

The financial crisis, which started in 2007, and the subsequent crisis in the euro area have led to far-reaching changes in financial regulation and supervision in the EU, and therefore also in Germany. This section does not attempt to detail all the numerous changes, but will rather give an overview of the most important ones and discuss some of Germany's concerns and preoccupations with the new regulations.[29] As a direct response to the financial crisis, substantial revisions to banking and securities market regulations were made. Among others, regulations concerning capital requirements, deposit insurance, large exposures, consolidation, corporate governance, credit rating agencies, investment funds and accounting were affected. A novelty in this process was the aim to establish a single rulebook for the EU as a whole. In practice this meant that some key regulations were not passed in the form of a directive, which would leave substantial national discretion (e.g. the Capital Requirement Directive (CRD) III had more than 100 national options), but in the form of EU regulation, which is directly applicable.

An area that received particular attention in public discourse was the reform of capital requirements, which were first changed by the CRD II (2009) and then by CRD III (2010). Eventually, substantial amendments were made by the CRD IV in 2013, which introduced the internationally agreed Basel III regulations. As a major change to previous EU regulation it substantially increased the eligibility criteria for regulatory capital, and increased the total amount of risk-weighted capital banks need to hold. Additionally, it made some minor amendments regarding the use of internal risk models (Detzer, 2015; Masera, 2014).

As shown above, there are large numbers of public and cooperative banks active alongside the private sector in Germany. They are integrated in specific group networks and are central to the German economic model, providing bank finance to a large part of the non-financial corporations. However, these banks are in parts highly leveraged and local governments and cooperative members may have difficulties with increasing the equity of public and cooperative banks quickly. Also, private German banks are relatively highly leveraged in international comparison.

According to Howarth and Quaglia (2013) these specific features made Germany an advocate of softening the Basel III rules when they were implemented as CRD IV. In addition, the high leverage ratio of its banks led Germany to oppose the introduction of a binding unweighted leverage ratio, which in the end was not included in the CRD IV. This opposition was also based on the importance of trade credit for German companies, which is high in volume but regarded as low risk.

A further problem occurred due to the fact that Basel III was developed with large listed commercial banks in mind. The German banking sector includes a huge number of non-listed public and cooperative banks. For these banks, alternative forms of capital, such as silent participation, play a major role. Germany pushed for amendments, so as not to put these banks at a disadvantage. In particular, the classing of silent participation as tier-1 capital was a key concern. Originally, as a hybrid form of capital, it was not counted as tier-1 capital in the Basel framework. Finally, the generally higher importance of bank credit for German firms, in particular small and medium ones, led to a heightened opposition to overly strict equity measures, as these would be more severe in Germany than in more market-based economies. Overall, Germany succeeded in getting exceptions into the CRD IV that took into account the specifics of the German banking system.

Later on, when the euro area crisis unfolded, the general structure of financial supervision and regulation in the euro area was challenged. As an answer to the problems associated with banking failures and sovereign debt problems, discussions on a Banking Union became prevalent in 2012. The Banking Union contains a Single Supervisory Mechanism (SSM) and a Single Resolution Mechanism (SRM), closely related to the Banking Recovery and Resolution Directive (BRRD). Initially, a common deposit guarantee scheme was discussed, but due to strong national interests, it is no longer being considered in current political discussions. With the SSM the ECB took over direct supervision of the large systemically important banks, and indirect supervision for all banks in the euro area. The framework for dealing with troubled banks in the areas of prevention, early intervention, and resolution was set with the BRRD for all EU member states. With the SRM a central mechanism has been established that is applied when a bank under the direct supervision of the ECB is endangered. Additionally, a resolution fund will be established, with the purpose of covering the costs of a resolution process.

The start of the Banking Union was originally envisaged for 2013, and has been considerably delayed. The ECB could only assume its role in November 2014, due to concerns and opposition of some member states, among them Germany. Concerns in Germany included the issues of the legal validity of the SSM and the SRM without a change of the EU Treatise, as well as practical concerns about potential conflicts of interest arising from the combination of monetary policy and supervision within the ECB. The legal structure of the SRM leads to relatively complex decision-making mechanisms, which has raised doubts about its speed and effectiveness during a crisis (Deutsche Bundesbank, 2014; Die Deutsche Kreditwirtschaft, 2013; Hartmann-Wendels, 2013; Schäuble 2014; SVR, 2013). Additionally, as a likely net-contributor to the support and resolution mechanisms established with the SRM, there were worries about moral hazard, from both member states as well as financial institutions (Howarth and Quaglia, 2014). In the policy discussions there were worries about costs that occur due to past supervisory failure, often referred to as legacy assets, in particular, which would be shifted to the new institutions (Deutsche Bundesbank, 2014; Schäuble, 2013; Bundesverband Deutscher Banken, 2013).

However, one of the main issues was the scope of supervision of the ECB and the SRM. Germany was in favour of assigning real investigative and supervisory powers to the ECB, but only in regard to the biggest banks. Savings and cooperative banks, mostly small and medium-sized institutions, were concerned that centralized supervision may be designed for large, systemically important banks while smaller banks might be overburdened with inappropriate regulation, and may have to pay for the risks incurred by those big banks. Therefore, they advocated national supervision for the non-systemic banks, which can take into consideration the specific structure of the German financial system. They were supported in this regard by the Ministry of Finance and the Bundesbank. Part of the opposition also stemmed from the impression that European regulation is geared largely towards capital market based finance, and that this might damage or substantially change the successful and robust German bank based system (Bundesverband der Deutschen Volksbanken und Raiffeisenbanken, Deutscher Sparkassen und Giroverband, 2014). During the negotiations, Germany followed this line of argument and advocated a relatively high threshold regarding which banks to include under the ECB direct supervision. Eventually, the threshold was set at €30 billion of bank assets. This will put the public Landesbanken under direct ECB supervision, which Germany originally tried to prevent. However, as a compromise, it has been agreed that the supervision will be 'differentiated' and carried out in 'close cooperation' with the national supervisors (Howarth and Quaglia, 2013a). For the SRM, Germany also succeeded at advocating a solution in which the smaller local banks remained the responsibility of the national authorities. Only those banks under direct supervision of the ECB, or in cases where the resolution fund should be tapped, fall under the responsibility of the SRM.

5 Detailed look at the financial regulation in specific areas

5.1 Deposit insurance

The system of deposit and investor protection in Germany is rather complex. Today's system is divided by type of institution (deposit taking or not), ownership type (cooperative, private, public), type of insurance (deposit insurance, institutional insurance), and whether the schemes are voluntary or statutory (see Table 3.2 for an overview).

The complexity of today's system stems from its historical development. Until 1931 there was no system of deposit insurance. The Banking Act of 1961 also did not include any regulations in these regards. However, cooperative banks (in 1937) as well as private banks (in 1966) had organized funds for deposit insurance among themselves on a federal level (Nolte and Schöning, 2004). A government report published in 1968 stated that general deposit protection was necessary and that existing schemes were not seen as sufficient. The lack of a legal claim for depositors, and the low capacity of the funds were criticized, in particular. In general, the report recommended the introduction of a general statutory scheme if the existing schemes were not restructured in a way that made them more effective and neutral regarding competition. Threatened by statutory regulation, the private banks reacted promptly with an improvement of their existing funds (Zimmer, 1993). Also, as a reaction to the report, the German Savings Bank and Giro Association established twelve regional savings bank guarantee funds in 1969. Those regional funds were connected due to joint-liability agreements.[30] Before, deposits in savings banks were protected indirectly and to the full amount due to public guarantees[31] and the institutional liability[32] local and regional governments provided for those institutions. However, the report demanded the establishment of funds to reduce the competitive advantage that saving banks had due to their public guarantees (Krätzner, 2002). Despite the fact that central demands of the report (like establishing a legal claim for depositors) were not met, the proposed law for a statutory scheme was withdrawn (Zimmer, 1993).

One of the main differences between the schemes was that savings and cooperative banking groups' schemes both aimed at guaranteeing the survival of member institutions. Therefore, all kinds of deposits were indirectly insured without limitation. In contrast to this, the fund operated by the private banks explicitly did not have the aim of protecting institutions, but only protected certain deposits up to a certain amount.[33]

A further impetus for the development of the deposit insurance schemes came from the default of the Herstatt Bank in 1974 and subsequent problems at other banks. Existing schemes were unable to cope with the situation. The government at that time, under the lead of the social democratic finance minister Hans Apel, was already discussing the introduction of a statutory deposit insurance scheme, if banks were not able to establish sufficiently effective voluntary schemes (Zimmer, 1993).

This threat, as well as an active trend among depositors to transfer deposit to savings banks, which were guaranteed by the state, made private banks react promptly. A guarantee fund was established at the German Association of Private Banks in May 1976 (Krätzner, 2002). The coverage was more encompassing (all sight-, time- and saving deposits were covered) and much higher (30 per cent of the bank's equity per depositor) than in the previous fund (Deutsche Bundesbank, 1992). In the same period, the *Landesbanken* and central clearing organisations of the savings banks were also forced to establish their own insurance scheme. They established the Guarantee Fund of the Central Savings Banks and Central Giro Institutions, which was also aimed at the viability of its members and joined the existing joint liability agreements of the savings banks. The plan for a statutory regime was abandoned. The schemes proved successful during the management of some problem banks and were regarded with high confidence from the general public thereafter (Krätzner, 2002).

With these three protection schemes in place only a few banks were not covered, such as for example some state-owned development banks. Public banks that did not belong to the savings banks sector only introduced a scheme in 1994. This scheme was a deposit insurance scheme similar to that of the private banks, and did not prevent institutions from failing.

At the same time in 1994, the Deposit Guarantee Schemes Directive 94/19/EC[34] was passed, against the vote of Germany. Despite some amendments that made the directive more compatible with existing German deposit insurance schemes (like exemption of banks that belong to an institutional insurance scheme, and the scrapping of a limit to deposit insurance), Germany filed a law suit at the European Court of Justice against the directive. The cited reasons were mainly the incompatibility of some elements of the directive with existing German provisions. First, the directive envisaged an encompassing compulsory membership, while the German system was based on voluntary membership. Additionally, Germany was worried about the so-called 'topping up', which mandated that the subsidiary of a foreign bank had to be enabled to join domestic deposit insurance schemes to increase its protection to the level of the host country. German politicians were concerned about the fact that a foreign subsidiary could join the German scheme but would be supervised by a foreign authority. Additionally, Germany did not agree to the 'export-ban', which limited the cover that German banks' subsidiaries could offer to the level prevailing in the host country. However, the lawsuit was rejected by the European Court of Justice in 1997.

In the same year Directive 97/9/EC[35] on investor-compensation schemes was passed. Since Germany had to introduce the directive 94/19/EC after the rejection of the European Court of Justice, the introduction of both directives in one law suggested itself. This was done with the Deposit Guarantee and Investor Compensation Act[36] of 1998. For the first time a statutory system of deposit insurance was introduced in Germany. Since the German authorities were confident about the existing schemes, the law introduced a scheme which fulfilled the minimum requirements of the directives, while it kept the existing schemes largely unchanged. Three different statutory schemes were introduced. One for private deposit-taking institutions, one for public deposit-taking institutions and one for non-deposit-taking institutions (securities trading banks, financial services institutions, investment companies).

In regards to covered claims and the amount of protection, the statutory systems were mainly oriented at the absolute minimum requirements of €20,000 prescribed in the directive. However, private insurance schemes were amended so that they worked subsidiary to the statutory schemes. Therefore, the protection level did not change, at least for deposit-taking institutions. Due to the absolute minimum in the statutory schemes, concerns regarding the 'topping up'-rule and the 'export ban' were circumvented. By 1999 the 'export ban' had been abandoned by the European Commission (Deutsche Bundesbank, 2000).

Legal limits of the statutory schemes were increased in line with the EU Directive 2009/14/EC, first to €50,000 in 2009 and then to €100,000 in 2011 (Schich, 2009). With this amendment, increased focus was put on early identification of imminent compensation cases, by demanding regular audits by the respective insurance funds of their members and increased information exchange with supervisors. Additionally, the new rules demand that the intensity and frequency of audits, and contributions to the funds should be oriented at the individual risk of institutions (BaFin, 2010).

In 2011 private sector banks decided to reduce the maximum amount covered by their private scheme from 30 per cent of liable capital to 8.75 per cent (which means a minimum of €437,500 per depositor). From 2015 to 2025 this will be gradually implemented (Handelsblatt, 2011).

One additional policy action is worthwhile mentioning. In the course of the financial crisis of 2008, when the Bundesbank informed the government about increasing cash withdrawals, Chancellor Angela Merkel and finance minister Peer Steinbrück guaranteed all bank deposits, without any limit, in a public declaration. This guarantee was renewed when the loss participation of depositors in Cyprus was discussed in 2013 (Die Zeit, 2013).

Table 3.2 Overview of deposit and investor protection schemes in Germany in 2013

Organization	*Institutional protection or statutory depositor/investor protection*	*Voluntary deposit protection*
Deposit taking institutions		
Under private law		
Credit cooperatives and regional institutions of credit cooperatives	Institutional protection (operated by the Federal Association of German People's Banks and Raiffeisen Banks, regional cooperative associations)[1]	
Other deposit-taking institutions (private commercial banks)	Statutory cover of a deposit[2] (maximum 100,000 euro) and up to 90% of a claim arising from investment business[3] (maximum 20,000 euro) (operated by the Compensation Scheme of German Banks (*Entschädigungseinrichtung deutscher Banken GmbH*))[1]	Supplementary cover for deposits not covered by depositor/investor protection[4] per depositor up to 20%[8] of the liable capital[5] of the institution concerned (operated by the Deposit Guarantee Fund of the Federal Association of German Banks)[1]
Under public law		
Savings banks, Landesbanken, public building and loan associations	Institutional protection (operated by the German Savings Bank and Giro Association, regional savings bank associations)[1]	
Other deposit-taking institutions	As in the case of other deposit-taking credit institutions under private law (operated by the Compensation Scheme of the Association of German Public Sector Banks (*Entschädigungseinrichtung des Bundesverbandes öffentlicher Banken Deutschlands GmbH*))[1]	Voluntary supplementary cover of a deposit[6] up to the full amount (operated by the Federal Association of Public Banks)[1]

Continued

Table 3.2 Continued

Organization	*Institutional protection or statutory depositor/investor protection*	*Voluntary deposit protection*
Other institutions		
Credit institutions with principal broking underwriting Credit institutions and financial services institutions with investment broking contract broking portfolio management own-account trading Investment companies with asset management for others	Statutory cover up to 90% of a claim arising from investment business[3] (maximum 20,000 euro) (operated by the compensation scheme of securities trading firms (*Entschädigungseinrichtung der Wertpapierhandelsunternehmen*) at the Reconstruction Loan Corporation)[1,7]	

Source: Deutsche Bundesbank, 2000; our amendments

Notes
1 Administration of a fund's assets for the settlement of claims, compulsory contributions by the cooperating/assigned institutions.
2 Protected deposits mainly account balances and registered debt securities denominated in euro or an EEA currency. Issued bearer bonds in particular, are among the items which are not protected. The protected group of depositors/investors consists mainly of individuals; financial institutions, public bodies, medium-sized and large incorporated enterprises, in particular, are not protected.
3 Protected claims arising from investment business are mainly claims to ownership or possession of funds (denominated in euro or an EEA currency) or financial instruments. Protected group of investors, see footnote 2.
4 Protected deposits are mainly sight, time and savings deposits as well as registered debt securities, irrespective of the currency in which they are denominated (amounts owed to customers). Issued bearer bonds, in particular, are not protected. The protected group of depositors includes all non-banks (especially individuals), business enterprises and public bodies.
5 Sum of core capital and prudential supplementary capital, with the latter being included only up to 25% of the core capital.
6 See footnote 4; certain public bodies (Federal Government, Regional Governments (Länder), their special funds) do not belong to the protected group of legal persons.
7 Unless an institution is assigned to another scheme in specific cases.
8 30% until 2015, 20% until 2020, 15% until 2025 and 8.75% after 2025.

5.2 Capital requirements

Capital requirements have a long tradition in Germany. A provision for capital requirements was already included in the law of the German Reich on banking in 1934. In 1951 the Bank of the German States[37] (the central bank before the Deutsche Bundesbank was founded in 1957) compiled a range of guidelines that specified capital requirements banks should fulfil if they wanted to use the central bank as a refinancing facility. The Banking Act established in 1961 stated that banks had to ensure that their endowment of liable funds was adequate to guarantee the fulfilment of their obligations to their creditors, and to safeguard the assets entrusted to them. The details were laid down for the first time in 1962 in an ordinance named Principle I. It effectively enforced a capital ratio of 5.56 per cent of assets[38] (Deutsche Bundesbank 1962). The balance sheet positions eligible to fulfil equity requirements were quite narrow, and had to comply with three central principles: they needed to be fully paid up, capable of meeting current losses and had to be permanently available to the bank (Deutsche Bundesbank 1988). Therefore, the following positions could be included in the capital base: paid-in capital, open reserves, and capital contributions of silent partners. An exception was special provisions for cooperative banks to add their members' uncalled liabilities to their regulatory equity by up to a maximum of 50 per cent of the amounts of paid up member shares and reserves (Deutsche Bundesbank, 1962).

In two revisions conducted in 1965 and 1969, the range of institutions covered by the Banking Act was extended. More importantly, a simple system of risk weights for loans to certain debtors (e.g. government, other banks) or for a particular type of business (e.g. guarantees) or with certain collateral (e.g. real estate and ship mortgages) was introduced. (Deutsche Bundesbank, 1964, 1969).[39]

The next large amendments were triggered by the crises of Herstatt bank in 1974 (see above). As a consequence of this crisis in 1976, a new Principle Ia was introduced which limited the net exposure to foreign currencies to 30 per cent of a bank's equity (Deutsche Bundesbank 1976). Here for the first time market price risks[40] became explicitly subject to banking regulation.

Caused by the failure of the Bankhaus Schröder, Münchmeyer & Hengst (see above) and due to an EC initiative, a consolidation principle was introduced in 1985, which aimed at preventing credit pyramids, which allowed banks to use equity within a group multiple times (Deutsche Bundesbank 1985).

In the first half of the 1980s savings banks campaigned to have their public guarantees acknowledged as part of equity similar to the cooperative banks' allowance for their members' uncalled liabilities. While the support of the regional governments was mixed, the Bundesbank and the central government opposed the idea (Deutscher Bundesrat, 1984). Eventually, the proposal was rejected. Instead, with the third amendment of the Banking Act in 1985, the allowance of cooperative banks was gradually reduced to 25 per cent. At the same time, the eligibility criteria for capital provided by dormant partners were tightened. A proposal to include subordinated liabilities was rejected as well, because they do not correspond to the three principles for regulatory equity (see above). The only concession made was that certain forms of jouissance right capital[41] were allowed to count as regulatory equity (Deutsche Bundesbank 1985). The discussion shows that there was a strong resistance to lower equity standards, in particular at the federal level and at the Bundesbank.

Also, while the discussion was much about levelling the playing field for the different banking groups in Germany, there was no concern about international competitiveness. The main focus at the time was on stability.

With an amendment of Principles I and Ia in October 1990, the exorbitant growth of off-balance sheet operations in derivative markets was addressed so that, on the one hand, regulatory capital had to be held against the counterparty risk stemming from those trades and, on the other hand, the total amount of open position was limited to 60 per cent of equity (Deutsche Bundesbank, 1990).

The Basel Committee was originally supposed to ensure international cooperation in banking supervision. When, in an environment of increasing international exposure taken on by banks, capital ratios of international active banks declined, its main focus shifted towards developing a common framework for minimum capital requirements. The result of this work was presented as the Basel Capital Accord in 1988 (Basel Committee on Banking Supervision, 2013). The, at that time, European Economic Community (EEC) adopted the results and based the Solvency Directive[42] and the Own Funds Directive[43] on the Accord. However, while the Basel Accord was developed for internationally active banks, the directives applied to all banks in the EEC. They were translated into German law in 1992. The changes mainly contained an extension of the assets that had to be backed by capital[44] and an adaption of the risk weights in line with the directive. In addition the capital ratio was raised from 5.56 to 8 per cent (Deutsche Bundesbank, 1993a).

As a compensating measure for the broader asset base and the higher capital ratio, the eligible forms of capital were expanded. This can be seen as a major change in the overall direction of capital regulation in Germany. The new rules allowed banks to include positions as capital that did not conform to the three principles (mentioned earlier) that were stressed so intensively during prior national discussion. The 8 per cent of the risk-weighted assets now had to be backed with core and additional capital, whereby the minimum amount of core capital had to be 50 per cent of total required equity capital (Deutsche Bundesbank, 1993). Core capital, in line with the three principles, consists only of items that are available to the institution for unrestricted and immediate use, to cover risk or losses as soon as they occur. Additional capital can be regarded as lower quality than core capital, since it is either not visible on the balance sheet or not directly liable or repayable. In particular, the recognition of unrealized reserves as regulatory capital was a highly debated issue in the German discussions. The Bundesbank and German supervisory authority were opposed to the acknowledgement of unrealized reserves, since they expected procyclical effects. The government envisaged only very restrictive use of unrealized reserves in its original proposal. Lobbying by the banks, mainly with the argument that too strict rules would put them internationally at a competitive disadvantage, led to a compromise, which, while softer than the original proposal, was still tougher than what was demanded by the directive. (Deutsche Bundesbank, 1993a).

Further changes were introduced in 1997 when the Banking Act and Principles I and Ia were adjusted to the Capital Adequacy[45] the Financial Services Directives.[46] Also parts of the anticipated Second Capital Adequacy Directive[47] were already implemented. There were four main changes relevant for capital requirement regulation in Germany. A change of the eligible own funds for required equity holdings, the introduction of the trading book, the introduction of capital requirements for market price risks and the allowance for banks to use internal risk models to calculate those market risks (Deutsche Bundesbank, 1998).

While the Financial Service Directive mainly aimed at creating a level playing field for investment firms and banks, the Capital Adequacy Directive introduced the same capital requirements for the same business when carried out by banks or by investment firms. The business of investment firms is largely related to securities transactions. Now banks had to put this type of business in a so-called 'trading book,' while the rest of a bank's business remains in the so-called 'banking book'. All own-account positions in financial instruments, marketable assets and equities taken on by the institution with the intention of profiting from short-term price variations had to be included in the trading book. The own-funds requirements for the trading book were then equally valid for banks and investment firms (Deutsche Bundesbank, 1998).

One of the most relevant changes was that the eligible capital base was extended again. Tier-3 capital, defined as net profits of the trading book and short-term subordinated liabilities, was introduced and could be used to cover certain risk positions of the trading book (Deutsche Bundesbank, 1998). Different to earlier discussion on eligibility criteria for regulatory equity, this amendment gained little attention.

A further important change was made in the regulation of market price risks in 1998. Until then banks had to back their counterparty and credit risks with capital according to Principle I, whereas Principle Ia limited the positions exposed to market price risks as a ratio to equity. This was now changed. Principle Ia was abandoned and assets weighted for market price risks now had to be backed with funds according to Principle I. For the computation of risks the institutions could choose between using a standardized method, or internal risk models. Originally, the proposal of the Basel Committee included only a standard method to determine market risk. Only after heavy lobbying by banks, which argued that the standard method did not encourage improvement of risk management systems and did not acknowledge risk diversification, as well as the internal risk measurement systems of banks sufficiently, a second proposal was released. In this banks were allowed to use internal models to calculate risk for supervisory purposes. If institutions decided to use internal models, the supervisory authority had to approve them. The Bundesbank supported this risk valuation method with the argument that internal risk models avoid multiple calculations for internal and supervisory purposes and so save costs and avoid problems of the standard methods like the misallocation of credit (Deutsche Bundesbank, 1998). In substance the risk models allowed banks to reduce their equity holding substantially, and privileged big banks which could use own risk models (Hellwig, 2008). The criticism against those models, which ranges from their procyclical character, their fundamental failure to capture systemic risk, their technical flaws, to certain incentive problems,[48] has received little attention in the policy debate. This is scandalous, and one is led to suspect that the intense lobbying by the banks, and what Hellwig (2008) terms regulatory capture by sophistication, must be at play here.

Few banks in Germany use internal risk models to determine market risk. In 1997 three banks were using internal risk models, a number that increased to 16 by 2006, after which it fell to 11 by 2012. However, since the banks using the models are most likely big banks, the share of the banking sector, in terms of assets, that uses these models can still be substantial.[49]

Another major change followed the release of Basel II in 2004. The EU Commission translated its content into the directives 2006/48/EC[50] and 2006/49/EC,[51] which had to be implemented by 2007 and 2008 (Deutsche Bundesbank 2006). During the discussion German negotiators had two main goals. One was related to loans towards small and medium enterprises, where Germany pushed for lower capital requirements, and the second was related to intergroup liabilities in the saving and cooperative banking groups, where they pushed for a zero risk weight. They succeeded in both issues (Deutscher Bundestag 2006). The directives were implemented in Germany in 2006 through changes in the Banking Act, in the German Large Loans Regulation,[52] in the Minimum Requirements for Risk Management[53] and the Solvency Regulation,[54] which replaced Principle I.

The main change regarding the eligibility criteria for regulatory capital was the introduction of so-called modified available capital, which became the new key indicator of the Solvency Regulation and therefore for the calculation of capital adequacy. Compared to the liable capital consisting of core and additional capital, the modified available capital has some add-ons and deductions resulting from the use of certain calculation procedures.[55] Regarding the determination of risk, the main changes introduced were capital requirements for operational risk and new calculation methods for credit risks. Following the logic of the calculations of market risk, the standard approach for the determination of credit risk[56] was replaced by two options. Banks could choose to use a standardized approach, which is based on external ratings of rating agencies. Depending on the external rating, different risk weights are applied. For certain types of loans, such as retail loans, loans to small and medium enterprises, or loans collateralized with residential mortgages, preferential risk weights are applied across the board, without considering external ratings (Deutsche Bundesbank 2006). As a second option, banks can use the so-called internal rating based approach (IRB-approach), which is based on internal risk models. Also, for the calculation of risk exposures in derivatives, the range of calculation approaches was extended and the calculation can be based on internal risk models (Deutsche Bundesbank 2006). Again, only a few institutions use internal risk models. At the end of 2010 only 47 institutions used an IRB approach while 1,846 institutions used the standard approach (BaFin, 2011).[57]

The first revisions of capital requirements after the crisis came with the CRDII in 2009. It established definite rules for the eligibility of hybrid capital in the form of a principles-based approach, so that eligibility depends on the characteristics of an instrument, not its form. This led to a need for revisions of the German rules, which were hitherto based on the capital instrument's form. Additionally, it included some technical amendments to internal risk models (BaFin, 2011, Deutsche Bundesbank 2009). The subsequent CRDIII rules, which followed in 2010, included some amendments to the use of internal risk models for the calculation of trading book risks, which had proven problematic during the crisis. Additional capital has to be held based on a stressed Value at Risk, which is calculated based on crisis scenarios. This measure aimed at reducing the procyclicality of the models. Furthermore, a risk charge addressing migration and default risk, which played an important role during the crisis, has been introduced. Additionally, since the ability of banks to evaluate the risk of securitized assets was drawn into doubt during the crisis, the use of internal models for the determination of risk was limited, and overall capital requirements for some trading book positions, in particular resecuritized assets, was increased (European Banking Authority, 2012a). The most relevant change, however, came with the introduction of Basel III. On a European level, the new Basel rules were adopted in the form of the CRDIV and the CRR (Capital Requirement Regulation). A major distinction from former EU legislation in this area was that a large part of the new rules were passed in form of a regulation, which means that the rules apply directly and do not need to be implemented at the national level. As an important change, the new rules break with the trend, which prevailed before the crisis, to allow for ever weaker forms of capital, and sets stricter eligibility requirements for regulatory capital. Three categories of capital remain: common equity tier-1 capital, additional tier-1 capital and tier-2 capital. Compared to the former rules, tier-2 capital has declined in significance and tier-3 capital has been abandoned. The overall amount of tier-1 capital within the 8 per cent capital requirement has been increased. Additionally, a range of buffers has been introduced, which increase overall capital requirements and address procyclicality, systemic risk and takes a more macro-prudential perspective. A flexibility package gives the member states a range of new instruments to address macro prudential risks. Those include higher capital requirements, which can be applied in a discretionary manner, but have to be coordinated with the EU institutions. Of particular relevance for Germany is that, to attenuate negative effects of the new regulations on credit availability or credit cost for small- and medium-sized enterprises (SME), a so-called 'SME-factor' was introduced. This factor neutralizes the higher requirements of the new capital conservation buffer of 2.5 per cent for loans to SMEs (Deutsche Bundesbank, 2013a; Luz et al.,

2013). Overall these regulations remedy some of the problems of the regulations in the tradition of Basel II. However, the trust placed in risk models is unbroken, in spite of their weaknesses.

6 Conclusions and summary

Germany has been the prototype of a bank based financial system. The banking system became strictly regulated after World War II. Capital markets played an unimportant role and were largely controlled by a system of self-regulation. Until the 1980s the Bundesbank, as well as the German government, played an important stabilizing role, preserving the existing system. Financial innovations, which could make the financial system less stable, and new types of financial institutions, like money market funds and hedge funds, were not allowed. This changed moderately in the 1980s and more strongly from the 1990s onwards.

The wave of deregulations in the banking industry, more capital market friendly regulations, and the support of financial innovations as well as the aim of making Germany an internationally important financial centre reflected a change in German government policy. Especially after 1998, under the red-green coalition, the deregulation of financial markets and labour markets became an economic and political project, which was supported by the financial industry and the Bundesbank. The big private banks wanted to go global and take part in the high profits earned in booming financial markets with myriads of innovations. Some of the Landesbanken also wanted to get a part of the seemingly big cake of financial markets. The Bundesbank no longer resisted the deregulation of financial markets and, as many other central banks in the world, may have started to believe in the doctrine of efficient financial markets which became mainstream in that time. From the 1980s on, the international competitiveness of German financial institutions also became a topic, and led to laxer and more market-friendly regulations. At the same time, the regulatory system in Germany became more and more influenced by EU regulation, which was almost entirely in the spirit of the belief in efficient financial markets, and the belief that deregulation of markets would increase efficiency and growth. Germany was reluctant to take over such rules at first, but gave up most of its resistance from the 1990s on.

In spite of the large and positive role of the bank-based financial system in the 'German miracle' after World War II, the change to a more market-based system was attempted in the 1990s and 2000s. While EU legislation had some influence on these changes, the pressure for reform came largely from within. Banks, large firms, social democrats and conservatives all pushed for these changes. Only when the effects became clear with the Vodafone-Mannesmann deal, did tides turn and did further adoption of Anglo American practices into the German system come to a halt. Nevertheless, the German system has undergone substantial changes and many elements, typically associated with market-based Anglo-Saxon financial systems, have been adopted. The German capital market has become more transparent and more easily accessible for foreign investors. The German corporate network has been partly untangled, outsider control has increased, and the market for corporate control has been strengthened.

A key example of the development of German banking regulation is capital requirements for banks. Until the 1990s, banking regulation was largely a national issue. While international coordination attempts picked up shortly after the Herstatt crisis in 1974, those only directly affected German capital requirement regulation in 1992 through EEC-directives. As risk weights were introduced in Germany relatively early the adoptation of this part of Basel I was unproblematic.

In 1998 a major change occurred. While before, the standard approach had dominated capital requirements, new regulations allowed banks to use risk models to calculate risks and regulatory capital. The new rules applied initially for market risks and were later extended to credit risks, and, since 2007, to operational risks. This meant that in an increasing number of areas, internal risk models were allowed for the determination of risk weights for the determination of capital requirements. Intense lobbying by the big banks, as well as the belief in efficient financial markets, stimulated this development. These models suffer from enormous problems: they can be used to significantly manipulate equity requirements, they support procyclical boom-bust cycles, and can destabilize the financial system. It is thus telling that there were barely any debates about their adoption.

In addition, a stepwise softening of the eligibility criteria for regulatory capital could be observed in Germany. This development can be divided into two phases. During the first and largely national period after World War II the eligibility criteria for capital were oriented along three principles: that of being fully paid up, capable of meeting current losses, and being permanently available. The Bundesbank, politicians, and the supervisory authorities strongly resisted pressures to soften these rules. The parliamentary discussions were largely concerned with the stability of the banks, or with the level playing field for different parts of the national financial system. Concerns about German banks' international competitiveness were limited. Starting from 1992, when Basel I was implemented, the eligibility criteria for capital were gradually relaxed. While in the beginning the German legislators used the leeway of the directive to establish stricter regulations than demanded by the directive, the argument of international competitiveness became more and more prevalent in the discussion, so that in 2007, when the Basel II rules were adopted, only the necessary minimum of regulation was introduced 'to avoid overburdening of the banks' (Deutscher Bundestag, 2006).

Overall, from a legal perspective the German regulatory framework has changed and provides the floor for a bigger role of financial markets. The big private banks and some of the Landesbanken used this new freedom, mainly for doing business abroad, and were also heavily affected by the sub-prime financial crisis. The domestic financial system, however, only changed moderately. Savings and cooperative banks play a big and important role, and did not change their general business models. Private wealth owners only temporarily showed more interest in stock markets during the new economy bubble of the 1990s. Cross-holding of shares between financial institutions and industrial companies decreased, and markets for corporate governance were established, but due to strong co-determination rights in almost all big firms a stakeholder corporate governance model prevails, rather than a shareholder approach.[58]

Notes

1 We are grateful to Jim Masterson, Enisa Serhati and Roel van Geijn for helpful editing. Remaining errors are, of course, ours.
2 For an overview regarding research on profitability and efficiency see Detzer et al. (2013), chapters 8 and 9.
3 *Kaiserliches Aufsichtsamt für Privatversicherung.*
4 *Reichsgesetz über das Kreditwesen.*
5 *Bundesaufsichtsamt für das Kreditwesen.*
6 *Landeszentralbanken.*
7 *Zweite Finanzmarktförderungsgesetz.*
8 *Bundesaufsichtsamt für den Wertpapierhandel.*
9 It has to be distinguished from the supervision of individual stock and securities exchanges, which is still in the responsibility of the German states.
10 *Bundesanstalt für Finanzdienstleistungsaufsicht.*
11 *Bundesanstalt für Finanzmarktstabilisierung.*
12 *Finanzmarktstabilisierungsfonds.*
13 *Restrukturierungsfonds.*
14 *Ausschuss für Finanzstabilität.*
15 *Reichsgesetz über das Kreditwesen.*
16 *Gesetz über das Kreditwesen.*
17 CDU Cristian Democratic Union, FDP Free Democratic Party.
18 Social Democratic Party.
19 Bündnis 90/Die Grünen.
20 *Erstes Finanzmarktförderungsgesetz.*
21 *Verkaufsprospektgesetz.*
22 *Gesetz zur Kontrolle und Transparenz im Unternehmensbereich.*
23 It is interesting to note here that, eventually, the banks got the tax exemptions demanded in 2001, without having to accept limits on their cross shareholdings.
24 If banks hold an equity share above 5 per cent, they have to choose between exerting either their own voting rights or the proxy votes of shares deposited with them. It also includes some information duties for the banks.
25 *Steuersenkungsgesetz.*
26 *Wertpapiererwerbs- und Übernahmegesetz.*
27 Deutsche Mark.
28 Topping up describes the practice of introducing stricter national rules than the respective international agreement demands.
29 For a detailed discussion of the changes by policy area see Detzer and Herr (2014).
30 *Haftungsverbund.*
31 *Gewährträgerhaftung.*
32 *Anstaltslast.*

33 The early version of the fund only protected savings as well as wage, salary and pensioners' accounts with balances of up to DM 10,000. This was later extended to all sight and time-deposits and was raised to balances of DM 20,000.
34 Directive 94/19/EC of the European Parliament and of the Council of 30 May 1994 on deposit-guarantee schemes
35 Directive 97/9/EC of the European Parliament and of the Council of 3 March 1997 on investor-compensation schemes
36 *Gesetz zur Umsetzung der EG-Einlagensicherungs-Richtlinie und der EG-Anlegerentschädigungs-richtlinie (Einlagensicherungs- und Anlegerentschädigungsgesetz);* 16 July 1998.
37 *Bank Deutscher Länder.*
38 Some assets could be excluded, e.g. loans to domestic and foreign local and federal governmental entities or some specific collateralized loans.
39 The capital ratio is calculated as $\frac{\textit{regulatory equity}}{\textit{risk weighted assets}}$. Later also market and operational risks multiplied by a certain factor were included in the denominator.
40 Market price risks relate to the risk of losses due to the changes in market prices, while credit risk refers to the risk that a borrower defaults on his contractual obligations to repay.
41 *Genussrechtskapital.* This is a liability, which combines elements of equity and debt instruments.
42 Council Directive 89/647/EEC of 18 December 1989 on a solvency ratio for credit institutions
43 Council Directive 89/299/EEC of 17 April 1989 on the own funds of credit institutions
44 For example, securities were now treated like regular book loans.
45 Directive 93/6/EEC on the capital adequacy of investments firms and credit institutions
46 Directive 93/22/EEC on investment services in the securities field
47 Directive 98/31/EC amending Council Directive 93/6/EEC on the capital adequacy of investment firms and credit institutions
48 For an overview of these problems see Detzer (2015), Hellwig (2008), Herr (2011).
49 For the number of banks using risk models see the yearly reports of the BaFin for the respective years.
50 Directive 2006/48/EC relating to the taking up and pursuit of the business of credit institutions.
51 Directive 2006/49/EC on the capital adequacy of investment firms and credit institutions.
52 *Großkredit- und Millionenkreditverordnung.*
53 *Mindestanforderungen an das Risikomanagement.*
54 *Solvabilitätsverordnung.*
55 For more details regarding the calculation of modified capital see the table 'How to calculate modified available capital' in Deutsche Bundesbank (2006, p. 71).
56 In the standard approach, risk weights between 0 and 100 per cent were allocated to a bank's assets, according to the type of asset and borrower, so that for example for borrowing to banks located in OECD countries a 20 per cent, or for loans collateralized with mortgages a 50 per cent, risk weight applied.
57 According to the Bundesbank, banks using internal approaches are either big and internationally active or specialized small- or medium-sized institutions. While the number of institutions using the IRB approaches for credit risk is small, in terms of balance sheet size they covered 62 per cent of the banking sector (Deutsche Bundesbank 2009).
58 See for further elaboration on this point for example Vitols (2004), Cioffi (2006).

References

BAFIN (2010) Jahresbericht der Bundesanstalt für Finanzdienstleistungsaufsicht 2009. May. Bonn: Bundesanstalt für Finanzdienstleistungsaufsicht.

BAFIN (2011) Jahresbericht der Bundesanstalt für Finanzdienstleistungsaufsicht 2010. April. Bonn: Bundesanstalt für Finanzdienstleistungsaufsicht.

BAFIN (2014) Bankenaufsicht. Available from: www.bafin.de/DE/DieBaFin/AufgabenGeschichte/Bankenaufsicht/bankenaufsicht_node.html

BASEL COMMITTEE ON BANKING SUPERVISION (2013) A brief history of the Basel Committee. Bank for International Settlements.

BECKER, H. P. and PEPPMEIER, A. (2011) *Bankbetriebslehre*. 8th edition, Herne: NWB.

BRADLEY, M. and SUNDARAM, A. (2003).The emergence of shareholder value in the German corporation, *EFA 2004 Maastricht Meetings Paper*. no. 1467.

BUNDESVERBAND DER DEUTSCHEN VOLKSBANKEN UND RAIFFEISENBANKEN, DEUTSCHER SPARKASSEN UND GIROVERBAND (2014) Erklärung der Genossenschaftsbanken und Sparkassen zur Europawahl: Stabilität sichern, Subsidiarität stärken – für die Schaffung einer mittelständischen Bankenpolitik in Europa. 24.03.2014. Available from: www.bvr.de/p.nsf/809BF3015C7C52EBC1257CA50045900C/$FILE/140324_Gemeinsame_Erklaerung_DSGV-BVR.pdf.

BUNDESVERBAND DEUTSCHER BANKEN (2013) Stellungnahme zum Vorschlag für eine Verordnung zur Festlegung einheitlicher Vorschriften und eines einheitlichen Verfahrens für die Abwicklung von Kreditinstituten und bestimmten Wertpapierfirmen im Rahmen eines einheitlichen Abwicklungsmechanismus und eines einheitlichen Bankenabwicklungsfonds sowie zur Änderung der Verordnung (EU). No. 1093/2010 des Europäischen Parlaments und des Rates. 27.09.2013. Berlin. Available from: http://bankenverband.de/themen/stellungnahmen/stellungnahme-zum-vorschlag-fuer-eine-verordnung-zur-festlegung-einheitlicher-vorschriften-und-eines-einheitlichen-verfahrens-fuer-die-abwicklung-von-kreditinstituten-und-bestimmten-wertpapierfirmen-im-rahmen-eines-einheitlichen-abwicklungsmechanismus-und/stellungnahme-deutsch.

CIOFFI, J. W. (2002) Restructuring 'Germany Inc.': The Politics of Company and Takeover Law Reform in Germany and the European Union. *Law and Policy*, 24, 355–402. October 2002.

CIOFFI, J. W. (2006) Corporate Governance Reform, Regulatory Politics, and the Foundations of Finance Capitalism in the United States and Germany. *German Law Journal*, 7, 533–562.

DEEG, R. (2002) Finance *Capitalism Unveiled: Banks and the German Political Economy*, Ann Arbor: Michigan University Press.

DEEG, R. (2005) The comeback of Modell Deutschland? The New German Political Economy in the EU. *German Politics*, 14(3), 332–353.

Der Spiegel (1983) Wie die neuen Rothschilds von Frankfurt. Der Spiegel 45/1983. 07.11.1983. Available from: www.spiegel.de/spiegel/print/d-14022332.html.

DERMINE, J. (2003). Banking in Europe: Past, Present, Future. In: Gaspar, V., Hartmann, P., Sleijpen, O. (eds), *The Transformation of the European Financial System*, 31–96. Available from: www.ecb.europa.eu/pub/pdf/other/transformationeuropeanfinancialsystemen.pdf.

DETZER, D. (2015) Financial Market Regulation in Germany – Capital Requirements of Financial Institutions. *PSL Quarterly Review*, 68(272), 57–87.

DETZER, D. and HERR, H. (2014) Financial Regulation in Germany. *FESSUD Working Paper* Series, No. 55, University of Leeds.

DETZER, D., DODIG, N., EVANS, T., HEIN, E., and HERR, H. (2013) The German Financial System. *FESSUD Studies in Financial Systems*, No.3, University of Leeds.

DEUTSCHE BUNDESBANK (1961) Deutsche Bundesbank Monthly Report. August. Frankfurt am Main: Deutsche Bundesbank.

DEUTSCHE BUNDESBANK (1962) Deutsche Bundesbank Monthly Report. March. Frankfurt am Main: Deutsche Bundesbank.

DEUTSCHE BUNDESBANK (1964) Deutsche Bundesbank Monthly Report. December. Frankfurt am Main: Deutsche Bundesbank.

DEUTSCHE BUNDESBANK (1969) Deutsche Bundesbank Monthly Report. January. Frankfurt am Main: Deutsche Bundesbank.

DEUTSCHE BUNDESBANK (1976) Deutsche Bundesbank Monthly Report. July. Frankfurt am Main: Deutsche Bundesbank.

DEUTSCHE BUNDESBANK (1985) Deutsche Bundesbank Monthly Report. March. Frankfurt am Main: Deutsche Bundesbank.

DEUTSCHE BUNDESBANK (1988) Deutsche Bundesbank Monthly Report. January. Frankfurt am Main: Deutsche Bundesbank.

DEUTSCHE BUNDESBANK (1990) Deutsche Bundesbank Monthly Report. August. Frankfurt am Main: Deutsche Bundesbank.

DEUTSCHE BUNDESBANK (1992) Deutsche Bundesbank Monthly Report. May. Frankfurt am Main: Deutsche Bundesbank.

DEUTSCHE BUNDESBANK (1993) Deutsche Bundesbank Monthly Report. January. Frankfurt am Main: Deutsche Bundesbank.

DEUTSCHE BUNDESBANK (1993a) Deutsche Bundesbank Monthly Report. March. Frankfurt am Main: Deutsche Bundesbank.

DEUTSCHE BUNDESBANK (1998) Deutsche Bundesbank Monthly Report. May. Frankfurt am Main: Deutsche Bundesbank.

DEUTSCHE BUNDESBANK (2000) Deutsche Bundesbank Monthly Report. July. Frankfurt am Main: Deutsche Bundesbank.

DEUTSCHE BUNDESBANK (2006) Deutsche Bundesbank Monthly Report. December. Frankfurt am Main: Deutsche Bundesbank.

DEUTSCHE BUNDESBANK (2009) Deutsche Bundesbank Monthly Report. January. Frankfurt am Main: Deutsche Bundesbank.

DEUTSCHE BUNDESBANK (2013) Deutsche Bundesbank Monthly Report. April. Frankfurt am Main: Deutsche Bundesbank.

DEUTSCHE BUNDESBANK (2013a) Deutsche Bundesbank Monthly Report. June. Frankfurt am Main: Deutsche Bundesbank.

DEUTSCHE BUNDESBANK (2014) Deutsche Bundesbank Annual Report 2013, Frankfurt am Main. Deutsche Bundesbank. Die Deutsche Kreditwirtschaft.

DEUTSCHE BUNDESBANK (2015) Time Series Database. Available from: www.bundesbank.de/Navigation/EN/Statistics/Time_series_databases/Macro_economic_time_series/macro_economic_time_series_node.html.

DEUTSCHER BUNDESRAT (1984) 545. Sitzung. 20 December. Bonn.

DEUTSCHER BUNDESTAG (2006) Plenarprotokoll 16/18. 15 February. Berlin.

Die Deutsche Kreditwirtschaft (2013): Stellungnahme an den Finanzausschuss des Deutschen Bundestages zu dem 'Entwurf für ein Gesetz zum Vorschlag für eine

Verordnung des Rates zur Übertragung besonderer Aufgaben im Zusammenhang mit der Aufsicht über Kreditinstitute auf die Europäische Zentralbank' (Drucksache 17/13470), Öffentliche Anhörung am 3. Juni 2013.

Die Zeit (1986) Intelligente Bankiers oder Gauner? 10 January, 3.

Die Zeit (2013) Merkel garantiert für Spareinlagen in Deutschland. 18 March.

DOMANSKI, D. (2003) The impact of financial regulation on financial structures in post-war Germany. *Quaderni di Ricerche.* No. 45. Ente Luigi Einaudi for monetary, banking and financial studies. Available from: www.enteluigieinaudi.it/pdf/Pubblicazioni/Quaderni/Q_45.pdf.

European Banking Authority (2012) EBA Guidelines on the Incremental Default and Migration Risk Charge (IRC) EBA/GL/2012/3, May, London.

FISCHER, K. and PFEIL, C. (2004) Regulation and competition in German banking: An assessment. In Krahnen, J. P. and Schmidt, R. H. (eds), *The German Financial System.* Oxford: Oxford University Press.

FRACH, L. (2008) *Finanzaufsicht in Deutschland und Großbritannien. Die BaFin und die FSA im Spannungsfeld der Politik.* Wiesbaden: Verlag für Sozialwissenschaft.

FRANKE, G. (1998) Notenbank und Finanzmärkte. In Deutsche Bundesbank (ed.). *Fünfzig Jahre Deutsche Mark. Notenbank und Währung in Deutschland seit 1948.* München: Beck.

HANDELSBLATT (2011) Privatbanken senken Garantien für Sparer. 17.10.2011. Available from: www.handelsblatt.com/unternehmen/banken/einlagensicherung-privatbanken-senken-garantien-fuer-sparer/5149040.html.

HARTMANN-WENDELS, T. (2013) Stellungnahme zum „Entwurf für ein Gesetz zum Vorschlag für eine Verordnung des Rates zur Übertragung besonderer Aufgaben im Zusammenhang mit der Aufsicht über Kreditinstitute auf die Europäische Zentralbank'.

HEINRICH, T. and HIRTE, H. (2009) Bankrechtskoordinierung und –integration. In Derleder, P., Knops, K.-O. and Bamberger, H. G. (eds). *Handbuch zum deutschen und europäischen Bankrecht.* Berlin: Springer.

HELLWIG, M. (2008) Systemic risk in the financial sector: An analysis of the subprime-mortgage financial crisis. *Preprints of the Max Planck Institute for Research on Collective Goods 2008/43*, Bonn.

HERR (2011) Money, expectations, physics and financial markets: Paradigmatic alternatives in economic thinking. In: Ganssmann, H. (ed.). *New Approaches to Monetary Theory: Interdisciplinary Perspectives.* London: Routledge.

HOWARTH, D. and QUAGLIA, L. (2013) Banking on stability: The political economy of new capital requirements in the European Union. *Journal of European Integration*, 35(4), 333–346.

HOWARTH, D. and QUAGLIA, L. (2013a) Banking Union as Holy Grail: Rebuilding the single market in financial services, stabilizing Europe's banks and 'completing' economic and monetary union. *Journal of Common Market Studies*, 51(9), 103–123.

HOWARTH, D. and QUAGLIA, L. (2014) The steep road to European banking union: Constructing the single resolution mechanism. *Journal of Common Market Studies*, 52(9), 125–140.

KRÄTZNER, D. (2002) Einlagensicherungsfonds Aufsichtsrechtliche und kartellrechtliche Fragen. Institut für Deutsches und Internationales Bank- und Kapitalmarktrecht. Available from: www.uni-leipzig.de/bankinstitut/dokumente/2002-02-20-01.pdf.

KRUPP, H.-J. (2001) Umorganisation der Bankenaufsicht, Mittelstand und Bundesbankstruktur. *Wirtschaftsdienst. Zeitschrift für Wirtschaftspolitik*, 81(2). ZBW.

LAMBSDORFF, O. G. (1989) Die Macht aus den Hinterzimmern. *Die Zeit*, 27 October, 44.

LÜTZ, S. (2002) *Der Staat und die Globalisierung von Finanzmärkten. Regulative Politik in Deutschland, Großbritannien und den USA*. Frankfurt, 116–133.

LUZ, G., NEUS, W., SCHABER, M., SCHNEIDER, P., WAGNER, C.-P. and WEBER, M. (2013) *CRR visuell. Die neuen EU-Vorschriften der Capital Requirements Regulation*. Stuttgart: Schäffer Poeschel.

MASERA, R. (2014) CRR/CRD IV: The trees and the forest. *PSL Quarterly Review*, 67(271), 381–422

NOLTE, B. and SCHÖNING, B. (2004) Die Reform des Haftungsverbunds der Genossenschaftsbanken: Abkehr von Solidarprinzip. paper presented at International cooperatives forum. September 2004. Münster. Available from: http://www-wiwi.uni-muenster.de/06/igt/papers/Workshop16/Abstracts/Dr_S_Sch%C3%B6ning_B_Nolte/ELS-IGT2.pdf.

PAUL, S. and UHDE, A. (2010) Einheitlicher europäischer Bankenmarkt? Einschätzung der Wettbewerbssituation vor und nach der Finanzkrise. *Wirtschaftsdienst*, 90(13), 26–34.

PFEIL, U. C. (1996) Finanzplatz Deutschland: Germany enacts insider trading legislation. in *American University International Law Review*, 11(1), 137–193.

SCHÄUBLE, W. (2013) The Banking Union: Another step towards a tighter-knit Europe. 23 October. Federal Ministry of Finance.

SCHÄUBLE, W. (2013a) Wir sind auf dem richtigen Weg. 19 March. Federal Ministry of Finance.

SCHÄUBLE, W. (2014) Mit gesünderen Banken in die Bankenunion. 5 March. Federal Ministry of Finance.

SCHICH, S. (2009) Challenges associated with the expansion of deposit insurance coverage during Fall 2008, Economics: The Open-Access. *Open-Assessment E-Journal*, 3, 2009–2020.

SHIRIKAWA, M. (2011) What is so special about financial innovation?. Keynote Address at the Conference on 'Welfare Effects of Financial Innovation'. Held by the De Netherlandsche Bank, 11 November. Available from: www.boj.or.jp/en/announcements/press/koen_2011/data/ko111114a.pdf.

SVR (2013) Gegen eine rückwärtsgewandte Wirtschaftspolitik. *Jahresgutachten*. 2013/14, November. Wiesbaden: Statistisches Bundesamt.

VITOLS, S. (1995) Inflation versus central bank independence? Banking regulation and financial stability in the U.S. and Germany. *WZB Discussion Paper FS I 95-312*. Berlin.

VITOLS, S. (2004) Negotiated shareholder value: The German variant of an Anglo-American practice. In *Competition and Change*, 8(4), 357–374.

VITOLS, S. (2005) Changes in Germany's Bank-Based Financial System: implications for corporate governance. In *Corporate Governance: An International Review*, 13(3), 386–396.

ZIMMER, K. (1993) *Bankenregulierung: Zur Begründung und Ausgestaltung der Einlagensicherung. Eine ordnungstheoretische Analyse auf der Grundlage der Modernen Institutionenökonomie*. Baden-Baden: Nomos.

4 Financial regulation in Italy

Liberalizations, prudential rules and governance

Giampaolo Gabbi, Massimo Matthias and Pietro Vozzella

Introduction

In Italy the key changes of banking and financial regulation before the crisis were the liberalization and privatization process within the financial system, the radical change from a structural regulation aimed at maximizing stability to a prudential regulation whose purpose is to optimize efficiency. After the crisis, regulatory interventions have been focused on internal governance, managers' remuneration and the banking crisis resolution.

The literature on financial stability argues that increased competition causes riskier banking behaviour and deteriorates bank assets. Consequently, financial liberalizations are a source of instability. The literature is generally in favour of the view that competition causes riskier banking. Chan et al. (1986) demonstrate that the marginal benefit of credit screening will be reduced when loan rates decrease. Gehrig (1998) shows that banking competition reduces screening efforts when the benefits from identifying profitable projects exceed the benefits of avoiding unprofitable projects. According to Schnitzer (1999) the overall loan quality, in a competitive banking market, declines. Dell'Ariccia (2000) shows that competition may lead to reduced screening. Hellmann et al. (2000) demonstrate that increased competition lowers banks' franchise values and thus encourages risky behaviour. There is also evidence of a positive link between financial liberalization and financial crises (Demirguc-Kunt and Detragiache, 1998; Gruben et al., 1999).

In the past two decades, many financial markets have resorted to financial liberalization in order to foster financial deepening. In the meantime, the frequency and degree of harshness of financial crises have increased. The question is whether there are inherent trade-offs between efficiency, indicated by lower loan rates, and soundness of the financial system, and between financial deepening and stability.

The purpose of Italian regulation was addressed by the Banking Law (article 5): reaching towards efficiency while maintaining the stability experienced during the period 1936–1985, when very few idiosyncratic banking failures occurred.

Our analysis shows that most of the regulatory effort, both in banking and in financial systems, was devoted to reducing entry barriers and to increasing competition strength. On balance, regulators failed to achieve both their goals, efficiency and stability. On one side, no significant positive effects due to increased competition were recorded; on the other side, the weakness of financial institutions when the crisis struck their resilience appears to be one of the most relevant in Europe, as confirmed by asset quality review and the stress test run by the European Central Bank in 2014.

1 Liberalizations. capital movements, credit market and financial services

Italian financial regulation experienced a long period, from 1936 to 1985, characterized by a structural approach, based on the hypothesis that, by modelling banking market structure, regulators would be able to manage banks' performance and help them reach their goals. The Italian regulatory priority has been stability for the period between 1936 and 1985. The goal has been pursued through the design of an oligopolistic market structure. One (un)intended consequence was the inefficiency of banking activity. To handle the issue, Italian regulators, partly forced by the EU framework, introduced some innovations aimed at liberalizing most of the financial processes, such as capital movements, banking and financial activity, and financial advisory services.

In this section we describe how these reforms have radically transformed the Italian financial system environment.

1.1 The liberalization of capital movements

To understand the process of the Italian progressive removal of its system of currency payments controls and, more generally, on capital liberalization we refer to the general principle contained in the Currency Act (no. 786/1956), which stated that 'all exchange transactions are prohibited unless specifically permitted'.

The 1970s were characterized by a phase of increasing financial protectionism, including some restraining measures imposed by Italian authorities on purchase of foreign securities, international loan and credit transactions, and access to forward hedging. On April 1976, in order to prevent capital outflows and speculation against the Italian lira, Law no. 159/1976 introduced some of the most important offences such as exporting currency and holding capital in foreign accounts. In the 1980s, the Italian Authority used capital controls with the purpose of ensuring the necessary degree of monetary autonomy and reducing the risk of speculative attacks against the currency stability and central banks' reserves.

In 1985 the European Council clearly identified free capital movements as one of the main goals to reach a full economic and monetary integration and set the end of 1992 as the deadline for the completion of an internal market with free movement of goods, persons, services and capital. Italy complied in a very short period; the main step towards the liberalization process was set with Law no. 599/1986 that changed the previous principle 'all is prohibited' into 'freedom of economic and financial relationship with abroad'. Some important restrictions, such as investment of foreign securities, were removed.

Before Directive 88/361, the liberalization process was triggered by the New Exchange Control Act (no. 148/1988), in which the principle 'all exchange transactions are prohibited unless specifically permitted' was substituted by 'all exchange transactions can be carried out unless specifically prohibited'. All the restrictions on commercial and financial transactions by residents with non-resident agents were abolished, with few exceptions; the full liberalization process was realized in 1990. Its adoption stated the end of the exchange controls monopoly, the abolition of restrictions on authorized bank's foreign exchange management and all remaining foreign exchange restrictions.

The impact on financial agents was prompt and noteworthy: the net position of investment dynamics, that is international investments Italian residents hold (at least 10 per cent of the ordinary shares or voting power) in a foreign company. It is a proxy of capital movements, which rapidly increased from 2000 (Figure 4.1).

During last two decades, net direct investments in Italy have recorded a stable increase until 2006 when they reached the peak (about €31 billion). In 2008 world flows of direct investment were powerfully affected by the financial crisis, owing both to the deterioration in the economic outlook and to firms' reduced self-financing capability and access to credit. The net inflows of direct investments (new investments net of disinvestments) towards Italy dramatically fell from €29.4 billion in 2007 to a negative value in 2008.

The liberalization of capital movements has been a source of weakness for public debt management. The freedom to take exposure in foreign markets and the elimination of the currency risk within the euro area caused the dependence from foreign institutional investors, for about 40 per cent of the total public debt from 2–3 per cent in 1998.

1.2 The liberalization of the banking market

The reduction of the Italian banking market entry barriers began in 1985 when the First Banking Directive was transposed (D.P.R. 350/1985). Since then, the liberalization of the market characterized the number of players, their businesses, the geographical distribution and concentration, and their organizational models. Cross-border competition was pursued as a goal to increase efficiency and, at the same time, market completion in terms of monetary, credit and financial services.

The Second Banking Directive (89/646/EC, hereafter SBD) has represented the most important EU legislative initiative concerning cross-border

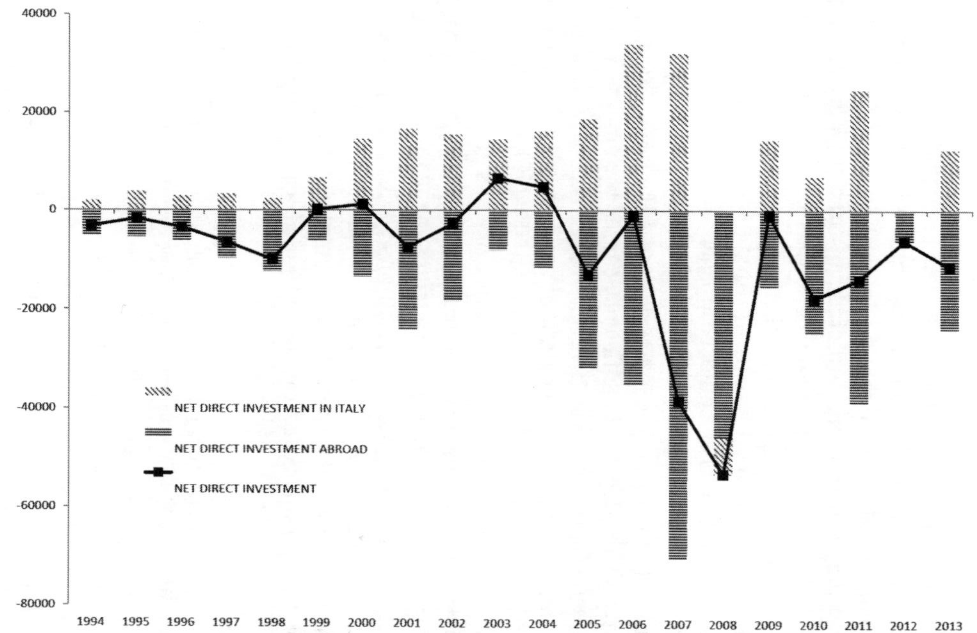

Figure 4.1 Net direct investment (millions of euros) (1994–2013)

competition and permitted activities and subsequent liberalization of credit activities. The aim of the Directive was twofold: a short-term goal was to create enforceable minimum standards regarding the conduct of financial affairs in Europe and a long-term goal was oriented to the coordination of monetary policy to favour economic and monetary union in Europe. With the introduction of the mutual recognition principle, each member state had to recognize the licences from other member states. The 'single banking licence' was the cornerstone of the SBD.

Before its adoption, in Italy this issue was regulated by the 1936 Italian Banking Act, which was based on the separation between commercial and investment banking, the constraints on maturity mismatch and the public governance of credit institutions. All credit institutions were regulated and supervised by the Bank of Italy and the Ministry of Finance Committee (CICR). The supervision was based on the principle of stability and competition was substantially ignored because it could be a source of instability. As a consequence, new branches could be opened or transferred only after a specific (and discretionary) authorization established by the Bank of Italy.

At the end of the 1980s, the common idea was the Italian banking system suffered from a strong degree of inefficiency caused by public governance and structural-based regulation.

The first step towards the elimination of entry barriers was introduced by the Bank of Italy's banks' branch planning of 1982 and by the Decree no. 350/1985, that introduced for banks the nature of firms (instead of institutions) with the purpose of inducing a change from an oligopolistic to a competitive market through the introduction of a prudential regulatory approach.

More precisely, the purpose of regulation (1993 Banking Act, article 5) was not only finalized to maintain financial stability, but also to reach a higher level of efficiency. The paradigm was that, in liberalizing the market with a capital constraint based on risk weighted assets, banks could reach both goals.

The concentration process accelerated in terms of size: between 1990 and 1995 the total assets held by the five largest banks was around 30 per cent of the total system; in 1999 this value rose to 48 per cent. At the same time, with the banking system liberalization, from 1996 to 2008 the number of branches increased by about 40 per cent (Figure 4.2). The distribution of lending activity confirms the small share of southern regions that received a small portion of resources, ranging from 15 to 18 per cent of total loans.

The Italian banking system, as it was until the end of the 1980s, was not able to face the impact of liberalization and the opening of the market to European banks. The legal status of most banks, which were not adapted to firm activity, their very small size that was prohibitive of acquisitions abroad, and the operating constraints which characterized Italian banks' activity, made for difficulty in reacting to the competition of European banks.

In the early 1990s, a few legislative bills deeply modified the structure of the Italian banking system. Law 218/1990 ('Amato Law') was aimed

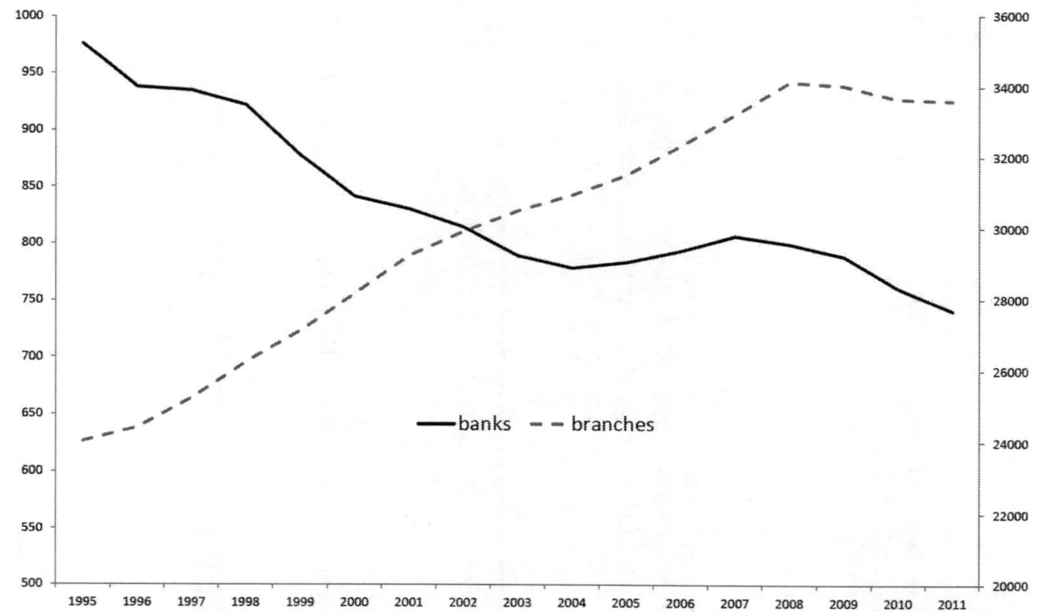

Figure 4.2 Banks (left hand scale) and banking branches (right hand scale) (1995–2011)

at privatizing the banking system by transforming public credit institutions into joint-stock companies: the saving banks, which until then were operating in the short-term sector, transferred their banking activities to ad-hoc joint stock banking; companies were converted into foundations assuming all the socially oriented tasks provided for by the status of the savings banks.

By 1993 the largest privatization process had been implemented. The most important state banks and insurance companies had been sold and listed through IPOs. Most of them were directly controlled by banking foundations, with a public nature. At the beginning of the 1990s neither banks nor institutional investors played a significant role in Italian companies' ownership (Table 4.1).

Whereas banks still showed a limited presence in non-financial companies capital, ownership by institutional investors significantly increased over the years between 1990 and 2010.

The structure of corporate regulation allowed banks to be capitalized during the financial turmoil after 2007. Nonetheless, in some cases, the excessive asset concentration and the strategic model to hold the bank control stimulated their leverage, with a doubtful sustainable perspective.

Thanks to tax incentives, merger operations, very rare until the end of 1980s, starting from 1990 recorded a remarkable increase and justified the introduction of the 'gruppo polifunzionale' (bank conglomerate).

The legal adoption of the SBD took place in 1992 when the principles of mutual recognition and of the home country control were finally introduced with the Legislative Decree n. 481. The distinction between savings banks and credit special institutions was abolished and the model of universal banking was addressed as the best solution to pursue.

Table 4.1 Ownership structure of listed banks (percentages, weighted by market capitalization)

Shareholder	*1990*	*1998*	*2007*	*2011*
Insurance	0.6	3.2	2.1	2.7
Bank	5.8	11.3	3.5	7.3
Foreign	1.8	8.5	6.1	7.8
Foundation	11.1	17.4	13.8	14.5
Institutional investor	0.5	0.1	0.0	0.0
Private non-financial companies	2.1	0.9	4.2	2.3
State	36.8	1.0	0.0	0.0
Individual[1]	2.6	1.4	2.0	6.9
Dispersed ownwership[2]	38.7	56.4	68.3	58.5

Source: Del Prete (2008) and our elaborations on Consob data.

Structural supervision was substituted by prudential supervision. In order to allow the credit institution to freely operate its choices from ones of political economy, the supervision was not directed at the market but at the company.

For the first time, in addition to the traditional purpose of stability and efficiency, competitiveness was listed as a primary goal. This is a first issue which could have originated a strong driver towards speculative behaviours finding banks unable to survive with the capital levels estimated before the crisis.

1.3 The liberalization of the financial services

The European Community achieved its goal to regulate security markets with the adoption of the Investment Service Directive (ISD) in 1993. Similarly to the SBD, the ISD, reaffirming the principle of mutual recognition based on home country control, was aimed at harmonizing essential minimum prudential standards of behaviour.

It was addressed not only to investment firms but also to banks and other financial institutions providing investment services.

The core of the Directive was the principle of mutual recognition: to the extent that an investment firm was authorized by its home national regulator to provide specified investment services, it was able to supply this latter in any other member state. No other authorization was requested.

With the purpose to fully realize an European single market, investment firms authorized by the authorities of their States to perform the listed activities in the Directive, could become members, or have access, to the exchanges of the host member states.

Before the introduction of the ISD in Italy, the first existing regulation was Law no. 2/1991 on brokerage activity. It stated that this activity was reserved to specialized financial firms (SIMs) along with banks. Moreover, it was allowed only to companies with legal head office in Italy, completely prohibiting cross-border activities. With the purpose of improving the transparency of the securities trades, the Italian legislator stated the principle of *stock exchange trading concentration*, that is the obligation to trade the transferable securities traded exclusively in regulated markets.

The most important changes of Eurosim Decree, like the Second Banking Directive, were the adoption of the *home country control* principle to the financial sector also, the abolition of the stock exchange concentration principle to which followed a new regulated market structure and organization, the privatization of the stock exchange and new rules concerning supervision activity.

Again, as for banks, the ISD aimed 'at transparency and accuracy of the conduct and the sound and prudent management of the supervised subjects having regard for to the investor protection and to the stability, to the competition and good operating of the financial system'. It was possible, therefore, to identify two intermediate goals: (i) transparency and accuracy of the conduct of the supervised subjects, (ii) sound and prudent management. The purpose of this strategy was to achieve the final goals of investors' protection, stability, competition and, finally, good operating of the financial system (Pontolillo, 1997).

Technological innovations and increasing complexity of financial markets did impose a review of the previous rules. In 2004, Directive 2004/39/ECC on markets in financial instruments (also known as MiFID) was approved. Differently from the ISD, MiFID stated the principle of *maximum harmonisation*, which provided the same rules to be applied across the EU and single countries could only impose additional requirements in limited circumstances.

The Directive was addressed to entities whose regular business was to provide investment services and perform investment activities on a professional basis; the most important rules were aimed at ensuring investor protection (*conflicts of interest* and *best execution rules*); reinforcing integrity and transparency market; promoting the competition between regulated market and other negotiation systems.

MiFID was adopted in Italy in 2007, involving important changes in national legislation, such as the introduction of the 'investment advice' and the 'multilateral systems of negotiation'. According to the Finance Act 'investment services and activities' refer to dealings for own account; execution of orders for clients; subscription and/or placement with firm commitment underwriting or standby commitments to issuers; placement without firm or standby commitment to issuers; portfolio management; reception and transmission of orders; investment advice; management of multilateral trading systems.

The liberalization for the activity of investment advice activity was complete, because it was considered among 'ancillary services' and, therefore, without the need of any authorization.

With the purpose of allowing investors to acquire a full awareness both of their rights and their duties deriving from investments, a client classification was adopted that did not have any corresponding concept in the legislation previous to the Legislative Decree 164/2007. Financial clients were classified as public professional costumers, private professional or retail customers. Although 'all information, including advertising and promotional notices, addressed to customers and potential customers by intermediaries must be correct, clear and not misleading', this customer classification is aimed at protecting clients characterized by lower financial knowledge or expertise. The Consob Regulation n. 16190/2007 stated that intermediaries must provide customers and potential customers with appropriate information about the nature of the investment service, the specific types of financial instruments involved and related risks, on the intermediary and his services, on the safeguarding of financial instruments and sums of money of the customer, on costs and charges involved in the provision of services, and about their classification as retail customer, professional customer or qualified counterparty.

The obligation to act in clients' best interests has meant for investment firms the need to conduct specific tests about the nature of the investment services offered to, or demanded by, customers. Particularly, the Consob Regulation n. 16190/2007 stated that in order to recommend the investment services and financial instruments suited to the investor, the intermediaries must obtain necessary details from the client in relation to both its awareness and experience of the investment sector relevant to the type of instrument or service and the financial position and the investment objectives. Moreover, intermediaries must verify that the client has the necessary level of experience and awareness to understand the risks deriving from the instrument or investment service offered or requested.

Given that the client, generally, is not able to supervise the accuracy of the investment firms activity, the 'best execution' rule has been introduced. Intermediaries must adopt all reasonable measures to achieve the best possible result for their clients, in terms of price, cost, speed and probability of execution and settlement, size and nature of the order and any other relevant consideration to the execution.

The elimination of the trading concentration obligation originated the explosion of trading venues, such as 'regulated markets', 'multilateral trading systems management' and 'systematic internalizers', with the liberalization of the opportunity for banks and other financial firms to address the trade in different kinds of markets. The new market environment appears to be more difficult to supervise, having been designed with the purpose of maximizing price competition. Nevertheless, it showed the unintended consequence of reducing liquidity and traceability of banks' behaviour.

Finally, Italy applied different kinds of administrative measures and fines, and criminal sanctions, such as violations of good repute, experience, independency requirements, failure to ensure sound/prudent management. Administrative fines and criminal sanctions actually appeared to be decided in very few cases.

Within the policy to modernize the Italian financial market and coherently with the liberalization framework, the investor protection against market abuses was adopted for the first time with Law 157/1991, which implemented Directive 89/592/ECC concerning regulations on insider trading and manipulation.

In Italy, Directive 2003/6/ECC was adopted with Law 62/2005. The major changes introduced in the Finance Act of 1998 were relating to the *disclosure of inside information* and the *market abuse* with particular reference to *insider dealing*.

To disclose market abuses, listed issuers and the entities controlling them *had to* make available to the public, *without delay*, the inside information that directly concerned them and their subsidiaries. In some cases, properly regulated by CONSOB, the listed issuers could, under their own responsibility, delay the communication of privileged information to the public, in order to avoid prejudice to their legitimate interests.

According to the Italian rules, inside information was the information of a precise nature which has not been made public relating, directly or indirectly, to one or more issuers of financial instruments or one or more financial instruments and which, if it were made public would be likely to have a significant effect on the prices of those financial instruments (price sensitive information.

It was considered of precise nature if (i) it refers to a set of circumstances which exists or may reasonably be expected to come into existence or an event which has occurred or may reasonably be expected to occur; (ii) … b) it is specific enough to enable a conclusion to be drawn as to the possible effect of the set of circumstances or event referred to in paragraph a) on the prices of financial instruments.

Differently to the previous legislation, the effect of the inside information on prices should be measured with regard to normal use within an investor's decision-making process.

Law 62/2005 distinguished between primary insiders ('any person who possesses inside information by virtue of his membership of the board, management or supervisory bodies of an issuer, his holding in the capital of an issuer or the exercise of his employment, profession, duties, including public duties, or position') and secondary insiders ('any person who, possessing inside information and knowing or capable of knowing through ordinary diligence its inside nature, carries out any of the actions referred to therein').`The alleged crimes were, (a) use of inside information, (b) disclosure unjustifiably of inside information (tipping ban) and (c) use of inside information by subjects who have obtained, directly or indirectly, such information by the primary insider.

An important innovation (the first in Europe) concerned the *duties of disclosure* provided for rating agencies which, for the first time, were required to take reasonable care in producing or disseminating the information related to issuers, ensuring that the information was fairly presented.

The market manipulation referred to the financial instruments listed in a regulated market. According to the Italian Financial Act, market manipulation referred to 'any persons who disseminates false information or sets up sham transactions or employs other devices concretely likely to produce a significant alteration in the price of financial instruments'.

With Law 62/2005, differently to the previous rules and to be compliant with provisions provided by Directive 2003/6, in addition to the penal sanctions, administrative penalties both for insider trading and market manipulation crime were introduced.

Finally, financial intermediaries were asked to communicate to the supervisory body abnormal investment cases, by customers or employees, in terms of amount, price, concentration, in order to ease the way regulators could identify abuses.

2 The introduction of prudential rules in Italy

In this section, we explore the way Italian regulators have designed the regulation concerning capital requirements, within the European framework, from Directive 1989/299, through Basel II and, finally, with the Basel III proposal, enhanced in the CRD IV.

2.1 Regulation before Basel II

The purpose of the adoption of Directive 89/299/CEE was to implement the Community legislation concerning prudential supervision of operative credit institutions that refers to the concept of own funds covering normal banking risks.

Italy decided to activate the option to include subordinated loan capital in own funds. This decision was based on the assumption that, in the event of liquidation of the credit institution, they are not to be repaid until all other debts have been settled.

Subordinated debts accepted as regulatory capital must fulfil a few criteria. First of all the funds must be totally deposited, their maturity must be at least of five years and, if the maturity is not fixed, those debts are refundable previous a notice of five years or with an agreement of the competent authorities. The subordinated debts are considered own funds with a graduated reduction over five years. Lastly the lending contract must not contemplate clauses stating that the debt can be refunded before the maturity except of the liquidation event.

On the asset side, risk weighted assets (RWAs) were compliant with the Basel Committee proposals. Italian regulators also allowed the bank to include fixed-term cumulative preferential shares in own funds. Off-balance sheet items are converted into on-balance sheet exposures in order to contribute to the RWA calculation. The application of this regulation has been criticized for many reasons: the assumption that banks were exposed only to credit risk; the same consideration for hedged and unhedged exposures; the same weight for small and large exposures; adverse selection and moral hazard behaviour problems (Gabbi, 1994).

With Directive 93/6/CEE, the credit risk was associated to market risk within the capital requirement set of rules. In 2000, with a new Legislative Decree (259/2000), the Italian prudential regulation introduced for the first time the opportunity to adopt a validated internal model for market risk exposures as an alternative solution to the standard formula for determining the capital requirement.

The Bank of Italy introduced some prerequisites to substitute the standard formula with the internal model. The bank must adopt value at risk models with a holding period of 10 days or less and with a confidence interval of least 99 per cent. Moreover, they ought consider the highest value between VaR(t-1) and the average VaR of the 60 days before and multiply this value by a multiplier ranging between 3 and 4 based on the number of violations appearing from backtesting.

Regarding qualitative and organizational requirements, directors and senior managers must be committed, risk managers must be independent, specialized and able to report frequently tests on results.

Along with prudential regulations, the banking system has reformed its accounting; the most relevant event was the implementation of IAS/IFRS standards, based on the use the mark-to-market approach. The most relevant innovations introduced with the adoption of new accounting principles are: (i) the fair value approach with results on income statement for trading exposures and minority interests; (ii) the fair value approach affecting the capital for available-for-sale securities; (iii) amortized cost for held-to-maturity exposures and loans; (iv) nominal value for liabilities. It is specified that a market to market approach refers to accounting for the 'fair value' of an asset or liability based on the current market price, or for similar assets and liabilities, or based on another objectively assessed 'fair' value.

2.2 The evolution of prudential rules with the New Capital Accord (Basel II)

In 2006 with Directives 2006/48/EC and 2006/49/EC (Capital Requirements Directive – CRD), Community legislation adopted the principles developed in Basel II. Italy implemented these directives in 2006, introducing a new definition of regulatory capital based on two components: 'base capital' and 'supplementary capital'. The supplementary capital cannot be higher than the base capital. The minimum capital requirement remains 8 per cent of RWAs.

While the market risk management approach confirmed the same approved in 2000, the credit risk capital requirement can be estimated either with the standard formula or with Internal Ratings-Based (IRB) approaches. A common feature of these approaches is the allocation of exposures across different portfolios ('asset classes'), typically differentiated by type of counterparty to which different risk weights are assigned. Italy allowed banks to use both approaches simultaneously, though on different portfolios and/or portions and only for a certain amount of time (7 years) so as to allow them to become familiar with the more advanced metrics. The options adopted by the national Italian regulator are the following:

- within the Standard Formula, for loans to banks allocated in countries rated between BB+ and B- or without rating, the coefficient is 100 per cent; the regulator can increase the weight for borrowers without rating when justified by previous critical events; to apply the deduction of 25 per cent for retail loans, the regulator will check the diversification of credit portfolios; non-residential mortgages can be applied with a 50 per cent weight instead 100 per cent, in case the collateral is a commercial real estate.

- within the Internal Models, minimum capital requirement is required to ensure the bank stability; liabilities linked to the share's value can be excluded by the capital definition; banks can extend progressively the IRB to other legal entities within the group or they can use a partial IRB permanently; there is a different definition of small and medium enterprises (total assets instead of sales); some short-term assets are valuated not on yearly basis but coherently with their duration.

Other minor options have been applied to covered bonds, mapping and rating agencies recognized by other countries.

Following the Basel proposal and the Directive content, operational losses are covered by a capital requirement whose estimation should be calibrated either with a standard formula (basic and standardized approaches) or with advanced/internal approaches.

Significant regulatory changes deserved deepening of the treatment of large exposures and the Bank of Italy implemented them with Instruction no. 263/2006.

A large exposure is a credit to a client or group of connected clients whose value is equal to or superior than 10 per cent of own funds. The maximum limit of 25 per cent and the total amount of large exposures must not exceed 800 per cent of own funds.

Both on-balance and off-balance sheet exposures were considered. Moreover, credit protection providers writing insurance or derivatives contracts (e.g. CDS) must be added to the total of all the other exposures to the same counterparty. Fixing the limits for banks, the Bank of Italy choose the most favourable of options, indeed the limit can be surmounted in the case of exposures to a bank in three situations: (i) the amount is within €150 million; (ii) the global exposure to bank-related customers, if not banks, is lower than 25 per cent of the capital; (iii) the bank estimates the exposures is within the risk appetite and, in any case, below the limit of 100 per cent of capital. In addition when the counterparty is a banking group the limit is 40 per cent. Moreover, in case of intra-group loans, the Bank of Italy applied a zero weight when involved legal entities are under home country control (only for EU banks).

2.3 Prudential regulation changes after the crisis

A few months after the introduction of Basel II, one of the first effects of the financial crisis was that regulators realized that previous definitions of regulatory capital were inadequate to cover bank losses. The previous prudential approach has not changed, it was only empowered by new capital and liquidity constraints. The only exception was the introduction of the leverage ratio, which is not based on RWAs (Gabbi et al., 2015).

The new capital requirements rules (after Directives 2006/48/CE and 2006/49/CE have been changed by Directive 2010/76/CE – CRD III) were introduced in the Italian regulatory system in spring 2011.

Bank capital is empowered, especially because of the introduction of the automatic cancellation of interest payment when the bank is under the minimum capital requirement. The clause to pay the interest delivering shares (ACSM) is not allowed. Innovative instruments will include nominal value cut or transformation in share mechanisms. The limit to include these instruments has increased from 20 per cent to 50 per cent. In case of payment in advance or with a contract maturity the limit is 15 per cent. The contingent convertible bonds or bail-in bonds (bond obliged to be converted into common equity in contingency situation) have a computational limit equal to 50 per cent. Banks can apply the prudential treatment provided by article 49 CRR concerning the possibility 'not to deduct the holdings of own funds instruments of a financial sector entity in which the parent institution, parent financial holding company or parent mixed financial holding company or institution has a significant investment'. In this case, the shareholdings will be considered as equity exposures. Finally, banks authorized cannot exercise the discretion to use Advanced Measurement Approaches to hold a floor lower than the Basel I floor (8 per cent).

Significant new rules regarding deductions for the calculation of regulatory capital have been introduced, such as: (i) the capital of banks' insurance subsidiaries above a 10% threshold; (ii) the minority excess capital of banking subsidiaries; (iii) the value of any defined-benefit pension fund asset; (iv) their investments in unconsolidated financial institutions above a 10% threshold; (v) all deferred tax assets that arise from net-loss carry-forwards. Most expected solutions for compliance and for raising capital quality include(i) buying out minority stakes or reducing the excess capital of banking subsidiaries; (ii) reducing unconsolidated investments below the thresholds defined by the regulator for capital deductions; (iii) reviewing pension contracts for a more precise understanding of the amount of pension assets that can be easily and promptly liquidated; (iv) rationalizing portfolios of deferred tax assets in detail in respect to both their composition and their amount.

In addition, the Basel Committee introduced several changes to the market risk treatment above all regarding the general and specific risk measures for the internal model. The general risk, which applies across all products, has had the addition of a stressed VaR to the standard VaR calculation; for the Italian banks the stressed period has been defined as the year 2011, when credit ratings affected the value of sovereign bonds.

Another innovation introduced is that all securitized products, including synthetic ones, will now have to use the ratings-based standard model. This means collateralized synthetic obligations (CSOs) will be treated like assets in the banking book, and their risk weights will depend on ratings and seniority. The risk weights for resecuritizations, such as leveraged super-seniors (LSS) or CDO squared products, will also increase significantly.

For correlation products (such as liquid credit derivatives, index tranches, and nth-to-default baskets) banks can also use an alternative risk-based approach: the Comprehensive Risk Measure (CRM).

The CRM must capture all price risks including: incremental default risk, migration risk, spread risk, basis risk, volatility of implied correlations and so forth. The capital charge for the CRM is the maximum between CRM at time (t-1) and the 12-week average value of the CRM. However a minimum floor is imposed fixed as a percentage of the charge that would be applied using the ratings-based approach.

For all positions in the trading book with migration/default risk, banks also must calculate weekly the Incremental Risk Measure (IRC) through an internal model. Here the regulator requires that P&L is derived from a dynamic strategy, where each position is rolled over after the end of its liquidity horizon; the liquidity horizon is position-dependent and is greater than or equal to three months; the equity instruments can be incorporated at the bank's discretion; the IRC must be back-tested and does not apply to securitization products and, finally, the counterparty risk is not measured.

No specific risk charge needs to be added if the supervisor agrees that VaR already incorporates specific risks and the bank's internal model already captures incremental default and migration risks.

The main implications of the reform are that the specific risk surcharge is abandoned; there is not diversification between VaR incremental risk and VaR market; the bank has to rebalance its portfolio for every liquidity period; it assumes 'constant level of risk' rather than buy-and-hold for one year; the correlation between credit losses and market losses is perfect; there are issues of double-counting of risks between the 10-day VaR capital calculation and the IRC calculation.

Regarding the settlement risk, the Bank of Italy has decided to exercise discretion, allowing the prior netting between a convertible and an off-setting position in the instrument underlying it. For this purpose, the Bank of Italy has established two different procedures by which banks are obliged to process the convertible. In the first case, convertibles are included among debt securities, in the second case they are included either among debt securities or among equity securities based on the likelihood of being converted (delta equivalent value).

Moreover, before the full application of the regulatory technical standards established by EBA, for the purposes of the assessment of the own funds requirements for position risk, foreign exchange risk and for commodity risk, the Bank of Italy has exercised discretion, allowing the national treatment existing before 31 December 2013 to apply to options and warrants.

Improving the banking sector's ability to absorb shocks arising from financial and economic stress and improving liquidity management are the core of the Basel III framework, translated into the 2013/36/EU Directive – CRD IV.

For its adoption, the Bank of Italy established the use of a large amount of discretion to ease the introduction of capital deduction and conservation buffer, along with the application of capital requirements foreseen in the last stage (e.g. tier 1 at 5.5 per cent instead of 6 per cent and a phasing-in for deductions).

The main changes refer to treatment of capital and liquidity requirements. On the capital side, the follow buffers are provided: (i) the Capital Conservation Buffer that is composed of common equity for an amount that varies from 0 per cent to 2.5 per cent of RWAs at the discretion of the bank. Constraints on a bank's distributions will be imposed when a bank falls into the buffer range; (ii) the Countercyclical Buffer that is imposed within a range of 0–2.5 per cent comprising common equity, when authorities judge credit growth implies an uncontrolled increase of systematic risk.

Moreover, within the standardized framework, the Bank of Italy has decided to fix a 0 per cent risk weight factor for banking exposures with counterparties belonging to the same banking group, with exceptions of those giving rise to tier-1 and tier-2 items.

Regarding the preferential treatment of covered bonds, with Circular no. 285, the Bank of Italy has stated that institutions investing in covered bonds should communicate to the competent authority the value of outstanding covered bonds, their geographical distribution, loan size, interest rate and currency risks, and their maturity structure.

For these items there are specific risk weights when a credit assessment drawn by an elected ECAI is available, otherwise they refer to those assigned to senior unsecured exposures to the issuing company.

Finally, regarding the exposures secured by mortgages on residential property or by commercial immovable property, the Bank of Italy can set a risk weight higher in case of relevant considerations relative to the financial market stability. The risk weight factor can increase to 150 per cent.

Whilst for the IRB approach, the Bank of Italy can set, without compromising financial system stability, higher minimum values of exposure weighted average LGD for exposures secured by property being located within Italy.

Finally, the Bank of Italy has exercised the national discretion on the treatment of equity exposures allowed by article 495 (1) CRR, stating that, until 31 December 2017, the national authority can state that certain categories of equity exposures held by EU institutions until at 31 December 2007 are exempt from IRB treatment.

One of the most relevant innovations introduced by Basel III is related to the liquidity risk measurement and management, with the liquidity coverage ratio (LCR) and the Net Stable Funding Ratio (NSFR). The Bank of Italy allows banks belonging to a banking group not to apply the provisions on liquidity coverage requirements on an individual basis. In this case, the liquidity requirements provided by CRR have to be followed by the parent institution on a consolidated basis.

The Bank of Italy has exercised the discretion concerning the liquidity outflows establishing an outflow rate of 5 per cent for trade finance off-balance sheet related products and allows the banks to apply a lower outflow percentage, on a case-by-case basis. Banks that intend, fully or partially, to exempt themselves from the limit of 75 per cent inflows, where the provider is a parent institution, need the Bank of Italy's prior authorization. Many options have been adopted by the Bank of Italy to ease the adoption of the new rules allowing Italian banks to maintain their portfolio mix and reduce the impact of the prudential rules.

Italian banking appears to be suffering more than any other large European country in case of stress, because of the large sovereign bond and non-performing loans exposure (Table 4.2).

Table 4.2 Baseline and adverse scenarios for banks' core tier 1 by country after the ECB stress test

Country	*2013*	*2016*	*2016*
		Baseline	*Adverse scenario*
Italy	9.5	9.3	6.1
Austria	10.5	10.6	7.4
Belgium	14.0	11.9	7.4
Cyprus	4.4	9.5	–1.0
Denmark	14.2	15.4	11.7
Finland	16.4	17.6	12.0
France	11.3	11.8	9.0
Germany	12.8	12.8	9.1
Greece	9.9	8.0	2.0
Hungary	15.9	17.0	11.9
Ireland	13.2	12.2	7.0
Latvia	9.8	10.5	7.7
Luxembourg	15.9	15.1	11.2
Malta	10.7	13.2	8.9
Netherlands	11.6	12.2	8.9
Norway	11.3	14.4	11.3
Poland	13.3	15.4	12.3
Portugal	11.1	10.1	5.9
Slovenia	15.9	14.4	6.1
Spain	10.4	11.6	9.0
Sweden	15.3	16.9	13.7
United Kingdom	9.8	11.2	7.6

Source: European Banking Authority (2014).

The EU average value of CT1 in 2013 was 11.1 per cent, the worst-case scenario in 2016 should be 8.4 per cent. Only Portugal, Greece and Cyprus show capitalization values lower than Italy. Even though these results could depend on many factors, such as the public bailouts, or the risk-weighted assets methodology, this shows that Italian banks after two decades of prudential regulation appear to be particularly weak in case of worst case scenarios.

3 Governance, compensation and safety net of financial intermediaries: the Italian perspective

The financial crisis brought forward many issues among regulators and economists about the robustness of the assumptions behind the regulatory model. As seen in the previous section, the prudential regulation approach has not been dismissed, only reinforced. Along with the new rules designed after the crisis, we describe some of the most relevant features of the regulatory framework to recalibrate the internal governance of control processes, to remove executive compensation incentives to increase risk appetite and to manage banking crises.

3.1 Internal governance and executive compensation

In the last decades both regulators and supervisors have focused their attention to the rules concerning the business conduct within financial firms, for a better safeguard of financial consumers, generally characterized by inadequate financial knowledge.

The crucial issue of Corporate Governance has triggered a series of initiatives at international level (OECD, 1999; BCBS, 1999) aimed at identifying principles that would have had to represent a reference point for policymakers to build and develop good corporate governance with a sound legal and regulatory basis.

The deficit of harmonization rules and the adoption among countries of different legal framework and standards has particularly affected large financial companies where financial difficulties resulting from corporate governance failures have involved widespread problems in the financial system. The international financial crisis has highlighted these deficiencies.

On March 2008, the Bank of Italy issued a regulation regarding banks' internal organization and corporate governance according to which banks would have had to choose the corporate governance model which was most likely to ensure the efficiency of operations and the effectiveness of controls, taking into account the costs involved in each model. On July 2013, new relevant rules to enforce the effectiveness of the internal control system were introduced. Banks were asked to separate compliance and risk management, to ask their owners to report directly to the board, as well as the audit function. Even though these new rules represented an improvement in terms of a real prudential banking behaviour, many concerns remained (Gabbi, 2012): control managers cannot report directly to the Bank of Italy in case the business decisions could damage the bank's safeness; the separation between compliance and risk management could weaken the control process; the composition of the boards is still far from recognizing the importance of a technical background able to realize the assumptions behind most of the risk and capital metrics.

An important part of the wider problem of the separation between ownership and control is represented by the issue of executive compensation, and therefore of the remuneration policies.

Many studies have analysed the relationship within the ownership structure (Barontini and Bozzi, 2011) or the corporate governance (Mehran, 1995; Ferrarini and Moloney, 2004; Fahlenbrach, 2009; John et al., 2010) and the remuneration of executive directors. Many critics have underlined the role of short-term incentives implied in the structure of the remuneration systems, which did not ensure the alignment between executives' goals and prudent risk-taking functions and the creation of economic value, at the root of the last financial crisis. The opinion that the structure of the remuneration system and incentives has been the main factor that triggered the financial crisis is widely shared (Brunnermeier, 2009; Davies, 2010; Jannuzzi, 2011; Winter, 2011). Other studies found no evidence that short-term incentives led to excessive risks (Ferrarini and Ungureanu, 2011). A good remuneration system could play an important role in increasing the economic value of a firm if it is able to attract and hold within the company skilled human capital and if it is built so that the management choices are consistent with the shareholders' risk profile. Conversely, if it is designed to incentivize short-time oriented policies, a remuneration system can encourage behaviours characterized by higher levels of risk than those compatible with a safe and sound management and, therefore, not in compliance with shareholder's interest. In fact, short-time oriented business conduct is, generally, characterized by a risk profile aligned neither to shareholders' interests nor to the principle of sound and prudent management and, as a consequence, it can lead to the loss of the economic value of the company (short-termism) (Dallas, 2011).

The issue of executive compensation has also received wide attention during the crisis because of the its great social impact. The increasing in inequality recorded in the last years has made public opinion very sensitive to this issue. 'This is probably because remuneration is not just a technical issue but has everything to do with perceived fairness, which leads people to make moral judgements' (Winter, 2011, p. 5).

In April 2009, the Financial Stability Forum (then Financial Stability Board) issued 'Principles for sound compensation practice' aimed to discuss an effective governance of compensation and to align the compensation systems with risk management and risk governance (FSF, 2009). According to the 'one size does not fit all' principle, the proposal was to reduce incentives towards excessive risk taking that may arise from the structure of remuneration systems.

Directive 2010/76/EU (CRD III), in order to harmonize the remuneration policies of banks and other financial firms across countries, made the standards prescribed by the Financial Stability Board in 2009 binding rules in the European system.

The main goal of the CRD III's remuneration rules was to encourage effective risk management and to avoid the pursuit of short-term gain at the expense of long-term results. The directive prescribed a set of rules which covered all relevant issues referring to remuneration system such as the balancing between fixed and variable remuneration, unsustainability of the guarantee variable remuneration and the possibility to activate either 'malus' mechanisms or clawbacks clauses. The 'malus' systems are mechanisms operating during deferred periods as a result of which variable remuneration can be reduced in relation to the dynamics of the risk-adjusted results or to the capital levels. The clawback clause refers to the return of a payment already paid to a staff member and it refers to both up-front and deferred portions.

In Italy, general principles on remuneration policies were already present before the crisis although they were particularly or exclusively addressed to listed companies.

On August 2004, banks were obligated to provide themselves with a corporate governance model where the remuneration mechanisms and incentive systems were aimed to dissuade managers from undertaking management choices not aligned with the bank's strategies. In 2008 with the purpose of making the Treasury Decree effective, the Bank of Italy issued a supervisory regulation particularly relevant for banks and other financial intermediaries that adopted the two-tier governance system.

In relation to the crucial issue of executives' compensation and incentive mechanisms, the general principle sponsored by the Bank of Italy maintained that, although

> the remuneration of persons responsible for the internal control function and of the manager responsible for preparing the financial statements must be commensurate with their considerable responsibilities and commitment ...

at the same time

> remuneration schemes must not conflict with a bank's prudent risk management policies or its long-term strategy. In particular, equity-based incentives (e.g. stock options) or performance-linked pay must take account of the risk borne by banks and be structured so as to avoid generating incentives that conflict with their long-term interests.

In March 2011, to implement the CRD III, the Bank of Italy issued a new regulation 'Supervisory provisions concerning remuneration and incentive policies and practices in bank and banking groups'. The structure of the remuneration systems and incentives mechanism represented the core of the regulation. The total amount of any remuneration had to be split into fixed and variable quotas and the distinction between these two components had to be strict. The evaluation of the ratio between fixed and variable components, although balanced, had to be made according to the complexity of the bank activities and to the features of staff member, with particular regards to the relevant personnel. Moreover, it was established that the employee's fixed compensation had to represent a sufficiently high proportion of his total remuneration, providing for the possibility to completely eliminate the variable part when the risk-adjusted performance, effectively obtained, was not aligned with the targets.

Detailed criteria to be followed for determining the variable component of the remuneration were introduced: (a) at least 50 per cent had to be balanced between shares, share-linked instruments or, for not listed banks, equivalent financial instruments and where appropriate, non-innovative capital instruments limited to 50 per cent of tier-1 capital, (b) an appropriate retention policy (with regards to the up-front portion of the variable remuneration component, the retention period had to be at least 2 years whereas for financial deferred instruments, the retention period could be shorter allowing for the duration of the evaluation period of performance) should be provided for all of these instruments, (c) the payment of at least 40 per cent of the variable remuneration component had to be deferred over a period not less than 3 to 5 years so that the remuneration was coherent with risks undertaken by the bank over the time (for executives or, more generally, for personnel and business areas characterized by a higher risk profile, the deferred part had to be increased at least 60 per cent), (d) in order to ensure that its total amount was sustainable regarding the financial situation of the bank and did not limit its ability to strengthen its capital base, ex-post correction mechanism had to be provided for, (e) for banks and banking groups receiving special government support, the variable remuneration was strictly limited as a percentage of net revenue when it was inconsistent with the maintenance of a sound capital base and timely exit from government support.

The task to define the remuneration and incentive systems, referred to executive managers, general directors and staff members having internal control functions, was attributed to the body having strategic supervision functions, which was obliged, on a yearly basis, to find out the implemented remuneration policy.

To increase the awareness of the overall costs and underlying risks of the chosen remuneration system, the task to approve the remuneration policies addressed to the bodies having supervisory, management and control functions was given to shareholders.

Large banks, as well as listed banks, were obliged to constitute a 'remuneration committee' whose members would have had to be non-executives and, the majority of them, independent. This is based on Fernandes (2005) who found that while firms with more non-executive board members paid higher wages to their executives those with zero non-executive board members had less agency problems and a better alignment between shareholders' and managers' interests. The committee was attributed both advisory and proposals tasks regarding the remuneration of corporate officers and advisory tasks related to the top managers' compensation. The mission to check the congruence between the remuneration practices and the provisions of the national supervisory authority was assigned to internal audit.

As in the Directive, the implementation of the new rules provided for a some flexibility depending on the characteristic, size and complexity of the activity of the bank (principle of proportionality). While large banking groups were obliged to fully comply with the community rules, some of the relevant provisions, in particular those referred to the structure of the incentive systems, were not binding for smaller banks.

In order to give application to the proportionality principle, the National Supervisory Authority, outlining the Supervisory Review and Evaluation Process (SREP) divided intermediaries into five macro-categories: (a) intermediaries having a significant international presence; (b) 'nationwide systemically relevant intermediaries': entities – including those controlled by foreign-based intermediaries – with total assets of no less than €20 billion and, conventionally, other intermediaries, other than those referred to in point (a), which are allowed to use internal risk-measurement systems for calculating capital requirements (intermediaries with 'authorized systems'); (c) 'medium-large intermediaries': entities – not falling within macro-categories (a) and (b) – characterized by at least one of the following conditions: (1) total assets between €3.5 billion and €20 billion (banks and financial firms as defined by the article 107 of the Banking Act), (2) assets under management exceeding €10 billion (intermediaries mainly involved in asset management) and (3) annual turnover – dealing for own account or for the account of a third party – exceeding €150 billion (intermediaries mainly involved in dealing for own account or for the account of a third party); (d) 'minor intermediaries': entities characterized by at least one of the following conditions: (1) total assets of 3.5 billion euro or less (banks, mainly mutual banks, and financial firms), (2) assets under management of €10 billion or less (intermediaries mainly active in asset management), (3) annual turnover – dealing for own account or the account of a third party – of €150 billion or less (intermediaries mostly involved in dealing for own account or for the account of a third party); (e) entities subject to specific regulations as EMIs, and intermediaries such as leasing, factoring and consumer credit (defined by article 106 of the Banking Act). According to the Bank of Italy provisions the term 'major banking groups' only includes intermediaries within the first macro-category SREP.

In December 2013, in order to adopt the rules introduced by Directive 2013/36/EU, the Bank of Italy submitted to public consultation the revision of the Regulation of March 2011 on remuneration policies. As a consequence, on 18 November 2014 a new chapter 2 (Remuneration and incentive policies and practices) was introduced to the Circular n. 285 of 17 December 2013.

Although the framework of the discipline remains unchanged, some important innovations have been introduced: a capped ratio of 1:1 between the fixed and variable component of remuneration (it may be raised to 2:1 with shareholders' approval, complying with the conditions and within limits set by the Directive); the reinforcement of the provisions concerning the ex-post risk adjustment mechanisms (malus and clawback arrangements) where an individual is responsible for serious misconduct which has resulted in significant losses to the institution; narrower limits on the ability of firms to award guarantee variable remuneration because it is not consistent with sound risk management or the pay-performance principle; limits to variable remuneration when banks do not respect capital requirements.

3.2 Deposit insurance and crisis resolution plans

The last financial crisis has highlighted how a banking crisis can become systemic because of strong interconnections among banks both within and across countries. The management of banking crises is more difficult the higher the contagion risk in banking and the greater the differences across countries in management processes and available instruments.

In Italy, most of the instruments available to deal with a banking crisis date back to Banking Law of 1936, which remained into force until 1993. The 1993 Banking Act provided two types of interventions to deal with banking crises: the first refers to the less difficult crisis situation where the recovery of banks through reorganization is possible (special administration), whereas the second involves the shutdown of banking activity (compulsory administrative liquidation).

The role of the Supervisory Authority represents the core of the crisis management discipline.

The most important element concerns the application of the home country control principle. This principle applies to the EC bank branches in the case of special administration whereas for branches of non-EC banks the competent authority is the Supervisory Authority of the host member state. As an exception, notwithstanding the home country control principle, in order to prevent possible crises it is possible to adopt special proceedings towards EC banks.

In relation to the compulsory administrative liquidation the Italian Banking Act attributed to the Bank of Italy the power to instruct proceedings at the expense of branches of EC banks (secondary winding-up proceedings).

The need for having a harmonized discipline on reorganization and winding up of credit institutions across countries arose after the collapse of BCCI in 1991 (Dale 1994). Finally, with Directive 21/2004/EC, for the first time a legislative measure was specifically addressed to banks, recognizing the peculiarity of banking crisis procedures. When it was adopted in Italy with Legislative Decree 197/2004, banking crisis management process underwent a few important changes. Although the institutional setting for regulation and supervision did not change, the Bank of Italy was asked to notify, by any means and before the beginning of the procedure or immediately after, the supervisory authorities of member states hosting branches of non-EC banks of the opening of the special administration procedure.

The measures and procedures for the reorganization and winding up of EC banks had to be regulated and produce their effects, without additional formalities in Italy, in accordance with the law of the home member state. Moreover, the measures and procedures for special administration, provisional management and compulsory administrative liquidation of Italian banks would be applied and would have produced their effects in the other member states and, on the basis of international agreements, in non-member states.

Finally, as a consequence of the principle of universality, with Legislative Decree 197/2004 the end of ring-fencing practice was set forth and also in Italy the principle of the *par condicio creditorum* was fully adopted.

The new rules introduced by Legislative Decree 197/2004 have allowed some waivers from the principle of the home member state concerning employment contracts and relationships, contracts on the right to use or acquire real property, the exercise of the property rights and other rights attaching to some financial instruments, the netting and novation agreements. Finally, the law of the home member state does not apply to the voidability, voidness or unenforceability of acts prejudicial to creditors where the beneficiary of such acts proves that the prejudicial act is regulated by the law of a member state which does not allow any form of challenge.

The management of banking crises is strictly linked with two important topics on which both European and national legislators and public opinion have focused much attention during the last financial crisis: deposit insurance schemes and corporate governance and executive remuneration policies.

The strong interconnection between financial and real economy highlighted by the last financial crisis, has called attention to consumer confidence and protection and therefore on deposit insurance schemes.

In Italy two deposit guarantee systems were created a long time before the intervention of European legislators on this issue and represented the first case of banking self-regulation: the Central Guarantee Fund (for cooperative banks, 1978) and the Interbank Deposit Protection Fund (1986). The voluntary membership and ex-post contribution system were the principles that characterized both funds.

In order to harmonize the main elements of the deposit guarantee schemes, but without aiming at overcoming the differences of their institutional framework across countries (minimum harmonization principle), Directive 94/19/EC stated the mandatory membership for all credit institutions to the DGS as a prerequisite for banking activity. To allow non-subscription to the fund, indeed, would implicitly introduce an asymmetric protection for unaware depositors and, in case of a large institution, cause a contagion process.

With Legislative Decree 659/1996 (4/12/1996), which partially modified Legislative Decree 385/93, in Italy membership to the DIS also became mandatory for all banks.

In full compliance with the Home Country Control, the Italian Banking Law allowed EU banks' branches in Italy to subscribe, on a supplementary basis, to the Italian guarantee scheme along with the one of their home country. In this case, the intervention of the guarantee schemes is mandatory when the compulsory administrative liquidation of a bank authorized in Italy occurs and payments shall be made when the guarantee scheme of the home member state has already intervened (topping up clause).

The channels provided for by Italian legislators through which deposit guarantee schemes can deal with bank failures are the compensation of depositors, interventions to transfer assets and liabilities, and other support interventions.

In the first case, as provided by Directive 94/19, the protection is referred to depositor and not to deposit. The coverage level granted to depositors was €103,291, much higher than the harmonized minimum guarantee level set by Directive and the highest level of deposit protection among EU Countries (Figure 4.3).

Such a high insured deposit level was aimed both at protecting small depositors and at strengthening the confidence in the stability of the banking system and, therefore, at avoiding the risk of a bank run in the event of financial crisis

In fully compliance with the European Directive, the Italian Banking Act stated that the reimbursement would have had to be satisfied, up to an amount equivalent to €20,000, within three months of the date of the decree of administrative liquidation. The time limit could be extended by the Bank of Italy in exceptional circumstances or special cases for a period not exceeding nine months.

The other two instruments made available to DIS, the transfers of assets and liabilities to another bank and support interventions when special administration occurs, aim at maximizing the stability of the banking system either by preserving the continuity of banking activity (first case) or by avoiding extreme procedures such as compulsory administrative liquidation supporting M&A operations (second case). The Interbank Deposit Protection Fund (IDPF), from the year of its constitution (1986) to 2011, has put into effect only one reimbursement (Table 4.3). In most of the cases, the fund intervened supporting the transfer of the assets and liabilities of the distressed bank to other banks.

The contribution base for members of IDPF consists of reimbursable funds (covered deposits), whereas for Cooperative Credit Banks it is determined taking into account, in different percentage, the amount of deposits

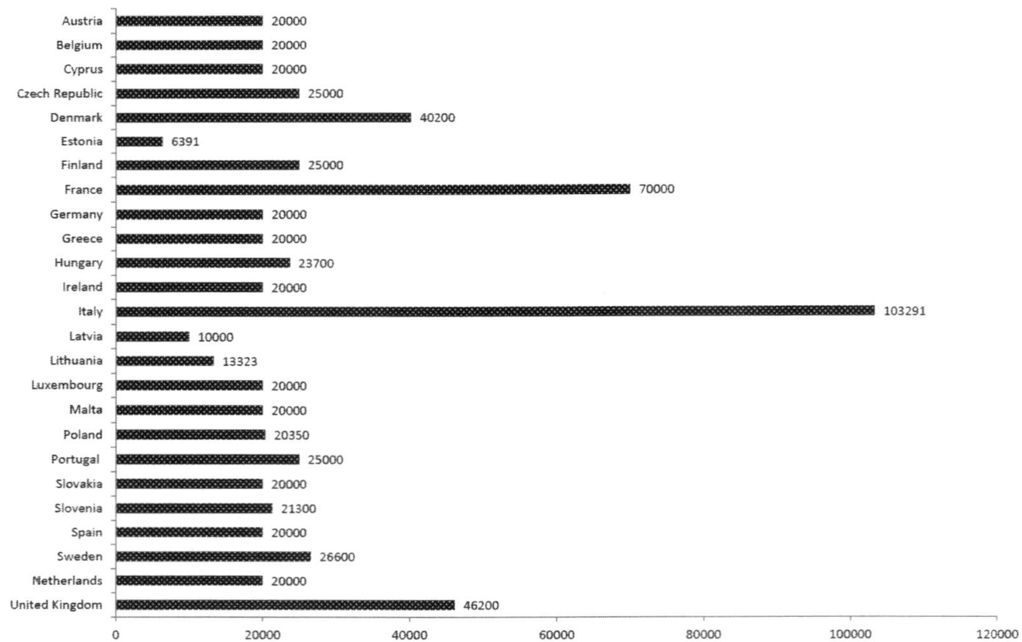

Figure 4.3 Level of deposit coverage in EU-25 at the end of 2005 (values in €)

Table 4.3 The IDPF interventions authorized by Bank of Italy since 1987

Name	*Type of interventions*	*Size of interventions €*
C.R. Prato (1988)	Support to banks	413 ml
Banco Tricesimo (1990)	Reimbersement of depositors	4 ml
Banca di Girgenti (1991)	Transfer of assets and liabilities	37 ml
Banca di Credito di Trieste (1996)	Transfer of assets and liabilities	78 ml
Credito Commerciale Tirreno (1997)	Transfer of assets and liabilities	52 ml
Sicilcassa (1997)	Transfer of assets and liabilities	516 ml
Banca Valle d'Itria e Magna Grecia (2010)	Transfer of assets and liabilities	5 ml
BER Banca (2011)	Support to banks	16 ml
Banca MB (2011)	Transfer of assets and liabilities	40 ml

Source: De Cesare et al. (2013) Interbank Deposit Protection Fund.

and the cash loans with the deduction of the regulatory capital. These contributions are not risk-based but determined on a proportional quota of insured deposits. Then, a regressive mechanism applied to the proportional quotas determines the 'regressive quotas' which will be adjusted by an increase or decrease correlated to the value of the weighted average aggregate index. The level of commitment each bank undertakes to pay annually ranges between 0.4 and 0.8 per cent of the repayable funds.

The minimum harmonization principle stated by Directive 94/19/EC showed its deficiency when the last financial crisis hit, since the great differences across countries involved an asymmetric loss of confidence of European citizens within the EU's single financial market. Moreover, the Northern Rock bankruptcy (2007) and the Icelandic banking system crisis (2008) highlighted the unfairness and ineffectiveness of the EU safety net.

In order to restore the confidence on the functioning of the financial system, on October 2008 the European Commission proposed a higher convergence among the deposit guarantee schemes of the different countries (Directive 2009/14/EC). However, many relevant issues such as the scope of coverage, funding mechanisms, fund size, co-insurance, trigger events and powers of supervision remained to be addressed.

With Legislative Decree no. 49/2011, Italy totally complied with Directive 2009/14/EC in terms of coverage level and pay-out delay. In the first case, the maximum payment for each depositor may not be less than €100,000.

The Bank of Italy can update such a limit to align it to further changes that could be introduced by the European Commission to make it adequate to the inflation rate. The rights of depositors would have to be processed within 20 working days from the date in which the administrative compulsory liquidation produces its effects.

Conclusions

Italian regulatory goals as described in our chapter were efficiency and stability. The supposed trade-off between them should have been reached through capital adequacy calibrated on risk-weighted assets. Actually, stability within the prudential regulation framework was not effective, as proved by the ECB comprehensive assessment run on 2014 (Table 4.2). Not only the capital adequacy failed its purpose, but the validation of internal models as allowed by the Basel II Accord, particularly for credit risk (internal rating based approaches), drove banks to a capital savings which during the crisis became a boomerang for their solvency ratio.

Besides the general criticisms to this approach (underestimation of risks whose unexpected losses cannot be covered by capital, such as liquidity, strategy, reputation), the style of Italian regulators and supervisors appeared to be excessively aimed at easing banks role in the financial system, without any serious incentive to reduce their risk appetite. A second dramatic factor was the corporate governance and the quality of board members, often unskilled in banking basics.

Girardone et al. (2004) show that banks' inefficiencies are inversely correlated with capital and positively related to the level of non-performing loans. Moreover, their analysis also shows that there is no clear relationship between assets size and bank efficiency. One of the reasons is that competition was introduced with a safety net inducing inefficient banks to survive, even in a highly risky environment, and increasing their moral hazard.

After the crisis many changes have been adopted by regulators. Among them, only the rules on internal governance appear to be oriented to improve banks stability and empower the internal control processes. The remaining set of new rules, fundamentally designed within the Basel III framework and contained in the capital requirement regulation and directive – CRR/CRD IV, are based on the attempt to improve the effectiveness of prudential regulation, whose ineffectiveness was behind the Italian banking system's weakness and inefficiency.

References

BANK OF ITALY (2013) Supervisory provisions concerning remuneration and incentive policies and practices in bank and banking groups. *Public Consultations*. December.

BARONTINI, R. and BOZZI, S. (2011) Board compensation and ownership structure: empirical evidence for Italian listed companies. *Journal of Management and Governance*, 15(1), 59–89.

BASEL COMMITTEE ON BANKING SUPERVISION (BCBS) (1999) *Enhancing Corporate Governance for Banking Organisations.* September. Revised February 2006.

BRUNNERMEIER, M. K. (2009) Deciphering the liquidity and credit crunch 2007–2008. *Journal of Economic Perspectives*, 23(1), 77–100.

CHAN, Y.-S., GREENBAUM, S. I. and THAKOR, A. V., (1986) Information reusability, competition and bank asset quality. *Journal of Banking and Finance*, 10, 243–253.

DALE, R. (1994) Regulatory consequences of the BCCI Collapse: US, UK, EC, Basle Committee – current issues in international bank supervision. In: Norton, J. J., Cheng, C.-J. and Fletcher, I. (eds), *International Banking Regulation and Supervision: Change and Transformation in the 1990s.* International Banking and Finance Law Series, 1, pp. 377–397.

DALLAS, L. (2011) Short-termism, the financial crisis and corporate governance. *Journal of Corporation Law*, 37, 265–321.

DAVIES, K. (2010) Regulatory responses to the financial sector crisis. *Griffith Law Review*, 19(1), 117–137.

DELL'ARICCIA, G. (2000) Learning by lending, competition, and screening incentives in the banking industry. Unpublished manuscript.

DEMIRGUC-KUNT, A. and DETRAGIACHE, E. (1998) Financial Liberalization and Financial Fragility. International Monetary Fund Working Paper, No. 98/83.

FAHLENBRACH, R. (2009) Shareholder Rights, Boards, and CEO Compensation. *Review of Finance*, 13(1), 81–113.

FERNANDES, N. (2005) Board compensation and firm performance: The role of 'independent' board members. *ECGI Working Paper Series in Finance.* 104.

FERRARINI, G. and MOLONEY, N. (2004) Executive remuneration and corporate governance in the EU: convergence, divergence and reform perspectives. *European Company and Financial Law Review*, 1(3), 251–339.

FERRARINI, G. and UNGUREANU, M. C. (2011), Economics, politics, and the international principles for sound compensation practices: An analysis of executive pay at European banks. *Vanderbilt Law Review*, 64(2), 431.

FINANCIAL STABILITY FORUM (FSF) (2009) *Principles for Sound Compensation Practice*. April.

GABBI, G. (1994) Coefficienti patrimoniali e 'Moral Hazard' degli intermediari bancari *Università Bocconi Working Paper*, 13.

GABBI, G. (2012) Il risk management e i suoi stakeholder. *Bancaria*, 3.

GABBI, G., IORI, G., JAFAREY, S. and PORTER, J. (2015) Financial regulations and bank credit to the real economy. *Journal of Economic Dynamics and Control*, 50 (January), 117–143.

GEHRIG, T. (1998) Screening, cross-border banking, and the allocation of credit. *Research in Economics*, 52, 387–407.

GIRARDONE C., MOLYNEUX P., and GARDENER E. P. M. (2004) Analysing the determinants of bank efficiency: The case of Italian banks. *Applied Economics*, 36(3), 215–227.

GRUBEN, W. C., KOO, J., and MOORE, R. R. (1999) When does financial liberalization make banks risky? An empirical examination of Argentina, Canada and Mexico. Federal Reserve Bank of Dallas, Research Dept. Working Paper. No. 99-05, pp. 1–27.

HELLMANN, T. F., MURDOCK, K. C., and STIGLITZ, J. E. (2000) Liberalization, moral hazard in banking, and prudential regulation: Are capital requirements enough? *American Economic Review*, 90(1), 147–65.

JANNUZZI, A. (2011) Soundness and disclosure of remuneration practice in the financial industry: an empirical analysis for Italian listed banks. *Mimeo.*

JOHN, K., MEHRAN, H. and QIAN, Y. (2010) Outside monitoring and CEO compensation in the banking industry, *Journal of Corporate Finance* 16, 383–399.

MEHRAN, H. (1995) Executive compensation structure, ownership, and firm performance. *Journal of Financial Economics*, 38(2), 163–184.

OECD (2004) *Principles of Corporate Government*. April. Originally Issue on June 1999.

PONTOLILLO V. (1997) Commento all'art. 4, in Capriglione F. (a cura di) *La disciplina degli intermediari e dei mercati finanziari*, Cedam, Padova.

SCHNITZER, M. (1999) On the role of bank competition for corporate finance and corporate control in transition economies. *Journal of Institutional and Theoretical Economics*, 155, p. 22–46.

WINTER, J. (2011) The financial crisis: Does good corporate governance matter and how to achieve it? *DSF Policy Paper Series*, 14.

5 Financial regulation in Spain

Santiago Carbo-Valverde and
Francisco Rodriguez-Fernandez

1 Introduction

This paper analyses the regulatory framework for the financial system in Spain. Particular attention is paid to the adoption of the EU directives on this matter and the way they have been transposed to Spain from 1986 to the present, including the regulatory developments in the last few years from the onset of the financial crisis. The Spanish case appears particularly interesting as it has shown one of the most significant transformations during the period considered in the structure of regulation. Spain joins the European Community in 1986 and a significant adaptation is then required to the European directives and regulations. This process goes in parallel to the development of a number of liberalization movements that were initiated in Spain since the late 1970s. Although this papers covers the regulatory initiatives that were confronted from 1986 onwards, in this introduction we make a brief analysis of the grounds of financial regulation in Spain before 1986 in order to provide a broader picture of the magnitude of the regulatory challenge that the country has faced since then.

The main reference for banking regulation before the liberalization process started was the Banking Regulatory Law of 1946. This law was characterized by intervention as it set strict controls and made banks become instruments of government industrial policy. The law of 1946 gave the Ministry of Finance ample discretionary powers to grant or to deny bank charters. Entry was at the discretion of the Ministry of Finance that used its authority rather arbitrarily. The era of easy entry came to an end. A new Banking Record Office was established. Only existing banks were allowed to register and to continue in the industry. Newcomers had to demonstrate the need for banking services in a specific geographic area. The banks' capital structure, its potential earnings, its management and the convenience and needs of the community were elements the new regulators considered before approving the establishment of a new bank. Furthermore, a favourable report of the Supreme Banking Council, also under the control of the government, was needed. Branching expansion depended on the financial density of each region, the existence of unattended financial demand or well-proven insufficient financial services. The concession of branches was linked to the volume of capital and reserves of each bank. The larger the bank the higher the likelihood it had to obtain authorization to open a new branch. As a result, financial concentration increased.

In 1962, the 1946 Banking Law was replaced by a new Banking and Credit Regulatory Law. The Bank of Spain was nationalized and old and new monetary instruments were put in place. Monetary policy, however, remained in the hands of the Ministry of Finance. This ministry kept its fully comprehensive powers over the financial system.

A first timid attempt towards deregulation began in 1969. Interest rate restrictions on long-term (two years or more) loans were lifted. Barriers to entry were loosened and branching restrictions were partially removed. These more relaxed chartering and branching policies enhanced competition. After 1974, deregulation sped up. Discrimination between banks and savings banks was eliminated. Banking operations were liberalized and the obstacles to competition among financial institutions were progressively suppressed.

The late 1970s and early 1980s saw the largest failures of the Spanish financial system in the 20th century. Because of its depth and the number of institutions affected this crisis has been included in the group of the so-called recent 'Big Five Crises' (see, for example, Reinhart and Rogoff, 2008). The resolution of the banking crisis imposed significant costs on the taxpayer. The total gross fiscal costs of the rescue operation were approximately 4–5 per cent of GDP. Deregulation and competitive pressures were other causes of the banking crisis. The number of banks increased slightly after the partial liberalization of the 1962 law, reversing the steady decline of the previous period. Moreover, there was a rapid expansion in the number of branches at existing commercial banks following the liberalization of the authorization to establish branches.

The interventions on banks took place from 1977 to 1983. To provide limited guarantees to depositors and to have a quick and adequate mechanism to intervene on banks a Deposit Guarantee Fund was established in November 1977.

In 1980 the Law of Governing Bodies of the Bank of Spain,transferred all responsibilities for bank supervision, discipline and sanctions to the central bank, that at the same time was given ample political autonomy. The following step came with the Autonomy of the Bank of Spain Law (Law 13/1994 of 1 June 2013), in order to comply with EU legislation.

In the following sections we cover the regulation from the mid-1980s to 2007, covering relevant issues such as the liberalization of capital movements (section 2), cross-border competition and permitted activities (section 3), capital requirements (section 4), supervision on a consolidated basis (section 5), supervision of financial groups and conglomerates (section 6), large exposures (section 7), investment services (section 8), deposit guarantees (section 9), crisis management schemes (section 10) and accounting (section 11). The paper ends with some conclusions (section 12).

2 Liberalization of capital movements

The liberalization of capital movements was a fundamental change in financial regulation in Spain after the country joined the European Community in 1986. However, it took a few years for the full implementation of Directive 88/361/EEC. As noted by Dell'Ariccia et al. (2008) the liberalization of capital movements in Spain was gradual and with occasional reversals, in particular, controls on inflows abolished in February 1992 and temporarily reintroduced in 1992–93 during the European Monetary System (EMS) crisis. Various legislative actions were undertaken to complete the liberalization. Some of them dealt with capital movements in general, as the Ministerial Order on 27 December 1990, on the liberalization of capital movements with foreign countries. Other measures specifically dealt with bank contracts and transactions such as the Bank of Spain Circular 1/92 (15 January 1992) on the bank accounts in foreign countries of country residents, the Bank of Spain Circular 2/92 (15 January 1992), on international loan and credit transaction.

3 Cross-border competition and permitted activities

Cross-border competition and permitted activities have a reference in the Second Banking Directive (89/646/EEC), which was supposed to be effectively implemented in EEC countries by no later than 1993. The implementation in Spain took place during 1994 and 1995. It started with Law 3/1994 (14 April 1994) to adapt Spanish law in relation to credit institutions to the Second Banking Co-ordination Directive and to make other amendments in relation to the financial system. This law was fully developed within Royal Decree 1245/1995 (14 July 1995) on the formation of banks, cross-border activity and other issues relating to the legal regime for credit institutions,

Law 3/1994 establishes the free opening of branches in Spain to banks from other member states of the European Union. In practical terms, an information and authorization system by the Bank of Spain was created in coordination with supervisory bodies of other member countries. Complementarily, it also regulated the information and authorization rules for Spanish banks to operate in other EU countries.

Royal Decree 1245/1995 modified the regulations on the formation of banks contained in Royal Decree 1144/1988. The importance attached to the suitability of shareholders with significant holdings and to the soundness of the administrative and accounting procedures of newly formed banks should be stressed. Secondly, other provisions were implemented that relate not only to banks but to all credit institutions. Thus, the rules governing the cross-border activity of both Spanish and foreign credit institutions, whether or not carried on through a branch, were specified. For European Union institutions, the so-called 'Community passport' was regulated in detail. This allowed a credit institution that is authorized to operate in one Community country to operate in all the other Community countries without needing the authorization of the authorities of the latter. There were also rules implementing the arrangements for so-called 'significant holdings', already extensively regulated in the previous Law 26/1988.

Cross-border activities and the formation of banks were also affected by the Investment Services Directive-ISD (93/22/EEC) that was expected to be fully adopted by member states by 1995, while in Spain it was adopted in 1998.

In accordance with the distinction made in the Investment Services Directive between regulated and non-regulated markets, a key element of the Spanish reform in 1998 was designing the operation of the single securities market, the official secondary markets existing in Spain were declared to be regulated and the distinction between official and unofficial organized markets was eliminated. The reform also introduced amendments to the admission and exclusion of listed securities. In particular, the questionable pre-existing equivalence of requirements for issuing and listing was eliminated; this equivalence had generated undesirable effects when there was a slight delay between issuing and listing and the law now sought immediate listing of securities so that they could begin trading as soon as possible.

4 Capital requirements

The initial stages of the adoption of EU regulation on capital requirements by Spain refer to Directive 89/299/EEC on the own funds of credit institutions in accordance with the 1988 Basel Capital Accord, and Directive 89/647/EEC on the solvency ratio for credit institutions, also in accordance with the 1988 Basel Capital Accord. Both directives were implemented in Spain through Law 13/1992 (01 June 1992) on solvency requirements and supervision on a consolidated basis of financial institutions, Royal Decree 1343/1992 (06 November 1992) (which develops Law 13/1992) and the Bank of Spain Circular 5/1993 (26 March 1993), on the determination and monitoring of financial institutions' own funds. Combining the three regulatory developments and organizing them in different areas of solvency regulation, these were the major changes made:

Basic solvency regulation for consolidatable credit institution groups is established in Law 13/1992 on own funds and consolidated supervision of financial institutions. This law was in part a redrafting of Law 13/1985, which had already introduced own funds requirements sensitive to the level of risk of assets and memorandum accounts in anticipation of what would subsequently become the new international practice.

Royal Decree 1343/92 reinforced and developed some of the principles in Law 13/1992 and reinforced the solvency ratio by a number of provisions limiting the negative effects of risks to which credit institutions were exposed, particularly in terms of credit risk. In particular, it limited major risks with an individual or economic group representing more than 10 per cent of the own funds of the consolidatable group. It also limited tangible fixed assets to 70 per cent of own funds. Additionally, it introduced penalties, via deduction

Table 5.1 Composition of own funds in Spain in accordance to Basel I principles

Capital stock
The initial fund (fondo fundacional)
Reserves
Generic banking provisions
Credit cooperative training and promotion funds
Subordinated financing and all other receivable or non-receivable items to be used to cover losses
All losses and any assets that may reduce the effectiveness of said resources in covering losses shall be deducted from these resources

Source: Law 13/1985.

from own funds, of excess qualifying holdings in non-financial institutions. Credit institutions were also required to control interest and liquidity risks and these controls had to be verifiable by and available to the Bank of Spain. In any event, the main composition of own funds was that of Law 13/1985, which stipulated that own funds of credit institutions and consolidatable credit institutions' groups shall comprise all the items shown in Table 5.1.

There were some important exceptions to the required capital ratios that were established by the above-mentioned Bank of Spain Circular 5/1993. In particular, lower individual ratios were set for Spanish credit institutions that form part of consolidated groups. These requirement reductions could total as much as 50 per cent based on the group's holdings in the Spanish credit institutions' affiliates.

After Directives 89/299/EEC and 89/647/EEC, solvency regulation is further developed with Directive 93/6/EEC (Capital Adequacy Directive of CAD) on capital requirements for market risk resulting from trading in securities, derivatives and foreign exchanges. The implementation of this Directive was due by 1996 but was anticipatively adopted in Spain in 1993 by means of the Bank of Spain Circular 11/1993 (17 December 1993).

Additional changes were undertaken following Directive 98/31/EC (CAD2) on the revision of the Capital Adequacy Directive 93/6/EEC, in accordance with the amendment of the Basel Capital Accord to incorporate market risk, allowing for the use of internal models. CAD2 was due to be implemented by 2000 and in Spain the transposition was effectively completed in 2001 with Royal Decree 1419/2001 (17 December 2001) which partially modifies the above-mentioned Royal Decree 1343/1992 (06 November 1992). In relation to the solvency of credit institutions, Royal Decree 1419/2001 made three changes:

- The scope of the rules applicable to government debt in relation to the capital ratio was widened to cover debt securities issued by local authorities;

- The definition of the securities trading book was widened to include positions in gold (which were given a similar treatment to positions in foreign currencies)
- Finally, and most importantly, Spanish credit institutions were allowed to use internal risk management models to calculate their capital requirements to cover market and foreign-exchange risks.

The 2004 Basel II Capital Accord issued by the Basel Committee on Banking Supervision on 26 June 2004 (known as Basel II) established a set of structured measures based on three mutually reinforcing pillars: the adoption of uniform rules to determine minimum capital requirements on the basis of the risks assumed (Pillar 1); supervisory review to foster improved internal risk management by institutions (Pillar 2); and market disclosure of the key features of their business profile, risk exposure and risk management practices (Pillar 3). These measures had to be taken into account simultaneously so that the level of own funds held by institutions was in keeping with their overall risk profile. Basel II principles were implemented in the EU through 2006/48/EC and 2006/49/EC (Capital Requirements Directive of CRD I) implementing Basel II on credit institutions and investment firms. The transposition was expected by 2007/8 and Spain effectively did it in due time. In particular with Royal Decree 216/2008 (15 February 2008) on the own funds of financial institutions, the Bank of Spain Circular 3/2008 (22 May 2008) on the settlement and monitoring of minimum capital requirements and the Securities and Exchange Commission (CNMV) Circular 12/2008 (30 December 2008) on the solvency of investment services firms.

Circular 3/2008 was the main step for full implementation. The minimum capital requirements for credit risk remained at 8 per cent of risk-weighted assets, including the off-balance-sheet items that entail credit risk and have not been deducted from own funds. The main new features of the Circular arise from the implementation of Royal Decree 216/2008. In particular, to calculate credit risk, institutions may choose between the standardized approach or, if authorized by the Bank of Spain, the internal ratings based approach. For the standardized approach, the Circular determines the weights applicable to the various risk exposures and sets the requirements to be met by external credit assessment institutions.

Most recently, there have been two important directives related to capital regulation in the crisis environment and linked to Basel III developments. In 2009, Directive 2009/111/EC, also known as CRD II and, in 2010, Directive 2010/76/EU, also known as CRD III. As for CRD II the most important issues were related to the removal of some national options and discretions as regards prudential regimes for large exposures, inter-bank exposures, and connected clients, harmonization of eligibility criteria of hybrid capital instruments and limits to inclusion in tier I, as well as the retention by originator or sponsor of an 'economic interest' no less than 5 per cent of the nominal value of the securitized exposures. In the case of CRD III the most relevant contents referred to the general principles applicable to remuneration policy in the financial services sector, the remuneration policies (which should aim at aligning the personal objectives of staff members with the long-term interests of the financial undertaking concerned), the assessment of performance-based components of remuneration and some amendments to capital requirements for trading book and for resecuritizations. Although some of the issues were already considered in previous regulations in Spain mentioned above, most of the contents were adopted by both Law 6/2011 (11 April 2011) on the amendment of the law on credit institutions' own funds and on credit institution deposit guarantee funds and the Securities and Exchange Commission (CNMV) Circular 5/2011 (12 December 2011) on the amendment of solvency regulations and accounting standards for investment firms.

The purpose of Law 6/2011 was to commence transposition of Directive 2009/111/EC. As one of the most important features this law makes it compulsory for credit institutions and investment firms to meet certain requirements to allow them to assume exposures to securitization positions and to initiate a securitization. Under these requirements, which were set out in Royal Decree 771/2011, a credit institution, other than when acting as an originator, a sponsor or original lender, shall be exposed to the credit risk of a securitization position in its trading book or non-trading book only if the originator, sponsor or original lender has explicitly disclosed to the credit institution that it will retain, on an ongoing basis, a material net economic interest.

5 Supervision on a consolidated basis

Supervision on a consolidated basis referred initially to the implementation of Directive 83/350/EEC on supervision of credit institutions on a consolidated basis in line with the 1983 Basel Concordat, which was made through Law 13/1985 (25 May 1985) on investment coefficients, own funds requirements and information disclosure rules for financial intermediaries. The developments of Law 13/1985 have been already widely commented in the previous section.

A significant change however came with the implementation of Directive 92/30/EEC 92/30/EEC on supervision of credit institution on a consolidated basis in accordance with the 1988 Basel Capital Accord.. The due implementation date was 1993 but in Spain it was transposed earlier, in 1992, through Law 13/1992 (01 June 1992) on solvency requirements and supervision on a consolidated basis of financial institutions, Royal Decree 1343/1992 (06 November 1992) on the development of Law 13/1992 and the Ministerial Order of 30 December 1992.

Law 13/1992 simply recognized the need of implementing the principles of Directive 92/30/EEC. The preamble of the law acknowledged the importance of being cautious and not imposing a stricter regulation on Spanish banks compared to their European counterparts. Following the Directive, Law 13/1992 pays particular attention to consolidated banking groups defined the general type of consolidated groups although it leaves to a lower-order regulation (Royal Decree 1343/1992) the full development of the definitions and the required own funds for each group. Importantly, Law 13/1992 and Royal Decree 1343/1992 were largely modified by Law 5/2005 on supervision of financial conglomerates and Royal Decree 1332/2005, on the development of Law 5/2005. For this reason, we make a joint treatment of these regulations. In implementation of Law 5/2005 on supervision of financial conglomerates, the Royal Decree established the obligations of groups in which banking or securities firms coexist with insurance companies, but which do not meet the requirement of significant sectoral diversification. These groups are required to send to all Spanish relevant competent authorities the information required to verify, first, that they are not subject to the supplementary supervision regime and, second, the supplementary capital they would have to hold if they became subject to it.

Royal Decree 1332/2005 also specified the criteria to be taken into account in subjecting to supplementary supervision, on one hand, those financial conglomerates that meet the aforementioned requirement of significant sectoral diversification in the second of the ways defined in the law, i.e. by having a balance sheet total in the smallest sector of the group that exceeds €6 billion, and, on the other, those regulated entities (as defined in Law 5/2005) that, not constituting a group, are investees or under notable influence of one or more physical or legal persons and have significant activity both in the banking and investment services sector and in the insurance sector. The conditions to be met under these criteria shall be decided by common agreement between the coordinator and the relevant competent authorities.

As for Directive 95/26/EC on reinforced supervision of financial institutions it only required the development of some definitions for what are called in Spain credit financial establishments and this was done in 1998 (with some delay to the supposed implementation data of 1998) with the approval of Law 37/1998 (16 November 1998), amending Law 24/1988 on the Securities Market Royal Decree Law 692/1996 (26 April 1996) on the legal regime for credit financial establishments ('establecimientos financieros de crédito').

6 Supervision of financial groups and conglomerates

The initial step in a common framework for a supervision of financial groups and conglomerates took place with Directive 2002/87/EC 2004 on rules for supplementary supervision for credit institutions, investment firms and insurance companies pertaining to a financial conglomerate. The implementation was due in 2004 and in Spain was finally done in 2005 with Law 5/2005 (22 April 2005) on the supervision of financial conglomerates, amending other financial sector legislation and the Royal 1332/2005 (11/11/2005) implementing Law 5/2005.

The main developments of Law 5/2005 have been mentioned in the previous section and responded to the fundamental aim of providing for a specific prudential regime applicable to financial conglomerates. However, it also had a secondary aim. Namely to progress towards greater consistency between the different sectoral legislations applicable to uniform groups, and between the sectoral legislation applicable to the latter and that applicable to financial conglomerates. The full development of Law 5/2005 was made through Royal Decree 1332/2005, as described in the previous section. The Royal Decree established how a financial conglomerate shall calculate its eligible own funds and what its minimum level will be. Also, the regulated entities of financial conglomerates must inform the coordinator with the periodicity specified by the latter, which must be at least once a year, of any significant intra-group transaction by the regulated entities in the financial conglomerate and of any significant concentration of risk; the coordinator must examine the possible risk of contagion and of conflict of interest within the financial conglomerate and the risk of evasion of sectoral rules and regulations. The regulated entities of financial conglomerates must send the coordinator such periodic or non-periodic information as the latter may require of them to verify compliance with their obligations. Also, they must cooperate with the coordinator in what it asks of them and facilitate any inspections, although the competent authorities responsible for supervision of the entities of groups included in the conglomerate may approach these directly, in exercise of the powers of individual or consolidated supervision of the entities included in the conglomerate. Finally, financial conglomerates must have adequate risk management procedures and internal control mechanisms. Other regulations were affected. The final provisions, continuing the amendments made to Law 5/2005, revise the sectoral (banking, securities and insurance) rules of regulatory rank in order to make them consistent with each other and bring them into line with the new regime for financial conglomerates. These provisions, most of them included for the sake of fine-tuning, include most notably the definition of the scope of consolidation for supervision purposes and the changes made to the calculation of eligible own funds. Most important among the latter are, on the deductions side, the need to subtract the amount of participating interests in insurance and reinsurance companies and in entities engaged primarily in holding investments in insurance companies, whenever the participating interest exceeds 20 per cent of the capital of the investee, and, on the eligible components side, the admissibility of including the accounting balance of the general allowance/provision for credit losses attributable to the customer, up to a limit of 1.25 per cent of risk-weighted assets, and the gains recognized in the assets of the company in application of the fair value criterion, although the Bank of Spain may reduce the gross amount by two-thirds, depending on the volatility of the different types of assets.

As for the implementation of Directive 2007/44/EC, which tightens supervision on M&A in the financial sector, it was transposed in 2009, the due year, through Law 5/2009 (29 June 2009) on the regime for the acquisition of significant holdings. This law reformed the regime for qualifying holdings in the financial sector, clarifying the procedures and evaluation criteria applicable for the prudential assessment of acquisitions and increases of such holdings. The aim was to enhance both the legal certainty and the practical effectiveness of the regime, making it more consistent with the ultimate aim, which was to ensure the stability of financial institutions and of the markets in which they operate. To this end, the Law envisages that a qualifying holding is held if it amounts to 10 per cent (up from 5 per cent previously) or more of the capital or voting rights of the institution acquired, or if there is a possibility of exerting notable influence in the institution (deemed to exist when there is a possibility of appointing or dismissing a board member). Moreover, all holdings of 5 per cent or more of the capital or voting rights, even if they are not considered qualifying holdings, must be notified to the supervisor.

Law 5/2009 also outlined a new assessment procedure that is clearer and more transparent and has shorter time limits, and establishes the criteria on which financial supervisors should base their opposition to any acquisitions proposed (the standing and solvency of the acquirer, the standing of the future administrators of the institution and the capability and solvency of the institution). It also reinforces the collaboration between the supervisor of the acquiring institution and that of the institution acquired throughout the assessment process, and simplifies the limits determining the need to notify any increases or reductions in qualifying holdings, which are set at 20 per cent, 30 per cent and 50 per cent of the capital or voting rights. Royal Decree 1817/2009 complemented Law 5/2009, implementing its more technical aspects.

7 Large exposures

Directive 92/121/EEC on the monitoring and control of large exposures of credit institutions set a transposition deadline by 1994. In Spain, it was implemented in 1993 with two circulars of the Bank of Spain: Circular 5/1993 (26 March 1993) on the determination and monitoring of financial institutions' own funds and Circular 12/1993 (17 December 1993) which modified Circular 5/1993.

Circulars 5/1993 and 12/1993 set four important rules regarding large exposures:

- They consider 'large risks' as those positions with a face value larger than 10 per cent of the own funds of the financial institution.
- The value of all the risk positions of an institution with the same subject or economic agent could not exceed 25 per cent of its own funds.
- If the risks were maintained with non-consolidated institutions within the same economic group, the limit was 20 per cent of the own funds.
- The sum of all the large exposures of a bank will be lower than eight times the own funds of the financial institution.

Directives 2006/48/EC and 2006/49/EC (CRD) Capital Requirements Directive implementing Basel II (credit institutions and investment firms) also incorporated various principles regarding large exposures. The due implementation date was 2007/2008 and that was the date met by Spanish regulators. The principles were mainly transposed through Law 36/2007 (16 November 2007) which modified Law 13/1985 (25 May 1985) on investment coefficients, own funds requirements and information disclosures rules for financial intermediaries, Royal Decree 216/2008 (15 February 2008) on the own funds of financial institutions, Bank of Spain Circular 3/2008 (22 May 2008) on the settlement and monitoring of minimum capital requirements, and the Securities and Exchange Commission (CNMV) and Circular 12/2008 (30 December 2008) on the solvency of investment services firms.

The two circulars of the Bank of Spain contained the main changes regarding large exposures. As for Circular 3/2008, it maintained the definitions previously mentioned for Circular 5/1993. In particular, it defined a large exposure as one whose value exceeds 10 per cent of a credit institution's own funds. The value of all the exposures of a credit institution to a third-party person or economic group may not exceed 25 per cent of its own funds. Where the exposures are to non-consolidated entities of a credit institution's economic group, this limit shall be reduced to 20 per cent. Finally, the total large exposures may not exceed eight times a credit institution's own funds.

Additionally, Circular 3/2008 made some changes to the measures in place to return to compliance with solvency regulations. Thus it equates a shortfall of 20 per cent of minimum own funds with a shortfall of 50 per cent in tier 1 capital, so that where a credit institution or group or subgroup of credit institutions has a regulatory capital shortfall exceeding 20 per cent of the minimum requirement, or its tier 1 capital falls below 50 per cent of that minimum requirement, the individual institution or each and every institution in the group or subgroup must allocate its net profit or surplus in full to reserves.

As for Circular 12/2008 the limits on large exposures (those exceeding 10 per cent of a credit institution's own funds) do not undergo any significant changes. The amount of all the exposures of a credit institution to a single third-party client or economic group may not exceed 25 per cent of its own funds; if the risk exposure is to unconsolidated institutions of the reporting institution's own economic group, this limit shall be 20 per cent.

A related key fundamental instrument of control for large exposures is the Bank of Spain's Central Credit Register (CCR). The CCR holds the credit records of natural and legal persons in order to facilitate institutions in their credit risk analysis. Generally speaking, reporting institutions (credit institutions and others) are obliged to report on direct risks with residents for sums of €6,000 and over for the whole of their businesses in Spain or of €60,000 or more in any other country. Non-residents however are obliged to report amounts of €300,000 or more. The main regulations concerning the Spanish CCR are shown in Table 5.2.

Table 5.2 Spanish regulations concerning the Central Credit Register

Bank of Spain Circular 3/1995 on the Central Credit Register
Law 44/2002 (22/11/2002) on "measures to reform the financial system)
Ministerial Order ECO/697/2004 (11/32004) on the reform of the Central Credit Register
Ministerial Order ECC/747/2013 (25/4/2013) which modifies Ministerial Order ECO/697/2004 (11/32004) on the reform of the Central Credit Register Bank of Spain Circular 1/2013 (24/05/2013) on the reform of the Central Credit Register

Source: Bank of Spain and own elaboration.

The reported information allows the Bank of Spain to know the total lending granted, which enables it to perform its banking supervision obligations. For their part, the institutions that report their risks to the CCR of the Bank of Spain receive monthly aggregate information on the risk contracted by the natural and legal persons that they have reported ('account holders'). Nevertheless, any institution may request specific information about an account holder if the account holder applies for a risk operation (such as a loan) or appears as liable for payment or as a guarantor in negotiable or credit documents which the institution has been requested to acquire or trade.

The CCR is used both to support on-site inspections and to carry out off-site monitoring of credit and concentration risk. The information held in the CCR also permits off-site monitoring. The obligation of all credit institutions to report defaulted obligors works as a disciplinary element that helps to maintain the quality of the information received and is a basic input for accurately assessing the risk incurred by each bank.

8 Investment services

The Investment Services Directive (ISD 93/22/EEC) was a fundamental change for financial services in Europe. Its due date implementation was 1995 while in Spain it was not fully transposed until 1998. The main reason is that Spain did a complete reform of its Securities Market Law (by that time Law 24/1988 on Securities Markets). Hence, the implementation of the ISD was made through Law 37/1998 (16 November1998), amending Law 24/1988 on the Securities Market.

Law 37/1998 introduced several changes on Law 24/1988. Firstly, as a result of the wide range of financial instruments included under the scope of the new market regulations, which go beyond the category of transferable securities, all financial instruments became subject to the discipline applicable to transferable securities, in order to adapt the new financial reality (e.g. swaps, FRAs, options, futures, etc.) in Spain's markets. Another significant aspect is the abolition of the monopoly on keeping book entry records for transferable securities not traded in official secondary markets, which was previously held by broker-dealers and brokers. There were also significant changes in the regime of the National Securities Market Commission (CNMV) Advisory Committee (Comité Consultivo). Firstly, its composition was amended to enable the admission of representatives of all of Spain's official secondary markets. Secondly, the Committee's powers were accommodated to the new provisions of the law regarding market subjects and the markets themselves.

Important new features in the regulation of the official secondary securities markets were also introduced. In addition to incorporating the provisions of the Investment Services Directive into Spanish law, it also incorporated market regulations such as those concerning derivatives, which had not been implemented within the Spanish financial system in 1988.

The classification of market transactions in accordance with the decentralizing principles which guide the regulation within the Investment Services Division is particularly noteworthy. It resulted in a basic distinction between market transactions and non-market transactions. Market transactions are those which result in a transfer, by purchase and sale or otherwise for a consideration, within the market. A distinction is also made between ordinary and extraordinary market transactions. Ordinary market transactions are subject to the basic market functioning rules (in particular, participation of members and the routing of transactions via ordinary trading systems).

Another fundamental aspect of the reform, which was made necessary by the Investment Services Directive, was that both Spanish investment services firms and those authorized in other European Union countries qualified to become members of official secondary markets, with the capacity to trade.

Focusing on market-specific regulations, in the stock markets, the execution of transactions in stock exchanges and in the electronic market (SIBE) was made subject to current regulations; therefore, the free access envisaged in the Directive is achieved by acquiring membership of a stock exchange management company. For this reason, some amendments had to be made to the rules regarding the acquisition of holdings in these management companies.

Several highly significant new elements were introduced in the public debt market represented by book entries. Firstly, securities listed in the Central Book-Entry Office can now be traded in parallel in any other official secondary market, thus offering a wider scope for trading and interrelation between markets.

Secondly, the fundamental market regulatory standard was called the 'Market Regulation' (Reglamento del Mercado). In addition, the existing Market Advisory Commission (Comisión Asesora del Mercado) would include representatives of market members and of the Autonomous Regional Governments.

The working of the market is structured in two distinct areas: registration, clearing and settlement; and trading. Therefore, this opens several categories depending on the vocation of each market subject. The derivatives market, already developed in the Spanish financial system, has been placed on a firm legal footing.

A specific treatment was made to 'Investment Services Firms', in accordance with the statutory equivalence of investment services firms and credit institutions as defined in the Investment Services Directive. Previously, investment services firms were defined by their financial institution status and by offering professional investment services to third parties. In accordance with the ISD, the activity status of investment services firms is categorized with regard to the investment services and ancillary services offered in connection with financial instruments, which, in the final instance, determine their implementation under the community passport. In compliance with the new objective and subjective regulation of financial market operators, the Law confers the status of investment services firm, in its strict sense, on broker-dealers and brokers, and on portfolio management companies.

Importantly, Law 37/1998 incorporated regulation of a new mechanism in the Spanish securities markets, the 'Investor Compensation Scheme' (Fondo de Garantía de Inversiones). This regulation transposes Directive 97/9/EC into Spanish law. The regulation of this fund also responds to one of the requirements of the Investment Services Directive and, like deposit protection schemes for credit institutions, it compensates investors in the event of insolvency or bankruptcy of investment services firms where the cash or securities entrusted by an investor are no longer available; however, in no way does the fund cover credit risks or any losses to the value of a market investment.

The reform made by Law 37/1998 also included more comprehensive regulation on preference shares, particularly non-voting shares. The aim of the legislation is to enable financing via markets (taking into account the practical circumstances of corporate control) with sufficient guarantees to investors, using formulae to allow investment in capital without involvement (through voting rights) in the running of the company. The reform distinguishes between listed and unlisted companies, providing more flexibility to the former due to the greater transparency requirements imposed in the securities markets.

9 Deposit guarantee

Deposit guarantee schemes are a cornerstone of financial architecture and they have suffered several regulatory developments in Spain over the last three decades. Directive 94/19/EC on deposit guarantee schemes was transposed to Spain in 1996, one year after the EU official transposition date by Royal Decree 12/1995 (28 December 1995) on urgent matters on budgetary, fiscal and financial issues (seventh additional measure: Deposit Guarantee Fund).

Royal Decree-Law 12/1995 introduced the first important novelties such as obligatory membership of a deposit guarantee fund for Spanish credit institutions, the conditions for exemption from this duty, together with the reasons for expulsion. However, the main principles of the reformed deposit guarantee regulation were introduced by Royal Decree 2606/1996. The decree established the legal regime covering deposit guarantee funds for banking institutions, savings banks, and credit cooperative banks. A new feature was the definition of the system of contributions to the funds and the mechanisms for the reduction and suspension of contributions, such that each of the funds is fed via the annual contributions of its member credit institutions and, exceptionally, by contributions from the Bank of Spain, the amount of which must be set by law.

The most novel features were the following:

- Voting is required as the means of electing members of the bodies governing the funds, i.e. this is to be the means whereby associations representing credit institutions elect their representatives on the respective deposit guarantee fund's management committee.
- The concept of the representatives of the associations is established according to two criteria: They must represent more than 80 per cent of the member institutions of the corresponding fund and more than 90 per cent of the deposits held by these institutions. If these percentages are not reached the appointment of representatives shall be carried out by means of a direct vote held by all the member institutions of the fund.
- The definition of the guaranteed deposits involves a delimitation which is as much positive as negative, in accordance with the guidelines foreseen in the Directive that it implements. Deposits not guaranteed on account of their nature and which, therefore, are not included in the calculation of the contributions, are distinguished from those which, although covered in principle, and so included in the calculation, may be excluded from the obligation to pay under certain circumstances. On the other hand, the maximum guaranteed amount in relation to deposits is limited to the equivalent in pesetas of €20,000, although up until 31 December 1999 this limit remained set at €15,000.
- The adoption of the so-called 'principle of guarantee by the country of origin' which implies obligatory coverage by deposit guarantee funds in the country of origin in the case of Spanish branch offices of credit institutions based in other countries of the European Union.
- The system of membership of the banking institution deposit guarantee fund for foreign branch offices of credit institutions is also defined, and an essential distinction is drawn. Institutions based in other member states of the European Community are permitted voluntary membership so that they may offer their depositors a complementary guarantee in addition to their own.
- The regulation of procedural aspects relating to the causes or circumstances that give rise to the liability for payment and those governing payment itself stand out. A traditional purpose of Spanish deposits

> guarantee funds has been to ensure the stability of the financial system, avoiding a crisis afflicting one credit institution affecting the rest of the institutions operating in the market. A noteworthy feature of the new regulations was the so-called 'action plan', which may include both preventive measures and measures for the reorganization of the institution. These measures may entail a range of actions intended to restructure the institution's assets, in particular subscription of capital increases by the fund, and various types of financial assistance and management measures.

In 2009, Directive 2009/14/29 on Deposit Guarantee Schemes was issued. This was implemented in Spain by Royal Decree 628/2010 (14/05/2010) on the amendment of legislation on depositor and investor guarantee scheme. The Royal Decree maintains the level of protection remains at €100,000 in DGFs and those guarantees continue to apply per depositor or investor, whether a natural or a legal person, regardless of the number and type of cash, securities or financial instrument deposits in the holder's name at the same institution.

With Royal Decree 628/2010, credit institutions have to make available to customers information on the functioning of the DGFs of which they are members, specifying the amount and scope of the cover offered. Also, they must inform about the conditions and the formalities which must be completed to obtain compensation payouts. The surplus held by DGFs in excess of the amount needed to fulfil their objectives shall remain in their assets and may not be distributed or returned to member institutions. DGFs have to conduct regular operational tests to assess their ability to cope with a possible crisis at an institution. Lastly, it is expressly specified that investor coverage schemes (ICS) will not cover investors holding a securities account with an institution not covered by the ICS, even if that institution had in turn deposited the securities in an account at one covered by the ICS.

Most recently, Royal Decree 771/2011 also introduced some changes by amending Royal Decree 2606/1996 by introducing a new regime for additional contributions to these funds based on the remuneration of the deposits in them. Specifically, the amounts of the deposits whose agreed remuneration exceeds the limits specified below shall be weighted at 500 per cent (i.e. 400 per cent more than the weight they would have if they were included in that base) for the purpose of calculating the contributions of the credit institutions belonging to the related deposit guarantee funds.

10 Crisis management schemes

The full implementation in Spain of the Directive on reorganization and winding-up of credit institutions (2001/24/EC) which was due by 2004 was actually undertaken in 2005 with Law 6/2005 (22 April 2005) on the clean-up and liquidation of credit institutions. In line with its cross-border focus, this Law 6/2005 was applicable to credit institutions authorized in Spain which have at least one branch or provide services without a permanent establishment in another member state of the European Union; to credit institutions authorized in another member state which also have at least one branch or provide services without a permanent establishment in Spain; and to the branches in Spain of foreign credit institutions not authorized in an EU member state, when such credit institutions have at least one branch in another member state. The reorganization measures referred to by this Law do not include those actions that, with the same name (preventive and reorganization measures), can be adopted by credit institution deposit guarantee funds in accordance with Royal Decree 2606/1996 of 20 December 1996. Rather, they only include those adopted by the administrative or judicial authorities of an EU member state that are intended to preserve or restore the financial situation of a credit institution

Since 2009, the Spanish banking sector has undergone some of the most ambitious and intense reforms since the financial liberalization of the 1970s and 1980s. The first important milestone in the bank restructuring process in Spain took place in June 2009, with the approval of Royal Decree-Law 9/2009 (26 June 200), which created the so-called Fund for the Orderly Restructuring of the Banking Sector (FROB). The FROB is one of the main pillars of the banking reform in Spain. Royal Decree 9/2009 included a set of measures to address some of the weaknesses shown by Spanish banks at that time. The text of the decree provided the following rationale for reform implementation:

> the situation of the Spanish banking sector cannot be described as normal, although given their size, those individual institutions likely to encounter difficulties are not systemic.

Nonetheless,

> if we consider their viability problems overall, a potential systemic risk could be created. The potential risk justifies the provision of early instruments and public resources in the event that circumstances make their use necessary … and the sector would find hard to sustain such losses through reliance on the three Deposit Guarantee schemes.

As for the functioning of Royal Decree 9/2009, it required Spanish banks to present viability plans to identify if they were in need of any of the solutions considered. The Bank of Spain itself released a statement that FROB was a

> painstaking process because of the variety and significance of the regulatory adjustments required and because of the complex decisions and negotiations entailed … the restructuring of the savings banks sector was unavoidable … since the sector had several structural limitations associated with its legal nature, such as the legal restrictions on raising high quality

capital other than via retained earnings and a complex and rigid system of governance not conducive to best corporate governance practices.

Reform emphasis from that moment onwards was placed on savings banks. However, as it has been shown by the most recent developments in the Spanish banking sector, the solvency problems were not exclusive to the savings banks. In fact, most Spanish banks are currently affected by restructuring processes on some level.

In any event, the implicit focus made on savings banks was reinforced by a new law in 2010 that was explicitly oriented to savings banks, Royal Decree-Law 11/2010 (9 July 2010). Prior to the this law, savings banks relied mostly on retained profits to increase their solvency ratios. Given that one of the main regulatory responses to the crisis has been requiring more bank capital (i.e. Basel III requirements) the limitations of savings banks to access market financing had to be removed. Royal Decree-Law 11/2010 addressed these limitations in two main ways. First, it increased the flexibility of rules governing existing core capital instruments, *cuotas participativas* (capital certificates) to allow for these instruments to carry voting rights. However, reliance on this type of financing since 2010 has been very limited. Second, and most important, it allowed for alternative ways for a savings bank to transfer all its banking activities to a bank (a public limited company) and remain as a holding institution or even an ordinary foundation, dedicated to the promotion of social works. This was a critical step during the Spanish bank restructuring process, as far as savings banks were concerned, for two main reasons:

- Savings banks were able to maintain their foundational nature and, therefore, the institutional diversity of the Spanish banking sector was legally guaranteed.
- The decree enhanced the development of larger savings bank groups, with a core financial centre that took the form of a commercial bank. This permitted the new banking groups to have better access to capital markets and liquidity, while the regional scope and relationship-banking nature of the savings banks' model was maintained within the banking group.

A third important regulatory event that comprised the Spanish bank reforms was Royal Decree-Law 2/2011 on the strengthening of the Spanish financial system. The aim of the recapitalization of the banking sector was that all Spanish banks should have a core capital ratio of at least 8 per cent (10 per cent if they were not a listed company and, hence, had difficulty accessing to equity markets, as experienced by some of the savings banks). Those that did not meet the new minimum requirements had until 30 September 2011 to increase their capital, either through reliance on private investors or through the FROB.

Towards the end of 2011, the debate on the likely impact of a potential clean-up of assets in the Spanish banking sector was very intense. In February 2012, the government approved Royal Decree-Law 2/2012 (3 February 2012). The rationale stated was that the measures were 'designed to clean up institutions' problematic exposures to construction and real estate developers in Spain – particularly land – from their balance sheets ... as well as to consider potential migrations of assets from normal to problematic portfolios.'

Most of the reform was directed at introducing new provisions and fostering further sector consolidation. Through this approach, the government was giving priority to private sector based solutions before imposing additional costs on taxpayers. The new provisioning scheme seems simple but there are several exceptions and specific features with very relevant implications.

The new banking reform gave preferential treatment to institutions that present merger plans. In order to facilitate these processes, the FROB was allowed to buy shares of the institutions. These shares must be sold through a competitive procedure within a maximum period of three years. Importantly, the FROB was also allowed to provide funds to facilitate the processes through CoCos (convertible into shares within five years).

On 9 June 2012, the Eurogroup published a statement in which they set up contingent financial aid for the recapitalization of Spanish banks for €100 billion. The aid was defined as a 'loan amount' that 'must cover estimated capital requirements with an additional margin of safety'. Importantly, following the formal request for aid by the Spanish authorities – effectively made 25 June 2012 – an assessment needs to be provided by the European Commission, the European Central Bank, the European Banking Authority and the International Monetary Fund. The conditionality is embedded in a Memorandum of Understanding (MoU). As specified in the Eurogroup statement, the financial assistance is expected to be provided by the European Financial Stability Facility (EFSF) or the European Stability Mechanism (ESM). Importantly, the Spanish government was expected to retain the full responsibility of financial assistance. Additionally, the Eurogroup considers that the policy conditionality of the financial assistance should be 'focused on specific reforms targeting the financial sector, including restructuring plans in line with EU state-aid rules and horizontal structural reforms of the domestic financial sector.'

On 31 August 2012, the Spanish government approved Royal Decree-Law 24/2012 on 'a new framework for the restructuring and resolution of financial institutions'. The title is quite illustrative on the aim of getting from restructuring measures to a final resolution setting for the banking crisis in Spain. Royal-Decree 24/2012 constitutes the first main step of the compliance with the MoU requirements, to meet, as a minimum, the following conditions:

- Introduce legislation to ensure the effectiveness of SLEs, (by End-August 2012).

- Upgrade of the bank resolution framework, i.e. strengthen the resolution powers of the FROB and the Deposit Guarantee Fund (DGF) (by End-August 2012).

Importantly, even if the MoU agenda was quite specific and clear in both its content and progress, Royal Decree 24/2012 acknowledges that the implementation of the MoU is taking place within an environment of significant foreseeable regulatory changes in Europe that may force Spain to adopt some of these ongoing measures to a new EU legal framework, in particular where the provision of EU funds and the functioning of the available funding mechanisms (the EFSF and/or the ESM) are concerned. Specifically, in the motivation of the Royal Decree it is said that 'as soon as the EU agrees on a legal text for a Directive on bailout and resolution mechanisms for banks, this decree will be adapted to that Directive'.

Royal Decree-Law 24/2012 included measures on six main subjects:

(i) A new and strengthened framework for crisis management of financial institutions that allows for effective restructuring and orderly resolution if necessary.
(ii) Reinforcement of the FROB's intervention tools at all stages of crisis management.
(iii) Strengthening of the protection of retail investors.
(iv) Establishment of an Asset Management Company (AMC).
(v) Burden sharing between the public and private sector of the cost of restructuring resulting from the restructuring of entities.
(vi) Other aspects, such as the strengthening of capital requirements, new limits on executive compensation and transfer of competences to the Bank of Spain.

As for the strengthened framework for crisis management of financial institutions, early intervention of a bank would take place in any of the following situations:

- Solvency requirements are not being met or there is a reasonable expectation that they will not be met.
- Liabilities of the bank are (or are expected to be) larger than the assets.
- Banks cannot (or are expected not to be able to) meet their financial commitments.

The decree provides the Bank of Spain with the power to directly remove the board of directors and other executive representatives of a bank. The Bank of Spain may also force the board of directors to set a board meeting and may force the board to negotiate a programme of debt restructuring with the debtors of the institution. The orderly resolution of an institution might also take the form of partial business sales or an asset and liability sale to a bridge-bank (a bank where the assets are transferred and managed by the FROB) or to an asset management company.

As mentioned above, a troubled bank may be required to make asset sales and/or to transfer assets to the AMC. Additionally, the FROB may require the transfer of all assets to a so-called bridge-bank that would be controlled and managed by the FROB itself. The FROB should dispose of its capital shares in the bridge-bank in five years.

The FROB could also decide to provide financial aid to the acquirers of troubled banks to help in the restructuring of the bank without taking control of it. This way the FROB could eventually minimize the public funds used.

In the cases where the FROB decides to inject funds in a bank as part of a restructuring process or to support the acquirers of a troubled institution, the funds could be provided as ordinary shares or as CoCos (convertible bonds). As far as CoCos are concerned, the FROB can convert them into capital in the six months following the fifth year of their subscription. The six months deadline can be increased to two years depending on the entity's situation. As for the ordinary shares – as in the case of the bridge bank – the FROB should dispose of them in five years.

The decree reinforced the FROB's powers, sharing some important supervision and discipline powers with the Bank of Spain. The decree highlights that 'the FROB will be in charge of managing the restructuring and resolution processes in the Spanish banking sector'. As described earlier, the FROB – in coordination with the Bank of Spain – may determine and monitor a number of early intervention actions and the current decree gives the FROB full rights to take control of financial firms and effectively manage them if necessary.

Another very relevant and controversial issue in the MoU was the burden sharing regime between the public sector and the private stakeholders. Royal-Decree Law 24/2012 defines this burden-sharing as the owners of hybrid capital instruments being forced to bear part of the losses of a troubled institution. According to the decree, 'the objective is to reduce, to the maximum extent possible, the cost for taxpayers of restructuring, according to the European rules of state aids'. The troubled banks themselves will be able to offer a number of possibilities to the owners of hybrid capital including haircuts on the value of the outstanding debt, the early buy back or anticipated sale of the debt instruments at discounted prices, a conversion of hybrid capital to any other form of equity capital or 'any other instrument offered by the bank'. Importantly if the FROB considers that the loss absorption by private owners is not enough, it will be able to impose on them specific exchange exercises. These exercises could consist of exchanges into capital instruments, direct or conditioned cash repurchases, or reduction and anticipated amortization of the nominal value of the instrument. All these actions will take into account market values, applying a haircut as established in the European rules.

Importantly, with Royal Decree Law 24/2012 came a new minimum capital requirement. Specifically, the tier-1 capital requirements of 8 per cent and

10 per cent at that time (8 per cent as a general rule and 10 per cent for entities with difficult access to capital markets and for those for which wholesale funding is predominant) became a single requirement of 9 per cent that all the entities must comply with as of 1 January 2013. The new regulation adapts the definition of the tier-1 ratio to the one established in the European Banking Authority.

The approval by the European Commission of the plans for the four banks in which the Fund for the Orderly Restructuring of the Banking Sector (FROB) has a majority stake on 28 November 2012 was a key milestone in the resolution of the banking crisis in Spain. These banks – classified as Group 1 according to the MoU criteria – were then set to receive the necessary equity funds to meet their capital requirements.

As for the effective implementation of the EU financial assistance programme, the MoU text included 32 milestones to be completed over 2012 and 2013.

As previously stated, one of the latest recommendations of the MoU referred to the improvement in the decision-making and resolution powers of the Spanish supervisors. A major step in this direction was taken by the Bank of Spain in late September 2013, when the Executive Commission of the Bank of Spain approved an internal Circular of Procedures applied in the Directorate of General Banking Supervision (Internal Circular 2/2013), updating the rules that were in force at that time (Internal Circular 7/2011). The new Circular included a number of mandatory procedures that were undertaken by early 2014. In any event, the Bank of Spain acknowledged that the new procedures will very probably have to be updated once the Single Supervisory Mechanism (SSM) within the European Banking Union is in place in late 2014.

Also following the principles of the MoU- the FROB approved a 'general framework for action to supplement its decision-making powers in relation to possible corporate operations'. This general framework was announced in October 2013. This new framework is set to facilitate the success of corporate operations 'to resolve credit institutions.' The principles approved by FROB are mainly the following:

(a) The main aim is to avoid problems of 'fairness for the creditors or shareholders' of a bank resulting from the general rules applied.
(b) A clear economic justification should be provided – and validated by an independent expert – to demonstrate the preservation of value for the FROB and the minimization of costs for taxpayers.
(c) The principles set by the FROB should comply with the European rules on State aid.

Many of the principles of the MoU were effectively implemented in Spain by Law 9/2012 (14 November 2012) on restructuring and resolution of credit institutions, which raised the content of Royal Decree-Law 24/2012 and Royal Decree-Law 9/2009.

11 Accounting

Changes in accounting principles have been transversally introduced in several regulations in Spain. However, as for the transposition of the main EU principles, the first reference is Directive 86/635/EEC on annual and consolidated accounts of banks and other financial institutions. The due transposition date was 1993 but in Spain it was transposed earlier, in 1991. In particular, from 1988 to 1991 with Law 26/1988 (29 July 1988), on the Discipline and Administration of Credit Institutions, the Bank of Spain Circular 18/89 (13/12/89) on financial repos and options, Royal Decree 1564/89 (22 December 1989) on public limited companies, Royal Decree 1643/1990 (20 December 1990) which approves the so-called 'Plan General de Contabilidad' (General Accounting Rules) and, mainly, with Bank of Spain Circular 4/1991 (14 June 1991) on accounting rules and financial statement formats.

Bank of Spain Circular 4/1991 was largely modified by Bank of Spain Circular no. 4/2004 (22 December 2004) on the public and confidential bank reporting rules and financial statements formats in accordance to the transposition (due in 2004 and made by that date) of EC 1606/2002 (Regulation) and 2003/51/EC on the application of International Accounting Standards to annual and consolidated accounts of banks, financial institutions and insurance companies. The amendments of Circular 4/2004 do not alter significantly the guiding principles of on Circular 4/1991 in this area, namely to promote healthy, sound accounting and to minimize the costs and uncertainty that the coexistence of numerous accounting criteria would entail. The accounting criteria and approaches of Circular 4/1991 of 14 June 1991 on Accounting Rules and Financial Statement Formats were mostly retained in Circular 4/2004 and they were in general in accordance with International Financial Reporting Standards (IFRS).

The adoption of the IFRS by the EU is part of the project to promote the formation of a European capital market, and to increase convergence with US accounting standards. However, the compatibility of Circular 4/2004 with the Community Regulation is no obstacle to its broader application with the aim of covering both accounting issues for external use and issues relating to the exercise of the powers and requirements of the Bank of Spain, especially in relation to supervision.

12 Conclusions

This paper analyses the implementation of the most important EU regulations regarding the financial system in Spain since the early 1980s to present. Overall, the implementation has been successful and has been timely. In any event, some specific observations can be made for the Spanish case:

- The implementation process was particularly intense after 1986, when Spain joined the European Community. Spain was then going through an intense process of liberalization and some of the Directives that had to be transposed completed that process and set up the pillars of what we know today as the modern Spanish financial system.

- The implementation has been particularly intense and fast where the solvency regulation is concerned. Some of the Directives on Capital Regulation following – Basel I and Basel II in particular – were implemented in advance in Spain.
- However, some other regulations, in particular those concerning capital markets, have normally required more time to be transposed or have had to be gradually implemented.
- Banks' supervision and prudential regulations have also been carefully implemented in Spain and some specific features not yet included in EU regulations – such as countercyclical provisions for bank losses – were already implemented in Spain since the early 2000s.
- The financial crisis has brought a number of significant changes beyond EU regulations for Spanish banks and it has shown that there was still substantial room for improvement in supervision and prudential regulations.
- The recapitalization and restructuring process and, in particular, the financial assistance programme of the EU for Spanish banks, have brought a number of regulatory changes beyond EU Directives, in particular those concerning early-prompt corrective actions and bank resolution mechanisms, including burden-sharing rules and other principles that will facilitate the adaptation of Spanish regulations to the forthcoming environment of the European Banking Union.

References

BANK OF SPAIN (2014) Financial stability report: www.bde.es/bde/en/secciones/informes/boletines/Informe_de_Estab/anoactual/.

BANK OF SPAIN (2013 and 2014) Economic bulletin (financial regulation section).

DELL'ARICCIA, G., DETRAGIACHE, E. and RAJAN, R. (2008) The real effect of banking crises. *Journal of Financial Intermediation*, 17(1), 89–112.

REINHART, C. M. and ROGOFF, K .S. (2008) Is the 2007 US subprime crisis so different? An international historical comparison. *American Economic Review*, 98(2), 339–344.

REPORT OF BANKING SUPERVISION IN SPAIN (2002, 2003 2004, 2005, 2006, 2007, 2008 and 2009) Bank of Spain: www.bde.es/bde/en/secciones/informes/Publicaciones_an/Memoria_de_la_Su/anoactual/.

6 Financial regulation in Estonia – a 'world of "dead letters"'

The interplay of Europeanization process and national idiosyncrasies

Egert Juuse

1 Introduction

The 2008 financial crisis revealed the shortcomings of financial policies on both national and international levels. Though views have differed on the exact causes of the crisis and policy failures, meagre requirements in trading, lack of transparency in complex financial instruments and freedom left to unregulated non-bank actors have been presented as some of the reasons behind the turmoil in the financial markets (see European Commission, 2010; Montanaro and Tonveronachi, 2011). Still, deeper understanding of the implications of regulatory environments has been a challenging task, in particular, in the European Union (EU) context, where limited real convergence of policies and institutions has been observed, that is, inconsistencies in the adjustment to EU policies and more specifically to the *acquis communautaire* across policy areas and countries (see Kohler-Koch and Eising, 1999; Héritier, 2001; Jacoby, 2004).

Inside the EU, Central and Eastern European countries (CEEC) stand out for deep integration with international markets, including for capital markets and various financial services, which explains why and how they were hit to greater or smaller extent by the 2008 global crisis. The crisis itself revealed several vulnerabilities of these economies, particularly dependence on high-volume cross-border funding via internal capital markets within the banking groups (De Haas and Naaborg, 2005, 2006; Lehmann et al., 2011; see Bohle and Greskovits, 2012). That being the case, CEECs have found themselves in a position where the governance of finance, dictated by regional or global regimes, has disabled national governments to shield their economies against the crises as evidenced by their unsuccessful attempts to control the credit boom of the 2000s (see Pistor, 2009). Therefore, the challenges in the governance of finance for CEECs arise from the multidimensionality of financial regulation in terms of the interplay of national and supranational actors as well as institutions that could be addressed from both the Europeanization and 'regulatory state' thesis (see Majone, 1996).

So far, the scope of the eastward Europeanization research has been rather wide with the focus on the entire *acquis* without any single country or issue on the agenda. Most of the research attention has been also placed on the output level, that is, legislative decisions with the focus on explanatory factors that affect the correct and timely transposition of the EU policies, and not so much on outcomes in terms of implementation performance (see Falkner et al., 2005; Treib, 2008). Hence, in light of the regulatory failures in finance and the impact of the EU on the evolution of financial policies at the national level, the current paper addresses the development of the banking legislation in one of the CEECs – Estonia – during the period of 1991–2011. Compared to other CEECs, the peculiarity of the Estonian financial system stems from the operation of the currency board system operating until 2011 and substantial foreign ownership in the banking industry with the four largest foreign-owned banks controlling over 95 per cent of the market in terms of both total assets and share capital (OECD, 2011). Furthermore, the tendency of Estonia to outperform Western European counterparts, but also other CEECs, when it comes to compliance with the EU regulation (see Sedelmeier, 2008; Toshkov, 2008) presents the grounds for a study on the effectiveness of regulatory harmonization in terms of potential divergence between legislation and 'real-life' developments in the banking industry. In this regard, the current chapter aims to explain the factors affecting the formation of the regulatory practices and also to understand the implications of the alignment with the EU banking regulation for financial supervision and overall stability.

The following analysis will be undertaken within the conceptual framework of Europeanization and the institutionalist tradition. The first section will present a brief overview on the current theoretical literature and presents the analytical framework for understanding the dynamics in regulatory and supervisory practices. The second section of the study presents the development of Estonian banking legislation to be followed by the sections discussing the factors affecting it and the implications for the banking sector supervision.

2 Multifaceted concept of Europeanization

Europeanization as a reflection of the convergence process has been presented in several ways: (1) the impact of the EU on countries through the absorption of EU norms and logic, that is, the transposition and implementation of European legislation in EU member and non-member states (Grabbe, 2006; Schimmelfennig and Sedelmeier, 2005a; Kaeding, 2006), (2) the substitution of national policymaking with supranational policymaking that modifies patterns of political and administrative behaviour (Radaelli, 2000; Majone, 1996), or (3) more narrowly, conceived of as the impact of individual EU policy measures on the existing policies, political and administrative processes, and structures of both member and non-member states (Héritier, 2005; Pollack,

2010). Even though all three interpretations are applicable in the analysis of banking regulation, it is the mechanisms of the Europeanization and the constructs behind them that give a better understanding of the dynamics in the field of study. In the context of the CEECs, these mechanisms have transformed throughout the (pre-/post-)accession period since 1989, starting with lesson-drawing, also imitation or institutional isomorphism, and ending with coercion, that is, conditionality and eventual membership obligations (see Grabbe, 2006; Jacoby, 2006). In that respect, theoretically informed studies on the Eastward Europeanization reason that compliance, enforcement and policy changes could be built around: (1) a rational choice institutionalist tradition, that is, the 'external incentives model', which captures the dynamics underpinning the EU's conditionality, (2) an institution-based historical (constructivist) tradition, that is, the 'social learning model' that emphasizes identification with the EU and persuasion of the legitimacy of EU rules as conditions for rule adoption, and (3) an ecological organization tradition, that is, the 'lesson-drawing model' with the focus on the adoption of EU rules as induced by the CEECs themselves through copying, emulation, combination or inspiration (see Radaelli, 2000; Schimmelfennig and Sedelmeier, 2002; Börzel and Risse, 2003; Schimmelfennig and Sedelmeier, 2005a; Pollack, 2010; Etienne 2011).

Schimmelfennig and Sedelmeier (2005b) claim that in the early transition period CEECs were receptive to lesson-drawing and social learning approaches due to the widespread perception of policy failure and the need to replace socialist legacies or to adopt new rules in areas where none existed before. This was evidenced by selective and limited EU-induced rule adoption (see also Andonova, 2003; Grabbe, 2002). However, they concede that the external incentives model, associated with EU membership conditionality, generally explains the broader patterns of rule adoption in CEECs from 1995 onwards. Despite the fact that the EU's influence worked through the conditionality for accession during the pre-2004 period, the given set of institutions once established has influenced and constrained the behaviour of the actors who adopted them. Perception of the embeddedness of national policies, institutions and regulation in line with EU requirements and accompanied significant 'sunk costs' in the adjustment process highlight the explanatory strength of the historical institutionalist tradition. In this regard, CEECs have eventually got locked in the Europeanization process in terms of setting in path-dependencies in externally directed policy formulation and implementation (Grabbe, 2006; Fink-Hafner, 2007).

Most of the research on the Europeanization process along these three main traditions has mainly focused on explanatory factors like misfit ('goodness of fit'), veto players or national bureaucracies, including administrative capacity and coordination as more broadly defined independent variables affecting the transposition of EU legislation and explaining deadlocks as well as delays (see Knill and Lenschow, 1998; Haverland, 2000;

Héritier, 2001; Falkner et al., 2005; Berglund et al., 2006; Hille and Knill, 2006; Steunenberg, 2006; Toshkov, 2007, 2008; Pollack, 2010; Young 2010). By criticizing the veto player argument and misfit hypothesis, Falkner et al. (2005, 2007) and Falkner and Treib (2008) have proposed an alternative approach that theorizes on the intuitive notion of the culture. They presented four worlds – obedience, domestic politics, neglect and 'dead letters' – as typical patterns in implementing EU policies, where national cultures, ideology and preferences on both political and administrative levels significantly affect the implementation performance. In their analysis, a world of 'dead letters' applies to new member states, where formal rules exist as a result of transposition ('obedience'), but they do not get implemented in practice ('neglect'). In a similar way, Goetz (2002) identifies 'four worlds of Europeanization' – Nordic world, north-west world, Mediterranean world, and Central and Eastern European world – by focusing on the timing of the adoption of the EU requirements by member states and links this categorization of member states to varying patterns of domestic behavior and effects. Also, Jacoby (2004) identifies four different types of impact that the EU can have on the CEECs' attempts to emulate EU rules, ranging from 'open struggle' and 'scaffolding' to 'continuous learning' and 'homesteading' by domestic groups.

However, as already stated, existing theoretical and empirical studies on Eastward Europeanization within all these traditions have had a rather narrow scope with the focus on factors affecting the implementation process in universal, homogeneous areas of study, such as social policy (e.g. Falkner et al., 2005; Linos, 2007) and environment (e.g. Héritier, 2001). The eastward Europeanization as a field of study falls short of the analysis on the effectiveness of externally induced policies and relevance of the Europeanization process for the CEECs, in particular in banking and finance. Hence, the following analysis tries to shed some light on these missing pieces in the discussion on Europeanization with the case of the banking regulation in Estonia.

3 Twenty years of the banking regulation in Estonia

Already in the early years of the independence in the 1990s, there was a clear tendency towards a 'regulatory state' model in socio-economic reforms in Estonia, as public institutions were not supposed to intervene in the economy other than to regulate (see Bohle and Greskovits, 2012). As one of the key reformers at the time, Siim Kallas, who was in charge of the central bank then, has argued that this choice was a conscious one, as there was low trust in government's ability to get interventions right (Kallas, 2003, p. 511). Further, the preference for the principle of firmly rooted rules instead of discretionary policies was reasoned with the need to stop past practices of socialist management and reduce uncertainties in a highly risky environment of the transition process (see Steinherr and Gilbert, 1994). This was manifest in the monetary institutions, that is, the currency board arrangement, which in essence depoliticized monetary policy and limited the function of the central bank as lender of last resort, but also was evidenced by the strict approach taken to the bank and bad-debt restructuring that resulted in bankruptcies and liquidations in the early 1990s with a clear message from public authorities in terms of not bailing-out commercial banks (Lainela and Sutela, 1994; OECD, 2000). It can be argued that one of the underlying motives behind both limiting the role of the central bank and the strict approach to crisis resolution in the early 1990s was to divide two main functions of the banking sector between domestic and external actors. Domestic actors (banks) should enable functioning and safe payment systems; external actors, through foreign direct investments, should enable the financing of productive investment into restructuring of the economy.

Though 1995 marks the beginning of the integration process into the international (banking) community, when the modern Credit Institutions Act, Accounting Act and Commercial Code were adopted, the starting point for Estonian banking regulation could be considered 1989, when a bill was passed to allow the establishment of commercial banks. On the grounds of the specifics of main reforms and legislative amendments, the following 25 years of the evolution of Estonian banking regulation and supervision can be divided into six periods (see also Zirnask, 2002; Sõrg and Tuusis, 2008), punctuated by critical junctures in both Europeanization and institutional progress of the banking sector, as presented in Table 6.1 at the end of the chapter:

1990–1992 – a period of monetary reform and a multitude of restrictions on capital account transactions, including a legal prohibition on foreign ownership of local banks, but no measures adopted to restore the solvency of banks in light of the first banking crisis (Sõrg, 2003; Lainela and Sutela, 1994). The main problems at that time lack of supervision and lenient requirements for establishing a bank due to the objective of public authorities to enhance competition by granting an easy entry via fairly low minimum capital requirements and lax review process of applications for a licence (OECD, 2000).

1993–1994 – the first attempts at regulating banking activities with prudential ratios – solvency ratio,[1] liquidity ratio,[2] risk concentration ratio,[3] net foreign exchange position ratio – in order to restrict the excess risks taken by banks (Bank of Estonia, 1994a). Also, new methods were adopted in the supervision of credit institutions that included a complex assessment of the quality of the bank's assets, the strength of capital base, profitability and the effectiveness of administration, while pre-emptive control was strengthened in the stage of issuing licences to credit institutions by approving the members of management (Bank of Estonia, 1995). Initially, the Bank of Estonia followed the recommendations of the Basel Committee on Banking Supervision, but later the requirements of the EU directives in elaborating prudential ratios (Bank of Estonia, 2003).

1995–1997 – qualitative changes in the regulatory framework with the enactment of the *Credit Institutions Act 1995*. Legislation on credit institutions established the basis for a universal banking model and enabled banks to own and finance other financial institutions, which also entailed the introduction of principles for consolidated financial statements. Aside from provisions on the establishment, management and supervision of the bank, tighter regulation of different risks (credit, foreign exchange, market, etc.) was adopted. One of the aims of the 1995 law and following amendments was to restrict lending to bank staff and owners as well as to prevent large exposures.

1998–2004 – a modern banking period with the focus on requirements arising from macroeconomic and international, in particular, the EU developments. In the aftermath of the 1997–1998 banking crisis, Estonia introduced the institution of deposit guarantee and adopted a European-type Credit Institutions Act 1999, based on the EU banking directives and materials from the Basel Committee on Banking Supervision. The new Credit Institutions Act was more specific in establishing the roles and responsibilities of the Banking Supervision Department at the central bank in executing oversight by stipulating specific rights for obtaining information, executing on-site inspections, demanding revitalization plans and issuing prescriptive orders, including the removal of a member of the Executive Management or Supervisory Board of the credit institution. By 2000, Estonian legislation on banking activities, accounting practices and organization of supervision was harmonized with Western practices, except for the deposit guarantee system. Amendments made in the early 2000s were mostly related to continuous harmonization of national legislation in banking to achieve full integration with the EU directives for joining the EU in 2004.

2005–2008 – continuous adaptation to the existing and new banking regulation of the EU. Further strengthening of capital adequacy regulation was caused by the need to adopt the new Basel II framework.

2009–... – the post-crisis period with reactive measures to the global financial crisis of 2008, including the improved guarantee of deposits and establishing a framework for granting emergency liquidity assistance to troubled credit institutions (OECD, 2011). Also, the rights of the Financial Supervision Authority were expanded for intervention into and inspection of the activities of banks in crisis. Moreover, the state was granted the right to consider expropriating the shares of banks operating in Estonia (Bank of Estonia, 2011). The most significant development was the enforcement of the Debt Restructuring and Debt Protection Act in 2011 to enable individuals in financial difficulty to restructure their debts. As a consequence of joining the eurozone, the minimum reserve requirement had to be lowered from 15 per cent to 2 per cent in 2010 (ibid.).

This periodization corresponds to three general stages in the banking sector's development: (1) a rapid increase in the number of banks as result of the liberalization of the banking environment in 1991–1992, (2) a decrease in the number of banks and a stabilization period until 1997–98, as the regulatory environment was made stricter, and (3) a growth phase after 1998 with increasing share of foreign ownership through organic growth and takeovers (Myant and Drahokoupil, 2011, p. 261). Such a periodization of institutional developments with general trends in the banking sector also reveals potential factors that have affected the banking legislation.

3.1 National idiosyncrasies and perseverant Europeanization

In light of the developments in the banking sector, the challenge in the 1990s was the establishment of institutions in both private and public sector by finding compromises between international regulatory trends and *ad hoc* country-specific needs, while the post-1997/98 period set the regulators the task of adjusting the regulatory and supervisory environment to suit a multinational cross-border context (Ross, 2013). Also, one has to bear in mind that Estonian banking regulation in the early 1990s was accompanied by the elimination of restrictions on capital movement and full convertibility of current account transactions under the general liberalization agenda (see De Castello Branco et al., 1996; Kattel and Raudla, 2013). The late-1990s and the following years, on the other hand, saw convergence with the EU banking directives that implied either extensive regulation of uncovered issues or re-regulating. In this regard, de- and re-regulatory cyclicality can be observed to some extent. For instance, approach taken in authorization of credit institutions was very loose in the early 1990s, followed by more stringent licensing requirements in the mid-1990s, but then again loosened due to adoption of the principles of the Second Banking Directive on cross-border banking activities.

Thus, different motives and situational circumstances in the early and late 1990s as well as the 2000s account for varying explanatory strength of theoretical concepts within the institutionalist approach on the matter of eastward Europeanization.

Although the build-up of the regulatory environment in the early 1990s was aligned with the international framework, specific domestic circumstances, such as a currency board system, influenced its design, while banking crises led to stricter regulations than international minimum standards (Ross, 2013). Thus, the crises-wrecked banking system needed a pragmatist approach in policymaking for finding solutions to single episodes of failing banks, but at the same time building an institutional environment from scratch (see De Castello Branco et al., 1996). In the conditions of reoccurring banking crises, policymaking was of a rather reactionary nature that was manifest in rule amendments after every major crisis and mostly related to practical issues in accounting, reporting, reserve and capital requirements. Consequently, attention was turned to international practices and example was taken from other Central and Western European countries in forming banking legislation, e.g. practices of Germany, Austria, Denmark, Finland, Iceland and Hungary were relied upon in drafting the legal acts, but also the Basel I principles and the EU directives were used as source of inspiration to the extent it was appropriate and possible, given the circumstances at that time (Bank of Estonia, 1994b, 1998; Khoury and Wihlborg, 2006). This indicates to the predominance of a bottom-up imitative-copying approach, associated with the 'lesson-drawing model'. The 'external incentives model', on the other hand, has cogency in explaining banking regulation from 1995 onwards, when the EU gained the leverage to spell out the content of legislation that had to be adopted as a precondition for membership, implying a rather political commitment and reasoning in adjusting the legislation to the *acquis*. Thus, the start of pre-accession negotiations can be considered as a critical juncture in the institutional adaptation. First, the adaptation to the EU banking directives was one of the key aspects of the Association (Europe) Agreement reached between the EU and Estonia in 1995 that foresaw the right for EU financial institutions to operate in Estonia by the end of a transition period at the latest, although the Europe Agreement contained transitional rules (see EBRD, 1998; Tison, 2002, p. 39; also Table 6.1 on specific examples). A second and more important development was the inclusion of Estonia in the first group of membership negotiations in 1997 and the enforcement of Association Agreement in 1998, which explain major harmonization efforts in banking legislation around the turn of the millennium in 1998–1999, as can be seen from the Table 6.1. Hence, the EU's impact on the alignment process intensified especially once the EU opened accession negotiations, which signalled the credibility of EU's membership incentive (see Sedelmeier, 2010). Moreover, EU banking policies have become embedded in Estonian legislation due to an expectation on fulfilment of conditions without opt-outs in an asymmetrical relationship and a dependence on EU's input (see Grabbe, 2006; Schimmelfennig and Sedelmeier, 2005b on asymmetry issue in the EU governance) that has allowed the EU an unprecedented influence on domestic institutions and policies in private finance. In the words of Bohle and Greskovits (2012) the period of 1989–1998 included the historical turning points with key decisions shaping the post-socialist legislative order, while the following period until the 2008 crisis brought about consolidation and further embeddedness of created structures. Such a path-dependence in adopting the EU banking directives is witnessed in the adoption of institutions and legislating financial instruments that were non-existent before the harmonization with the EU rules was initiated. For instance, investment firms and agents, financial conglomerates, securitization transactions, hybrid capital instruments, etc. were introduced into the legislation only as a result of the EU's influence, although the necessity of provisions on these notions could be questioned (see below). In that respect, Estonian banking legislation has been exposed to path-dependence in policy formulation from the late 1990s and essentially being locked in the Europeanization process, supported by the statements by the Ministry of Finance and the FSA:

> Since financial sector regulation is pretty much harmonized with European Union law, then all the reforms and changes generally start from there. In this sense, one cannot talk about specific changes and reforms …Financial stability policy is quite successful in Estonia [given the developments in the banking sector for the last 15 years], but there are also indirect external factors [operational in Estonia] that are beyond the control of the Estonian state.
>
> (Senior civil servant at the Ministry of Finance, 2014)

> If we look at Estonian legislation on financial markets, 95 per cent is comprised of European Union law, while the share of the domestic input is minuscule. The domestic component consists basically of two things: the second pillar of the pension system, even though it is partly built upon the UCITS Directive, and the Estonian Central Register of Securities …
>
> (Member of the Management Board at the Financial Supervision Authority, 2014)

This kind of embedded socialization in terms of the 'stickiness' of formal rules and institutions transposed to Estonia, emphasized in the historical institutionalist tradition, has been also supported by the prevalence of a 'simple polities' approach. Namely, policymakers seek to govern with the means for constructing communicative discourses, the purpose of which has been the persuasion of the legitimacy of policies and regulations on the grounds of the EU's accession or membership obligations (see Bohle and Greskovits 2012; Kattel and Raudla, 2013).

It can be concluded that despite the strengths of both rationalist and constructivist arguments in explaining the adoption of the EU rules in the 1990s and 2000s, the realization of several idiosyncratic risks during these times caused *ad hoc* reactive actions and were guided by more pragmatic considerations due to high political salience of the issue, namely dealing with several rounds of banking crises in the 1990s. Hence, in the 1990s the legislative development in the banking sector was driven by the interplay between the Europeanization process as an exogenous factor and the post-communist transition process, seen as an endogenous factor. One could argue, then, that the regulation in finance, and in banking in particular, has been consistent with the differentiation thesis, that is, simultaneous Europeanization, liberalization and (re-/de-)regulation (see Eberlein and Grande, 2005). However, none of the theoretical discourses has addressed the issue of potential impact, not to mention the significance of discussed regulatory tendencies for the institutional development of the banking sector.

3.2 Peculiarities and direct implications of the harmonization process

Veto player and goodness of fit propositions, associated with the aforementioned theoretical concepts, are of little significance in explaining transposition of EU banking directives into national legislation. First, the rationale underlying the misfit argument never emerged in banking regulation, as regulatory philosophies or deeply entrenched models were only taking shape and were largely missing prior to the harmonization process. This could be also reasoned with the new regulation and re-regulation of the banking sector, while the communist legacy endowed no institutional resistance to EU policies (see Schimmelfennig and Sedelmeier ,2005b; Grabbe, 2002 on misfit and veto player discussion in CEECs). Second, as already stated, it was common to justify policies by referring to EU norms and expectation in the harmonization process with the *acquis*. Moreover, the nationalist logic of integration required efficient work in order to guarantee a positive evaluation in the Commission's Progress Reports (see Laar, 2000). Similarly, nationalist sentiments on the premise of safety nets against the 'eastern' influence implied openness to foreign ownership in the banking (Bonin et al., 2009; Bohle and Greskovits, 2012). Consequently, the transposition of directives, including in the field of banking, has been excluded from daily political struggles, implying technocratic policymaking, that is, the persistence of a simple polity stance of the government and depoliticization of EU matters (Kaik, 2002; Börzel, 2010; Bohle and Greskovits, 2012; Kattel and Raudla, 2013). Estonian political leadership tended to make integration an elite project because of its complexity or importance for wider democratic politics with legitimation coming from the EU rather than from citizens. This explains the diminished role of the Parliament that was supposed to be a mere enforcer of legislation without actual influence on the formulation of legal acts, and hence, the executive bias in the overall accession process (see Grabbe, 2006).

> The whole legislative body embraces to large extent, and will do it even more in the future, European Union law. Legislation will become directly applicable and the role of the Estonian parliament and ministries here disappears altogether.
>
> (Member of the Management Board at the Financial Supervision Authority, 2014)

However, because of low administrative capacity and priority given to speed in improving banking regulation, legal acts were of low quality with technical inaccuracies (Kasemets, 2000; Bonin et al., 2009). This implied prolonged transposition of the EU directives into national legislation, evidenced by several rounds of amendments in banking-related legal acts in consequent years in the late 1990s and the early 2000s.

Such an approach in dealing with the EU affairs has reduced both political and administrative capacity to address the developments in the financial sector that have not been dealt with on the EU level, such as issues related to non-bank credit providers (SMS-loan providers), new forms of financing (P2P platforms), etc. The first credible measures for regulating pervasive activities of non-bank financiers, who have extended so-called ninja loans, that is, high interest rate loans to no-income and no-job borrowers via easily accessible electronic channels, including mobiles phones, were drafted only at the beginning of 2014 (Valdre, 2014).

> As distinctive from European Union reforms, the Ministry of Finance has developed a regulation on how SMS-loan providers would go under the supervision of the Financial Supervision Authority. This is not directly related to financial stability, as the SMS-loan providers do not pose a risk to financial stability ... rather, as their behavior has caused social problems, and secondly, the business is relatively opaque, then the state has decided to pinch a bit and take control over their activities. The supervision of these loan providers is related to more social issues, where there is clearer political will and agenda, while in the case of major [EU level] reforms, no political pressure has been felt.
>
> (Senior civil servant at the Ministry of Finance, 2014)

3.2.1 'Dead letters' manifestations

Grabbe (2006) raised concerns over the encouragement of institutional isomorphism for gaining political legitimacy for institutional and policy changes during the post-communist transition period, as that could lead to functional dualism whereby institutions resemble the EU ones, but are not functional. Hence, questions have been raised about the real impact of the adopted formal rules with the possibility of a mere existence of regulations on paper, that is, 'formal structures without substance' (see Bugaric, 2006). Dimitrova (2010) raises the danger of the EU rules being created for a different set of preferences and economic conditions that might not fit the domestic economic conditions, when transferred to candidate states. In a similar line of argument, institutionalization is undermined if there is a mismatch between formal and informal rules, meaning that the adopted formal rules will remain rather rules-on-the-books than rules-in-use without any real effects. In addition, Jacoby (1999) has observed a specific kind of superficial domestic change through 'Potemkin harmonization', where political and regulatory changes were carried out for the purpose of EU monitoring without significant institutionalization.

Similar developments are present in the field of banking regulation in Estonia. For instance, financial conglomerates, 'significant branches', e-money institutions and their practices have been regulated in detail, but without real use in practice due to the lack of such institutions operating in the Estonian financial market. Similarly, provisions on hybrid capital instruments, credit risk mitigation techniques, securitization transactions and instruments were legislated, although being not practised in the banking sector (Rahandusministeerium, 2010a). Neither banks nor investment firms in Estonia conclude any complicated financial transactions. The types of financial instruments and transaction negotiable on the Estonian market have been restricted, and trading activity has been very low, implying non-existent speculative transactions in Estonia (see Oja, 2012, 2013; Auväärt, 2013). For instance, foreign debt securities have been the dominant assets in the portfolio of banks, the shares held for trading staying at low levels (3 per cent of securities portfolio in 2001) (Lepik and Tõrs, 2002). Essentially, mortgages denominated in foreign currency, not complex financial structured instruments such as CDOs, CDSs etc., were considered as innovative financial products that proved to be risky practices in Estonia and other CEECs (EBRD, 2012). The insignificance of some of the capitalization regulation regarding the trading book and counterparty risks is due to the fact that the banking sector operates in mostly commercial banking field.

> As the Estonian financial sector is still small and we do not have quite a number of these financial services or sophisticated financial instruments on the local market as found in the rest of the world, we do not possess any significant expertise here to have an opinion on one or another EU proposal or impact ... And there is really no one to discuss [these issues] with. Estonia's problem is that in some areas there is not really any knowledge.
>
> (Senior civil servant at the Ministry of Finance, 2014)

In addition, banking policies do not allow any claim that managers of the Estonian financial institutions have been paid unreasonable salaries or bonuses in light of the recent EU's attempts at reining excessive remuneration episodes (Rahandusministeerium, 2010b). In principle, one can witness nominal (legislative) convergence with the EU legislation, but to some extent divergence between adopted rules and real life practices. This, in turn, raises the question on the effectiveness of financial policies and regulations in addressing real-life financial practices.

Furthermore, when analysing the cases of the worlds of 'dead letters', Falkner and Treib (2008) found that literal translation of EU Directives at the expense of careful adaptation to domestic conditions implied frequent shortcomings in enforcement (see also Sissenich, 2002; Schimmelfennig and Sedelmeier, 2007). In this regard, the basic elements of the EU banking regulation, including the risk-weighted capital adequacy requirement, large exposure limits, the initial minimum capital requirement, etc. were copied into Estonian legislation in the 1990s (Ross, 2013). This explains the lack of analysis and assessment of banking legal acts in the 1990s, evidenced by the limited consultation with outside organizations as well as civil society (Kasemets, 2000) and low-quality explanatory notes that accompanied legislation (European Commission, 1999).

It could be argued that the regulatory evolution of the banking sector was driven by pragmatic considerations in the 1990s, only to be permeated by the embedded formalist approach afterwards, that is, mechanical adoption of EU legislation in this policy field. In principle, one can observe both path-dependence in terms of a continuous alignment with the EU policies, and 'dead letters' in the evolution of the EU-led banking regulation in Estonia. Hence, one of the problems in Estonian banking regulation is related to its isolation from the underlying economic substance, as rules have not been adapted to the market structure.[4] Consequently, operational functionality of regulation has been reduced with repercussions for financial supervision.

3.3 Supervisory obstacles and challenges

In contrast to the transposition of prudential regulation, the EU directives have left ample room for national discretion in supervisory intrusiveness without any clear quality standards to be followed (Tonveronachi, 2010). This has been evident in the failures to enforce policies, including transposed EU legislation, due to constrained administrative and judicial capacities in new EU member states. Weak enforcement of contracts, legal restrictions on disposal of assets backed by real estate, difficult access to collateral and low collateral recovery were just a few examples of problems in the 1990s and early 2000s (see De Castello Branco et al., 1996; Steinherr, 1997; EBRD, 1998; Scholtens 2000; Schimmelfennig and Sedelmeier, 2005a; Falkner and Treib, 2008; Sedelmeier, 2008). Even banks perceive legal enforcement as the weakest area, although capital regulation in Estonia is seen as strict and the local legal system considered as adequate (EBRD 2011). In the words of Wagner and Iakova (2001), the effectiveness of financial regulations was lagging behind the extensiveness of regulatory coverage.

By the mid-1990s banking regulation in Estonia was considered to be on par with international standards, but adequate implementation was lacking by public authorities and also bank owners. Although the central bank established basic rules for commercial banks such as minimum capital requirements, capital ratios, exposure requirements, etc., the scope of adherence to the rules was undetermined due to ineffective supervision (Lainela and Sutela, 1994). This was evident in several cases of mismanagement, like incorrect reporting of the value of the securities and non-performing loans. For instance, at the Hoiupank, equity was pledged by senior managers to back a loan to finance purchases of the bank's shares by the very same managers, while at Eesti Maapank, mismanagement of the bank's equity portfolio, including fraudulent behaviour, brought about losses that resulted in the bank's bankruptcy (see EBRD, 1998). *Eesti Maapank* reported the higher face value of the securities instead of marking them to market – as required by the Bank of Estonia – thus inflating both its assets and profits. Essentially, the bank abused the option given by the central bank to undertake sophisticated transactions with forward contracts and also managers could make deals with themselves (Khoury and Wihlborg, 2006). Aside from cases of engagement in extensive insider and connected lending, banks also violated standard prudential banking norms by using illegal mechanisms such as shell companies in order to disregard or actively circumvent legislative restrictions (Lainela and Sutela, 1994; Hansson, 1995, p. 156; De Castello Branco et al., 1996; Myant and Drahokoupil, 2011, p. 266). Thus, fraud was present mostly due to lax enforcement of laws in the 1990s, which in turn was caused by institutional and human capital constraints. For instance, in 1992 there were only ten officials at the Bank Inspection department in the central bank, who were mostly inexperienced newcomers, to supervise over 40 banks (see Hansson, 1995, p. 159). General weaknesses in supervision were also related to a lack of adequate training arrangements for upgrading of skills and knowledge in new financial products (Khoury and Wihlborg, 2006). Problems were further aggravated by limited reporting requirements and the lack of specificity in rules for transparency, disclosure of information and insider trading (Bank of Estonia, 1997). Thus, the banking problems in the 1990s were to great extent attributable to lacking supervision as well as inexperience of supervisors.

In the 2000s, the rights of the Financial Supervision Authority were expanded for intervention into and inspection of the activities of banks. Particularly in 2010 and 2011, the powers of the Financial Supervision Authority were expanded by giving authority to require a reduction of performance pay, amendments in internal rules, an increase in own funds in the reorganization plan, including increase in share capital, and to make a proposal to amend or supplement the organizational structure of a credit institution among others (Finantsinspektsiooni seaduse, investeerimisfondide seaduse, krediidiasutuste seaduse ja tagatisfondi seaduse muutmise seadus, 2010; Investeerimisfondide seaduse ja sellega seonduvate seaduste muutmise seadus, 2011). Yet, most of the actions have been taken against investment firms as well as insurance companies and have been related to withdrawal of licences (mostly on the request of investment firms themselves), issuing recommendations on credit policies of banks, notifications on misleading advertising and violations of information requirement, and dealing with complaints filed against financial institutions (Financial Supervision Authority, 2014). Essentially, precepts have mostly addressed the issues in relation to consumer protection. This indicates that the emphasis has been laid on market conduct supervision by the FSA, whereas prudential supervision has been challenged by the broader internationalization of banking activities.

3.3.1 Challenges in addressing cross-border banking activities

As suggested by Pollack (2010) and Bohle and Greskovits (2007), the substantial presence of foreign ownership in the banking sector has implied that policy priorities in CEECs have been influenced by the outside players form other EU member states. Similarly, Lenschow (2006) has attributed domestic changes to forces other than the impact of the Europeanization process, such as the increasing internationalization of finances and markets. Further, Andonova (2003) has shown the absence of opposition by potential veto players to the EU's demands, if a policy area lacks institutional legacies or the regulated sector is highly internationalized, as is the case with the banking industry in Estonia.

Sweden and other Nordic countries as home countries of banks operating in Estonia have been proactive in guiding subsidiaries and thus endowing Estonian authorities with coordination and supervision challenges (see Lehmann et al., 2011). The dominance of foreign capital in the Estonian banking sector renders all banks subject to consolidated supervision by the home country authorities. In that respect, the division between consolidated and delegated supervision is not so distinct, given the provisions in the legal acts that provide the opportunity to transfer the supervisory duty to the home country authorities (Credit Institutions Act, 1999). Further, the local supervision of subsidiaries is rendered ineffective, given that banks tend to treat subsidiaries increasingly as branch offices. Within the vertically integrated financial groups, centralized strategies are being implemented in a manner that is oblivious of national legislation and where subsidiaries remain relevant only for tax and accounting purposes (see ECB, 2005; Pistor, 2009). Consequently, the cross-border dimension of banking activities and supervision has allowed for political risks, associated with regulatory and fiscal policies (see Kudrna and Gabor, 2013 on political risks). Moreover, political risks are present due to two unaddressed issues in the current regulatory regime: the misallocation of regulatory responsibility and a related lack of accountability for failures in markets beyond the home regulator's jurisdiction (Pistor, 2010).

Potential legal loopholes in Estonia exist in the area of the reallocation of capital and liquidity through internal capital markets, which enable banks to evade taxes and undermine any countercyclical financial (monetary) policies at the disposal of the Bank of Estonia. The duty of corporate income tax that has been levied in Estonia only in case of profit distribution (reinvested profits exempted from taxation) has been circumvented by substituting repatriation of retained earnings with lending to parent companies (Sulg, 2014; also Vedler, 2010). As of 2009, the accumulated retained earnings of the banking sector amounted to €1461.5 million or 10.6 per cent of GDP, compared to €400,000 and 0.006 per cent of GDP in 2000 (author's calculation based on Bank of Estonia, 2012), and none of the foreign subsidiaries had paid out dividends before 2014. Out of €1.4 billion as net profit of the four largest banks for the period of 2010–2013 (3rd quarter), only €21 million were paid in income tax (Arumäe, 2014).

Similarly, the effectiveness of entity-based regulation in Estonia, such as higher capital and reserve requirements, in curbing the credit growth has been impaired by the possibility of parent banks to circumvent Estonian legislation and prudential policies by providing cross-border financial services to local businesses or lending to leasing,[5] asset management and other non-bank financial institutions within the same group that are not included in the banking statistics (Pistor, 2010; Lehmann et al., 2011; Atanas and Sanne, 2013; Ross, 2013). This, in turn, has been made possible by the universal banking model, stipulated in both Estonian legislation and EU banking directives. Financial intermediation was envisaged to be built around universal banks that eventually resulted in credit institutions growing into banking groups (Lepik and Tõrs, 2002; EBRD, 1998).

Therefore, effect-based regulations have been curtailed within the established regulatory framework, particularly in relation to the cross-border provision of financial services and the activity of branches. Banking supervision has focused on the solvency of individual institutions, but not on macro-prudential issues, such as dynamic systemic risks in the whole system (see Kregel, 2014 for a general discussion of this issue). This, however, has not been seen as a problem by the public authorities.

> In the case of a small environment, this [micro and macro-prudential regulation] is nebulous … actually, one can achieve with micro-prudential instruments the same as with macro-prudential instruments, because there are few market participants and they have such a large market share. Therefore, this issue is not so important to deal with …
>
> (Member of the Management Board at the Financial Supervision Authority, 2014)

Nonetheless, in the established legislative framework, the potential danger for Estonia lies in insufficient interest of a home country regulator in a subsidiary that might have an insignificant part at the banking group level but entails systemic risks for the financial sector in Estonia (see Bonin et al., 2009; EBRD, 2012). In that respect, the liquidity and credit squeeze pose significant threats to the Estonian financial sector and the economy as a whole, should the liquid assets be repatriated from Estonia, when parent banks face funding difficulties. Such an international dimension of banking activities has put Estonia in a complicated position in guaranteeing financial stability (see Begg, 2009). All in all, the overall outcome of financial liberalization, the dominance of financial groups from Nordic countries and the systematic 'outsourcing' of regulatory supervision to home country authorities has been a form of financial governance that emphasizes *positive* integration, but is void of feasibility to control the risks associated with exposure to capital flows (Pistor, 2009; Khoury and Wihlborg, 2006). The outsourced nature of supervision was exemplified during the crisis by the emergency loan taken by the Swedish central bank to cover the potential losses of Swedish banks in Estonia and elsewhere in the Baltic States. Hence, Estonia has been lacking an effective governance regime for finance that has addressed only the credibility aspect of finance (and thus, security of the payment systems), but not money supply – two sides of the same coin that are conventionally interlinked. As stated above, this division of labour within the banking sector follows in Estonia the dividing line between domestic and foreign actors.

And even if any 'bottom-up' domestic regulatory efforts for financial stability could be well reasoned on economic grounds, the Europeanization process has put brakes on these initiatives. For instance, in relation to higher capital requirements for mortgage lending and to counter overheating, new EU level regulations meant for Estonia procyclical loosening of requirements as domestic regulations had to be scaled down in mid-2000s. Similarly, stricter rules could not be introduced in Estonia alone that would have made the equal treatment of branches and subsidiaries problematic, while the initiatives to introduce stricter risk weights on mortgage loans at the regional level would have contradicted the broader process of harmonization of regulations (see Sutt et al., 2011; Ross, 2013). As it happened, petition by the Estonian supervisors for stricter capital requirements, when the economy was booming, was rejected by the Swedish peers on the grounds of sufficient capitalization at the group level (EBRD, 2012).

As a response to the regulatory voids left by EU legislation in addressing cross-border financial stability and the allocation of responsibility, new types of informal institutions have been introduced such as the transnational regulatory network in the form of memorandum of understanding (MoU). As a coordination mechanism this informally harmonizes regulatory activities of regional members (Eberlein and Grande, 2005). The Baltic-Nordic MoU, signed in August 2010 has been considered as one of the most specific burden-sharing models, which considered the asset share of the financial groups in a given country and introduced exacerbating and mitigating factors (Kudrna, 2012).

> The monitoring of the entire group is located in Sweden … for which a college of supervisors has been established, where supervisors from Estonia, Latvia and Lithuania are invited … and basically information is exchanged on what is happening down here [in Estonia] and what we think of things. In such a debate or dialogue, decision-making takes place that is implemented across the group level. Sweden is good in the sense that this college system originates from the Nordic countries, where the culture of consensus prevails, which means that a lot is contributed to discussions and all taken decisions are implemented.
>
> (Member of the Management Board at the Financial Supervision Authority, 2014)

Compared to other similar agreements, it was peculiar for including *ex ante* burden-sharing procedures and for engaging ministries of finance along with central bankers and financial supervisors for introducing a permanent body – the Nordic-Baltic Cross-Border Stability Group (NBSG) – to oversee financial stability issues (EBRD, 2012). Yet, Märten Ross, the former deputy governor of the Bank of Estonia has acknowledged the difficulties in such a coordination of regulations in the region, although stressing the importance of cross-border coordination of banking supervision (Ross, 2013).

It has been established that within the emerged architecture of the financial regulation on cross-border banking activities, the presence of two supervisory authorities challenges the supervision as well as the application of macro-prudential measures. This was seen in the credit boom in the mid-2000s that was encouraged by the limited control by the Estonian authorities over the crediting of the economy and insufficient cross-border coordination that impaired prudential regulation to halt the overheating of the economy (see EBRD, 2012). This raises the question on the compatibility of two characteristics of the integration process, namely the simultaneous liberalization of external accounts and national responsibility for financial stability without the EU-wide lender of last resort facility.

4 Conclusions

Regulation of the banking industry in Estonia is theoretically significant in many respects. There is no clear straightforward model that would explain the evolution of banking legislation, as all theoretical concepts – lesson-drawing model, rationalist institutionalism and historical institutionalism – are applicable for understanding the dynamics at certain periods in the regulatory development trajectory. This is witnessed in the interplay of domestic features such as banking crises in the 1990s that required steadfast responses by public authorities,[6] and external factors such as the increasing presence of foreign financial intermediaries in Estonia from the late 1990s. Both the need to build up the institutional framework for private finance and address reoccurring crises anchored banking regulation and supervision (nominally) to the EU and other international principles and practices, as seen from the Table 6.1. This has been supported by the position of the Ministry of Finance:

> It could even be argued that the financial sector is overregulated ... In the past 5–10 years, a lot of new rules or new proposals have been adopted that we considered as excessive regulation ... especially considering that our market is small and the new requirements or charges may be too hard to deal with. So, we have tried to fight as much as possible against such a heavy regulation, which we have not been very successful at.
>
> (Senior civil servant at the Ministry of Finance, 2014)

Nonetheless, Estonia has been 'accused' of meticulous punctuality in applying the EU regulations, in some cases directly copying from external legal sources and setting even stricter requirements than the EU would dictate. For instance, Estonia has implemented a reserve requirement on liabilities of 11–15 per cent and a 10 per cent capital requirement throughout the accession and post-2004 period, compared to the ECB's minimum requirement of 2 per cent on liabilities with maturity up to two years and an 8 per cent capital requirement in most Western European countries (ECB, 1998). This, however, has created a paradox of exemplary compliance with the EU standards in terms of its extensiveness, but meagre effectiveness in addressing real-life developments in the banking industry. This chapter has shown the pragmatic approach to establishing regulatory and supervisory framework in the 1990s in the context of crises, internationalization of banks and also EU-accession aspirations, while the 2000s marked gradual outsourcing of oversight and embedded formalism or regulatory 'autopiloting' in terms of deepening reliance on external (EU, Basel) normative standards with insignificant economic substance, given the local circumstances. As indicated, several institutions and prudential norms were introduced in Estonia only due to the harmonization process with EU legislation with little or no intersection with practices in the banking sector. Furthermore, given the ideological (neoliberal) position of government coalitions on the one hand and the necessity to establish new institutions from scratch on the other hand, the evolution of the regulatory framework in Estonia has been a mix of deregulation and re-regulation at the same time. Particularly, this was the case in the early 1990s, when several institutions were established and corresponding regulations implemented but with gradual easing of the overall supervisory grip.

One of the peculiarities of the Estonia banking industry has been a high degree of internationalization, which has entailed important ramifications for the local financial system. Foreign acquisitions in Estonia have changed the institutional landscape and deepened the financial sector's cross-border integration, but also posed the economy new challenges. As a result of the institutional transformation and internationalization of the Estonian banking sector throughout the last 20 years, several challenges for the regulatory and supervisory framework have emerged in addressing the problems in cross-border banking-crisis management such as insufficient information, limited power and conflict of interest (see Kal Wajid et al., 2007). Moreover, the general tendencies toward supervisory consolidation based on the home-country principle and the centralization of key business functions such as liquidity and risk management have made separate assessments of subsidiaries more difficult. This in turn compromises the government's responsibility for general financial stability run along national borders. Thus, deep Europeanization in terms of both normative but also industry-wide convergence has locked Estonia into dependency in terms of decreasing political and economic autonomy, essentially trapping the economy into settings that tend to reproduce, but also contribute to financial fragility.

Table 6.1 Transposition of the EU banking directives and the Europeanization of the Estonian banking sector, 1992–2011

	1992	*1994*	*1995*	*1996*	*1997*	*1998*	*1999*	*2000*	*2001*
Institutional developments and crises	1st banking crisis	2nd banking crisis. Repeal of capital controls	First Credit Institutions Act		Stock market crash & 3rd banking crisis. Take-over of banks by foreign investors. Introduction of the deposit guarantee institution in 1998		Second Credit Institutions Act		Creation of joint banking, insurance and securities supervision: FSA
Internationalization and the EU accession process	Joining the IMF		Signing Association (Europe) Agreement with the EU		Opening of accession negotiations with Estonia	Estonia's Europe Agreement entered into force			
Transposition of the EU banking directives		88/361/EEC on liberalization of capital movements (1)							
			Second Banking Directive 89/646/EEC on the coordination of laws, regulations and administrative provisions relating to the taking up and pursuit of the business of credit institutions (2)						
			89/229/EEC on the own funds of credit institutions (3)						
			89/647/EEC on a solvency ratio for credit institutions (3, 4)						
			92/121/EEC on the monitoring and control of large exposures of credit institutions (5)						
				92/30/EEC on the supervision of credit institutions on a consolidated basis (10)					
				86/635/EEC on the annual and consolidated accounts of banks and other financial institutions					
						94/19/EEC on deposit-guarantee schemes (13)			
							95/26/EC on amending Directives 77/780/EEC and 89/646/EEC (11)		
						93/6/EEC on the capital adequacy of investments firms and credit institutions (6)			
									93/22/EEC on investment services in the securities field

	2002	2003	2004	2005	2006	2007	2008	2009	2010	2011
Institutional developments and crises				Division of FSA's work: Supervision of capital and Services		Collapse of real estate and consumption bubble			The Baltic-Nordic MoU, signed in August	
Internationalization and the EU accession process			Estonia joining the EU							Estonia joining the euro-zone
Transposition of the EU banking directives			2001/24/EC on the reorganisation and winding up of credit institutions (14)					2007/44/EC on acquisitions and increase of holdings in the financial sector		
				2004/39/EC on markets in financial instruments					2009/111/EC on amending Directives 2006/48/EC, 2006/49/EC and 2007/64/EC (8)	
					2006/48/EC relating to the taking up and pursuit of the business of credit institutions and 2006/49/EC on the capital adequacy of investment firms and credit institutions (7)					2010/76/EC on amending Directives 2006/48/EC and 2006/49/EC (9)
	92/121/EEC on the monitoring and control of large exposures of credit institutions									
	2002/87/EC on supplementary supervision in a financial conglomerate (12)									
									2009/14/EC amending Directive 94/19/EC	
	98/31/EC on amending the Directive 93/6/EEC (6)									

Source: author's elaboration, based on the comparison of the Estonian legal acts and the EU directives

Notes to Table 6.1

(1) Implicit transposition of the directive by repealing the legislation on restrictions on non-residents' possession of shares of the Estonian commercial banks, on foreign currency transactions (inflow and outflow of foreign cash), requirements on registration of foreign loans and on residens' foreign accounts. The obligation to renounce capital account restrictions stemmed also from the IMF Agreement.

(2) The transposition process lasted until 204 due to harmonization with the amending directive 2000/12/EC. In 1995, mostly the principles of the First Banking directive 77/80/EEC were transposed, while the regulation on authorization and supervision of foreign branches according to the principles of mutual recognition of banking licenses and home country control was adopted in 1999. Estonia had much broader and stringent requirements for application for authorization and bases for refusal as well as withdrawal of authorization and acquiring a holding, but also on the principles of the management, that is, requirements for the members of and tasks for council and board of credit institutions. Also, provisions on the cross-border establishment of subsidiaries and branches of foreign credit institutions were specified in 2004 pursuant to amended articles of the Directive 2000/12/EC.

(3) Although the principles on own funds, risk exposures and risk categorization on the balance-sheet assets for the calculation of the solvency ratio were present already in 1993, they did not comply fully with the principles of the EU directives. Given the non-membership in the EU and the development level of the banking sectors at that time, these directives were adopted gradually by broadening the regulatory principles according to the needs and possibilities, and often being even stricter than EU regulation, e.g. in relation subordinated liabilities, possibility to exceed the thresholds and limits, etc.

(4) Estonia did not adhere to the same allocation of asset items between 4 categories as was stated in the directive and in comparison with the directive, not all listed assets items were incorporated into the legislation. Solvency regulaton was again stricter in terms of applying higher weightings on particular assets and capital adequacy ratio set at 10 percent level (8 per cen was the EU's minimum).

(5) Strictness position in the transposition of the directive, e.g. renouncing the possibilities for exemptions in the calculation of exposure limits and transitional provisions relating to exposures in excess of the limits.

(6) Introduction of regulation on market risks and capital requirement in relation to trading-book business. Furhter, the possibility to delegate the responsibility for supervising solvency of subsidiary of a parent undertaking situated in another member state to a competent authority that authorized and supervised the parent undertaking, which was adopted in 1999 in Credit Institutions Act. 2002 amendments in the regulation included the introduction of specific definitions of previously undefined financial instruments (warrants, repos, OTC financial derivatives, underwriting commitments, etc.), regulation on commodities trading and commodity instruments, the possibility for contractual netting, and elaboration on option risk, commodity risk, trading-book credit and counterparty risks, based on the Directives 93/6/EEC and 98/31/EC, the latter being essentially translated into the Estonian legislation with its annexes.

(7) Introduction of credit risk mitigation, operational risk, internal ratings based approach, the regulation of securitization transactions with majority of the provisions of the directives being implemented into the Estonian law by more or less identical provisions. Several regular provisions were not transposed due to irrelevance and peculiarities in the institutitonal structure of the Estonian financial system, e.g. FSA has not been responsible for any supervision on a consolidated basis or existence of any credit institution whose parent company would be an investment firm.

(8) Amendments included the grounds for common decision-making procedures for ensuring capital adequacy of banking groups operating cross-border, defining significant branches, and operating in the colleges of supervisors. The inclusion of the so-called hybrid instruments in the calculation of own funds. The acts also specified the requirements related to securitization.

(9) Amendments in the Credit Institutions Act were mostly related to the principles of remuneration of managers and employees, requirements on the disclosure of securitization instruments and trading-book portfolios, the regulation of "re-securitization", capital requirement for additional – default and migration – risks (calculation, methods, risk mitigation), and capital requirement on counterparty credit risk from unregulated securities transfers/transactions.

(10) Principles of the directive adopted in the national legislation concerned the consolidated and sub-consolidated supervision, calculation of large exposures, delegation of supervisory

responsibility, cross-border cooperation between competent authorities that were introduced for the first time in 1999 for supervisory purposes.

(11) Legal harmonization included the introduction of a notion 'close links', the grounds for an exchange of information between competent authorities and other authorities (information from and an obligation to provide information to the central bank and the Ministry of Finance), and the regulation on professional secrecy and confidential information.

(12) The regulation covered the thresholds for identifying a financial conglomerate with regulation on intra-group transactions, internal control, and supplementary supervision on a group-wide basis. Regulation on financial conglomerates was only provided in the Insurance Activities Act that copied the structure and the the wording of the directive. Regulation on financial conglomerates was introduced into Credit Institutions Act in 2013.

(13) The Deposit Guarantee Act of 1998 was harmonized with the directive, but the full implementation of the directive was not undertaken due to transition period until 2007. Provisions on definitions, range and scope of the guarantee coverage, membership conditions in the guarantee scheme, host-home country guarantee schemes in case of cross-border banking activities were adopted during that period.

(14) Before the 2004 amendments in the Credit Institutions Act, the regulation on winding-up and reorganization was too narrow and did not address the cases of cross-border banking, including information sharing and disclosure between the competent authorities of different member states. The new sections in the act established uniform procedures, publication and language requirements with regard to winding-up operations, and provided the basis for cooperation between competent authorities of member states, associated with liquidation proceedings.

Notes

1 The ratio of a bank's own means to the total of risk-weighted assets and liabilities.
2 The ratio of a bank's liquid assets to current liabilities.
3 The ratio of total liabilities of high risk-concentration clients to the bank's own means.
4 In a study on the Hungarian banking sector, Petrick (2002) found that neither *acquis communautaire* nor the Basel rules were similarly appropriate to deal with the situation that Hungary was faced with, that is, dominating state-ownership, a newly formed but financially weak and inexperienced banking sector, and a pervasiveness of inter-enterprise debt relations.
5 In 2004, credit provided by bank-owned leasing companies accounted for 15.4 per cent of GDP in Estonia (Mihaljek, 2006).
6 Estonia was a 'path-setter' not only in the number of banking sector bankruptcies in the whole of Eastern Europe in the early 1990s, but also the responsiveness by the central bank to the growing problems of the banking sector (Lainela and Sutela, 1994). In 1992, the authorities closed one bank without rescuing its depositors and merged two banks with a partial bailout. Further, after the prudential measures were introduced in 1993–1994, the Bank of Estonia did not renew the licences of eight banks, while ten banks were forced to merge into one bigger bank, two smaller banks were forced into bankruptcy with dire consequences for depositors, and three banks declared a moratorium as a result of not meeting new requirements. Similarly, in 1998 and 1999 the central bank initiated bankruptcy proceedings and some banks were merged in order to prevent possible instability in the Estonian banking sector (Hansson, 1995, p. 143; Khoury and Wihlborg, 2006).

References

ANDONOVA, B. L. (2003) *Transnational Politics of the Environment: The European Union and Environmental Policy in Central and Eastern Europe*. Cambridge, MA: MIT Press.

ARUMÄE, L. (2014) Pangad maksavad pea olematut tulumaksu. Postimees. [Online] 27 January. Available from: http://e24.postimees.ee/2675912/pangad-maksavad-pea-olematut-tulumaksu. [Accessed: 2 February 2014.]

ATANAS, K. and SANNE, Z. (2013) Introduction. In: Atanas, K and Sanne, Z. (eds). *Banking in Central and Eastern Europe and Turkey Challenges and Opportunities*. European Investment Bank.

AUVÄÄRT, T. (2013) Finantstehingute maks: palju lahtisi otsi. Äripäev. [Online.] 6 May. Available from: www.aripaev.ee/Default.aspx?PublicationId=1046fa95-1bc6-420f-b5bb-e875321025b8. [Accessed: 22 October 2013.]

BANK OF ESTONIA (1994a) Eesti Pank Annual Report 1993. [Online] Tallinn: Bank of Estonia. Available from: www.eestipank.info/pub/en/dokumendid/publikatsioonid/seeriad/aastaaruanne/_1993/. [Accessed: 11 June 2013.]

BANK OF ESTONIA (1994b) Krediidiasutuste seaduse eelnõu seletuskiri. Tallinn: Bank of Estonia.

BANK OF ESTONIA (1995) Eesti Pank Annual Report 1994. [Online] Tallinn: Bank of Estonia. Available from: www.eestipank.info/pub/en/dokumendid/publikatsioonid/seeriad/aastaaruanne/_1994/. [Accessed: 11 June 2013.]

BANK OF ESTONIA (1997) Eesti Pank Annual Report 1996. [Online] Tallinn: Bank of Estonia. Available from: www.eestipank.info/pub/en/dokumendid/publikatsioonid/seeriad/aastaaruanne/_1996/. [Accessed: 11 June 2013.]

BANK OF ESTONIA (1998) Seletuskiri Krediidiasutuste seaduse eelnõu juurde. Tallinn: Bank of Estonia.

BANK OF ESTONIA (2003) Eesti Pank Annual Report 2002. [Online] Tallinn: Bank of Estonia. Available from: www.eestipank.info/pub/en/dokumendid/publikatsioonid/seeriad/aastaaruanne/_2002/. [Accessed: 16 June 2013.]

BANK OF ESTONIA (2011) Eesti Pank Annual Report 2010. [Online] Tallinn: Bank of Estonia. Available from: www.eestipank.info/pub/en/dokumendid/publikatsioonid/seeriad/aastaaruanne/_2010/. [Accessed: 20 June 2013.]

BANK OF ESTONIA (2012) Statistics. [Online] Tallinn: Bank of Estonia. Available from: www.eestipank.ee/en/statistics. [Accessed: 12 July 2013.]

BEGG, I. (2009) Regulation and supervision of financial intermediaries in the EU: The aftermath of the financial crisis. *Journal of Common Market Studies*, 47(5), 1107–1128.

BERGLUND, S., GANGE, I. and VAN WAARDEN, F. (2006) Mass production of law. routinization in the transposition of European directives: A sociological-institutionalist account. *Journal of European Public Policy*, 13 (5), 692–716.

BOHLE, D. and GRESKOVITS, B. (2007) Neoliberalism, embedded neoliberalism and neocorporatism: Towards transnational capitalism in central-eastern Europe. *West European Politics*, 30 (3), 443–466.

BOHLE, D. and GRESKOVITS, B. (2012) *Capitalist Diversity on Europe's Periphery*. Ithaca, NY: Cornell University Press.

BONIN, J., HASAN, I. and WACHTEL, P. (2009) Banking in transition countries. In: Berger, A. N., Molyneux, P. and Wilson, J. O. S. (eds). *The Oxford Handbook of Banking*. Oxford, NY: Oxford University Press.

BÖRZEL, T. (2010) Why you don't always get what you want: EU enlargement and civil society in Central and Eastern Europe. *Acta Politica*, 45(1/2), 1–10.

BÖRZEL, T. and RISSE, T. (2003) Conceptualizing the domestic impact of Europe. In: Featherstone, K. and Radaelli, C. (eds). *The Politics of Europeanization*. Oxford, NY: Oxford University Press.

BUGARIC, B. (2006) The Europeanisation of national administrations in Central and Eastern Europe: Creating formal structures without substance? In: Sadurski, W., Ziller, J. and Zurek, K. (eds). *Apres Enlargement: Legal and Political Responses in Central and Eastern Europe*. Florence: European University Institute, Robert Schuman Centre for Advanced Studies.

DE CASTELLO BRANCO, M., KARNMER, A. and PSALIDA, L. E. (1996) Financial sector reform and banking crises in the Baltic countries. IMF Working Paper. WP/96/134.

DE HAAS, R. and NAABORG, I. (2005) Foreign banks in transition countries: small business lending and internal capital markets. EconWPA Working Paper, International Finance. [Online.] Available from: http://128.118.178.162/eps/if/papers/0504/0504004.pdf. [Accessed: 24 September 2014.]

DE HAAS, R. and NAABORG, I. (2006) Foreign banks in transition countries: To whom do they lend and how are they financed? *Financial Markets, Institutions and Instruments*, 15(4), 159–199.

DIMITROVA, L. A. (2010) The New Member States of the EU in the aftermath of enlargement: Do new European rules remain empty shells? *Journal of European Public Policy*, 17(1), 137–148.

EBERLEIN, B. and GRANDE, E. (2005) Beyond delegation: Transnational regulatory regimes and the EU regulatory state. *Journal of European Public Policy*, 12(1), 89–112.

EBRD (1998) Transition report 1998. Financial sector in transition. Economic transition in Central and Eastern Europe, the Baltic states and the CIS. London, UK: European Bank for Reconstruction and Development.

EBRD (2011) Banking environment and performance survey II country profile. Estonia. [Online] Available from: www.ebrd.com/downloads/research/economics/microdata/beps/estonia.pdf. [Accessed: 12 February 2014.]

EBRD (2012) Transition report 2012. Integration across borders. London, UK: European Bank for Reconstruction and Development.

ECB (1998) The single monetary policy in stage three. General documentation on ESCB monetary policy instruments and procedures. [Online] Frankfurt am Main: European Central Bank. Available from: www.ecb.europa.eu/pub/pdf/other/gendoc98en.pdf. [Accessed: 3 October 2014.]

ECB (2005) Banking structures in the new EU member states. [Online] Frankfurt am Main: European Central Bank. Available from: www.ecb.europa.eu/pub/pdf/other/bankingstructuresnewmemberstatesen.pdf. [Accessed: 5 October 2014.]

ESTONIA. Credit Institutions Act. (1995) RT I 1995, 4, 36. Tallinn: The Parliament of Estonia.

ESTONIA. Credit Institutions Act. (1999) RT I 1999, 23, 349. Tallinn: The Parliament of Estonia.

ESTONIA. Finantsinspektsiooni seaduse, investeerimisfondide seaduse, krediidiasutuste seaduse ja tagatisfondi seaduse muutmise seadus. (2010) RT I, 21.12.2010, 3. Tallinn: The Parliament of Estonia.

ESTONIA. Investeerimisfondide seaduse ja sellega seonduvate seaduste muutmise seadus. (2011) RT I, 24.03.2011, 1. Tallinn: The Parliament of Estonia.
ETIENNE, J. (2011) Compliance theory: A goal framing approach. *Law and Policy*, 33(3), 305–333.
EUROPEAN COMMISSION (1999) Regular report on Estonia's progress toward accession. Brussels: European Commission.
EUROPEAN COMMISSION (2010) Regulating financial services for a sustainable growth. Communication from the Commission to the European Parliament, the Council, the European Economic and Social Committee and the European Central Bank. COM (2010) 301 final. Brussels: European Commission.
FALKNER, G. and TREIB, O. (2008) Three worlds of compliance or four? The EU-15 compared to new member states. *Journal of Common Market Studies*, 46(2), 293–313.
FALKNER, G., HARTLAPP, M. and TREIB, O. (2007) Worlds of compliance: Why leading approaches to European Union implementation are only 'sometimes-true theories'. *European Journal of Political Research*, 46, 395–416.
FALKNER, G. et al. (2005). *Complying with Europe: EU Harmonisation and Soft Law in the Member States*. Cambridge, UK: Cambridge University Press.
FINANCIAL SUPERVISION AUTHORITY (2014) Estonian Financial Supervision Authority, press releases. [Online.] Available from: www.fi.ee/?id=1080. [Accessed: 10 February 2014.]
FINK-HAFNER, D. (2007) Europeanization in managing EU affairs: Between divergence and convergence, a comparative study of Estonia, Hungary and Slovenia. *Public Administration*, 85(3), 805–828.
GOETZ, K. (2002) Four worlds of Europeanisation. Paper prepared for the ECPR Joint Sessions of Workshops. Turin. Italy. 22–27 March 2002.
GRABBE, H. (2002) Europeanisation goes east: Power and uncertainty in the EU accession process. In Featherstone, K. and Radaelli, C. (eds). *The Politics of Europeanization*. Oxford, NY: Oxford University Press.
GRABBE, H. (2006) *The EU's Transformative Power: Europeanization Through Conditionality in Central and Eastern Europe*. Houndmills, Basingstoke, Hampshire: Palgrave Macmillan.
HANSSON, A. (1995) Reforming the banking system in Estonia. In: Rostowski, J. (ed.), *Banking Reform in Central European and the Former Soviet Union*. Budapest: Central European University Press.
Haverland, M. (2000) National adaptation to European integration: The importance of institutional veto points. *Journal of Public Policy*, 20(1), 83–103.
Héritier, A. (2001) Differential Europe: The European Union impact on national policymaking. In Héritier, A., Kerwer, D., Knill, C., Lehmkuhl, D., Teutsch, M. and Douillet, A.-C. (eds), *Differential Europe. The European Union Impact on National Policymaking*. Boulder, CO: Rowman & Littlefield Publishers.
Héritier, A. (2005) Europeanization Research East and West: A comparative assessment. In Schimmelfennig, F. and Sedelmeier, U. (eds), *The Europeanization of Central and Eastern Europe*. Ithaca, NY: Cornell University Press.
HILLE, P. and KNILL, C. (2006) 'It's the Bureaucracy, Stupid'. The implementation of the acquis communautaire in EU candidate countries, 1999–2003. *European Union Politics*, 7(4), 531–552.
JACOBY, W. (1999) Priest and penitent: The European Union as a force in the domestic politics of Eastern Europe. *East European Constitutional Review*, 8(1–2), 62–67.

JACOBY, W. (2004) *The Enlargement of the European Union and NATO: Ordering from the Menu in Central Europe*. Cambridge, NY: Cambridge University Press.

JACOBY, W. (2006) Inspiration, Coalition, and Substitution: External influences on postcommunist transformations. *World Politics*, 58(4), 623–651.

KAEDING, M. (2006) Determinants of transposition delay in the European Union. *Journal of Public Policy*, 26(3), 229–253.

KAIK, K. (2002) Bureaucratization or strengthening of the political? Estonian institutions and integration into the European Union. *Cooperation and Conflict: Journal of the Nordic International Studies Association*, 37(2), 137–56.

KALLAS, S. (2003) Reminiscing with the 'Father of the Kroon': Interview with Siim Kallas. *Demokratizatsiya*, 11(4), 509–516.

KAL WAJID, S. et al. (2007) Financial integration in the Nordic-Baltic region. Challenges for financial policies. [Online] IMF, Monetary and Capital Markets Department. Available from: www.imf.org/external/np/seminars/eng/2007/nordbal/pdf/0607.pdf. [Accessed: 28 November 2013.]

KASEMETS, A. (2000) Seaduseelnõude seletuskirjade informatiivsus sotsiaalmajanduslike mõjude, eurointegratsiooni ja osalusdemokraatia valdkonnas. Riigikogu Toimetised. 1. 2000.

KATTEL, R. and RAUDLA, R. (2013) The Baltic republics and the crisis of 2008–2011. *Europe-Asia Studies*, 65(3), 426–449.

KHOURY, S. J. and WIHLBORG, C. (2006) Outsourcing central banking: Lessons from Estonia. *Journal of Policy Reform*, 9(2), 125–144.

KNILL, C. and LENSCHOW, A. (1998) Coping with Europe: The impact of British and German administrations on the implementation of EU environmental policy. *Journal of European Public Policy*, 5(4), 595–614.

KOHLER-KOCH, B. and EISING, R. (eds) (1999) *The Transformation of Governance in the European Union*. London, UK: Routledge.

KREGEL, A. J. (2014) Minsky and dynamic macroprudential regulation. Levy Economics Institute of Bard College Policy Brief. [Online] 131. Available from: www.levyinstitute.org/publications/?docid?=2036. [Accessed: 10 April 2014.]

KUDRNA, Z. (2012) Cross-border resolution of failed banks in the European Union after the Crisis: Business as usual. *Journal of Common Market Studies*, 50(2), 283–299.

KUDRNA, Z. and GABOR, D. (2013) The Return of Political Risk: Foreign-owned banks in emerging Europe. *Europe-Asia Studies*, 65(3), 548–566.

LAAR, M. (2000) The role of the government in the process of adoption of the acquis communautaire. Speech at the 7th International Conference 'Estonia and the European Union: Estonia on its way to a changing Europe', Tallinn, 2–3 November 2000.

LAINELA, S. and SUTELA, P. (1994) *The Baltic Economies in Transition*. Helsinki: Bank of Finland.

LEHMANN, A., LEVI, M. and TABAK, P. (2011) Basel III and regional financial integration in emerging Europe. An overview of key issues. EBRD Working Paper. No. 132. [Online] London, UK: European Bank for Development and Reconstruction. Available from: www.ebrd.com/downloads/research/economics/workingpapers/wp0132.pdf. [Accessed: 11 September 2014.]

LENSCHOW, A. (2006) Europeanization of public policy. In: Richardson, J. (ed.). *European Union: Power and Policy-Making*, 3rd edition. Abingdon: Routledge.

LEPIK, I. and TÕRS, J. (2002) Structure and performance of Estonia's financial sector. In: Christian, T. (ed.). *Financial Sectors in EU Accession Countries*. Frankfurt am Main: European Central Bank. July 2002.
LINOS, K. (2007) How can international organizations shape national welfare states? Evidence from compliance with European Union directives. *Comparative Political Studies*, 40(5), 547–570.
MAJONE, G. (ed.) (1996) *Regulating Europe*. London, UK: Routledge.
MEMBER OF THE MANAGEMENT BOARD AT THE ESTONIAN FINANCIAL SUPEVISION (2014) Interview with a member of the management board of the Financial Supervision Authority on 6 October 2014. Tallinn: Estonian Financial Supervision Authority. [Recording in possession of author.]
MIHALJEK, D. (2006) Rapid growth of bank credit in Central and Eastern Europe: The role of housing markets and foreign-owned banks. In the 12th Dubrovnik Economic Conference. Dubrovnik, 28 June–1 July 2006. Croatian National Bank.
MONTANARO, E. and TONVERONACHI, M. (2011) A critical assessment of the European approach to financial reforms. *PSL Quarterly Review*, 64(258), 193 – 226.
MYANT, M. and DRAHOKOUPIL, J. (2011) *Transition Economies: Political Economy in Russia, Eastern Europe, and Central Asia*. Hoboken, NJ: John Wiley & Sond, Inc.
OECD (2000) OECD majandusuurimused. Balti riigid: regiooni majandusülevaade. February.
OECD (2011) Estonia: Review of the financial system. October.
OJA, T. (2012) Tõnis Oja: finantstehingute maksu pole vaja, Postimees, E24. [Online] 17 November. Available from: www.e24.ee/1044052/tonis-oja-finants-tehingute-maksu-pole-vaja. [Accessed: 18 October 2013.]
OJA, T. (2013) Pangad finantstehingute maksu vastu sõjas. Postimees, E24. [Online] 13 March. Available from: www.e24.ee/1167394/pangad-finantstehingute-maksu-vastu-sojas. [Accessed: 17 October 2013.]
PETRICK, K. (2002) Hungarian banking in transition. In: Green, D. and Petrick, K. (eds), *Banking and Financial Stability in Central Europe: Integrating Transition Economies into the European Union*. Cheltenham, UK: Edward Elgar.
PISTOR, K. (2009) Into the void, governing finance in Central & Eastern Europe. UNU-WIDER conference on 'Twenty years on transition'. Helsinki, 18–19 September.
PISTOR, K. (2010) Host's dilemma rethinking EU banking regulation in light of the global crisis. Finance Working Paper. No. 286/2010. Columbia Law School and ECGI.
POLLACK, A. M. (2010) Theorizing EU policy-making. In: Wallace, H., Pollack, A. M. and Young, A. R. (eds), *Policy-Making in the European Union*, 6th edition. Oxford, NY: Oxford University Press.
RADAELLI, C. (2000) Whither Europeanization? Concept stretching and substantive change. *European Integration online Papers* (EIoP), 4(8), 1–27.
RAHANDUSMINISTEERIUM (2010a) Seletuskiri. Finantsinspektsiooni seaduse, investeerimisfondide seaduse, krediidiasutuste seaduse ja väärtpaberituru seaduse muutmise seaduse eelnõu juurde. RT I, 21 December, 6. Tallinn: Rahandusministeerium.
RAHANDUSMINISTEERIUMI (2010b) Seletuskiri. Investeerimisfondide seaduse ja sellega seonduvate seaduste muutmise seaduse juurde. RT I, 24 March 2011, 1.Tallinn: Rahandusministeerium.

ROSS, M. (2013) Regulatory experience in the Baltics. In: Atanas, K and Sanne, Z. (eds), *Banking in Central and Eastern Europe and Turkey Challenges and Opportunities*. European Investment Bank, January, 2013.

SCHIMMELFENNIG, F. and SEDELMEIER, U. (2002) Theorizing EU enlargement: Research focus, hypotheses, and the state of research. *Journal of European Public Policy*, 9(4), 500–528.

SCHIMMELFENNIG, F. and SEDELMEIER, U. (2005a) Introduction: Conceptualizing the Europeanization of Central and Eastern Europe. In: Schimmelfennig, F. and Sedelmeier, U. (eds), *The Europeanization of Central and Eastern Europe*. Ithaca, NY: Cornell University Press.

SCHIMMELFENNIG, F. and SEDELMEIER, U. (2005b) Conclusions: The impact of the EU on the accession countries. In: Schimmelfennig, F. and Sedelmeier, U. (eds), *The Europeanization of Central and Eastern Europe*. Ithaca, NY: Cornell University Press.

SCHIMMELFENNIG, F. and SEDELMEIER, U. (2007) Candidate countries and conditionality. In: Graziano, P. and Vink, M. P. (eds), *Europeanization: New Research Agendas*. Houndmills: Palgrave Macmillan.

SCHOLTENS, B. (2000) Financial regulation and financial system architecture in Central Europe. *Journal of Banking and Finance*, 24, 525–553.

SEDELMEIER, U. (2008) After conditionality: Post-accession compliance with EU law in east Central Europe. *Journal of European Public Policy*, 15(6), 806–825.

SEDELMEIER, U. (2010) Enlargement: From rules for accession to a policy towards Europe. In: Wallace, H., Pollack, A. M. and Young, A. R. (eds), *Policy-Making in the European Union*, 6th edition. Oxford, NY: Oxford University Press.

SENIOR CIVIL SERVANT AT THE MINISTRY OF FINANCE (2014) Interview with a senior civil servant of the Ministry of Finance on 25 September 2014. Tallinn: Estonian Ministry of Finance. [Recording in possession of author.]

SISSENICH, B. (2002) The Diffusion of EU social and employment legislation in Poland and Hungary. In: Linden, R. H. (ed.), *Norms and Nannies: The Impact of International Organizations on the Central and East European States*. Lanham, MD: Rowman & Littlefield.

SÕRG, M. (2003) Reformation of the Estonian banking system. Diskussionspapier 2/03. Greifswald: University of Greifswald.

SÕRG, M. and TUUSIS, D. (2008) Foreign banks increase the social orientation of Estonian financial sector. Diskussionspapier (1 – 43). Greifswald: Ernts-Moritz-Arndt-Universität Greifswald.

STEINHERR, A. (1997) Banking reforms in Eastern European countries. *Oxford Review of Economic Policy*, 13(2), 106–125.

STEINHERR, A. and GILIBERT, P. (1994) Six proposals in search of financial sector reform in Eastern Europe. *MOST: Economic Policy in Transitional Economies*, 4(1), 101–114.

STEUNENBERG, B. (2006) Turning swift policy-making into deadlock and delay. national policy coordination and the transposition of EU directives. *European Union Politics*, 7(3), 293–319.

SULG, J. (2014) Pangad, korporatsioonid ja riigijuhid ehk Eestist kaduvad miljardid. Ole Teadlik. [Online] 18 February. Available from: www.oleteadlik.ee/pangad-korporatsioonid-ja-riigijuhid-ehk-eestist-kaduvad-miljardid/. [Accessed: 20 March 2014.]

SUTT, A., KORJU, H. and SIIBAK, H. (2011) The role of macro-prudential policies in the boom and adjustment phase of the credit cycle in Estonia. World Bank Policy Research Working Paper. No. 5835. [Online] The World Bank. Available from: http://elibrary.worldbank.org/doi/pdf/10.1596/1813-9450-5835. [Accessed: 14 April 2014.]

TISON, M. (2002) Harmonisation and legal transplantation of EU banking supervisory rules to transitional economies: A legal approach. In: Green, D. and Petrick, K (eds), Banking and financial stability in Central Europe: Integrating transition economies into the European Union. Cheltenham, UK: Edward Elgar.

TONVERONACHI, M. (2010) Empowering supervisors with more principles and discretion to implement them will not reduce the dangers of the prudential approach to financial regulation. *PSL Quarterly Review*, 63(255), 361–376.

TOSHKOV, D. (2007) In search of the worlds of compliance: Culture and transposition performance in the European Union. *Journal of European Public Policy*, 14(6), 933–959.

TOSHKOV, D. (2008) Embracing European Law: Compliance with EU directives in Central and Eastern Europe. *European Union Politics*, 9(3), 379–402.

TREIB, O. (2008) Implementing and complying with EU governance outputs. *Living Reviews in European Governance*, 3(5), 1–30.

VALDRE, L. (2014) Riik kehtestab kiirlaenudele uued karmid piirangud. Postimees. [Online] 13 March. Available from: http://e24.postimees.ee/2726460/riik-kehtestab-kiirlaenudele-uued-karmid-piirangud. [Accessed: 24 March 2014.]

VEDLER, S. (2010) Välisfirmad viivad Eestist maksuvabalt välja miljardeid, Eesti Ekspress. [Online] 4 October. Available from: http://ekspress.delfi.ee/news/paevauudised/valisfirmad-viivad-eestist-maksuvabalt-valja-miljardeid.d?id=34572101. [Accessed: 11 March 2014.]

WAGNER, N. and IAKOVA, D. (2001) Financial sector evolution in the Central European economies: Challenges in supporting macroeconomic stability and sustainable growth. IMF Working Paper. WP/01/141. [Online] International Monetary Fund. Available from: www.imf.org/external/pubs/ft/wp/2001/wp01141.pdf. [Accessed: 27 September 2014.]

Young, R. A. (2010) The European policy process in comparative perspective. In: Wallace, H., Pollack, A. M. and Young, A. R. (eds), *Policy-Making in the European Union*, 6th edition. Oxford, NY: Oxford University Press.

Zirnask, V. (2002) *15 Years of New Estonian Banking. Achievements and Lessons of the Reconstruction Period*. Tallinn: Estfond.

7 Financial regulation in Hungary

Judit Badics, Károly Miklós Kiss, Zsolt Stenger and Szabolcs Szikszai

1 Introduction

Owing to the market-friendly attitude of Hungarian reform economists towards a market-based economy and Hungary's relatively early joining to international financial institutions, the reform of the banking system in Hungary preceded both domestic political reforms and similar reforms in Poland (1989) and Czechoslovakia (1990) (Takata, 2005; Szikszai, 2008), so, the preconditions for the operation of a modern banking system were in place years before the actual transition from a planned to a market economy.

In 1985 MNB's lending and central banking functions were separated within the organization, which prepared the ground for more profound financial reforms in 1986 when these lending departments were separated from MNB's organization. The subsequent creation of the two-tier banking system in 1987 replicated the structure of Western European financial systems, in which the central bank endowed with the task of maintaining financial stability, providing liquidity, supervising banks, managing foreign exchange reserves and making monetary policy while commercial banks were entitled to provide households, corporates and municipalities with financial services (Honvári, 2008; Szikszai, 2008). Following the creation of the central bank, the Hungarian state established three new big commercial banks in 1986, the Hungarian Credit Bank (MHB), the National Commercial and Credit Bank (OKHB) and Budapest Bank (BB), and some middle and small banks entitled them to extend loans to corporations. At that time, among commercial banks, besides state-owned banks there were already partly foreign-owned banks, such as CIB, Citibank and Unicbank. In the retail segment, Postbank, was set up in 1988 by the state-owned Hungarian Post and Dunabank, launched in 1987 by MHB, Merkantil Bank, registered in 1988 by OKHB and Takarékbank, established by savings cooperatives in 1989. However, none of these posed any real threat to National Savings Bank's (OTP) dominant position in the retail market. This latter was established in 1949 as MNB's retail sub-bank and had a monopoly position on the retail market. By the way, OTP, which also was the exclusive account-keeping bank of municipalities up to 1991, managed to hold its dominant position in the retail segment even after the complete liberalization of the bank system.

While Hungary was a forerunner in the transformation of the financial system, it lagged behind other Central and Eastern European (CEE) countries in the speed of bank privatization. The sell-off of large banks had already begun in 1992 and 1993 in the Czech Republic and in Poland, respectively, whereas in Hungary the process only started in 1994.

In line with Hungary's goal to join the European Union, it signed in 1991 and ratified in 1994 together with other CEE countries the so-called Europe Agreement, in which it obliged itself to open its domestic banking market to foreign competition (Agreement of 1993, §68, §83 and §98–103). The opening of the EU for aspirant CEE economies was announced in 1993 in Copenhagen, where the so-called 'Copenhagen criteria' including the economic standards of EU accession were published. These economic standards called for a restructuring of the banking sector to increase its competitiveness and enable it to operate in a highly competitive business environment. These documents provided incentive for CEE governments both to recapitalize domestic banks to prepare them for foreign competition from EU-based banks and to totally restructure the domestic business environment through privatization (Takata, 2005).

Indeed, Act LXIX of 1991 on Financial Institutions and Financial Activities included a passage that called for the decrease of the Hungarian state's share in the banking system to 25 per cent by 1997. This passage and the early experiences gained from the inefficient operation of domestic banks led policymakers to believe that the privatization process should be accelerated. This task was, however, a difficult one. While state ownership in the banking sector was 39 per cent in 1991, it increased back to 66 per cent after the consolidation and even after the bulk of privatization had happened by 1997 it was still 37 per cent (Várhegyi, 1998). Between 1994 and 1999 the Hungarian State sold the biggest domestic banks and cashed in 160 billion forints (1.4 per cent of 1999 GDP). While further smaller privatizations came afterwards, the privatization of Postabank in 2003 marked the end of the era of privatizations in the Hungarian banking sector.

Given the underdevelopment of the capital market at that time, it was a widely held belief that a higher sales price could be attained by inviting strategic investors rather than financial investors, thus, this had come to be viewed as the main form of bank privatization (Várhegyi, 1998).

The commitment to the specific form of bank privatization to strategic investors in the 1990s was a Hungarian specialty in the Central and Eastern European region. In Poland the number of initial public offerings through the stock exchange roughly equalled the number of sales to foreign strategic investors while the Czech Republic widely applied the alternative technique of voucher privatization in which previously distributed certificates could be exchanged for bank shares. The technique of employee buyout (EBO), in which the bank was sold to domestic owners, was used as an auxiliary method in only a few cases (Takata, 2005).

The only exception when this commitment to strategic investors was relaxed was the multi-stage public offering of OTP Bank shares to institutional investors in 1995. The main reason behind OTP's exceptional treatment was the fear that if one investor gets a dominant position in OTP,[1] it will have control over two-thirds of Hungarian household savings. As a consequence, OTP's ownership structure became highly fragmented, which ensured the lack of strategic ownership control over the management.

As a result of the privatization process, foreign investors have got hold of an overwhelming share of the banking sector, but the state stuck to its ownership in Hungarian Development Bank, Eximbank and MEHIB.

After the wave of privatization had passed the main trend in the banking sector was determined by the dynamics of the retail segment. Restructured domestic banks set out to compete with OTP for the retail segment. This new form of competition caused the rate of expansion of credit stock to double from an average 10 per cent in the second half of the 1990s to 20 per cent by the mid-2000s. The engine of growth was, due in part to the appearance of interest-subsidized forint housing loans, the growth of housing and consumer loans, growing by 46 per cent and 37 per cent on average, respectively, from 2001 to 2006. The ratio of household loans to GDP quadrupled from 8 per cent to 33 per cent between 2000 and 2008, which can be interpreted as convergence to West European levels (Szikszai, 2008).

In the meantime the state created legislation in 1997 that allowed its newly established mortgage bank (FHB) to issue mortgage bonds in order to finance long maturity mortgage loans with preferential interest rates using the intermediation of domestic banks. FHB's monopoly to issue mortgage bonds was broken in 2001 on pressure from OTP, which led to the establishment of two further mortgage banks in 2002 (OTP and HVB). Because the subsidy of housing loans went through the issue of mortgage bonds, the main beneficiary of this development was the OTP which extended two-thirds of interest-subsidized housing loans. The group not only benefited from the spread between its total interest revenue including subsidies and the interest paid on the mortgage bond but also from the spread between the latter and the interest paid on household deposits. This is because OTP Bank subscribed the mortgage bonds issued by OTP Mortgage Bank using deposits placed by its clients (Szikszai, 2008).

After 2004, the dynamics of the retail segment slowed temporarily due to the gradual phasing out of the housing loan interest subsidy scheme in 2004, the proliferation of more sophisticated risk assessment techniques and the climb of interest rates on forint denominated loans in 2004.

In an effort to revive the dynamics of the retail segment, banks turned to loans denominated in foreign currency. These were mainly Swiss franc denominated mortgage-backed housing or free-purpose loans. Although borrowing in foreign currency had already been very popular in the corporate sector, the spread of household foreign exchange loans was a new development, which was a consequence of the large interest rate spread, the relative stability of the exchange rate of forint and the overwhelming presence of well-funded, foreign-owned credit institutions, loose fiscal policy and the expected adoption of the euro. Thanks to these factors, banks' lending dynamics received new momentum from the household segment. In 2000 foreign currency loans only represented 4 per cent in the total retail loan portfolio. By 2007 the shares of outstanding foreign currency loans had surpassed that of forint denominated ones, which made the Hungarian bank sector rather vulnerable.

2 Liberalization of capital movement

Before the transition, financial transactions using foreign currency were limited in Hungary. All forward instruments between the domestic currency (forint, HUF) and foreign currencies and exchange foreign currencies was limited. Only licensed financial institutions were allowed to serve currency exchanges. Non-resident agents were prevented from undertaking foreign exchange transactions in the local market, or invest directly in Hungary.

These restrictions were removed gradually. In 1988 foreign direct investments in most sectors in Hungary were allowed, but prior authorization was required for full or majority foreign ownership. (Act XXIV of 1988, Art. 9) The prior authorization for full or majority foreign ownership was removed from 1991. (Act XCVIII of 1990, Art. 1) As a result, the number of foreign investments increased rapidly.

Hungary joining the Organization for Economic Cooperation and Development (OECD) in 1996 and Hungary's aspiration to join the European Union resulted in significant changes. At the time of joining the OECD, Hungary were assured that no further restrictions to those already in place in 1996 would be introduced, all restrictions would be removed by the time of the membership, and all other OECD members would be treated equally. Similar obligations were included within the agreement made with the European Union.

During the legal harmonization process, Hungary had the opportunity to choose the areas that wanted to protect. Hungary and the EU agreed that Hungary would restrict direct investment related to the ownership of agricultural land for seven years, and the ownership of a secondary place of residence for five years from the day of accession. During this period, citizens of other member states were allowed to own agricultural land only if they had been acting in Hungarian agriculture and residing in Hungary for at least three years. Nationals of other EU member states had to ask for a licence to buy a secondary abode in Hungary, unless they had been living in Hungary for at least four years. The reason behind these limitations was that land and abodes were much cheaper in Hungary than the average price in the European Union (Kolozs, 2008, pp. 285–300).

The limitations in foreign exchange were removed in 2001 by Governmental Decree 88/2001 (VI. 15.) on the Implementation of the Foreign Exchange Act. It perfectly liberalized the foreign exchange regime, and the Hungarian currency (HUF) became freely convertible and the barriers were removed. The main changes were the followings (MNB, 2002, p. 74):

- the repatriation of foreign currency from abroad was no longer prescribed,
- residents were allowed to maintain forint and foreign currency accounts abroad without the licence of the authorities,
- residents were allowed to use foreign currency without any restriction,
- not natural person residents could hold foreign currency without restrictions,
- there were no normative conditions of direct acquisition of enterprises, prior reporting was no longer required,
- residents did not have to apply for permission from the foreign exchange authorities, and they did not have to report about their foreign exchange transactions,
- gifts could be given freely to non-residents,
- domestic and foreign currency could be imported or exported to and from Hungary without limitations,
- payments in foreign currency within the territory of Hungary were allowed conditionally on the agreement between the parties, as forint remained the legal tender in Hungary.

Act XCIII of 2001 on the Elimination of Foreign Exchange Restrictions and on the Amendment of Certain Related Acts entered into force in 2002. Its most important provisions were the followings: (MNB, 2002, pp. 74–75)

- forint remained the legal tender of Hungary, which must be accepted as a means of payment within the country,
- any payment obligation to the state, or payments obliged by any authority or court must be carried out in forint,
- legal transactions may be made freely in foreign exchange, foreign currency or forint
- the Government was allowed to restrict international payments (excluding those which are related to bank accounts of natural persons) for at most six months in cases of economic difficulties, conditionally on the recommendation of the Hungarian central bank.

This act finished the harmonization of the Hungarian measures on foreign currencies to the provisions of Council Directive 88/361/EEC of 24 June 1988 for the implementation of Article 67 of the Treaty.

3 Cross-border competition and permitted activities

In Hungary financial and investment services are regulated by acts separately. The Banking Act[2] applies to financial services and auxiliary financial services, and the measures of the Act on the Capital Market[3] are applied to investment services and auxiliary investment services.

The notion of financial services and auxiliary financial services were introduced by the Banking Act in 1996, and its scope was widened by an amendment of the Banking Act in 1997 and 2000. (Act CLVIII of 1997, Art. 2(1); Act CXXIV of 2000, Art. 3(1))

Up to 2001 the Hungarian laws about cross-border financial services were ambiguous.

Act XXIV of 1988 on the Investments of Foreigners in Hungary did not allow cross-border services in any sector (not only in the financial one). It was amended by Act LXXII of 1998 on Foreign Private Entrepreneurs which permitted the cross-border services for some special activities (like education), but not for financial or investment services. (Act LXXII of 1998, Art. 2(2))

The Banking Act came into force in 1997 and stated that foreign credit institutions must not found branches or provide any cross-border financial services in Hungary. (Act CXII of 1996, Art. 224) Its amendment came into force in 1998 and declared that a foreign company may provide financial or auxiliary financial services only by its Hungarian branch. (Act CLVIII of 1997, Art. 3) The permitted activities for branches of a foreign bank included almost all financial and auxiliary financial services if it had a licence for such activities from the supervisory authority of its home country. The permitted activities for branches of a foreign financial enterprise were almost the same if it had a licence for such activities from the supervisory authority of its home country. In order to found a branch office in Hungary, the foreign company had to submit an application for foundation to the Hungarian regulatory authority (Act CLVIII of 1997, Art. 14).

An amendment of the Banking Act came into force on 1 January 2001 and permitted cross-border credit and loan operations and financial leasing for a foreign financial institution registered in a member country of the Organization for Economic Cooperation and Development (OECD) if such activities were permitted by its home country supervisory authority (Article Act CXXIV of 2000, Art. 4(3)). Other articles of this amendment which came into force on 1 May 2004, permitting cross-border financial or auxiliary financial services without the authorization by the Hungarian supervisory authority for credit institutions registered in another member state of the EU and financial enterprises that satisfy some specified conditions (Article Act CXXIV of 2000, Art. 4(4), 5, 13). From 1 May 2004, the rules of governing the permitted cross-border activities were equivalent to the relevant rules of Council Directive 89/646/EEC. (Act CXXIV of 2000, Art. 26–28)

The Hungarian legislation defined the investment instruments, investment and auxiliary investment services firstly in the Securities Act,[4] and later in the Capital Market Act.

Investment services and auxiliary investment services are subject to licensing by the Hungarian supervisory authority (Act CXX of 2001, Art. 91). Credit institutions and investment firms may apply for this licence (Act CXX of 2001, Art. 85(1)). Foreign investment firms are allowed to provide investment services only through their branches before the Hungarian accession (Act CXX of 2001, Art. 85(4)). After the accession investment service providers established in another state of the EU were allowed to provide cross-border services, and they are not required to apply for the licence of the Hungarian supervisory authority (Act CXX of 2001, Art. 85(5)). The same is true for the investment services provided by the Hungarian branch of such an investment service provider if licensed for the same activities by the supervisory authority in its home country (Act CXX of 2001, Art. 91(5)). From 1 May 2004 the rules of cross-border investment and auxiliary investment services provided by a firm of another member state of the EU were equivalent to the provisions of Council Directive 93/22/EEC of 10 May 1993 on investment services in the securities field.

4 Capital requirements

The first Hungarian provisions on capital requirements for credit institutions were motivated by the recommendations of Basel I. Later the changes in the regulation followed the relevant EU directives. The main idea remained the same: credit institutions, and later investment firms, too, had to maintain capital requirements to prevent risks. As the scope of the relevant risks widened, the calculation methods became more complex.

The notion of capital requirements was introduced by Act LXIX of 1991 on Financial Institutions and the Activities of Financial Institutions (Financial Institutions Act) in Hungary. This law defined the minimal amount of subscribed capital, the calculation of own funds, introduced the capital adequacy ratio according to Basel I, and included provisions on general reserves and risk reserves. It prescribed the lowest amount of subscribed capital for different types of credit institutions. It also stated that at least 50 per cent of the subscribed capital must be paid up in cash (Act LXIX of 1991, Art. 10). The amendment of the Financial Institutions Act increased this limit to 100 per cent in 1993 (Act CXII of 1993, Art. 8(1)).

The provisions of the Financial Institution Act and its amendment in 1993 stated that the own funds were the sum of the core capital and the additional capital reduced by the value of the holdings in other credit and financial institutions, they defined the positive and negative items of these components of core capital, and gave an upper limit on the amount of the additional capital in terms of the amount of core capital.

The provisions of the Financial Institution Act on the capital adequacy ratio stated that the ratio of the adjusted own funds and the adjusted balance sheet total must have been at least 8 per cent from 1993 as it is recommended by Basel I. The calculation method of the adjusted balance sheet total was defined by a decree of the supervisory authority (State Supervisory Authority of Banking Sector Governor's Decree 1/1992).

The provisions of the Financial Institution Act translated the recommendations of the Basel I into Hungarian law, and all of these measures went into force by the end of 1993. Although the Own Funds Directive[5] and the Solvency Directive[6] also were based on Basel I, one cannot say that these directives were implemented by the Hungarian provisions by 1993, because the Hungarian provisions were only motivated by Basel I and not by the directives of the EU. The first Hungarian banking law that was motivated by the translation of these directives of the European Union was Act CXII of 1996 on Credit Institutions and Financial Enterprises which went into force in 1997.

The Own Fund Directive was translated into Hungarian law by Act CXII of 1996 on Credit Institutions and Financial Enterprises which went into force in 1997. This law includes provisions on the minimal amount of the subscribed capital, the equity capital and the own funds for credit institutions. The act stated that the subscribed capital had to be paid up in cash, and gave its minimal amount. The own funds were defined as the sum of the core capital and additional capital the positive and negative items of which was listed.

The Hungarian legislation was more restrictive than the directive: the list of negative items of the own fund was broader than in the Own Fund Directive. At the same time some of the limits prescribed by Article 6 of the Own Fund Directive were not applied this time in the Hungarian legislation.

The Banking Act stated that for credit institutions the solvency ratio had to be at least 8 per cent (Act CXII of 1996, Art. 76(2)).

The numerator of the solvency ratio was defined as the own funds. The Banking Act also stated that the denominator of the solvency ratio was defined by a decree.

The Solvency Decree I[7] of the minister of finance entered into force in 1998, and was modified by Solvency Decree II[8] in 2001. The decrees gave the detailed methodology for deriving the denominator of the solvency ratio. Solvency Decree I made a distinction between countries of Zone A and Zone B identically to the Solvency Directive.[9] It also gave risk weightings for the different asset items. The main difference between the two decrees was that the first one was more restrictive: it assigned low weightings only to fewer types of assets, and it did not include the condition for the claims on credit institutions that these were not components of the own funds of those institutions. Solvency Decree II included also the special rules for credit institutions maintaining a trading book and for those which did not maintain a trading book. Those credit institutions which maintained a trading book had to use the market pricing approach for the positions not included within the trading book. The other credit institutions – without a trading book – were allowed to choose between two methods, the market pricing approach, and the original risk approach.

The Capital Adequacy Directive[10] 93/6/EEC and the Second Capital Adequacy Directive[11] were implemented in parallel (Seregdi, 2006, pp. 165–166).

Act CXI of 1996 on the Securities Trading, Investment Services and the Stock Exchange introduced the notion of an investment firm and gave the first capital requirements for them in Hungary. These requirements were about the calculation method of the own funds, and the minimal amounts of the subscribed capital and own funds for the different types of investment firms.

The positive and negative items of the own funds of an investment firm were almost the same as for the credit institutions defined by the Banking Act. The own funds had to be at least 8 per cent of the value of the risks of the investment undertakings. These risks were calculated by the investment firms daily according to the requirements of this act. These requirements were very simple, they were not equivalent to the prescriptions of the Capital Adequacy Directive.

One year later, an amendment of this act (Act CLI of 1997) introduced the concept of a trading book, stating that there were capital requirements for investment service providers maintaining a trading book. It was also stated that the market value of any position included within the trading book must have been evaluated on a daily basis. This act also defined those limits under which the credit institutions could have been relieved of maintaining a trading book (Act CLI of 1997, Art. 21). These limits were equivalent to the requirements of Article 4(6)-(7) of the Capital Adequacy Directive.

The detailed provisions for the maintenance of the trading book and for the capital requirements of market risks were included within a governmental decree which came into force in 2001 (Governmental Decree 244/2000). Investment firms and banks had to use a trading book for their positions in those financial instruments that were held to make a profit on them. The remaining business of banks was contained within the banking book.

The Trading Book Decree divided the market risk into four parts: (1) position risk, (2) counterparty risk, (3) commodities risk, and (4) the risk of large exposures. It also introduced the notion of the foreign-exchange risk. It imposed capital requirements of position risk, counterparty risk, commodities risk, the risk of large exposures for firms maintaining a trading book, and the capital requirement of the foreign-exchange risk for all financial institutions. Financial firms and institutions had to calculate the capital requirements of interest-rate risks and equities risk only for positions included within the trading book. The Trading Book Decree which came into force in 2001 required the calculation of the capital requirement of commodities risks only for those positions that were involved in the trading book (Governmental Decree 244/2000, Art. 12(1)), but an amendment of the Trading Book Decree stated that the capital requirement of the commodities risks had to be calculated for all positions of financial firms – irrespectively of maintaining a trading book or not – and institutions from 2003 (Governmental Decree 230/2003). Capital requirements of foreign exchange-rate risks had to be derived for all positions of financial institutions and firms – included those which did not maintain a trading book – from 2001 (Governmental Decree 244/2000, Art. 12(2), 12(6)).

The Amendment of the Trading Book Decree in 2003 also gave the detailed methodology of calculating capital requirements for those credit institutions and financial enterprises which were subject to supervision on a consolidated basis. Such provisions were not included within the Trading Book Decree in 2001, because the conditions of being subject to supervision on a consolidated basis were declared in the amendments of the Banking Act and Capital Market Act in 2003 (Act XXXIX of 2003, Art. 16; Act XL of 2003, Art. 17).

The Trading Book Decree gave the detailed methodology for the calculation of the capital requirements for the different types of the market risk. These methods were called standard methods for the calculation of the capital requirement. Subject to specified conditions, the supervisory authority was allowed to permit institutions to apply their own internal-risk management models to calculate capital requirements for general interest-rate risk, general equity risk, commodity risk, and foreign exchange-rate risk. From 2003, under the permission of the supervisory authority, the own internal-risk management models could be used to derive the capital requirements for position risks, commodities risks and foreign exchange risks. The Trading Book Decree also gave the conditions under which authorities might have allowed institutions to calculate their capital requirements applying their own internal risk-management models – these conditions were equivalent to those imposed by the Second Capital Adequacy Directive (Governmental Decree 244/2000, Art. 43; Directive 98/31/EC, Annex VIII, Point 2). The financial firms and institutions were allowed to decide to use their internal risk-management models in combination with the standard methods, too. So they had the opportunity to use their internal risk-management models to calculate the capital requirement for some types of risk, and the standard method for the other types of it.

Comparing the national measures and the Capital Adequacy Directives, one can find that national laws identically implemented the provisions of these directives in most cases, but there were little differences induced by the specialities of the Hungarian financial system (Seregdi, 2006, p. 166).

An amendment of the Banking Act in 2002 (Act LXIV of 2002) introduced the notion of supplementary capital, and stated that own funds are equal to the sum of the core capital, subsidiary capital and supplementary capital.

An amendment of the Banking Act (Act LI of 2007) implemented equivalently most of the measures of Directive 2006/48/EC on the scope of the provision against risk (Directive 2006/48/EC, Art. 68–73) and on the calculation of the minimum level of own funds (Directive 2006/48/EC, Art. 74–75; implemented by Act LI of 2007, Art. 28(1)).

An amendment of the Banking Act in 2007 stated that credit institutions may use the standardized method or may get the supervisory authority's permission to apply the internal ratings based approach calculating their risk-weighted exposure. (Act LI of 2007, Art. 29–30) The conditions under which the supervisory authority may allow the usage of the internal ratings based approach are specified according to the provisions of the directive.

The main provisions of the Hungarian legislation on the standardized method and internal ratings based approach are equivalent to those in the directive, but one can find slight differences in the classification of the off-balance-sheet items and the classification of exposures in the case of the standardized method, and also in the conditions of supervisory authority's approval for introducing the internal ratings based approach in the credit institution sequentially. (Act LI of 2007, Art. 29–31, 34–37, Annex I. Point 12; Governmental Decree 196/2007, Art. 11, 17, 24–28, 30, 32–33, 38–39)

The Credit Risk Decree[12] came into force in 2007 gives the classification of the off-balance-sheet items equivalently to the measures of Directive 2006/48/EC (Governmental Decree 196/2007, Art. 17; Directive 2006/48/EC, Annex II). The decree gives the list of medium risk, medium/low risk and low risk off-balance sheet items almost equivalently to the measures of the directive, and states that any other off-balance sheet item has full risk. The exposure classes given in the Amendment of the Banking Act do not include the items belonging to regulatory high risk classes (Act LI of 2007, Art. 29). In the case of exposures to institutions only the central government risk weight based method is transposed, so weighting is not individual, but it is based on the rating of the government (Directive 2006/48/EC, Annex VI. Part I, Points 26–28).

The amendment of the Banking Act gives the detailed conditions of the authorization of implementation of the internal ratings based approach to be carried out sequentially. Among these conditions one can find that the credit institution has to declare within the application for permission its commitment to use the internal rating based approach at least 60 per cent of the risk-weighted exposure amounts within 2.5 years following the date of the permission, and increase this ratio to 100 per cent within five years following the date of the authorization. (Act LI of 2007, Art. 30(9))

Most of the provisions on credit risk mitigation are equivalently implemented (Directive 2006/48/EC, Art. 90–93 and Annex VIII). Only the competent authorities can waive the requirement for credit institutions to comply with all conditions to recognize a real estate property as eligible collateral, because the Hungarian legislator does not wish to use the discretional right for it (Directive 2006/48/EC, Annex VIII. Points 14–19).

The measures on securitization (Directive 2006/48/EC, Art. 94–101 and Annex IX) and operational risk (Directive 2006/48/EC, Art. 102–105 and Annex X) have been implemented equivalently in most cases, the only exception is Article 105(4), so an EU parent credit institution or financial holding company and its subsidiaries may be allowed to use Advanced Measurement Approaches based on their operational risk measurement if the parent institution or company and its subsidiaries meet the qualifying criteria. These qualifying criteria are equivalent to the requirements of Directive 2006/48/EC, Annex X, Part 3.

The trading and trading book related provisions of Directive 2006/49/EC (Directive 2006/49/EC, Art. 11 and Annex VII) have been almost all implemented equivalently by the Investment Firms Act.[13] This act gives the definition of a financial instrument, which is a restrictive one: 'Financial instruments are free of any restrictive covenants on their tradability AND able to be hedged.' [14]

The provisions of Directive 2006/49/EC on own funds are fully implemented (Directive 2006/49/EC, Art. 12–17). Only the provisions of Art. 13(2) on alternative determinations of own funds conditionally on the permission of the supervisory authority has not been transposed, so the alternative determination method cannot be applied.

The transposition of Art. 18(1) of Directive 2006/49/EC on the minimal amount of own funds is restrictive: it states that own funds shall not fall under the sum of

- capital requirements for position risk, clearing and counterparty risk, and large exposures shown in the trading book,
- foreign-exchange risk and commodities risk in respect of all business activities,
- capital requirements for credit risk in respect of all business activities,
- capital requirements for the operational risk in respect of all business activities (Act CXXXVIII of 2007, Art. 105(1)).

As the last two items are not mentioned in Art. 18(1) of Directive 2006/49/EC, one can conclude that Hungarian regulation is more restrictive than is required by the EU.

The provisions of Directive 2006/49/EC on the calculation of the capital requirements for position risk, settlement and counterparty risk, foreign exchange risk, and on the internal models to calculate capital requirements have been transposed equivalently, but some options are not applied (Directive 2006/49/EC, Arts 18–20 and Annex I–VI). Three of them are about foreign exchange risk: in Hungary the competent authority may not allow institutions to provide lower capital requirements against positions in closely correlated currencies than those which would result from the standards, or to remove positions which are subject to legally binding intergovernmental agreement, and the institutions are not allowed to break down their net positions in composite currencies into the component currencies. (Directive 2006/49/EC, Annex III. Points 3–4). In the case of using internal based model for calculating capital requirements against commodity risk, the option of Directive 2006/49/EC, Annex V. Point 13 which states that the competent authority may allow institutions to use empirical correlations is not applied, too.

The implementation of the Capital Requirement Directives was successful. The main provisions of the Directives have been transposed identically or equivalently to the requirements of the Directives. Comparing the Directives and the Hungarian laws one can find only slight differences between them. Most of the discretions of the Directives have not been exercised in Hungary.

During the transposition of the measures of CRD II[15] the modifications of the Hungarian laws and decrees affected the following areas of capital requirements:

- eligibility criteria and limits for some types of hybrid capital instruments to involve them among the components of own funds of credit institutions,
- capital requirements for the risk arising from securitization exposures.

In Hungary hybrid instruments (called capital of mixed properties) are introduced as a component of core capital from 2011 by an amendment of the Banking Act (Act CLIX of 2010, Annex 2 and 3 modified Act CXII of 1996, Annex 5 and Act CXXXVIII of 2007, Annex 2).

Introducing the hybrid capital as an item of the core capital the implementation modified the components of own funds.

The notion of securitization has been defined by an amendment of the Banking Act in 2010 (Act CLIX of 2010, Annex 2). This definition states that it is a transaction with the following three properties:

- the credit risk of an exposure or pool of exposures is tranched,
- the payments in the transaction depend on the performance of the securitized exposure or pool of exposures,
- the distribution of losses during the ongoing life of the transaction is determined by the subordination of tranches.

Those credit institutions and investment firms which are the originators of a securitization have to take into account the following two restrictions calculating own funds (Act CLIX of 2010, Annex 2–3):

- net future gains arising from the securitized assets which improve credit quality of securitized positions cannot be taken into account as a positive component of own funds,
- the core capital and the supplementary capital have to be decreased by 50 per cent of that amount of securitization positions to which a risk weight of 1250 per cent is assigned, if the credit institution does not take it into account in the risk-weighted exposure amounts.

During the implementation of CRD III[16] the regulation on the calculation of capital requirements for credit institutions and investment firms changed in two aspects: the capital requirements of resecuritization positions were prescribed, and the standard for internal models used for the calculation of market risk capital requirements for the positions in the trading book became stricter.

The concept of resecuritization positions was introduced in a governmental decree of 2011 (Governmental Decree 348/2011). It stated that resecuritization is a securitization for which the credit risk of a pool of exposures is tranched where the pool of exposures involves at least one securitization position. The decree assigns higher risk-weights and higher capital requirements to the resecuritization positions than to the simple securitization positions. It also prescribes that the credit institutions and investment firms have to make a specified valuation for the risks of their resecuritization position without which a very high (1250 per cent) risk-weight should be applied.

The credit institutions using internal models to determine the capital requirement of the market risk for the positions within the trading book has to introduce a new methodology to calculate the risks of their securitization positions.

5 Supervision on a consolidated basis

The principles of consolidated supervision of financial groups existing in Hungary is covered by the Act on Credit Institutions (in the course of amendments of the Act CXII of 1996) and in the regulations of the Trading book (Governmental Decree 244/2000). Hungarian regulation of consolidated supervision can be divided into three main periods.

1 The first period from the 1987 modernization of the Hungarian banking system (when Hungary returned to the two-tier banking system) to the first attempt of harmonization with EU directives in 2000. In this term legal rules of consolidated supervision did not exist in Hungarian law.
2 In 2000 there was a legal harmonization: the amendment (Act CXXIV of 2000) of the Act on Credit Institutions (Act CXII of 1996) introduced a new chapter on consolidated supervision into the Act. But the legal rules of consolidated supervision was not really consistent in the law and practice of supervision in Hungary as far as the accession to the EU in 2004. As a next step forward, the trading book's regulations introduced similar prescriptions when formulating the capital requirements of market risks. Thus the provisions concerning group-wide supervision of credit institutions were formally harmonized. However, there were errors in both definition and procedure, which had the consequence that the substance of the Hungarian regulation did not meet either the purpose of legal harmonization or the goals of consolidated regulation. (Horváth and Szombati, 2002, p. 86)
3 The second main step of harmonization came into force in 2004 (Act XXXIX of 2003 on Amendment of Act CXII of 1996 on credit institutions and financial enterprises; and Act LXXXIV of 2004 on the Amendments of Financial Regulations Relating to the Supplementary Supervision of Financial Conglomerates). From 2004 the Hungarian regulation of these fields essentially corresponds with EU directives.

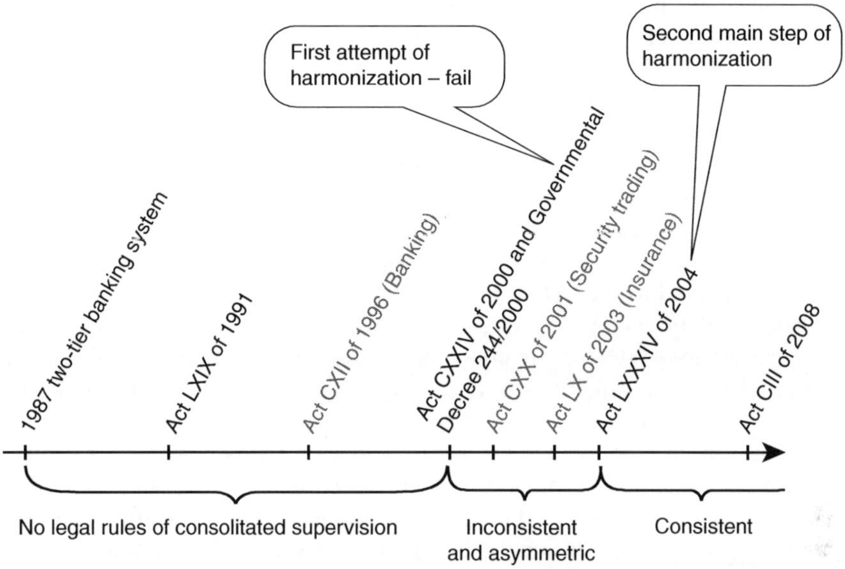

Figure 7.1 Essential milestones of the implementation of supervision on a consolidated basis in Hungary (up to the crisis)

The first attempt of harmonization came in 2000 when a new chapter was introduced on consolidated supervision into the Act on Credit Institutions. As a next step forward, the trading book's regulations introduced similar prescriptions when formulating the capital requirements of market risks. Thus the Hungarian legal rules of consolidated supervision of credit institutions would seem formally harmonized. However, these rules had some shortcomings, inconsistency and discrepancies, which had the consequence that the substance of the Hungarian regulation did not meet the goals of consolidated regulation in this term. A good signal of this problem was that the Hungarian Financial Supervisory Authority did not require consolidated data supply until 2002. Insufficiencies which deviated fundamentally from the logic of group-wide supervision, related basically to two areas: the scope of institutions to be consolidated with the purpose of prudential supervision and the method of calculation of consolidated own funds and capital adequacy. Only in 2002, the supervisory authority ordered an extraordinary supply of consolidated data, in line with the initiative of amendment legislation.

One element of inconsistency was the differences in definition of financial institutions (in Act CXXIV of 2000). The concept of financial institution, and the identification of financial holding company and mixed activity holding company were different in Hungarian provisions. In line with the EU regulation a financial institution is a non-credit institution undertaking with the main activity of acquiring participations or executing universal banking activities listed in Annex 1 of Directive 2000/12 with the exception of collecting deposits. But in Hungarian regulation the credit institution and the financial undertaking were denominated as a financial institution (executing certain activities from Annex 1 2000/12/EC), thus it included different scope of institutions and activities compared to the ones defined by the EU on the basis of activities.

The Act LXXXIV of 2004 changed these definitions of institution types. Although the definition of financial institution did not change in Hungarian rules (thus it continues to differ from EU definition), the definitions of financial holding company and mixed activity holding company have already become identical to the EU's.

Another deficiency was that 'close link' was not defined exactly. Although certain elements of the EU directives and a simplified formulation of close link was reflected in the Amendment of 2000 of the Act on Credit Institutions and the Act on Capital Markets. These Acts allowed for the supervisory authority to refuse a licence, if the activity of the applicant (owner or leading officer) endangers proper management of the credit institution or the financial undertaking, or if the activity, contacts or acquisitions of the applicant hinder the pursuit of efficient supervision. Even so, in contrast to the detailed explanations of the EU directives, it was not clarified what level of ownership participation and relationship might hinder efficient supervision and prudent management of the institution. Only the 2004 amendment of the Act on Credit Institutions introduced the definition of 'close link' and 'dominant influence'.

Furthermore, there was an asymmetry among the different types of institutions until 2004. On the one hand for investment fund managers no prescription required the investigation of owners, the owners' relations and their activities, involving the possible refusal of a licence. On the other hand, the provisions of the Act on Insurance Institutions did not authorize the supervisory authority – in parallel with the notification requirement of acquiring ownership participation or voting rights – to refuse licensing due to the activity or relationships of the owner.

The amendments adopted in spring 2003 affecting regulations on consolidated supervision pertaining to financial groups concluded a regulatory process lasting for several years. The resultant new regulations are fully compliant with EU requirements and provide for the possibility that each financial group can be assessed and supervised as one single unit.

5.1 Ranges of institutions in consolidated supervision of financial groups

The amendment (Act CXXIV of 2000) of the Act on Credit Institutions regulated the consolidated supervision of groups including credit institutions on three levels, relating to different ranges of institutions.

> *Data supply and the requirement of prudent operation* are to be met if there is at least one credit institution among the members of the group. This is

> the widest possible range of institutions and thus members of a banking group, a financial holding and mixed-activity holdings have to satisfy these requirements. A *register* is kept by the supervisory authority on banking groups and financial holdings, *group-wide risk exposure and capital adequacy requirements* were related to financial holdings or banking groups; the consolidated requirement stipulated in the trading book relates to investment firms or a financial institution controlled by a credit institution.
> (Horváth and Szombati, 2002, p. 90)

Since until 2004 the financial holding companies were defined by the Act on Credit Institutions only, a holding company might be a financial institution, which owns exclusively financial institutions and investment firms, and at least one of them is a credit institution. Consequently, a holding company which owns only investment firms and investment fund managers was not a financial holding company and was not subject to consolidated supervision.

Hungarian regulation dealt with the controlling relationship only in the case of a banking group (group led by a credit institution) when, of the share capital, more than 20 per cent is owned by an undertaking belonging to a banking group or which was controlled by a person together with an undertaking belonging to a banking group. But there was a crucial deficiency, that institutions not belonging to a banking group could have 20 per cent or more of *voting rights*, and another main deficiency, that the supervisory authority did not have the possibility of using *discretionary instruments*.

These shortcomings and discrepancies ceased following the 2004 amendment of the Acts concerned.[17] And an important development was that the Supervisory Authority was now entitled to deem the relationships identified at on-site inspections or upon examining documents as a close link and request that the credit institution or investment firm comply with consolidation requirements and prepare its calculations accordingly.

6 Supervision of financial groups and conglomerates

The provisions of consolidated requirement were one-sided until 2003 in Hungarian regulation, since only the Act on Credit Institutions dealt with this problem. Although from 2003 the Act on Capital Markets and Act on Insurance Institutions also contained the same rules of consolidated regulation, but these rules were applied only to homogeneous group members. The 2004 amendment of these acts introduced new chapters on supplementary supervision of financial groups and conglomerates into the legislation.

Before 2004, financial undertakings not belonging to any credit institution were not subjected to group-wide requirements, even formally. Therefore, in financial groups with no credit institution there was no consolidated requirement either. Hence, consolidated reporting rules did not relate to homogenous groups of investment firms or groups controlled by an investment firm, nor to insurance undertaking and asset management company group members.

Similarly, group-wide regulations relating to insurance undertakings did not exist in Hungarian regulation until 2003. The definition of different institutions, like insurance holding company or mixed activity insurance holding company, was also missing in this period.

Directive 2002/87/EC of the EU required the amendment of the Acts on credit institutions and financial enterprises, on the capital market and on insurance institutions and the insurance business. Act LXXXIV of 2004 introduced new chapters on supplementary supervision of financial groups and conglomerates into Hungarian regulation. Previous amendments (in 2003) also provided for supervision on a consolidated basis, but these rules applied only to homogeneous group members. In 2004 the adapted directive provided for the supplementary supervision of those groups which include insurance undertakings and credit institutions or investment firms simultaneously. Except for intra-group transactions, the new rules apply to those group members that have a parent–subsidiary company, participation or horizontal relationship. Thus, the rules cover those institutions that are considered parent and subsidiary companies from an accounting aspect and those that have a decisive influence on each other's operation based on the opinion of the supervisory authority. The legislation also covers institutions with a 'horizontal relationship', i.e. ones which are managed on a uniform basis or governed by a common executive body.

At the end of 2004, the HFSA identified 20 financial groups in Hungary.

> In these groups, a total of 231 organizations operated under the (direct or indirect) management of a Hungarian parent company or common foreign owner. These groups comprised 17 credit institutions, 15 insurance companies, 4 investment enterprises, 40 financial enterprises, 124 investment funds and 31 pension and health funds. In 13 of these twenty groups, the parent company is a credit institution, in five, an insurance company, while in two cases, an investment enterprise. As these 20 groups represent a growing proportion of the capital mediated by the financial sector, amounting to 84.5% in 2004, furthermore, as there are 10 financial institutions on average within a group, the management of groups and of intra-group risks has significance of systemic importance.
> (HFSA, 2004 p. 21)

But only one group was identified as a financial conglomerate (OTP group).

The increasingly intertwined and complex relations among credit institutions, financial enterprises, investment service providers, insurance institutions and funds in terms of ownership and activities provided the institutional reasons for consolidated supervision. In April 2000 the Hungarian Financial Supervisory Authority was founded integrating several former separate supervisions.

Three predecessor institutions were since the 1990s:

- Banking and Capital Market Supervision (that was also established through the early merger (1996) of Banking Supervision and Securities and Exchange Supervision),
- Insurance Supervision and
- Pension Fund Supervision.

Before the establishment of the single supervisory authority the regulation and supervision of these fields was fragmented with diverging levels of operative independence, different approaches and regulatory backgrounds to off-site and on-site examinations, low level and slow supervisory co-operation among institutions. The predecessor supervisory authorities employed different methods and had different supervisory cultures. The unification of supervisory methods has made it possible for the HFSA to conduct group-level inspections.

Unfortunately the independence of HFSA decreased from 2004: the Internal Operational Rules of the HFSA are proposed by the Board of HFSA, but approved by the minister, furthermore the director general and the deputies are appointed by the Prime Minister (for a fixed six-year term), no regulatory power, legally binding regulations cannot be issued by the HFSA.

7 Large exposures

Large exposure means exposures to one debtor (partner, client or group of connected clients), which – due to their size – may jeopardize an institution's stability, if the debtor cannot meet its payment obligation. In Hungary – in line with EU member states – an exposure to the same client or group of connected clients the amount of which reaches or exceeds 10 per cent of the regulatory capital is defined as a large exposure.

The 92/121/EEC directive has been implemented in Hungarian law by Act CXII of 1996 on Financial Institutions and Financial Undertakings. Until December of 1996 a credit institutions exposure to a single client or a group of connected clients would be considered a large exposure where its value is equal to or exceeds 15 per cent of its own funds and the sum of large exposures may not exceed six times the amount of own funds. From 1997 Hungarian regulation corresponds to EU legislation; in places it is more rigorous, because it does not contain several exemptions. The 2006/48/EC and 2006/49/EC directives have been implemented in Hungarian law by Act LI of 2007 on the Amendment of Act CXII of 1996 on Financial Institutions and Financial Undertakings and the Amendment of Laws on Specialized Credit Institutions.

A credit institutions exposure – that is to be taken into consideration for the calculation of capital requirement for credit risk using the standardized approach – to a single client or a group of connected clients shall be considered a large exposure where its value is equal to or exceeds 10 per cent of its own funds. The combined value of a credit institution's exposures to a single client or a group of connected clients, after taking into account the effect of the credit risk mitigation: (a) may not exceed 25 per cent of the credit institution's own funds, or (b) where that client is a credit institution, investment firm or where a group of connected clients includes one or more credit institutions or investment firms, 42 billion forints or the amount defined in point (a), whichever the higher, provided that the sum of exposure values, after taking into account the effect of the credit risk mitigation, to all connected clients that are not credit institutions or investment firms does not exceed 25 per cent of the credit institution's own funds (Act CXII of 1996, Section 79 (2)).

If a credit institution is under a dominant influence or a company holds a participating interest in a credit institution that has a dominant influence or participating interest in another credit institution or in a financial enterprise, investment firm or ancillary services company, calculations on a consolidated basis concerning the requirements for capital adequacy and for the control of large exposures must be made separately by each credit institution and financial holding company that is subject to supervision on a consolidated basis (Act CXII of 1996, Section 93).

Hungary is one of a few countries that do not operate either a national, non-profit, or a profit-oriented business-based complete mandatory credit information system (credit register), that could be a useful instrument to control large exposures. However, a partial credit register has been in place in Hungary: BISZ Ltd (owned by Hungarian financial institutions) was founded in 1994. BISZ was expected to design and operate the Interbank Debtor and Credit Information System (IDCIS). This partial database covers the most important data about all corporate loans (both performing and non-performing), but this database is not used in supervision. HFSA reclines upon its own collection of data.

The first survey of the adequacy of large exposure requirement was in 2002. The total value of large exposures taken on a consolidated basis was far below the statutory limit of eight times the regulatory capital, similarly to what was seen in case of individual banking calculations. The average is about 1.5 times the regulatory capital.[18] The ratio of large exposures on regulatory capital was only 3.4 and 3.7 even in case of the two banking groups with the highest figures. But from 2003 the HFSA had to provide against contravention of large exposure limits in every year at least in one case.

8 Investment services

Upon accession into the European Union, community legislation ensuring the obstacle-free operation of the internal market also entered into effect in Hungary. These laws provide a European single passport to all investment enterprises seated in a member state, allowing them to operate throughout the EU on the basis of authorization obtained from their home supervisor for investment services and supplementary services subject to mutual recognition.

Prudential supervision of the founder investment enterprise (which the branch office is an integral part of) shall be the responsibility of the competent authorities in the institution's home member state, including the supervision of activities for which the investment enterprise has a licence. This way, the operations of a Hungarian branch office (e.g. rules of organization and operation, internal auditing) are primarily subject to the legal provisions of the parent institution's home member state. The requirements set out in Act CXXXVIII of 2007 on Investment Firms and Commodity Dealers, and on the Regulations Governing their Activities, Act CXX of 2001 on the Capital Market and other financial regulations should only be applied where the legal provisions concerned explicitly provide so (HFSA, 2012, p. 23–4).

Pursuant to the interpretative provisions of Act CXXXVI of 2007 on the Prevention and Combating of Money Laundering and Terrorist Financing, branch offices qualify as investment service providers and as such they are required to develop internal rules and submit them to the HFSA for approval. The branch office's activities to prevent and combat money laundering are subject to scrutiny by the HFSA (HFSA, 2012, p. 24).

Pursuant to Section 2 of Government Decree 284/2001 (XII.26.) on the Mode of the Generation and Forwarding of Dematerialized Securities and the Relevant Rules on Safety, as well as on the Opening and the Keeping of the Security Account, the Central Securities Account and the Customer Account dematerialized securities are only allowed to be generated, recorded and forwarded subject to rules approved by the HFSA and using an approved computer system and storage media that ensures compliance with the referenced government decree (HFSA, 2012, p. 24).

Sections 79–81 of Act CXXXVIII of 2007 on Investment Firms and Commodity Dealers, and on the Regulations Governing their Activities set out mandatory provisions for investment enterprises that outsource activities. As the branch offices discussed herein operate in Hungary and serve Hungarian customers, in this respect they must also comply with regulations pertaining to outsourcing. As provided by law, the branch office needs to report to the HFSA on a regular basis the company name and principal office of its outsourcing partners along with the description of outsourced activities and the duration of outsourcing. Further, it must submit the outsourcing contract to the HFSA within 3 days after signing it (HFSA, 2012, p. 25).

Branch offices are entitled to use pending agents for their activities. In case a branch office already registered in the territory of Hungary intends to use, in the territory of the host member state, the services of a tied agent seated or permanently residing in Hungary, it shall inform the competent home supervisor of this. The home supervisor shall pass on this information to the host supervisor. When a tied agent is contracted for the intermediation of investment services, the HFSA must be notified of this within five days after contract conclusion. The notification must include the agent's name and principal office along with the description of intermediated services (HFSA, 2012, p. 25).

9 Deposit guarantee

Credit institutions seated in Hungary are required to join the National Deposit Insurance Fund (NDIF – OBA). Pursuant to Act CXII of 1996 on Credit Institutions and Financial Enterprises, the branch office of a credit institution seated in another member state is not required to join the NDIF if it has taken out deposit insurance as per Directive 94/19/EC of the European Parliament and of the Council. Vice versa, if said branch office does not have such deposit insurance as described above, it is required to join the NDIF in order to take out supplementary insurance as per Para (7) in Section 97 of the Act CXII of 1996 on Credit Institutions and Financial Enterprises (Act CXII of 1996).

The National Deposit Insurance Fund of Hungary has existed since July 1993. Previously the deposits of citizens were guaranteed and by establishing this institute the state extended this protection to the corporates. This state guarantee was almost entirely harmonized with the later implemented EU legislation (94/19/EC). Act CXII of 1996 on Credit Institutions and Financial Enterprises (§97-137) entered into force with the amount of the deposit guarantee to 1 million forints. The NDIF's main task is to start compensating the depositors within 15 days of their frozen (and insured) deposits at NDIF's member institutions. The indemnification period must be finished within three months. Credit cooperatives were not able to join to NDIF. Regular and compulsory contributions paid by credit institutions into a financial fund. Connection fee was 0.5 per cent of the share capital of the given institute. In case of insolvency of financial institutes or freezing deposits NDIF makes payment to the depositors from the fund. NDIF can make payments both in national and foreign currency, but solely on registered deposits.

Act LVI of 2008 was an Amendment for raise of coverage of Act CXII of 1996 on Credit Institutions and Financial Enterprises. Compensation can reach maximum 13 million forints. Act XLI of 2009 on the Amendment of deposit guarantee of Act CXII of 1996 on Credit Institutions and Financial Enterprises raised the amount of deposit guarantee further to €50,000. Act LVI of 2008 was also on the base of €50,000 but on a 260 forints/€1 exchange rate. Thanks to this change the compensation amount increased to 15 million forints (due to the fact the exchange rate became 300 forints/€1 in the meantime). Deposits in foreign currency are also protected up to €50,000 in total. At the same time the deadline of indemnification reduced from three months to 20 days. These 20 days were extendable once, with a maximum of 10 days.

The deposit insurance covers all deposits which were placed at the member institution of NFID by a clearly identifiable person or legal entity. Exceptions are government agencies, credit institutions, insurance companies and mutual funds. These institutions expected to have professional risk assessment. Bonds and depositary receipts issued after 1 January 2003 are also protected. Clients should not have to report the claim, the OBA payments are paid on the basis of banking system records. The base of compensation is the sum of the capital and interest of frozen deposits of an individual. The relevant foreign exchange rate is the Hungarian Central Bank's exchange rate on the day preceding the indemnification.

Act CLIX of 2010 on the amendment of certain financial acts (§55, Para 1) in accordance with 2009/14/EEC increased the coverage to €100,000 (Act CLIX of 2010).

10 Crisis management schemes

Act XLIX of 1991 on Bankruptcy Proceedings, Liquidation Proceedings and Voluntary Dissolution sets the basis of winding-up procedures and the supplements for financial institutes can be found in the following detailed at Act CXII of 1996 on Credit Institutions and Financial Enterprises. Act CXII of 1996 characterizes such cases which can be considered as crisis situation. Supervisory authorities should take (not specifically defined) action in the following cases (the most important ones) when the financial institution:

(a) has own funds that are less than 50 per cent of the capital requirements specified in this Act,
(b) wishes to pay or pays dividends in a situation where its own funds are below 50 per cent of the capital requirements specified in this Act,
(c) fails to meet its obligation to create provisions or the obligation of value adjustment, has insufficient provisions and inadequate value adjustments, meaning that the evaluation of off-balance sheet items and assets was incorrect, as a consequence of which its solvency ratio falls below 4 per cent, because the solvency margin was reduced by the amount of unaccounted accumulation of provisions and value adjustments (Act CXII of 1996).

None of the measures use the term crisis situation, but Act IV of 2006 on Business Associations does characterize such circumstances which can be interpreted as crisis situation:

(a) the company's equity capital has dropped to two-thirds of the share capital due to losses;
(b) the equity of the company has dropped below 5 billion forints (in case of banks this amount is 2 billion forints);
(c) the company has stopped making payments and its assets do not cover its debts (Act IV of 2006).

11 Accounting

Act XXXVII of 1875 on Commerce can be considered as the first recorded step of the development of Hungarian accounting. International rules, in practice the German law and trade patterns, were adapted to Hungarian economic relations. The provisions of the Act were gradually repealed from the existing rights at first by Decree-Law no. 33 of 1968 on Accounting. This Decree-Law was the first independent law on accounting which regulated the bookkeeping, cost accounting, balance sheets obligations and the reporting system. The second annulment entered into force by Decree-Law no. 34 of 1986 on Certain Provisions of Economic Associations. All provisions remain in force of Act XXXVII of 1875 on Commerce repealed by Act VI of 1988 on Business Companies.

Act LXXXV of 2003 on the Amendment of Act C of 2000 on Accounting entered into force on 1 January 2004. The regulation entrusted the member states of the application the possibility of extension regarding non-listed companies' consolidated annual accounts and individual accounts. The regulation after Hungary's EU accession (1 May 2004) became directly part of domestic law. Further regulation of the accounting law is required only on those cases where there is not specific ordinance or where there is an option or possibility to choose. Act LXXXV of 2003 on the Amendment of Act C of 2000 on Accounting applied the possibility of extension. Non-listed parent companies can prepare their consolidated accounts according to the Regulation. However, in the case of individual statements this option does not exist.

Act XCIX of 2004 on the Amendment of Act C of 2000 on Accounting was issued to fulfil the requirements of the 2003/51/EC Directive. Hungary has taken over all the provisions and options offered by the Directive into regulation. Act XCIX of 2004 on the Amendment of Act C of 2000 on Accounting clarifies the accounting standards for provisioning accordingly. The provisioning can take place only at such payment of liabilities and expected future costs where their existence or future occurrence is likely to be assumed on the date of the balance sheet. The Amendment expands – in accordance with the provisions of the Directive – the scope of data, the scope of information and details of them that should be included in the Business Report. Additional adaptations of the Directive are the regulations on the independent audit and the obligations related to the independent auditor's report as well. Further amendments to the international rule system approach are introduced in the rules on goodwill, on calculating exchange differences of outstanding long-term investments in foreign currency, on the exempted parent company in the case of higher-level parent companies at consolidation and on the disclosures on websites. In the case of goodwill the Amendment serves rectification at handling special effects on expected returns. It takes account of when goodwill value grows through business activity, as well as eliminating the possibility of 'inside' goodwill value at transition. The Amendment clarifies the law regarding the preparation of consolidated financial statements of the exemptible parent company in the case of higher-level parent companies. It also determines that specific information which should be presented separately during exemption (Act XCIX of 2004).

12 Conclusion

Hungary's financial system has undergone significant changes since 1987, the year when the foundations of the two-tier banking system were laid. Since the wave of privatization of state-owned banks between 1994 and 1999, large, foreign-owned, universal credit institutions have become the backbone of the financial system. Today not only do banks represent two-thirds of all institutional assets in the financial system and have substantial presence in all markets of financial intermediation but they also own major stakes in the capital market, insurance and fund sectors.

One of the key points in the financial regulatory changes in Hungary during the last two decades was the introduction of and changes to capital requirements. The introduction of capital requirements for the bank was motivated by Basel I in 1991; later its changes were induced by the EU directives on capital requirements. The idea was that Hungarian banks and later investment firms, too, had to maintain capital requirements to prevent risks. The scope of relevant risks has widened and calculation methods have become more complex.

The first provisions about capital requirements on banks in 1991 gave minimal amounts of subscribed capital for various types of banks. By 1997 the initial capital and own funds, the solvency ratio for credit institutions, were defined. The minimal amount of subscribed capital for various types of banks and also the minimal solvency ratio were regulated.

CAD and CAD2 were implemented at the same time, in 2001. From this year the notion of a trading book was introduced, and capital requirements of position risk, counterparty risk, commodities risk, risk of large exposures for firms maintaining a trading book, and the capital requirement of market risks and foreign-exchange risk for all financial institutions were imposed. The concept of an internal risk-management model was introduced. The conditions under which the authorities may allow institutions to calculate their capital requirements applying their own internal risk-management models were equivalent to the conditions imposed by Directive 98/31/EC.

In 2007–2008 the provisions of CRD were implemented by Hungarian laws and decrees. The new Hungarian provisions were equivalent in most points of these directives, but in some cases the Hungarian acts were a bit more restrictive ones than the EU directives. Most of the discretions were not applied.

During the transposition of the measures of CRD II the modifications of Hungarian laws and decrees affected the eligibility criteria and limits for some types of hybrid capital instruments to involve them among components of own funds of credit institutions, and capital requirements for the risk arising from securitization exposures.

During the implementation of CRD III the regulation on the calculation of capital requirements for credit institutions and investment firms changed in two aspects: the capital requirements of resecuritization positions were prescribed, and the standard for internal models used for the calculation of market risk capital requirements for positions in the trading book became stricter.

Hungary was in delay in the legislative process of implementing MIFID. Harmonization took place only from 2008 through Act CXXXVIII of 2007 on Investment Enterprises and Commodity Exchange Services and the rules governing the activities they perform and Act CXXXV of 2007 on the Hungarian Financial Supervisory Authority. Infringement proceedings started against Hungary in 2010 due to the incomplete implementation of 2004/39/EC and its regulations (2006/73/EC and 1287/2006 Regulation.) Hungary incorrectly transposed several provisions, including provisions relating to definitions, market transparency and licensing regime for investment firms (passport) and relating to the protection of investors. As a result, Hungarian firms do not provide services in other member states. Consequently, the chance is smaller for the Hungarian financial sector for economic growth and job creation. In addition, the investors are not guaranteed the same high level of competitiveness and the protection of financial markets as elsewhere in the EU.

Credit institutions seated in Hungary are required to join the National Deposit Insurance Fund. In case the branch office joins the deposit insurance system of its home member state, it must draw up a Hungarian-language guide with all the relevant information. Concerning legislation changed several times, the current compensation amount is 15 million forints and for deposits in foreign currency is €50,000. The deadline of indemnification is 20 days, which can be extended once, with a maximum of 10 days.

No Hungarian measures use the term crisis situation, but Act IV of 2006 on Business Associations does characterize such circumstances which can be interpreted as a crisis situation. Act CXII of 1996 on Credit Institutions and Financial Enterprises also declares some measures that HSFA should apply in different situations. These measures have different levels according to the seriousness of the situation.

The Hungarian legal system is almost fully harmonized with European legislation. Certain parts of the implementation took place slowly and still there are topics where in some aspects we can see divergences (for instance MIFID). However, these differences haven't impacted on the general attitude of financial institutes, and customers as well can safely perform their activities.

Notes

1 George Soros made a bid to buy 25 per cent of OTP in 1994 but was refused.
2 Act CXII of 1996 on Financial Institutions and Financial Enterprises.
3 Act CXX of 2001 on the Capital Market.
4 Act CXI of 1996 on Securities Trading, Investment Services and the Stock Exchange
5 Council Directive 89/299/EEC of 17 April 1989 on the own funds of credit institutions

6 Council Directive 89/647/EEC of 18 December 1989 on solvency ratio for credit institutions
7 Minister of Finance's Decree No. 28/1998 (X.21.) on the Solvency Ratio.
8 Minister of Finance's Decree No. 13/2001 (III.9.) on the Calculation of the Solvency Ratio.
9 Council Directive 89/647/EEC of 18 December 1989 on a solvency ratio for credit institutions.
10 Council Directive 93/6/EEC of 15 March 1993 on the capital adequacy of investment firms and credit institutions
11 Directive 98/31/EC of the European Parliament and of the Council of 22 June 1998 amending Council Directive 93/6/EEC on the capital adequacy of investment firms and credit institutions
12 Governmental Decree 196/2007 (VII. 30.) on Handling of the Credit Risks and Relevant Capital Requirements.
13 Act CXXXVIII of 2007 on Investment Firms, Commodities Exchange Service Providers, and Regulations on Their Operations.
14 Act CXXXVIII of 2007, Article 103(7). The definition of the financial instruments in Directive 2006/45/EC says that they are *either* free of any restrictive covenants on their tradability *or* able to be hedged.
15 Directive 2009/111/EC of the European Parliament and of the Council of 16 September 2009 amending Directives 2006/48/EC, 2006/49/EC and 2007/64/EC as regards banks affiliated to central institutions, certain own funds items, large exposures, supervisory arrangements, and crisis management.
16 Directive 2010/76/EU of the European Parliament and of the Council of 24 November 2010 amending Directives 2006/48/EC and 2006/49/EC as regards capital requirements for the trading book and for resecuritizations, and the supervisory review of remuneration policies.
17 Act XXXIX of 2003 on Amendment of Act CXII of 1996 on credit institutions and financial enterprises; and Act LXXXIV of 2004 on the Amendments of Financial Regulations Relating to the Supplementary Supervision of Financial Conglomerates
18 True, it is partly due to the fact that short-term exposure to credit institutions is only weighed at 20 per cent.

References

HONVÁRI, J. (2008) 20. századi gazdaságtörténet. [Twentieth century economic history] In Andor, L. (ed.), *Magyar Gazdaság* [*Hungarian Economy*]. Budapest: Pannonica. pp. 9–190.

HORVÁTH, E. and SZOMBATI, A. (2002): Risks and regulation of financial groups and conglomerates – Convergence of financial sectors. MNB Occasional Papers (25), 2002 Budapest.

HUNGARIAN FINANCIAL SUPERVISORY AUTHORITY (HFSA) (2004): Annual Report 2004

HUNGARIAN FINANCIAL SUPERVISORY AUTHORITY (HFSA) (2012): Informative Guide – To laws and other legal provisions regulating the provision of services in Hungary

KOLOZS, B. (2008): Some interesting issues regarding artices 56–58 EC Treaty, Annales Universitatis Scientiarum Budapestinensis De Rolando Eötvös Nominatae Sectio Iuridica, XLIX, pp. 285–300.

MNB (2002): Report on Financial Stability, June 2002

SEREGDI, L. (2006): Az Európai Unió hitelintézetekre vonatkozó szabályai és azok alkalmazása Magyarországon, In: Lentner, Cs. (ed.), *Pénzpiacok szabályozása Magyarországon*. Akadémiai Kiadó, pp. 121–184.
SZIKSZAI, Sz. (2008): Pénzügyi rendszer [Financial system] In Andor, L. (ed.), *Magyar Gazdaság* [*Hungarian Economy*]. Budapest: Pannonica. pp. 308–343.
TAKATA, K. (2005): Evolution of banking sector structures within Central-European countries during transition. Kyoto University Discussion Paper 065. 27 p.
VÁRHEGYI, É. (1998): Bankprivatizáció. [Bank Privatization] Budapest: ÁPV Rt. 142 p.

Acts, agreements, decrees

HUNGARY. Act XXXVII of 1875 on Commerce. Budapest.
HUNGARY. Act VI of 1988 on Business Companies. Budapest.
HUNGARY. Act XXIV of 1988 on the Investments of Foreigners in Hungary. Budapest.
HUNGARY. Act LXXXVI of 1990 on the Prohibition of Unfair Market Practice. Budapest.
HUNGARY. Act XCVIII of 1990 on the Amendment of Act XXIV of 1988 on the Investments of Foreigners in Hungary. Budapest.
HUNGARY. Act IL of 1991 on Bankruptcy Proceedings, Liquidation Proceedings and Voluntary Dissolution. Budapest.
HUNGARY. Act LXIX of 1991 on Financial Institutions and the Activities of Financial Institutions. Budapest.
HUNGARY. Act CXII of 1993 on the Amendment of Act 1991 on Financial Institutions and the Activities of Financial Institutions. Budapest.
HUNGARY. Act LVII of 1996 on the Prohibition of Unfair and Restrictive Market Practices. Budapest.
HUNGARY. Act CXI of 1996 on Securities Trading, Investment Services and the Stock Exchange. Budapest.
HUNGARY. Act CXII of 1996 on Credit Institutions and Financial Enterprises. Budapest.
HUNGARY. Act CLI of 1997 on the Amendment of Act CXI of 1996 on the Securities Trading, Investment Services and the Stock Exchange. Budapest.
HUNGARY. Act CLVIII of 1997 on the Amendment of Act CXII of 1996 on Financial Institutions and Financial Undertakings. Budapest.
HUNGARY. Act LXXII of 1998 on Foreign Private Entrepreneurs. Budapest.
HUNGARY. Act C of 2000 on Accounting. Budapest.
HUNGARY. Act CXXXVIII of 2000 on the Amendment of Act LVII of 1996 on the Prohibition of Unfair and Restrictive Market Practices. Budapest.
HUNGARY. Act CXXIV of 2000 on Amendment of Act CXII. of 1996 on credit institutions and financial enterprises. Budapest.
HUNGARY. Act XCIII of 2001 on the Elimination of Foreign Exchange Restrictions and on the Amendment of Certain Related Acts. Budapest.
HUNGARY. Act CXX of 2001 on Capital Market. Budapest.
HUNGARY. Act LXIV of 2002 on the Amendment of Financial and Capital Market Regulations. Budapest.
HUNGARY. Act XXXI of 2003 on the Amendment of Act LVII of 1996 on the Prohibition of Unfair and Restrictive Market Practices. Budapest.

HUNGARY. Act XV of 2003 on the Prevention and Combating of Money Laundering. Budapest.
HUNGARY. Act XXXIX of 2003 on Amendment of Act CXII of 1996 on credit institutions and financial enterprises. Budapest.
HUNGARY. Act XL of 2003 on the Amendment of Act 2001 on Capital Market. Budapest.
HUNGARY. Act LX of 2003 on Insurance Institutions and the Insurance Business. Budapest.
HUNGARY. Act LXXXV of 2003 on the Amendment of Act C of 2000 on Accounting. Budapest.
HUNGARY. Act XCIX of 2004 on the Amendment of Act C of 2000 on Accounting. Budapest.
HUNGARY. Act LXXXIV of 2004 on the Amendments of Financial Regulations Relating to the Supplementary Supervision of Financial Conglomerates. Budapest.
HUNGARY. Act LXVIII of 2005 on the Amendment of Act LVII of 1996 on the Prohibition of Unfair and Restrictive Market Practices. Budapest.
HUNGARY. Act IV of 2006 on Business Associations. Budapest.
HUNGARY. Act LI of 2007 on the Amendment of Act CXII of 1996 on Financial Institutions and Financial Undertakings and the Amendment of Laws on Specialized Credit Institutions. Budapest.
HUNGARY. Act CXXXV of 2007 on the Hungarian Financial Supervisory Authority. Budapest.
HUNGARY. Act CXXXVI of 2007 on the Prevention and Combating of Money Laundering and Terrorist Financing. Budapest.
HUNGARY. Act CXXXVIII of 2007 on Investment Firms, Commodities Exchange Service Providers, and Regulations on Their Operations. Budapest.
HUNGARY. Act LVI of 2008 on the Amendment for raise of coverage of Act CXII of 1996 on Credit Institutions and Financial Enterprises. Budapest.
HUNGARY. Act CIII of 2008 on the amendment of certain acts with effects on financial services. Budapest.
HUNGARY. Act CIV of 2008 on Promoting the Stability of the Financial Intermediary System. Budapest.
HUNGARY. Act XIV of 2009 on the Amendment of Act LVII of 1996 on the Prohibition of Unfair and Restrictive Market Practices. Budapest.
HUNGARY. Act XLI of 2009 on the Amendment of deposit guarantee of Act CXII of 1996 on Credit Institutions and Financial Enterprises. Budapest.
HUNGARY. Act CLVIII of 2010 on the Hungarian Financial Supervisory Authority. Budapest.
HUNGARY. Act CLIX of 2010 on the Amendment of Certain Financial Laws. Budapest.
HUNGARY. Act XCVI of 2011 on the Amendment of Certain Economic Laws. Budapest.
HUNGARY. Act CXLVIII of 2011 on the Amendment of Financial Regulations in Connection with the Restriction of Credit Interest Rates and Annual Percentage Rate. Budapest.
HUNGARY. Act CXCIII of 2011 on Investment Fund Managing Companies and Forms of Collective Investments. Budapest.
HUNGARY. Act CLI of 2012 on the Amendment of Certain Financial Laws. Budapest.

Agreement Free Trade between the European Communities and Their Member States and the Republic of Hungary of 1993

Council Directive 88/361/EEC of 24 June 1988 for the implementation of Article 67 of the Treaty

Council Directive 89/299/EEC of 17 April 1989 on the own funds of credit institutions

Council Directive 89/646/EEC of 15 December 1989 on the coordination of laws, regulations and administrative provisions relating to the taking up and pursuit of the business of credit institutions and amending Directive 77/78/EEC

Council Directive 89/647/EEC of 18 December 1989 on solvency ratio for credit institutions

Council Directive 93/6/EEC of 15 March 1993 on the capital adequacy of investment firms and credit institutions

Council Directive 93/22/EEC of 10 May 1993 on investment services in the securities field

Directive 98/31/EC of the European Parliament and of the Council of 22 June 1998 amending Council Directive 93/6/EEC on the capital adequacy of investment firms and credit institutions

Directive 2006/48/EC of the European Parliament and of the Council of 14 June 2006 relating to the taking up and pursuit of the business of credit institutions

Directive 2006/49/EC of the European Parliament and of the Council of 14 June 2006 on the capital adequacy of investment firms and credit institutions

Directive 2009/111/EC of the European Parliament and of the Council of 16 September 2009 amending Directives 2006/48/EC, 2006/49/EC and 2007/64/EC as regards banks affiliated to central institutions, certain own funds items, large exposures, supervisory arrangements, and crisis management

Directive 2010/76/EU of the European Parliament and of the Council of 24 November 2010 amending Directives 2006/48/EC and 2006/49/EC as regards capital requirements for the trading book and for the resecuritizations, and the supervisory review of remuneration policies

HUNGARY. Decree-Law no. 33 of 1968 on the Accounting. Budapest.

HUNGARY. Decree-Law no. 34 of 1986 on Certain Provisions of Economic Associations. Budapest.

HUNGARY. Government Decree 88/2001 (VI. 15.) on the Implementation of the Foreign Exchange Act. Budapest.

HUNGARY. Government Decree 244/2000. (XII. 24.) on the rules of establishing the capital adequacy of Positions registered in the Trading Book, Foreign Exchange Risk, Large Exposures and Risks. Budapest.

HUNGARY. Government Decree 284/2001 (XII.26.) on the Mode of the Generation and Forwarding of Dematerialized Securities and the Relevant Rules on Safety, as well as on the Opening and the Keeping of the Security Account, the Central Securities Account and the Customer Account. Budapest.

HUNGARY. Government Decree 230/2003. (XII. 16.) on the Amendment of Governmental Decree 244/2000. (XII. 24.) on the Rules of Establishing the Capital Adequacy of Positions registered in the Trading Book, Foreign Exchange Risk, Large Exposures and Risks. Budapest.

HUNGARY. Government Decree 196/2007. (VII. 30.) on Handling of the Credit Risks and Relevant Capital Requirements. Budapest.

HUNGARY. Government Decree 200/2007. (VII. 30.) on Handling of the Operational Risks and Relevant Capital Requirements. Budapest.

HUNGARY. Government Decree 234/2007 on Disclosure Requirements of Credit Institutions. Budapest.

HUNGARY. Government Decree 345/2007 (XII. 19.) on the Amendment of Governmental Decree 244/2000 on the Rules of Establishing the Capital Adequacy for Positions Registered in the Trading Book, Foreign Exchange Risk, Large Exposures and Risks Undertaken. Budapest.

HUNGARY. Government Decree 380/2007. (XII. 23.) on Securitization Capital Requirements of the Financial Institutions. Budapest.

HUNGARY. Government Decree 381/2007 on the Management of Counterparty Credit Risk. Budapest.

HUNGARY. Government Decree No. 22/2008 (II.7.) on the Mandatory Elements of the Rules of Business at Business Organisations Providing Investment Services, Auxiliary Investment Services and Commodity Exchange Services. Budapest.

HUNGARY. Government Decree 164/2008 (VI. 27.) on Publication of Information on Risk Management and Risk Assumption of Investment Firms. Budapest.

HUNGARY. Governmental Decree 301/2008 on Credit Risk of Investment Firms. Budapest.

HUNGARY. Government Decree 344/2010. (XII. 28.) on the Exposures to Transferred Credit Risk. Budapest.

HUNGARY. Government Decree 349/2010. (XII. 28.) on the Amendment of Certain Governmental Decrees on Finance. Budapest.

HUNGARY. Government Decree 131/2011 (VII. 18.) on the Application of Remuneration Policies with Regard to the Features Arising from the Size, Nature and Scope of Activities, and Legal Form of Credit Institutions and Investment Enterprises. Budapest.

HUNGARY. Government Decree 348/2011 (XII. 30.) on the Amendment of Certain Financial Governmental Decrees. Budapest.

HUNGARY. Minister of Finance's Decree No. 28/1998 (X.21.) on the Capital Adequacy Ratio. Budapest.

HUNGARY. Minister of Finance's Decree No. 13/2001 (III.9.) on the Calculation of the Capital Adequacy Ratio. Budapest.

HUNGARY. Minister of Finance's Decree No. 53/2005 (XII. 28.) on the Scope of Data to be reported by Credit Institutions to the Hungarian Financial Supervisory Authority and the Manner of Reporting. Budapest.

HUNGARY. Minister of Finance's Decree 27/2007 on Consolidated Own Funds and the Calculation of Consolidated Capital Requirements. Budapest.

HUNGARY. Minister of Finance's Decree 45/2008 (XII. 31.) on the Data to be Provided by Credit Institutions to the Financial Supervisory Authority of Hungary and the Method of Providing Data. Budapest.

HUNGARY. State Supervisory Authority of Banking Sector Governor's Decree 1/1992 (PK 5.) on the Principles of Capital Adequacy and Its Calculation. Budapest.

HUNGARY. State Supervisory Authority of Banking Sector Governor's Decree 3/1993 (PK 16.) on the Amendment of State Supervisory Authority of Banking Sector Governor's Decree 1/1992 (PK 5.) on the Principles of Capital Adequacy and Its Calculation. Budapest.

HUNGARY. State Supervisory Authority of Banking Sector Governor's Decree 4/1996 (PK 13.) on the Amendment of State Supervisory Authority of Banking Sector Governor's Decree 1/1992 (PK 5.) on the Principles of Capital Adequacy and Its Calculation. Budapest.

8 Financial regulation in Poland

Paweł Marszałek and Alfred Janc

1 Introduction

The history of the modern financial sector in Poland and its regulations is relatively short. The sector has been developing since the beginning of the 1990s, i.e. since the transformation of the Polish economy from planned into a market one. Apart from already existing banks, the first to develop was the interbank deposit market. The next to develop was the Treasury bill market. The introduction of partial convertibility of the Polish zloty in 1994 resulted in the emergence of the FX market. The stock exchange was developing simultaneously with the interbank market, mainly as a result of privatization (see Janc, Jurek and Marszałek, 2013). It must be stressed that the reconstruction of the financial system took place under circumstances of thorough and rapid changes in all, in principle, domains of political, economic and social life in Poland (Kowalski, 2010).

Before the economic transformation of 1989, the financial system in Poland and its regulations were poorly developed.[1] In fact, the sector consisted only of the banking system. Apart from banks, there was only one state-owned insurance company – the Polish Insurance Company (Polski Zakład Ubezpieczeń – PZU). No other types of financial intermediation existed nor other financial markets than the loan-deposit one. Moreover, banks acted under the non-market rules, with all significant parameters (interest rate, exchange rate, credit restrictions, etc.) determined and strictly regulated by the government.

During the years 1946–1982 predominant in Poland was the so-called monobank system, typical for communist countries with centrally planned economies.[2] In such a system privately owned banking institutions did not exist. At the same time state-owned banks were highly specialized, in principle not offering services to society. They just strictly adhered to government plans and decisions. The National Bank of Poland (NBP) acted as the main actor in the financial market. Apart from its activity as the subject of monetary policy, it made loans, accepted deposits and conducted payments and settlements, which proved to be highly ineffective solutions.

The weak performance of the Polish financial system was additionally reinforced, and simultanously contributed to, by ineffective functioning of the domestic currency, the Polish zloty. An informal dollarization occurred, altogether with money imbalances and hidden inflation. Thus, the financial system in Poland had to be reconstructed also in order to create the background for broader monetary reforms and to restore confidence in the currency (National Bank of Poland, 2001).

Institutional and political reforms turned out to be successful: since 1989 a modern and effective financial system has been built, encompassing different types of financial institutions (banks, insurance companies, investment funds, pension funds, etc.), conducive to economic growth and allowing for effective transformation and allocations of funds. Those institutional changes also required, in turn, changes in regulation, as domestic and foreign conditions have been changing on an ongoing basis and new types of risk and challenges for supervisors appeared. The situation was complicated additionally with the global financial crisis of 2008 and its consequences for financial systems and individual economies, also for Poland (National Bank of Poland, 2010, 2013).

The aim of the chapter is, against a background of reforms of the financial system and financial regulations in Poland, to characterize the main activities of supervisors and changes in financial regulations in Poland, being the aftermath of the global financial crisis. A short description of the Polish regulatory framework before 1997 is presented in section 2. Section 3 describes subsequent changes of regulations resulting from adjustments to changes in the EU directives, connected with the accession process. Sections 4 and 5 present the main changes in the regulatory frameworks, enforced in a way by crisis events and resulting from response to them from, respectively, European and domestic regulators. Section 6 concludes.

2 The first phase of the reconstruction of the Polish financial system and its regulations (1982–1997)

The transformation of the Polish financial system started even earlier than the overall systemic change. Moreover, changes in the domain of finance were much deeper and more complex than in other subsystems of the economy. The first, though only partial, attempts to rebuild the banking system were made in 1982, but more profound changes within the banking system were enforced at the end of January 1989 (that is, even before the Round Table Talks). Two new acts were passed then: the Banking Act that determined the creation and functioning of commercial banks, and the Act on the National Bank of Poland, redefining the role and responsibilities of the Polish central bank. Both acts made it possible to form a two-tier banking system, typical of market economies. Building such a system, consisting of universal instead of specialized banks, was recognized as the priority and the fundamental objective of banking reform (Janc, 2004).

At the same time nine commercial banks were created. Those new institutions had capital excluded from the regional branches of the NBP that ceased to make financial services for households and enterprises. At the same time all existing forms of by-operator and by-business-type constraints were lifted and clients became free to choose their banks and shape their relationship with banks on the contract basis. Another important step was the liberalization of the terms of entry into the banking system. Broad opportunities were provided for potential – domestic and foreign – investors to run banking activities in Poland, especially very mild licence policy – legal barriers to create a banks were relatively small.[3] As a result, in 1991 already 72 commercial banks functioned in the Polish market.[4] Parallel with the development of the banking sector, other types of financial intermediaries were also created, increasing competition in the financial market (National Bank of Poland, 2001, 2002).

Continuous evolution of the Polish financial system also required development of regulations connected with this domain. Brand new institutions were created, as well as the overall regulatory frameworks, and many already existing supervisors reformulated their objectives, instruments and responsibilities. Characteristic of the changes, the scale and scope of regulations increased systematically, along with growing complexity of the Polish financial market and more and more dynamic activity of financial intermediaries.

This process was additionally reinforced by ongoing integration of Poland with the European Union.[5] The integration also implied, among many other things, adjustments of financial regulations.

The integration process moved along with the transformation of the economic and political system. It was in a sense, convenient: many adjustment could have been made while creating a brand new legal environment. Thus, in many cases, no special modifications were needed – It was sufficient just preparing and introducing laws consistent with the EC regulations. It was also the case when one takes into account financial regulations. Moreover, since the very beginning of the transformation, financial institutions from the EC/EU were present in the Polish financial system, being one of the most active investors in the process of privatization. Thus, many links with financial systems of the EU countries were already established, even prior to Poland's formal accession to the EU.

However, some adjustments still had to be made. They involved implementation of the EU *acquis communautaire* relating to free flow of capital and services, as well as to functioning of individual types of financial intermediaries, the central bank and monetary policy, supervision authority, and settlements systems actions taken in order to reinforce the stability and strengthen the capitalization of the whole sector and to improve the quality of the legal, judicial and technological infrastructure.

With reference to the banking sector, the dominant part of the Polish financial system, the main part of adjustments was made with passing Poland's new Constitution of 2 April 1997 and, in the same year, the Act on National Bank of Poland and the Banking Act – both of 29 August 1997. These two adjusted almost entirely the organization and functioning of Polish banks to EU directives. All remaining differences were eliminated by amendments, passed by the Act of 18 December 2003, which entered into effect on 1 January 2004. Since then it can be stated that the domestic regulations blend in with those of the EU. Necessary legal adjustments were also enforced with reference to other parts of the Polish financial system.[6] The main elements of those regulations are described in the next section.

3 Financial regulations in Poland and their adjustments to EU requirements before the financial crisis – a short overview

The frameworks within which legal regulations of the financial services sector are created is specified in the Constitution of the Republic of Poland (1997). It introduces the principle of freedom of business activity as the basis for the whole economic system. As regards the financial sector, this freedom is expressed as:

- freedom to conclude contracts of any subject and of any contents;
- freedom to select business partners and a possibility to perform cross-border activities;
- freedom of competition.

According to the Constitution, provision of financial services is subject to control and supervision by the state, while 'entities put funds entrusted to them by other entities (natural and legal persons) at risk of their operations'.

The need – mentioned already – to adjust the Polish legal system to European Union law and to the commitments stemming from Poland's membership in the Organization of Economic Cooperation and Development (OECD) was the main reason for the amendments introduced to Polish financial legislation. The process of adjustment of Polish law was very dynamic, since regulations regarding the financial sector in European law have been frequently changed. This was reflected in numerous amendments to acts or in the creation of new acts (National Bank of Poland, 2004). Moreover, some changes have been introduced as a result of EU laws, and not of domestic legislation, like for example regulations which have introduced the single licence (passport) principle in the financial sector of EU countries.

The newly passed laws may be divided into three groups – those regarding the entire financial sector, those referring to its individual sectors: banking, insurance companies, capital markets, investment funds, pension funds, etc., and, finally, those regarding supervision over the financial sector.

Among the most important laws from the first group was the Foreign Exchange Law. It specified the rules of exchanging Polish currency to foreign currencies and procedures for the issuance of permissions to perform market operations that are related to spending in terms of the foreign currency.

Changes in the Foreign Exchange Law were mainly related to the fulfilment of Poland's obligations towards the OECD and the EU.

Until 2002, foreign exchange operations were regulated by the Act of 18 December 1998 – Foreign Exchange Law. The adopted legal solutions, despite their contribution to the liberalization of foreign capital flows, did not meet the standards of the European Union. Non-residents were not able to purchase short-term securities or financial derivatives in Poland without a foreign exchange permit. However, these restrictions did not pertain to purchases by non-residents of Treasury securities and financial derivatives offered on stock exchange markets, nor to the purchase of short-term securities and financial derivatives offered by authorized banks.

The new law (Act of 27 July 2002 – Foreign Exchange Law) implemented in 2002 had already met the obligations stemming from European Union law. The abolition of restrictions in the flow of capital to countries within the EU, countries within the European Economic Area and other countries in the OECD, made it possible for residents to freely invest in the capital markets of these countries. As a result of these changes, residents obtained the right to maintain accounts with foreign banks and to deposit funds on such accounts.

Since 2007 restrictions on capital flows have been additionally lifted. Amendments introduced in this very year to the Foreign Exchange Law (Act of 26 January 2007 Amending the Foreign Exchange Law Act and Other Acts) resulted from the obligation to ensure compliance of Polish legal regulations with EU law. The most important solutions lifted restrictions on the disposal and acquisition of securities and participation units of joint investment funds by non-residents from third countries, as well as granting and taking loans and lending facilities in trading between residents and non-residents (National Bank of Poland 2010).

The amendment to the Foreign Exchange Law did not remove restrictions on settlements in foreign currency between residents. Removing restrictions imposed on agreements and on performing other activities which result or may result in domestic settlements in foreign currency was put on hold.

Another important 'general' law was passed on 17 June 2010. Then the requirements of European Directive MiFID (Markets in Financial Instruments Directive) entered into force in Poland. The MiFID has been introduced into Polish law through the Act on Trade in Financial Instruments together with its implementing provisions. Its implementation means that agents investing in the financial market in Poland are entitled to the same level of protection as they are in other EU states. The protection offered to clients in line with the implementation of the MiFID in Poland consists of, among others:

- submission and preparation of detailed information on the products and services in a way which is comprehensible and not misleading,
- assessment of the client's understanding of the product, particularly the risks involved,

- verification whether the services or products to be provided are suitable by establishing the client's level of investment knowledge and experience.

Among all the 'sectorial' regulations, the most significant were those referring to the banking sector, dominating the Polish financial system. As it was mentioned, the reform of the banking sector was one of the crucial components of the 1989 transformation. In January 1989 the Sejm passed two acts: the Banking Act and the Act on the National Bank of Poland. The basic importance of the first of them was to be seen, among other effects, in the reconstruction of the banking sector, as the act allowed for the operation of state banks, joint stock banks and cooperative banks, an abolition of the mechanism of automatic lending for governmental purposes, as well as the extension of the catalogue of banking activities and services (National Bank of Poland 2001).

The Acts of 1989 were complex in the way they set out to regulate the operation of the banking system. However, as the time went by banking legislation became a component of a larger whole, which forced the introduction of new acts in 1997, specifically the aforementioned Act on the NBP of 1997 and the Banking Act of 1997. These acts have become the source of principles of conducting banking business, as well as the principles of performing banking supervision, and bank liquidation and bankruptcy procedures (National Bank of Poland, 2001).

Thus, one may consider the year 1998 as a kind of milestone for the legal and institutional framework for Polish central bank and the banking sector. This framework was first outlined by the new Constitution of the Republic of Poland of 2 April 1997, and then fleshed out by the two mentioned acts: the Act on the National Bank of Poland and the Banking Act, both adopted on 29 August 1997.[7]

Significant changes were introduced in the organisation of banking supervision, which was entrusted to the Commission for Banking Supervision (*Komisja Nadzoru Bankowego* – KNB), which took over the previous competence of the National Bank of Poland and its President. The General Inspectorate of Banking Supervision became the executive body of the Commission, remaining an organizational unit of the National Bank of Poland.

The *Banking Act*, like the preceding one, formed the regulations to perform certain banking operations. These included: bank accounts, bank settlements, loans, advances, bank guarantees, endorsements, letters of credit and also the issue of bank securities. Generally speaking, the regulations on individual operations were expanded as compared with the previous regulations resulting from the Banking Act of 1989.

The design of the licensing process, worked out on the grounds of previously binding regulations, was maintained. The establishment of a cooperative bank and a joint-stock bank required the founders obtaining the authorization of the Commission for Banking Supervision, granted in agreement with the Minister of Finance. A state bank may be set up by ordinance of the Council of Ministers at the request of the Minister of Treasury, which should obtain the opinion of the Commission for Banking Supervision. The Banking Act of 1997 specified also the capital requirements set to the founders. The initial capital provided by the founders shall not be less than the zloty equivalent of €5 million. A part of the initial capital might be contributed in kind, in the form of equipment and property holdings, if they are directly useful in the banking business; however in any case, the value of non-cash considerations cannot exceed 15 per cent of the initial capital. If the bank's capital is increased, the value of non-cash considerations shall not exceed 15 per cent of the bank's core capital.

The further significant changes appeared in the banking regulations with the Amendment of 23 August 2001. It assumed primarily the adjustment of Polish law to Directive 2000/12/EC of the European Parliament and of the Council relating to the taking up and pursuit of the business of credit institutions. Among many other things, it introduced into Polish law definitions of: a credit institution, a branch of credit institution, a branch of domestic bank, providing services within cross-border operations, as well as defining the principles of the taking up and pursuit of the business by credit institutions in Poland and by domestic banks in the EU.

More precisely, the amendment of August 2001 regulated and adjusted to EU standards such areas and issues as:

- making declarations of intent on electronic data media;
- introduction of a definition of electronic money;
- introduction of consolidated supervision;
- modification of regulations on the cooperation and exchange of information with domestic financial supervision authorities and with foreign banking supervision authorities;
- modification of regulations on the risk-based capital ratio and introduction of the grounds for the CBS to determine the principles of banks observing the capital requirements against individual risks, including the market risk;
- removing problems connected with the application of bilateral netting in case of insolvency; the amendment aims at protection of domestic financial system stability in case of bankruptcy of a major financial institution – in relation to deepening mutual relationships between individual institutions;
- introduction of regulations on cross-border transfers; the amendment introduces to the Polish system numerous provisions of Directive No. 97/5/EC of the European Parliament and of the Council relating to the performance of transfer orders within foreign relationships and Directive 98/26/EC of the European Parliament and of the Council relating to the finality of settlements within the payment and the securities settlement systems;

- introduction, for supervisory purposes, of definitions of: a financial institution, a financial group, a mixed-activity group, a parent undertaking, a significant influence, close links;
- extension of the catalogue of sanctions used by the Commission of Banking Supervision;
- modification of provisions on the control of joint-stock banks' shares transfer.

Thus, the changes that have been introduced to the Banking Act since 1997 have been largely a consequence of gradual adaptation of Polish regulation to EU requirements (Kowalski and Matysek-Jędrych, 2010). In consequence, significant regulatory changes took place in the Polish banking sector, especially with reference to capital requirements and risk management in banking institutions. These changes were related to the implementation of the New Capital Accord, prepared by the Basel Committee and incorporated then into the EU law (Directive 2006/48/EC, Directive 2006/49/EC).

The implementation of the CRD directive to domestic law was a very complex process due to its high complexity. In contrast to previous prudential regulation applied by banks, the CRD was implemented based on the maximum harmonization principle. To ensure the transposition of the directive provision to Polish law as soon as possible, the legislator decided to apply an analogical approach to the proposed in the Lamfallusy report. The Banking Act specified only those of the CRD directive provision that required statutory regulations. Other provisions were regulated in the resolutions of the (then) Commission of Banking Supervision. In detail, Directives 2006/48/EC and 2006/49/EC have primary been implemented into Polish law by the following regulations:

- the Act of 29 August 1997 (Journal of Laws of 2002, No. 71, Item 665 as amended) on banking law (the *Banking Act*);
- the Act of 21 July 2006 (Journal of Laws of 2006, No. 157, Item 1119, as amended) on the financial supervision (the *Financial Supervision Act*);
- the Act of 29 September 1994 (Journal of Laws of 2002, No. 74, Item 694, as amended) on accountancy (the *Accountancy Act*);
- the Act of 15 April 2005 (Journal of Laws of 2005, No. 83, Item 719, as amended) on supplementary supervision (the *Act on Supplementary Supervision*);
- the Ordinance of the Minister of Finance of 19 November 1999 on consolidated banking accounts;
- Resolution of the Banking Supervision Commission No. 1/2007;
- Resolution of the Banking Supervision Commission No. 3/2007;
- Resolution of the Banking Supervision Commission No. 4/2007;
- Resolution of the Banking Supervision Commission No. 5/2007;
- Resolution of the Banking Supervision Commission No. 6/2007;
- Resolution of the Banking Supervision Commission No. 10/2007.

In December 2008 a number of new resolutions of the newly created Polish Financial Supervision Authority (see further) were adopted, replacing the Resolutions listed above adopted in 2007. Since then, Directives 2006/48/EC and 2006/49/EC were implemented into Polish law by the following regulations:

- Resolution of the Polish Financial Supervision Authority No. 380/2008 KNF 3 (Resolution No. 380/2008 KNF*);*
- Resolution of the Polish Financial Supervision Authority No. 381/2008 KNF (Resolution No. 381/2008 KNF);
- Resolution of the Polish Financial Supervision Authority No. 380/2008 KNF (Resolution No. 385/2008 KNF);
- Resolution of the Polish Financial Supervision Authority No. 387/2008 KNF (Resolution No. 387/2008 KNF)

However, some changes in a domestic legislation have been introduced not for the purpose of adjustment to EU law. Among them, one can distinguish an amendment to the Polish banking legal framework not linked with EU legislation, being the Act on the so-called Prevention of Usury, which has been passed by the Polish parliament in 2005. According to the Act the maximum interest rate which can be charged on bank loans, trade credit and cash loans cannot be higher than four times the lending credit rate of the NBP. This regulation limits also the total value of all fees and commissions arising from a conclusion of a consumer loan agreement (excluding costs of credit insurance and security) to 5 per cent of the value of a consumer credit.

Significant changes have been introduced to the institutional structure of financial supervision since 2007. The Act on Financial Market Supervision, provisions of which entered into force on 19 September 2006, has changed the rules of supervision in Poland (Act of 21 July 2006 on Financial Market Supervision). The new solutions were aimed at integrating the supervisory bodies overseeing the financial market (the Commission of Banking Supervision, the Securities and Exchange Commission, the Insurance and Pension Funds Supervisory Commission). One organizational body is now responsible for the tasks and powers that formerly belonged to several bodies supervising the individual sectors of the financial market. The Polish Financial Supervision Authority comprises the chairperson, two vice-chairpersons and four members: the minister competent for financial institutions or his/her representative; the minister competent for social security or his/her representative; the President of the NBP or a delegated Deputy President of the NBP; a representative of the President of the Republic of Poland. The activity of the PFSA activity is being supervised by the President of the Council of Ministers.

The Polish Financial Supervision Authority (PFSA), which on 19 September 2006 replaced the Insurance and Pension Funds Supervisory Commission and the Securities and Exchange Commission, was entrusted with conducting integrated supervision. The PFSA initiated its activity on 19 September 2006. In the second phase of the merger of financial supervision, on 1 January 2008, the PFSA took over the powers of the Commission for Banking Supervision together with its office – the General Inspectorate of Banking Supervision. Thus, there occurred an establishment of authority separate from the structure of the National Bank of Poland and unifying all supervisory bodies into a single authority, the task of which is to provide surveillance over the financial sector (Kowalski and Matysek-Jędrych, 2010).

It must be stressed the Polish financial regulations were in principle assessed relatively high. Proof of their efficiency might be that in Poland no financial (banking, currency or debt) crisis occurred, even despite the changing environment and ongoing transformation processes, connected with high uncertainty. Moreover, the pace of the process, as well as the selection of goals and milestones during the development of regulation is perceived positively. Also, supervisory authorities were assessed to work satisfactory.[8] It has also been found that the banking legislation in force since January 1998 has ensured a high consistency with European Union regulations (National Bank of Poland, 2006a, 2006b).

4 Changes in regulatory frameworks after the crisis – incorporation of EU regulations

The onset of the global financial crisis did not directly influence Poland. The country avoided heavy losses brought about by the crisis and the Polish financial system remained relative stable. One reason – apart from the 'confidence package' implemented by the National Bank of Poland and the 'plan for stability and development', adopted by the Government – might be the stable institutional and regulatory framework (National Bank of Poland, 2010, 2011)

Some problems occurred and the growth rate was lower, but still the Polish economy functioned well, especially when compared to other European countries. But as the crisis escalated, it started to interfere with economic processes in Poland and negative tendencies occurred within the financial system. Those tendencies along with the need to incorporate new regulations introduced by the EU, brought another modifications of financial regulations.[9] The most significant changes took place within the years 2009–2011. Due to the dominant role of banks in the Polish financial systems, most changes addressed these very institutions. Among new regulations and modifications, the most important were those referring to banks' capital requirements, the deposit guarantee scheme and accounting.

4.1 Capital requirements

Since 2007, the PSFA, in several resolutions, adjusted the Polish regulations concerning capital requirements to laws introduced in the EU, aimed at straightening stability of the financial sector of individual member countries. The specific objective behind the adoption of those resolutions was to:

- adjust the Polish legal framework to the amended directives of the European Parliament and of the Council, i.e. Directive 2006/48/EC relating to the taking up and pursuit of the business of credit institutions, and Directive 2006/49/EC on the capital adequacy of investment firms and credit institutions (CRD), adopted by virtue of Directive 2009/111/EC of the European Parliament and of the Council of 16 September 2009, Commission Directive 2009/27/EC of 7 April 2009 and Commission Directive 2009/83/EC of 27 July 2009 (CRD II);
- adjust the Polish legal framework to the amended directives of the European Parliament and of the Council, i. e. Directive 2006/48/EC relating to the taking up and pursuit of the business of credit institutions, and Directive 2006/49/EC on the capital adequacy of investment firms and credit institutions (CRD), adopted by virtue of Directive 2010/76/EC of the Europe an Parliament and of the Council of 24 November 2010 amending Directives 2006/48/EC and 2006/49/EC as regards capital requirements for the trading book and for resecuritizations, and the supervisory review of remuneration policies (CRD III);
- reflect amendment proposals submitted within the PSFA Office and by the banking sector.

In 2010, the PFSA, acting on the basis of statutory delegations included in the Banking Act, adopted the following legal acts:

- resolution on the scope and detailed rules for determination of capital requirements for individual types of risk (Resolution No. 76/2010 of the Polish Financial Supervision Authority on the scope and detailed rules for determination of capital requirements for individual types of risk – Official Journal of the PFSA of 2010, No. 2, item 11, as amended). The Resolution came into force on 10 March 2010;
- resolution on other items of a bank's balance sheet included in tier-1 capital, their amount, scope and conditions of inclusion in a bank's tier-1 capital (Resolution No. 434/2010 of the Polish Financial Supervision Authority of 20 December 2010) that came into force on 31 December 2010.

The first of those resolutions replaced the previous resolution concerning these matters.[10] The measures adopted in the new resolution were a consequence of adapting domestic regulations with the requirements of CRD II (Directive 2009/111/EC of the European Parliament and of the Council of 16 September 2009 amending Directives 2006/48/EC, 2006/49/EC and 2007/64/EC as regards banks affiliated to central institutions, certain own funds items, large exposures, supervisory arrangements, and crisis management – EU

Official Journal L 320 of 2009, p. 97), as well as, inter alia, the aftermath of the amendments to that Directive, planned then.[11]

The second resolution repealed the provisions of the Resolution of the Polish Financial Supervision Authority of 14 October 2009 (Resolution No. 314/2009 on other items of a bank's balance sheet included in tier-1 capital, their amount, scope and conditions of inclusion in a bank's tier-1 capital – Official Journal of the PFSA of 2009, No. 1, item 8). The necessity of adopting a new resolution concerning banks' core funds also resulted from the need to adapt Polish law to the provisions of CRD II. This act limited the scope of financial instruments which may be included in own funds of credit institutions. As a consequence, pursuant to the new Resolution of the PFSA, from December, 31, 2010 banks cannot include financial resources raised from new issues of convertible bonds and long-term bonds in their tier-1 capital.

Article 2 of the Resolution provides that financial resources raised from the issuance of long-term bonds and already recognized as tier-1 capital pursuant to a decision of the PFSA (given in accordance with the resolution of the PFSA of 14 October 2009) can be included in tier-1 capital in amounts no higher than:

- 35 per cent of total tier-1 capital – from 31 December 2010 to 31 December 2020;
- 20 per cent of total tier-1 capital – from 1 January 2021 to 31 December 2030;
- 10 per cent of total tier-1 capital – from 1 January 2031 to 31 December 2040.

In 2010, the PFSA also adopted the following legal acts, amending previous regulations:

- Resolution No. 367/2010 of the PFSA of 12 October 2010 amending Resolution No. 381/2008 of the PFSA of 17 December 2008 on other deductions from original own funds, their value, scope and conditions for a deduction of these items from the bank's original own funds, other bank's balance sheet items that are included into the bank's supplementary own funds, their scope and conditions of their inclusion in the bank's supplementary own funds, reductions of supplementary own funds, their value, scope and conditions for a deduction of such items from the banks' supplementary own funds; and the scope and method of including banks' activities in holdings when calculating own funds (Official Journal of the PFSA of 2010, No. 8, item 36).
- Resolution No. 368/2010 of the PFSA of 12 October 2010 amending Resolution No. 385/2008 of the PFSA of 17 December 2008 on detailed principles and methods of publication of qualitative and quantitative information on capital adequacy by banks and the scope of published information (Official Journal of the PFSA of 2010, No. 8, item 37).

Both those amendments came into force on 31 December 2010. The first resolution increased, in accordance with the provisions of CRD II, the number of items reducing tier-1 capital, the number of items included in supplementary own funds and provided a precise specification of items included in a bank's regulatory capital account. The second resolution extended the scope of disclosed information on the application of the value at risk method (VaR) in calculating capital requirements and on the use of advanced measurement approaches (AMA) in calculating the capital requirements for operational risk. Moreover, banks which apply the AMA to calculate the capital requirements for operational risk will be obliged to disclose information not only on relevant insurance policies, but also on other risk transfer mechanisms (PFSA, 2011).

In 2011 resolutions of CRD II and CRD III Directives were introduced into the national legislation. In April 2011, the Parliament passed amendments to the Banking Act and to the Act on Trading in Financial Instruments, which were the first steps towards the implementation of Directive 2010/76/UE (the so-called CRD III). With reference to the banking sector they were included in the Banking Act and in resolutions of the Polish Financial Supervision Authority. The amendment to the Banking Act of 28 April 2011, introduced significant changes in supervisory limits of risk exposures. The total amount of a bank's claims – off-balance sheet commitments and shares or participations held by the bank directly or indirectly in another entity, contributions to a limited liability company or limited partner shares – depending on which of these amounts is higher – in a limited partnership or a limited joint-stock partnership (exposure), exposed to a single entity or to entities linked by capital or organisation structure may not exceed the exposure concentration limit which amounts to 25 per cent of the bank's own funds.

Moreover, the bank's exposure towards another domestic bank, credit institution, foreign bank or a group of entities linked by capital or organisation structure, comprising at least one domestic bank, credit institution or foreign bank may not exceed 25 per cent of the bank's own funds or the equivalent of €150 million, calculated in Polish zloty at the mid-rate published by the National Bank of Poland and ruling on the last reporting day – depending on which of the amounts is higher; and the aggregate amount of exposures towards all linked entities in the group which are not a domestic bank, credit institution or foreign bank may not exceed 25 per cent of the bank's own funds.

In 2011, the Polish Financial Supervision Authority adopted the following nine resolutions (PFSA 2012):

1 Resolution No. 153/2011 of the Polish Financial Supervision Authority of 7 June 2011, amending Resolution No. 76/2010 of the Polish Financial Supervision Authority on the scope and detailed procedures for determining capital requirements for particular risks – the resolution introduced an amendment that raised to 100 per cent the risk weight of

retail exposures for which the principal payment or interest payment depend on the exchange rate of currency or currencies other than the currency of the debtor's income for: retail exposures, exposures secured by residential real property as an actual or potential place of residence of the owner or his/her rental property. By increasing the capital requirement, the amendment was aimed to take into account a higher (than in the case of national currency or other currency of the debtor's income) level of risk associated with the above exposures.

2 Resolution No. 206/2011 of the Polish Financial Supervision Authority of 22 August 2011, amending Resolution No. 76/2010 of the Polish Financial Supervision Authority on the scope and detailed procedures for determining capital requirements for particular risks – the resolution introduced changes associated with the need to transpose CRD II and CRD III. CRD II was implemented through a change of reference to the Banking Act of 29 August 1998, with respect to exposure concentration limits and a large exposure limit, resulting from the amendment (also implementing the provisions of CRD II), implemented by the Act of 28 April 2011 amending the Banking Act, the Act on Trading in Financial Instruments and the Act on Financial Market Supervision (which entered into force on 12 July 2011).

3 Resolution No. 207/2011 of the Polish Financial Supervision Authority of 22 August 2011, amending Resolution No. 384/2008 of the Polish Financial Supervision Authority, on the requirements concerning identification, monitoring and control of concentration of exposures, including large exposures – the resolution introduced changes related to the implementation of CRD II, which amended the provisions on stress-testing concentration risk. The resolution: specified that the tests should cover the risks connected with possible changes in economic circumstances of the bank, including market conditions, which could have a negative impact on the adequacy of the bank's own funds; specified the rules and procedures that banks should include in their strategies to address concentration risk; took into account the transposition of the definition of a 'large exposure' from the Banking Act to the resolution superseding Resolution No. 382/2008 of the Polish Financial Supervision Authority on detailed rules and conditions for considering exposure when determining the observance of the exposure concentration limit and the large exposure limit.

4 Resolution No. 208/2011 of the Polish Financial Supervision Authority of 22 August 2011 on detailed rules and conditions for considering exposure when determining the observance of the exposure concentration limit and the large exposure limit – the amendment of CRD II also warranted amendment of the Banking Act. The amendments to the Banking Act were published on 27 June 2011 (Journal of Laws of 2011, No. 131, item 763) and became effective on 12 July 2011. The amendment of the Banking Act involved introducing a single exposure concentration limit

of 25 per cent of the bank's own funds. The delegation contained in the Banking Act required the PFSA to determine the rules and conditions for considering exposure when observing the exposure concentration limit, taking into account credit risk mitigation techniques and to specify the detailed conditions to be met by exposures excluded from the concentration limit so that they do not jeopardize secure conduct of business and proper risk management at the bank. Some of the most important changes introduced by Resolution No. 208/2011 included excluding from the concentration limit short-term exposures related to cash transfer, modifying reporting obligations, and excluding from the concentration limit exposures reserved by CRD II for the assessment of national regulators.

5 Resolution No. 258/2011 of the Polish Financial Supervision Authority of 4 October 2011 on detailed principles of the operation of the risk management system and the internal control system and detailed conditions for estimation of internal capital by banks and for reviews of the internal capital retention and estimation process and the principles of determining the policy of variable components of the remunerations of persons in managerial positions at banks – the resolution introduced changes associated with the need to transpose CRD II and CRD III. CRD II is implemented through a regulation that requires banks to include reputational risk (applicable to complex structures and products) in their securitization risk management procedures and also requires investing banks (in addition to sponsoring and originating banks) to develop such procedures. CRD III is transposed by regulations concerning the principles of determining the policy of variable components of the remunerations of persons in managerial positions at banks.

6 Resolution No. 259/2011 of the Polish Financial Supervision Authority of 4 October 2011 amending Resolution No. 385/2008 of the Polish Financial Supervision Authority on detailed principles and manner of disclosure by banks of qualitative and quantitative information pertaining to capital adequacy and the scope of information subject to disclosure – the resolution introduced changes associated with the need to transpose CRD III. The amendments to the resolution are associated with the regulations, introduced in Resolution No. 258/2011 of the Polish Financial Supervision Authority, transposing CRD III and concerning the principles of determining the policy of variable components of the remunerations of persons in managerial positions at banks. The new regulations introduced the requirement to publicly disclose: information concerning the process of determining the policy of variable remuneration components; most important information concerning changes in remunerations (in particular with respect to performance).

7 Resolution No. 324/2011 of the Polish Financial Supervision Authority of 20 December 2011, amending Resolution No. 76/2010 of the Polish Financial Supervision Authority on the scope and detailed procedures for determining capital requirements for particular risks and Resolution

No. 386/2008 of the Polish Financial Supervision Authority on determining liquidity standards binding on banks.

8 Resolution No. 325/2011 of the Polish Financial Supervision Authority of 20 December 2011 on other deductions from the capital base, their amount, their scope and conditions of their deduction from a bank's capital base, other balance sheet items included in the supplementary capital, their amount, their scope and the conditions of their inclusion in the supplementary capital, deductions from the supplementary capital, their amount, their scope and conditions of their deduction from the supplementary capital and the scope and manner of treating the activity of banks that are members of conglomerates in calculating own funds – the Resolution was a consolidated text prepared in connection with implementing CRD III. It superseded Resolution No. 367/2010 of the PSFA of 12 October 2010, which amended Resolution No. 381/2008 of the PSFA of 17 December 2008 and in order to eliminate any formal concerns, both resolutions were repealed.

9 Resolution No. 326/2011 of the Polish Financial Supervision Authority of 20 December 2011 amending Resolution No. 385/2008 of the Polish Financial Supervision Authority on detailed principles and the manner of disclosure by banks of qualitative and quantitative information pertaining to capital adequacy and the scope of information subject to disclosure The resolution introduced changes associated with the need to transpose CRD III.

In 2012, the PSFA adopted three subsequent resolutions, amending domestic regulation to the EU requirements:

1 Resolution No. 172/2012 of the Polish Financial Supervision Authority of 19 June 2012 amending the resolution on the scope and detailed rules for determining capital requirements for particular types of risk – the Resolution was adopted, among others, in order to:
   - follow the modified supervisory practice and the changes caused by implementation of EBA GL45 guidelines for AMA and the needs to make analogical changes for IRB and VaR approaches, aimed at revising and organizing the regulations for the content of the applications for approval to use the IRB approach, VaR method and AMA for operational risk;
   - ensure consistent approach to the duty to comply by the bank with the requirements as applicable for IRB approach, VaR method, mixed method and AMA as well as the procedure in case a bank no longer satisfies the application requirements for those models;
   - follow the revision of Resolution No. 208/2011 of 22 August 2011 on detailed rules and conditions for considering exposure when determining the observance of the exposure concentration limit and the large exposure limit – incorporation of the new title of the resolution.

2 Resolution No. 173/2012 of the Polish Financial Supervision Authority of 19 June 2012 amending the resolution on the detailed rules and conditions for taking account of exposure when determining compliance with the limit of exposure concentration and the limit of large exposures, and amending the resolution on the requirements for identifying, monitoring and controlling exposure concentrations, including large exposures – the Resolution amended Resolution No. 208/2011 of the PFSA on detailed rules and conditions for considering exposure when determining the observance of the exposure concentration limit and the large exposure limit. It introduced changes in response to the need to perform the activities whereby the Polish banking sector would be prepared for the planned regulatory changes following implementation of the new EU regulations: CRR/CRD IV (see PFSA, 2012).

3 Resolution No. 307/2012 of the Polish Financial Supervision Authority of 20 November 2012 amending the Resolution on the scope and detailed rules for determining capital requirements for particular types of risk – the Resolution extended the applicability period for the regulations on the calculation of the total capital requirement benchmark for the year 2013 so as to ensure continuity of those regulations' application, also included in the proposal for a regulation of the European Parliament and of the Council on prudential requirements for credit institutions and investment firms (CRR). Previously, the regulations were effective until 31 December 2012. The period was extended versus the one set out in Directive 2006/48/EC, since the effective date for CRR was then planned for 1 January 2013.

4.2 Changes in the deposit guarantee scheme

The reconstruction of the Polish banking system required, among other things, also the establishment of an institution that would deal with banking deposit guarantees. On February 1995 such an organizational body in form of the Bank Guarantee Fund (BGF) was established (the Act on the Bank Guarantee Fund of 14 December 1994). According to the law, the basic tasks of the Fund included, inter alia: reimbursement of funds accumulated on bank accounts in the event of the bankruptcy of a bank which is a participant in the deposit guarantee scheme as well as financial assistance to banks which have found themselves faced with a loss of solvency and are engaging in independent reforms. The entities covered by the guarantee system contribute compulsory annual payments to the Fund and are obliged to establish a protection fund for guaranteed funds.

In more detail, the Act covered the following specifics: principles of establishment and operation of obligatory and contractual guarantees of bank account funds, types of action that may be taken to assist entities covered by the obligatory system of funds guarantees in cases of dangers of insolvency, as well as principles for collecting and using information regarding entities covered by the guarantee system. The banks covered by the guarantee system contribute compulsory annual payments to the Fund and are obliged to establish a protection fund for guaranteed funds. Treasury securities and the National Bank of Poland money-market bills, deposited on a separate account, are assets that cover this fund. In addition, assets that cover the protection fund of guaranteed funds must not be pledged or be charged in any form and not be subject to a court or administrative enforcement.

The objective of the compulsory guarantee system of bank account deposits was to ensure that the depositors may be repaid funds collected on those accounts up to the amount specified by the Act. According to the initial provisions of the Act, deposits up to the zloty equivalent of €1000 were entirely covered by a full guarantee. The upper limit of funds guaranteed at 90 per cent rose in 2001 to €15,000 (in 2002 this rose to €17,000, and in 2003 to €22,500).

The legislator also specified the deposit guarantee principles. Deposits maintained in all banks with their registered offices within the territory of the Republic of Poland were covered by the Fund. In the event of the bankruptcy of a domestic bank, the BGF was obliged to pay the guaranteed funds up to the amount determined by law, except for the deposits of, inter alia: the State Treasury, banks, brokerage houses, pensions funds, investment funds, entities providing insurance services, managers of the bank and its main shareholders (holding at least 5 per cent of the shares).

The current legal provisions on the BGF are in full compliance with Directive 2009/14/EC of the European Parliament and of the Council of 11 March 2009, which amends Directive 94/19/EC on deposit-guarantee schemes. After the outburst of the global financial crisis the most important changes in the functioning of the BGF took place in 2010. In the very year two amendments to the Act on the Bank Guarantee Fund were adopted, that made the law consistent with changes in the EU legislation.

The first amendment of 10 June 2010 amended the principles for remunerating members of the Fund's Council. In accordance with the new regulations, remuneration for participation in a meeting of the BGF Council was replaced with a monthly remuneration consisting of a fixed part and a variable part. These measures made the amount of the variable part conditional on the presence of the member of the Council at its meetings and on the frequency of the meetings in a given month.

The second amendment to the Act on the Bank Guarantee Fund, dated 16 December 2010, was of much greater importance to the domestic financial market. It was aimed at fully adapting Polish law to the provisions of European law.[12] The most significant changes consisted in:

- raising deposit guarantees from the PLN equivalent of €50,000 to the zloty equivalent of €100,000;[13]
- shortening the period for paying out guaranteed funds to 20 working days;
- obliging banks to draw up and maintain an up-to-date list of depositors;

- shortening the period within which the PFSA is obliged to take a decision on the suspension of a bank's operations if for reasons directly related to the bank's financial standing the bank fails to fulfil its commitments with respect to paying out guaranteed funds.

The second amendment to the Act also changed the principles according to which the National Bank of Poland may extend a loan to the BGF. The provisions of Article 16a (6) of the Act specify that such a loan will be possible if the BGF exhausts the assets held in its dedicated funds allocated to the payout of guaranteed deposits and if the stability of the domestic financial system is at risk. Moreover, similarly as in the case of the previously applicable regulations, such a loan may be provided to the BGF on condition that appropriate collateral for the NBP is established.

4.3 Accounting

The adoption by the Sejm of the Republic of Poland of the Accounting Act in 1994 and issuing regulations based on it had a crucial importance for the development of principles of bank accounting throughout the 1990s. The regulations of special importance specifically concerned here were Regulation No. 1/95 of the President of the NBP on particular principles of bank accounting and the preparation of additional information of 16 February 1995 and Regulation No. 10/95 of the President of the NBP on particular principles of drawing up consolidated financial statements by banks of December 1995. The regulations were adjusted to the European Union requirements, including Directive 86/635/EEC.

On the basis of provisions of the Accounting Act, requirements on bookkeeping for banks, the drawing up of financial statements, assets and liabilities valuation and determination of earnings were specified in the regulations of the President of the NBP. The scope of information presented as notes to the financial statements was also defined. The requirements on auditing and publishing the financial statements were also specified.

The Regulations of the President of the NBP on bank accounting were then replaced in 1998, because of formal requirements, with resolutions of the Commission for Banking Supervision. The resolutions, however, did not change substantially the principles of bank accounting.

Another amendment to the Accounting Act was made in November 2000. Its implementation at the beginning of 2002 coincided with the issuance of specific provisions adjusted to it in the field of bank accounting. New regulations were to a larger extent adjusted to International Accounting Standards (IAS). The issues connected with the valuation and presentation of financial instruments were regulated in a more precise way. The accounting principles for hedging consistent with the concept provided in IAS 39 were admitted to use. The scope of notes to the financial statements was also expanded, e.g. by the information on hedging by banks against individual risks resulting from the banking operations.

Generally, according to the World Bank Report (2005), very significant progress was achieved by Poland in the area of accounting, financial reporting and auditing. It was stated in the report that financial companies were required to prepare their financial statements in conformity with Polish accounting requirements, based on the Fourth and Seventh European Union Company Law Directives, and provide a simplified financial reporting framework for small and medium-sized enterprises. Banks were required to prepare their consolidated financial statements in conformity with endorsed International Financial Reporting Standards (IFRS), and their legal entity financial statements in conformity, either with accounting regulations set by the Minister of Finance based on the Banking Accounts Directive, or with endorsed IFRS. Insurance companies were required to prepare their financial statements in conformity with accounting regulations set by the Minister of Finance based on the Insurance Accounts Directive.

After the outburst of the financial crisis some adjustments in accounting and auditing of financial institutions were, however, needed. The Regulation of the Minister of Finance on special accounting principles of banks, applicable since 30 October 2010, implemented new measures introduced by the Act on Trading in Financial Instruments in 2009. The Act repealed the obligation providing for a financial separation of brokerage activities carried out by a bank, the requirement to establish separate share capital for such activities, to keep separate accounting books and draw up separate financial statements.

The provisions of the Regulation were supplemented accordingly with relevant accounting principles, pertaining to:

- presenting operations related to the bank and the brokerage house in the accounting books;
- presenting and valuing financial assets and liabilities of banks, including financial instruments acquired for a bank and on its own account and held in the securities accounts of clients by the brokerage house,
- recording and valuing financial instruments of clients.

Another important amendment to this Regulation was the extension of the scope of additional information relating to significant events from previous years which were presented in the financial statements for a given period. It concerned, inter alia, the type of errors made and the amount of correction.

In order to achieve greater comparability of financial statements of banks, the Regulation introduced principles applied by the IAS. A new category 'financial assets and liabilities at fair value through profit or loss', including 'financial assets and liabilities held for trading' was introduced. The definition of financial assets and liabilities, as well as their classification, was adapted to the requirements of IAS 39. The obligation to disclose information concerning fixed assets held for sale and the requirement of valuation and disclosure in the financial statement of the value of shares held for sale in subsidiaries were also introduced.

In addition, the new provisions made it possible to reclassify financial assets from the category of 'financial assets and liabilities at fair value through profit or loss' to other categories of assets. The measures first applied to financial statements drawn up for the financial year starting in 2010.

5 Changes in regulatory frameworks after the crisis: selected domestic regulations

Apart from changes in regulations aimed at ensuring compatibility of the Polish law with the requirements of the EU, some specific additional regulations were also adopted in Poland. They included acts and directives, as well as recommendations of the PSFA. The latter ones have no strictly binding character, nevertheless, banks usually obey them.

In February of 2010 the Act on the Recapitalization of Certain Financial Institutions (Journal of Laws of 2010, No. 40, item 226) was adopted. It was aimed at creating a legal basis for the State Treasury to recapitalize financial institutions which are at risk of losing liquidity or becoming insolvent. The Act introduced two methods of recapitalization of financial institutions: the State Treasury granting guarantees of increasing the capital of financial institutions and, secondly, the right of the State Treasury to perform a compulsory acquisition of a financial institution.

The new provisions allowed domestic banks and insurance companies to obtain State Treasury guarantees when increasing their own capital under recovery proceedings. As a result, such financial institutions will be able to increase their share capital through the issue of shares, bonds or bank securities (in the case of banks) without the risk that such securities are not taken up by new investors or existing shareholders. A guarantee of the State Treasury may be obtained only on condition that the recovery programme is accepted by the Polish Financial Supervision Authority. In accordance with the provisions of the Act, the guarantee will be granted by the Minister of Finance at the request of a financial institution in the form of an agreement, after having consulted the PFSA and the President of the NBP and, in the case of banks, also the Bank Guarantee Fund.

The second recapitalization method involves the State Treasury acquiring a financial institution by means of a compulsory buyout of shares from its existing shareholders. Such a compulsory acquisition will be possible in the case where a financial institution is at risk of losing its solvency or in the case of the financial institution's serious infringement of the terms and conditions of the State Treasury guarantee agreement referred to in the previous paragraph. Only if statutory conditions specified in Article 14(1) and Article 9(2) are met, the Council of Ministers will be able to acquire the financial institution on behalf of the State Treasury by means of an administrative decision. Such a decision will be taken at the request of the Minister of Finance after having consulted the President of the NBP and the Chairperson of the PFSA and, in the case of banks, the BGF.

With reference to risk management and adequate functioning of banks in Poland, recommendations of the PSFA[14] are of crucial importance, despite their non-binding character. After the 2007 the PFSA, observing rapid growth of lending to retail banking clients and intending to avoid potential problems with liquidity and the growing scale of irregular loans, took actions aimed at limiting the excessive indebtedness of households and improving credit risk management at banks.

In order to increase protection for market participants, on 17 December 2008 the PFSA adopted a resolution introducing Recommendation S II. The Recommendation introduced suggestions that are additional to those included in Recommendation S, related to the obligation to inform customers about currency spread, burdens and risk related to differences between the sell rate and buy rate of foreign currencies before and during the period of validity of the credit agreement in the case of loans granted in foreign currency or indexed to foreign currency. In accordance with the new recommendations, the banks should permit the customer upon request to repay instalments in the indexation currency in the case of a loan indexed to foreign currency (change in the manner of repayment should cover all instalments from the date of amendment of the agreement, which means that it may occur only once throughout the agreement validity period). The PFSA expected that these amendments improve the relations between banks and customers, as the latter ones would have been better informed about the consequences of their decisions.

Another step in actions aimed at strengthening banks' positions and their stability was Recommendation T, adopted on 23 February 2010 (PFSA Resolution 52/2010). This recommendation was a collection of best practices in retail lending and was based on the principle of fair examination of customers' creditworthiness The recommendations contained in the document set forth the principles of analysis of creditworthiness of clients, the relation of collateral to debt for retail loans, including loans indexed to changes in FX rates, and introduce limits of the level of general debt in relation to the borrower's income. According to the guidelines of the PFSA, the loan repayment burden on income should not exceed the level of 50 per cent of net income in the case of borrowers with income not exceeding the average level in the economy. With respect to other borrowers, this threshold should not exceed 65 per cent of net income. A significant element of the Recommendation was the instruction that banks should also take into consideration debt limits of credit cards and limits of revolving credit facilities, even if they are not fully used, when calculating the client's creditworthiness. Recommendation T also introduced guidelines for banks concerning the verification of the value of the potential borrower's income, monitoring of the timeliness of the client's debt repayment and the use of databases containing information on the borrower's debt level and the history of repayment of their liabilities.

Another recommendation prepared by the PSFA that entered into force on 1 July 2010, was Recommendation I concerning the management of currency risk at banks and rules of execution of transactions carrying currency risk (PFSA Resolution 53/2010 of 23 February 2010). This Recommendation replaced the previous Recommendation I issued by the Commission for Banking Supervision in 2002. It was the amendment aimed at reducing the credit risk associated with the conclusion of foreign currency lending transactions and at improving management within banks of foreign exchange risk. The PFSA guidelines extended the process of currency risk management by requiring banks to examine the impact of changes in FX rates on the counterparty's credit risk. In order to enhance the protection of the client's interests, it is recommended that banks inform the client on potential liabilities towards the bank which may arise as a result of a significant change in the FX rate, and present a simulation of the effect of various changes in the FX rate on the result of the transaction before closing a transaction exposed to currency risk. The Recommendation also prescribed that banks offer clients primarily simple currency derivatives such as forward transactions and options. Moreover, it was assumed that banks, before concluding a transaction, should try to identify the character of the client's activities, their awareness of credit risk and the need to secure against that risk.

The third recommendation enforced in 2010 was Recommendation A on the management of risk related to derivatives transactions executed by banks (PFSA Resolution 134/2010 of 5 May 2010). The adoption of the recommendation by the PFSA was aimed at improving the quality of risk management associated with banks concluding derivative transactions or transactions with embedded derivatives, as well as at defining the principles for concluding such transactions by banks. The recommendations, which came into force on 1 August 2010, concerned the monitoring and control of risk (in particular, counterparty credit risk), the documentation and exchange of information with clients, as well as the introduction of procedures making it possible to streamline the information flow between the bank's units responsible for risk management.

Recommendation A specified also that banks should examine whether clients conclude transactions involving derivatives for speculative purposes or in order to hedge against risk related to their economic activities. Banks should also monitor whether such risk-hedging transactions involving derivatives lead to heightened risk in situations of adverse market parameters. Moreover, the Recommendation contained instructions according to which banks should conduct simulations of the valuation of the counterparty's exposures related to currency derivatives, including the hedged position.

In 2011 three other recommendation were adopted/amended. The first one was Recommendation H concerning internal control at banks. The need to amend Recommendation H resulted from implementing provisions concerning internal control at banks in the Banking Act of 29 August 1997 and Resolution No. 383/2008 of the Polish Financial Supervision Authority of 17 December 2008 on detailed principles of the operation of risk management and internal control systems and detailed conditions of estimating internal capital by banks and reviewing the process of estimating and maintaining such capital.

The second recommendation amended in 2011 was Recommendation S on good practices in the management of credit exposures financing real estate and secured by a mortgage. Among the reasons behind the amendment of the recommendation the following were indicated (PSFA, 2011):

- the risk associated with a growing share of the portfolio of mortgage-backed credit exposures and credit exposures financing real estate in dues from the non-financial sector;
- harmonization of Recommendation S II and Recommendation T concerning best practices in managing credit exposures financing real estate and mortgage-backed credit exposures;
- insufficient effectiveness of Recommendation S II;
- the need to protect the Polish banking sector against disruptions such as those suffered by a banking sectors of other economies in the CEE region, which were caused by unrestricted foreign-currency lending to households.

The last recommendation from 2011 was amended Recommendation R concerning the rules for identification of impaired balance-sheet credit exposures, calculation of impairment losses on balance-sheet credit exposures and provisions for off-balance-sheet credit exposures. The amendment of the recommendation resulted from the need to adjust it to current market practice and the fact that its then-current version was implemented at a time when the provisions of international regulations were only starting to be effective in Poland and banks did not yet have the requisite knowledge and experience in that regard.

Among the most important changes brought by this recommendation were: verification of the adequacy of the parameters used in calculating impairment losses, developing a methodology for applying balance sheet credit exposures to restructured balance sheet credit exposures, which, among other things, contained a definition of a restructured balance sheet credit exposure and the conditions for impairment of these items, and an indication of the conditions for reclassification of exposure as exposure without impairment, frequency of conducting reviews associated with banks' historical data.

Recommendation R was addressed to banks operating in Poland that prepare consolidated or separate financial statements in accordance with the IAS/IFRS. The guidelines contained in Recommendation R also applied to branches of a domestic bank and the bank's subsidiaries located outside of Poland, taking into account the legal environment of local markets and the feasibility of ensuring compliance with the good practices set forth in the recommendation (PSFA, 2011).

In 2012, the Polish Financial Supervision Authority adopted Recommendation J concerning the principles of gathering and processing real estate data by banks. Recommendation J provided the guidelines for creating and using external (interbank) real estate market databases by banks, which would contribute to improved risk management market standards for mortgaged-backed credit exposures. The main changes made subsequently to the amended Recommendation J encompassed recommendation of uniform standards for gathering, processing and making available real estate market data in reliable databases, description of the set of characteristics identifying real estates which should be gathered in the database and recommendation of use of statistical models to assess the risk of change in value of real estate-based collateral for the banks with significant mortgage-backed exposures.

6 Conclusions

Generally, described changes in the Polish financial regulatory frameworks turned out to be effective. Adoption of the new regulations (and modification of those already existing) helped to avoid turmoil in the Polish financial systems. No financial institution was bankrupted and there were no drastic tensions on the financial market. There were also no real threats for stability of the financial system nor any serious fears of insufficient liquidity of financial institutions.[15] Also non-performing loans were in principle under control (some problems occurred only temporarily). At the same time, the banks in Poland recorded significant levels of incomes (see Janc, Jurek and Marszałek, 2013 or National Bank of Poland, 2014). Moreover, performance of other types of financial intermediaries also may be perceived as satisfying.

In detail, according to the PFSA (2010, 2011), the new regulatory framework (combined with other factors, like for example high investment outlays made by the public sector, the floating exchange rate, relatively low development of the financial market and rather local character of the banking system) contributed, among other things, to:

- maintaining stability of individual segments of the financial system;
- securing liquidity of both the banking and insurance systems, as well as reinforcing their capital position;
- smaller demand for financing offered by the National Bank of Poland;
- growth of confidence in the financial institutions;
- adjustments leading to more favourable structuring of loans.

It must be noticed, however, that the introduction of the new regulations may be connected with some threats to the Polish financial institutions (mainly banks), Namely, the costs of implementation of some new mechanisms and rules might be too high, especially for smaller financial intermediaries. This applies also to participation in the European banking union.

Notes

1 It has to be stressed that some consequences of this underdevelopment (especially with reference to the cooperative banks) seem to last even until now (National Bank of Poland, 2014).

2 However, according to Kokoszczyński (2006), in the Polish banking system a classic example of a monobank had never existed. There were a few so-called specialized banks, formal monopolists in particular fields of banking activity (e.g. foreign currency operations or agriculture).

3 In 1989 initial capital required for establishment of a new bank amounted to only circa US$1 million.

4 Initially, there was only one bank with dominant foreign capital. However, the situation changed very fast and foreign investors started to prevail within the banking system, amounting currently to around two-thirds of funds, assets and equity (Jurek, 2014).

5 Poland finished the accession negotiations in December 2002. Then the Accession Treaty was signed in Athens on 16 April 2003. After the ratification of that Treaty, Poland became the member of EU on 1 May 2004.

6 For instance, the insurance market was re-regulated with the passing of the *Insurance Activity Act*, the *Insurance Brokerage Act* and the *Compulsory Insurance, Insurance Guarantee Fund and Polish Motors Insurers' Bureau Act* – all of them of 22 May 2003.

7 The third part of the legislative package passed then was the Act on Mortgage Bonds and Mortgage Banks (Journal of Laws, 1997, No. 140, item 940). It determined the principles of issue, purchase, and redemption of mortgage bonds as well as the principles of establishment, organisation, operation and supervision over mortgage banks.

8 Controversy arose only in 2006–2007 when legislation setting up a new integrated financial supervisory authority came into force.

9 A separate institutional solution, but of high importance, was the creation of a Financial Stability Committee. It existed informally since 2007 but officially it was established just in 2008.

10 Resolution No. 380/2008 of the Polish Financial Supervision Authority of 17 December 2008 on the scope and detailed rules for determination of capital requirements for individual types of risk and the detailed principles to be applied in determining those requirements, including but not limited to, the scope and conditions of applying statistical methods and the scope of information attached to applications for authorisation to apply them, principles and conditions of taking account of contracts on debt assignment, subparticipation, credit derivatives and contracts other than those on debt assignment, and subparticipation, in calculating the capital requirements, terms and conditions, scope and manner of making use of the ratings assigned by external credit assessment institutions and the export credit agencies, manner and specific principles for calculation of the capital adequacy ratio of a bank, the scope and manner of taking account of banks conducting their activities in groups in calculating their capital requirements as well as establishing additional items of bank balance sheets included in bank regulatory own funds in the capital adequacy account, the amount thereof and the conditions to be used in calculating them (Official Journal of the PFSA of 2008, No. 8, item 34, as amended).

11 For instance, Article 14 of the resolution included the planned amendment to Article 152 of Directive 2006/48/EC extending until 31 December 2011, the transition period during which banks applying advanced methods for determining the capital requirements for credit and operational risk (IRB, AMA) were required to maintain regulatory capital at a level no lower than 80 per cent of the comparative

total capital requirement calculated in accordance with the principles of the Basel I Accord.

12 Directive 2009/14/EC of the European Parliament and of the Council of 11 March 2009 amending Directive 94/19/EC on deposit-guarantee schemes as regards the coverage level and the payout delay (EU Official Journal L 68 of 2009, p. 3).

13 Since 2010, a deposit amount not exceeding the zloty equivalent of €100,000 has been guaranteed in full. The guaranteed amount is as before calculated from the total funds located in all the accounts of a single person in a given bank, while in the case of a joint account, each account holder is entitled to a separate guaranteed amount.

14 Before mentioned in Section 3. institutional changes in Polish supervision recommendations were prepared by the General Inspectorate of Banking Supervision. During the years 1996–2000, this body prepared 11 recommendations, concerning different aspects of risk management in banks.

15 It must be stressed that in Poland, unlike other countries of the region, the scale of foreign financing, providing by the parent banks to their subsidiaries operating in Poland, did not decrease. Contrary, its dynamics after 2008 even accelerated.

References

Act Amending the Banking Act and Other Acts of 1 April 2004, Journal of Laws No. 91/2004, Item 870.

Act of 12 February 2010 on the Recapitalization of Certain Financial Institutions, Journal of Laws No. 40/2010, Item 226.

Act of 21 July 2006 on Financial Market Supervision, Journal of Laws No. 157/2006, Item 1119.

Act of 26 January 2007 Amending the Foreign Exchange Law Act and Other Acts, Journal of Laws No. 61/2007, Item 410.

Act of 31 January 1989 – The Banking Law, Journal of Laws No. 72/1992, Item 359, as amended.

Act of 27 July 2002 – Foreign Exchange Law, Journal of Laws No. 141/2008, Item 1178 as amended.

Act on the Bank Guarantee Fund of 14 December 1994, consolidated text in Journal of Laws No. 84/2009, Item 711.

Act on Mortgage Bonds and Mortgage Banks, the Journal of Laws, 1997, No. 140, Item 940).

Act on the National Bank of Poland of 29 August 1997, Journal of Laws No. 140, Item 938, with later amendments.

Act on the so-called Prevention of Usury repealed Article 18 of the Bonds Act of 29 June 1995, consolidated text in Journal of Laws No. 1300/2001, Item 120, as amended.

Act on Compulsory Insurance, the Insurance Guarantee Fund and the Polish Motor Insurers' Bureau of 22 May 2003, Journal of Laws No. 124/2003, Item 1152.

Banking Act of 29 August 1997, Journal of Laws No. 140/1997, Item 939.

Insurance Intermediation Act of 22 May 2004, Journal of Laws No. 124/2004, Item 1154.

JANC, A. (2004) *Modern Banking in Transition Economies of Central and Eastern Europe*. Poznań: Poznań University of Economics Publishing.

JANC, A., JUREK, M. and MARSZAŁEK, P. (2013) *Financial System in Poland.* FESSUD Studies in Financial Systems. No. 7.

JUREK, M. (2014) *The Structure of Ownership in the Financial Sector across the European Union*. Poznań: Poznań University of Economics Publishing.

KOKOSZCZYŃSKI, R. (2004) *Modern Monetary Policy in Poland* (*Współczesna polityka pieniężna w Polsce*). Warszawa: PWE.

KOWALSKI, T. and MATYSEK-JEDRYCH, A. (2010) Changes in the banking law vs. the performance of banks in Poland in 1997–2008. In: Kowalski, T., Letza, S. and Wihlborg, C. (eds), *Insitutional Change in the European Transition Economies: The Case of Poland*. Poznań: Poznań University of Economics Publishing.

KOWALSKI, T. (2010) Comparative analysis of economic transformation in Poland and selected Central European Countries, in: Kowalski, T., Letza, S. and Wihlborg, C. (eds), *Institutional change in the European Transition Economies: The case of Poland*. Poznań: Poznań University of Economics Publishing.

NATIONAL BANK OF POLAND (2001) *The Polish Banking System in the Nineties*. Warsaw.

NATIONAL BANK OF POLAND (2002) *Financial Market in Poland 1998–2001*. Warsaw.

NATIONAL BANK OF POLAND (2004) *Financial System Development in Poland 2002–2003*. Warsaw.

NATIONAL BANK OF POLAND (2006a) *Financial Stability Report 2005*. Warsaw.

NATIONAL BANK OF POLAND (2006b) *Financial System Development in Poland 2004*. Warsaw.

NATIONAL BANK OF POLAND (2010) *Financial System Development in Poland 2007*. Warsaw.

NATIONAL BANK OF POLAND (2013) *Financial System Development in Poland 2010*. Warsaw.

NATIONAL BANK OF POLAND (2014) *Financial System Development in Poland 2011*. Warsaw.

PFSA (2010) Polish financial market in the face of the global financial crisis of 2008–2009. Warsaw.

PFSA (2011) Report on the activities of the Polish Financial Supervision Authority in 2010. Warsaw.

PFSA (2012) Report on the activities of the Polish Financial Supervision Authority in 2011. Warsaw.

Resolution No. 314/2009 on other items of a bank's balance sheet included in tier-1 capital, their amount, scope and conditions of inclusion in a bank's tier-1 capital –Official Journal of the PFSA of 2009, No. 1, item 8

Resolution No. 380/2008 of the Polish Financial Supervision Authority of 17 December 2008 on the scope and detailed rules for determination of capital requirements for individual types of risk and the detailed principles to be applied in determining those requirements, including but not limited to, the scope and conditions of applying statistical methods and the scope of information attached to applications for authorization to apply them, principles and conditions of taking account of contracts on debt assignment, subparticipation, credit derivatives and contracts other than those on debt assignment, and subparticipation, in calculating the capital requirements, terms and conditions, scope and manner of making use of the ratings assigned by external credit assessment institutions and the export credit agencies, manner and specific principles for calculation of the capital adequacy ratio of a bank, the scope and manner of taking account of banks conducting their activities in groups in calculating their capital requirements as well as establishing additional items of bank balance sheets included in bank regulatory own funds in the capital adequacy account, the amount thereof and the conditions to be used in calculating them (Official Journal of the PFSA of 2008, No. 8, item 34, as amended).

Resolution No. 381/2008 of the PFSA of 17 December 2008 on other deductions from original own funds, their value, scope and conditions for a deduction of these items from the bank's original own funds, other bank's balance sheet items that are included into the bank's supplementary own funds, their, scope, and conditions of their inclusion in the bank's supplementary own funds, reductions of supplementary own funds, their value, scope and conditions for a deduction of such items from the banks' supplementary own funds; and the scope and method of including banks' activities in holdings when calculating own funds

Resolution No.385/2008 of the PFSA of 17 December 2008 on detailed principles and methods of publication of qualitative and quantitative information on capital adequacy by banks and the scope of published information

The Constitution of the Republic of Poland of April 2, 1997 (1997).

World Bank (2005) *Report on the Observance of Standard and Codes (ROSC)*. Corporate Governance. Poland, June 2005, Washington DC.

9 Financial regulation in Slovenia

Creation, adaptation and collapse

Jože Mencinger

1 Introduction

1.1 The creation and development of the country

The proclamation of the country's independence on 26 June 1991 coincided with unresolved disputes over custom duties. Yugoslav federal authorities intervened by an attempt to grab the control of the borders. The army was, however, badly surprised by the resistance. After a week of fighting between the Yugoslav army on one side and Slovenian territorial defence and police on the other, the Brioni ceasefire was attained. In accordance with it, Slovenia had to defer the implementation of independence activity for three months. On 8 October 1991, the moratorium expired and Slovenia introduced its own currency – the Slovenian tolar; the country became 'fully independent'. This ended tense and uncertain political and economic developments in the 1980s and, definitely so, in 1990[1] when the political future of Slovenia was not yet firmly established and the shape of a future arrangement within Yugoslavia was unknown. Consequently, the new Slovenian government, installed after elections in April 1990, began cautious preparation for a likely collapse of Yugoslavia by gradually acquiring control over its economic policy and economic system. What remained unknown was the level of the disintegration, the way in which Yugoslavia would disintegrate, and when this would happen.[2] Indeed, separation from Yugoslavia was a kind of an 'emergency exit'.

Slovenia has been often considered 'a success story' of transition; early economic performances were satisfactory and the social costs of transition were rather low. The reasons for that can be sought in two major directions: initial conditions and patterns of transition. First, many essentials of a market economy were created before 1989; enterprises were autonomous, basic market institutions existed, and the government could use many standard economic policy tools. Second, Slovenia, the richest of former socialist CEE countries could afford to implement macroeconomic stabilization cautiously with pragmatism and risk aversion while refusing patronage of international financial institutions and foreign advisers.

Four periods can be distinguished in a brief economic history of the country: a short period of transitional depression (1991–1992), a decade of balanced economic and social development (1993–2004), the 'gambling' period (2005–2008), and the crisis period (2009–). In1993, Slovenia reached the bottom of transitional depression. After two years, the benefits of secession appeared to prevail over its costs. While the costs of reorienting trade from protected to competitive markets were significant, the secession intensified economic restructuring, pushed for sound economic policy, and enabled creation of a 'normal' economic system. GDP grew at a more or less constant rate of 4 per cent annually, inflation was gradually lowered, the state budget was nearly balanced, public debt amounted to 30 per cent of GDP only, surplus in trade of services outweighed the deficit in trade of goods, and foreign exchange reserves more than matched foreign debt. Social cohesion was retained.

Monetary policy was crucial for preserving the tolar and enhancing its role in a small currency area dominated by the Deutschmark as a measure of value, means of savings, and even transaction instrument. Foreign exchange transactions became the channel of money creation; the regulation of money supply and banks' liquidity shifted to open market operations and prudential regulation. After cautiously removing initial administrative restrictions on foreign exchange flows, monetary policy intervened sensibly to prevent substantial real appreciations of the tolar which would result from excess supply of foreign exchange. Thus, monetary policy became trapped in conflicting goals: to lower and keep inflation under control or to prevent real appreciation of the tolar. The Bank of Slovenia (BS) opted for prevention of excessive real appreciation as the major goal, leaving disinflation to be handled by increased competition.

'Back to Europe' was a slogan of the last decade of the twentieth century and the ultimate goal of all former socialist countries in Central and Eastern Europe, Slovenia included. A new 'emergency exit' appeared with a delay but continued rather smoothly. In 1999, the country began preparations for joining the EU and EMU which required changes in economic policies, particularly the opening of the capital market. When entering the EU in 2004, Slovenia already fulfilled four Maastricht criteria and immediately assumed ERM2 status. In February 2005, the national master plan for the introduction of the euro was formally adopted. Contrary to hasty and uncertain procedures in conversion from the dinar to the tolar in 1991, the procedures in the conversion from tolar to euro were precisely scheduled and the changeover on 1 January 2007 was smooth. However, in the process of accepting the EU 'aquis', Slovenia was gradually losing control of economic policies. By entering the EU in May 2004 and ERM2 in July 2004, Slovenia also formally lost its monetary policy and surrendered a large part of its fiscal policies. In a decade, a newly born national economy turned again to a regional economy. The entry into the EU and EMU coincided with the 'gambling' period; in four 'gambling' years 2005–2008, characterized by high but also extremely unbalanced growth, 'the success story' became questionable. Indeed, after years of steady convergence towards the EU average in terms of GDP per capita, the small and very open economy was severely hit by the global financial crisis.

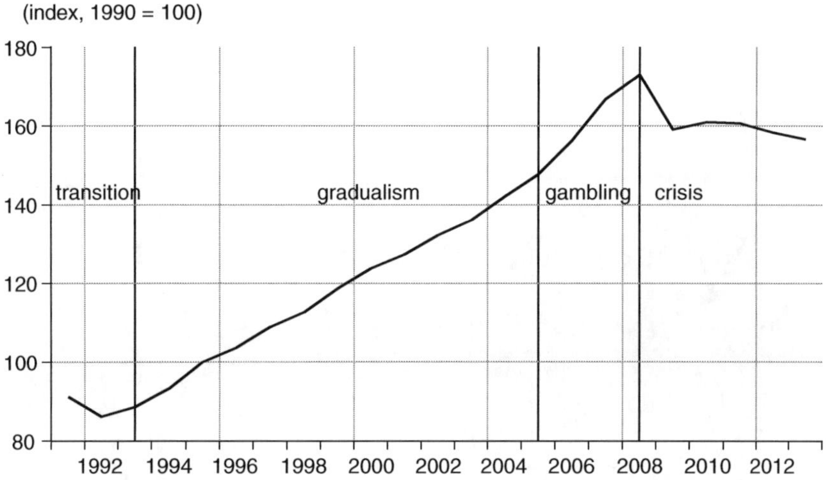

Figure 9.1 Economic development of Slovenia

The imbalances from the gambling years, growing political instability, and social discontent have also severely hindered recovery.

Slovenia's experience after the euro area entry could serve almost as a textbook example of possible outcomes. For example, the rounding up of prices and correction of relative prices which had been under control before conversion to the euro contributed to inflation which was, however, pushed upwards also by the increase of world oil and agricultural products prices. Previous constant growth in the Slovenian share of exports in EU exports disappeared and turned to stagnation of its share, which could be a consequence of the disappearance of exchange rate policy. The unprecedented increase of current account deficit which followed the entry can be explained by relaxation and the replacement of the 'old fashioned' philosophy that one can succeed by working hard with the 'modern' philosophy, by which wealth can be most efficiently created by 'financial deepening', looking for 'opportunities', and buying securities at home and abroad; savings turned to speculations. GDP growth strengthened to 7 per cent per year due to 15 per cent growth in the construction sector and financial services. This was enabled by credits growing at a rate of 30 per cent per year, and after entering the euro area, at a rate surpassing 40 per cent per year. Banks were enthusiastic to cooperate in the 'gambling' by borrowing cheap money in the EU or acquiring it from their mother banks; the inflow of capital in 2007 reached 12 per cent of GDP, half of it was used for buying securities abroad. Net foreign debt increased from €0 in 2005 to €10 billion at the end of 2008 when the crisis hit.

The global financial crisis did not affect Slovenia until the end of 2008. But when the financial and economic crisis deepened, the very open Slovenian economy was unable to avoid the decline. Manufacturing companies were

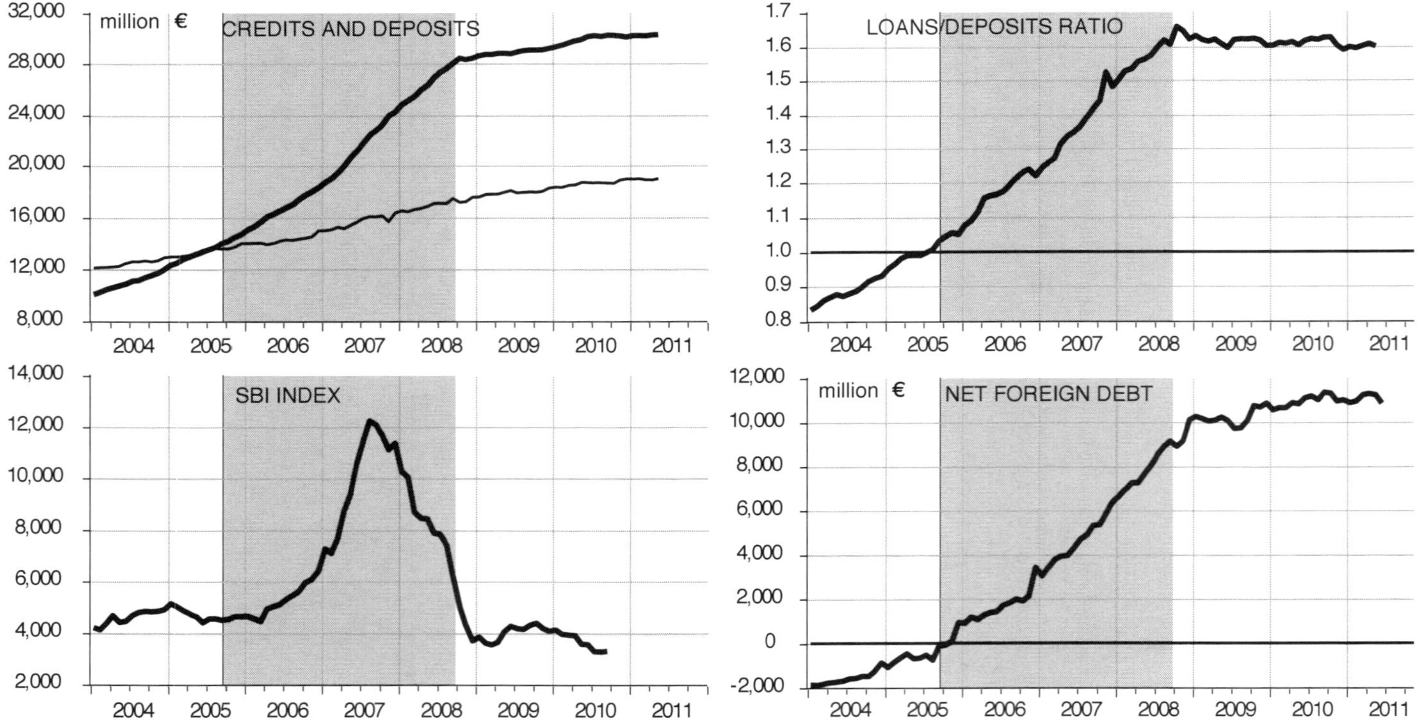

Figure 9.2 Gambling (financial deepening, creation of virtual wealth and foreign indebtedness)

hit by the drop of foreign demand, crippled investments congested construction activity. In 2009, GDP fell by 7.8 per cent, exports by over 15 per cent, gross fixed investments by more than 30 per cent. Active use of fiscal policy helped to make the fall in GDP in 2010 less than it would otherwise had been; the costs were high general government deficit and large increase in public debt. The crisis in domestic demand deepened in 2011, when government consumption declined alongside the contraction in investment and household consumption. The only contribution to GDP growth came from net trade surplus created by export-oriented manufacturing industries and weak domestic demand for imports. In 2012, economic activity in Slovenia declined again much more than in the eurozone. The decline was the result of an accelerated contraction in domestic consumption, caused by government austerity measures, difficult access to financing, and a high level of uncertainty. A yet more significant drop in GDP was again prevented by the positive contribution of net exports; the large current account surplus was largely a result of the narrowing of the merchandise trade deficit. After five years of the financial crisis, the Slovenian economy slid into deeper recession again in 2013; the reasons for the second wave were over-leveraging in non-financial companies and austerity measures.

1.2 Creation of the Financial System

The search for monetary independence in Slovenia began in June 1990 and concentrated on three issues: the consequences of unilateral decisions for the functioning of the financial system and for the relations with other countries and international institutions; the possibilities of a monetary system in a confederation which was at the time considered a viable political solution for Slovenia in Yugoslavia; and the prospects of eventual monetary independence. Actual developments between June 1990 and October 1991 reveal uncertainty and confusion. Already in October 1990, nameless provisional notes were secretly printed, and the debates shifted to the pattern and the most appropriate moment for the introduction of the Slovenian currency. The preparations for monetary independence in Slovenia were at the same time accompanied by attempts to handle the repercussions of a fixed overvalued dinar and to cope with advancing hyperinflation. These attempts are best illustrated by the Introduction of a Parallel Currency Act drafted on 4 February 4, 1991, which envisaged a parallel currency pegged to the Austrian schilling; the new currency would enter circulation through foreign transactions and would float against the dinar. The concept of parallel currency was abandoned in favour of 'the certificate of import privileges' solution which was less risky and would not expose Slovenian banks to the reactions of the federal authorities. The system functioned in the following manner: an exporting company, while obliged to sell foreign exchange to a bank at the official fixed exchange rate of 7 dinars to 1 deutschmark, would also receive a 'certificate' which was saleable and would allow its buyer the access to foreign exchange. The fixed exchange rate plus the price of the certificate totalled the flexible exchange rate. Earlier, in the middle of 1990, the black market of foreign exchange for individuals was abolished by its de facto legalization; anybody possessing foreign exchange (mainly guest workers in Germany and Austria coming from Croatia and Bosnia) could sell it on the streets of Slovenian towns at a market exchange rate which was fluctuating at the level twice the official exchange rate. This created an inflow of foreign exchange and an outflow of dinars from Slovenia, and also an undeterminable amount of 'foreign exchange reserves' kept by the population at their homes or in Austrian and Italian banks. After the so-called 'break' in the Yugoslav monetary system by Serbia at the end of 1990, Slovenia hastened in preparing acts for its own monetary system; all crucial acts were prepared in spring of 1991. The creation of the monetary system was interrupted for three months in July 1991 by the Brioni ceasefire to allow for negotiations on the future of Yugoslavia. Nothing happened, and on 8 October Slovenia introduced its own currency, using provisional notes for transactions in cash. Despite uncertainties and confusions before, the conversion from the dinar to a new currency, the tolar, was very smooth.

The Bank of Slovenia was established as the central bank within the framework of the legislation promulgated on 25 June 1991 when the Bank of Slovenia Act was adopted together with the Basic Constitutional Charter on Independence and Sovereignty of the Republic of Slovenia and the Constitutional Act on the Implementation of the Basic Constitutional Charter. Article 152 of the Constitution defined the Bank of Slovenia (BS) as an independent central bank responsible directly to the Parliament.

The responsibilities of the BS were traditional: stability of the national currency, liquidity of the banking system within the country, and general liquidity of the country with foreign countries. In order to carry out these tasks, the BS regulated money supply, liquidity of banks and savings banks, general liquidity in payments abroad, supervised banks, issued banknotes and put coins and banknotes in circulation, guaranteed for bank deposits of natural persons and carried out some financial services for the government. The BS also carried responsibilities and competencies set forth by the Banks and Savings Banks Act, Foreign Exchange Transactions Act, Credit Transactions with Foreign Countries Act, Pre-rehabilitation, Rehabilitation, Bankruptcy and Liquidation of Banks and Savings Banks Act and Agency for Deposit Guarantees Act.

Establishing the monetary system involved a choice between a fixed and floating exchange rate. While economic theory does not provide a definite answer as to which is preferable, the majority of experts supported the view that the fixed exchange rate system would suit a country in transition better, or they proposed the crawling peg or currency board as appropriate possibilities. The exchange rate regime and ensuing macroeconomic stabilization patterns were, beside privatization, fields of heated controversies. The 'pegging versus floating' issue also reflected two opposite approaches to transition in Slovenia: a radical and a gradualist. The 'shock therapists' supported by foreign advisers suggested an overwhelming package encompassing price stabilization, fixed exchange rate, balanced budget, administrative restructuring of manufacturing and of the banking system, and centralized privatization be part of the package of measures for independence.[3] The gradualists suggested that economic policy remains funded on a gradual construction of market institutions and separation of political independence from macroeconomic stabilization. There would be no formal stabilization programme and the government would have only an indirect role in the privatizing and restructuring of the economy. Economic policy instruments of this approach would be firm but for flexible wage policy, restrictive government spending enhanced by budget deficit, if required, monetary policy enabling tolerable liquidity, flexible exchange rate regime, reliance on foreign equity capital, and concessions for investments in infrastructure. It was argued that such policy would result in a smaller loss in product and lower unemployment on the account of higher inflation. Gradualists, who gathered in the governing board of the central bank, prevailed. However, Slovenia opted for floating for a very practical reason; a fixed exchange rate could not be preserved. First, the central bank had no foreign exchange reserves to defend the fixed rate. Secondly, monthly (!) inflation in October 1991 was 21.5 per cent. A moderate initial devaluation would therefore be overridden by inflation immediately while a large devaluation would stimulate inflation and again endanger the fixed rate. Thirdly, it was impossible to determine the starting equilibrium exchange rate in a new country. Fourthly, pegging would, in such circumstances, hinder accommodations of the equilibrium real exchange rate to a newly required volume of trade and trade patterns. Slovenia thus established a system of managed floating; the experiences which followed proved that managed floating was the right choice.

One of the features of the Slovenian financial market has been the prevalence of monetary financial institutions; the share of non-monetary financial institutions adds up to between 25 per cent and 30 per cent of aggregated assets of the financial system. At the end of 2013, the assets of monetary financial institutions amounted to 71.3 per cent of financial assets, while the share of non-monetary financial institutions, which included investment companies,[4] mutual funds and insurance companies, mutual pension funds, pension companies, and insurance agencies, was 28.7 per cent. The primary securities market remained underdeveloped. The dominant share issuers were non-financial companies (78 per cent of the total value), followed by banks, other financial intermediaries and insurance agencies, while the largest groups of shareholders were non-financial companies, followed by households, government, financial intermediaries, rest of the world, banks and insurance agencies. By far the most important bond issuer was the government, followed by banks, non-financial companies and insurance agencies. The main holders of bonds were banks, insurance agencies, households, the government, non-financial companies, other financial intermediaries, and the rest of the world.

2 Authentic post-independence financial regulation, 1991–1998

Most financial regulation was prepared in the beginning of 1991 following the so-called break in the monetary system by Serbia when it became certain that Slovenia would have to establish its own monetary system. The regulation was adopted by the parliament in the package of six acts together with the proclamation of independence in June 1991. Many provisions of Basel I were encompassed in the regulation though the Bank of Slovenia (BS) was not a member of BIS.

Foreign exchange shortage used to be a kind of 'normality' in a socialist shortage economy, a pillar in creating the financial system prior to independence and a reason for extreme cautiousness observed in the initial BS regulation. Namely, when the new currency tolar was introduced the BS had no foreign exchange reserves, the economic situation was extremely unstable and it was not possible to determine the rate which would assure balance of payments objectives. The rate of 32 tolars for 1 deutschmark was used as the initial rate and it was supposed to float with inflation. Floating quickly led to a high positive current account balance, and Slovenia soon faced abundance rather than shortage of foreign exchange. Actual development thus enabled very quick elimination of initial restrictions such as the mandatory sale of 30 per cent of foreign exchange to the BS. BS regulation nevertheless remained cautious regarding foreign exchange liquidity of the banks. The main reason for the restrictions of capital flows was prevention of real appreciation of the tolar. Base money was accordingly created through foreign exchange transactions and steady oversupply of foreign exchange required constant sterilization of foreign exchange inflows by BS bonds. Current account transactions were free, so were also transactions related to foreign direct investments. This was not the case with foreign portfolio investments which increased sharply following the relatively good country risk rating assigned to Slovenia for the first time in 1996 and the relatively high level of domestic interest rates. Given the small currency area and limited possibility of the BS to neutralize any big-scale pressures of capital inflows on the exchange rate, the BS required that non-resident portfolio transactions be channelled through custody accounts with fully licensed domestic banks and with committed long-term portfolio investments. BS also requested mandatory reserves of foreign exchange by banks (foreign exchange minimum) in the form of liquid assets on the accounts with first-class foreign banks, obliged banks to balance their foreign exchange assets with foreign exchange liabilities, and introduced a non-interest-bearing tolar deposit on non-trade related loans taken abroad.

The provisions dealing with the cross border competition were scarce. A bank could be set up by domestic and foreign legal and natural persons and the foreign bank could establish a branch as a legal person, business unit or representative office. Contrary to other CEE countries, there was not much demand for establishing foreign banks in Slovenia which can be explained by the reforms of the banking system in Yugoslavia. With these reforms, banks were functioning as banks elsewhere, and they had well defined 'owners' (non-financial companies). In addition, there were uncertainties linked to the rehabilitation of the banking system between 1993 and 1997.

The provisions which were directly or indirectly related to capital adequacy for banks and savings banks were set in the Banks and Savings Banks Act.[5] From December 1993, banks had to use the methodology of the Committee on Banking Regulations and Supervisory Practices in Basel (Basel I). From 1 August 1994, the generally accepted level of capital adequacy was put to 8 per cent. BS also adopted new rules on the method of calculating the capital adequacy of banks regarding classification of balance sheet assets and off-balance sheet items and the establishment of provisions for credit risk. Banks had to comply with the provisions on large and maximum loans and on the total amount of all loans. A bank, which collected deposits, had to insure them with an authorized institution up to the amount prescribed by the Ministry of Finance.[6]

The Crisis Management, Pre-rehabilitation, Recovery, Bankruptcy and Liquidation of Banks and Savings Banks Act provided solutions for handling crises in the banking system. Indeed, with the creation of an independent state the potential need to bail out some banks turned to reality. The major reasons were bad loans to companies in Slovenia and other former Yugoslav republics before transition and independence, and foreign currency deposits of the population. The capital adequacy was the basic criterion in the assessment of the needed recovery; according to it, the two largest banks were insolvent. Actual crisis management procedures were introduced by the Bank of Slovenia Directive on the Recovery of LB d.d. (27 January 1993) and KBM d.d. (30 March 1993). BS together with a newly established Agency for the Rehabilitation of Banks opted for a gradual introduction of the procedures in individual individual banks, taking into account their situation, available public financing, and effects on monetary policy. The procedure consisted of: writing off current losses against capital, replacing bad assets with government bonds, the transferring of assets to liabilities in the form of subordinated debt of former owners, recapitalization, and transfer of ownership to the Agency. Such a recovery procedure implied (at least temporary) nationalization. Replacing bad assets of banks with bonds solved the problem of insolvency and improved income, but did not solve the short-term liquidity problems. Initially, banks were only able to meet their obligations by making use of the BS's liquidity loans. The two banks were gradually able to comply with prudential rules, their cash flow and liquidity improved significantly during 1996; they were actually able to manage their own liquidity and concluded the year 1996 with profit and return on assets and equity well above the average. The BS therefore released them from the recovery process; the state owned banks could be privatized but have not been.

One more issue is linked to the recovery procedure. In 1994, it became apparent that there were no prospects for rapid conclusion of the negotiations on financial assets and liabilities of the former state. The Slovenian parliament therefore passed the Constitutional Act on the Constitutional Act Implementing the Basic Constitutional Charter on the Independence of the Republic of Slovenia (27 July 1994) and established NLB d.d. and NKBM d.d, which took over the operations of LB d.d. and KBM d.d. By it, the credits and liabilities of the former federal institutions, as well as obligations to depositors from other republics were retained by LB d.d. and KBM d.d. The issue has remained unresolved and the rather short-sighted decision has become the subject of law suits in domestic and international courts.

To cope with the consequences of extremely high inflation which required high nominal interest rates, Slovenia used indexation which was inherited from Yugoslavia. Real interest rates were defined as the real component above the indexation rate (base rate – BR, in Slovenian 'temeljna obrestna mera' -TOM) which was determined by inflation rate. As the BS pursued the stability of real exchange rate policy as the major goal while leaving gradual lowering of inflation to increased competition, the BS was reducing base rates gradually and in line with declining inflation and by gradual de-indexation of its monetary instruments. In 1995, the BS abolished indexation for its instruments with maturities of less than 30 days, and introduced a three-month average of inflation as the base rate for all other instruments. In February 1996, the revaluation clause was extended to a four-month average, and in December 1996 to a six-month average. Later, the reference period for calculation of TOM was extended to 12 months. In September 1998, the BS issued a 270-day bill at a nominal rate equal to the indexed rate for the same instrument, and on 1 January 1999, the BS abolished the 270-day instrument at an indexed rate of interest. These contributed to a reduction in the volatility of nominal interest rates, and the movements thereof became more closely linked with the real rate rather than with current movements of retail price inflation. The government treasury followed the example and issued bonds at a nominal interest rate.

3 Adaptations to and acceptance of EU regulation, 1999–2007

One of the rationales for the independence of the country was easier access of Slovenia to European associations, the EU in particular. Negotiations with the EU began in 1992. They were followed by the Association Agreement in June 1996. Before all EU member countries ratified the Association Agreement, the Interim Agreement on trade and trade-related matters was used. In January 1997, the EU introduced full liberalization of trade in industrial and agricultural products; Slovenia did that gradually up to the end of 2001. The agreement contained legal clauses and stipulations on capital flows, cooperation in the field of finance, prevention of fraud, etc. The core of the financial regulation for the new period was set by the Banking Act 1999 which was passed assuming that Slovenia would become a member state of the EU and EMU. This implied that banking legislation should be harmonized with corresponding directives and also with the Core Principles for Efficient Banking Supervision adopted by the Basel Committee on Banking Supervision in 1997 regarding: establishment of a bank, definition of financial services, common standards for banking licence, management, establishment and functioning of foreign banks, capital adequacy rules, identification and measurement of credit risk, stipulations on large exposures, stipulations on management of liquidity risk, interest rate risk, currency risk, and other market risks, limited investment of banks in equity and in real property, supervision of banks and banking groups.

In 1999, the government made a commitment that the legislative framework of Slovenia concerning free capital flows would be harmonized with the 'acquis communautaire' before the date of the country's accession to the EU. The agreement signed by Slovenia and the European Community and its member states came into force on 1 February 1999. A four-year transitional period relating to controls on short-term capital movements was agreed while the lifting of sector-specific restrictions was linked to amending legislation governing the respective areas. A significant step towards alignment with the 'acquis' in capital movement liberalization was made by implementing the new foreign exchange legislation in April 1999, which lifted a number of restrictions in the field of inward and outward capital flows. By the Foreign Exchange Act, cross-border credit transfers were liberalized, though some restrictions in short-term capital movements remained. The BS liberalized borrowing abroad and kept few controls which referred to short-term capital flows. In response to the appeal by the European Union to liberalize capital movements prior to accession, the BS adopted a timetable for the liberalization of cross-border capital movements and made a commitment to abolish the existing restrictions no later than by the milestones set out in the timetable. Major changes were introduced in 2001 and 2002. On 1 January 2002, all restrictions on purchases of non-residents in the domestic money market were lifted and transfers of domestic and foreign cash into and out of the country were fully liberalized if they were in accordance with the Money Laundering Prevention Act.

On 17 July 2002, the new Bank of Slovenia Act came into effect. The act established the core aim of the BS as price stability. While ensuring price stability, the BS should also support general economic policy and promote financial stability while adhering to the principles of an open market economy and free competition. The BS continued with efforts to ensure the harmonization of Slovenian with the EU regulation and the preparation of further negotiating positions with regard to the freedom to provide services, the free movement of capital, etc. Negotiations on Slovenia's entry to the EU were concluded in December 2002. Entering the EU and EMU implied the harmonization of extremely cumbersome financial regulations.[7]

After accession, Slovenia was required to act in accordance with the ultimate EU goal of introducing the euro. Less than two months after joining the EU, on 28 June 2004, Slovenia entered the ERM II regime; the central rate was set at 239.64 tolars to the euro, the nominal exchange rate was allowed to fluctuate within a standard band of ±15 per cent. On 11 July 2006, the council of EU finance ministers passed a resolution, abolishing the derogation, and a resolution on the tolar-euro conversion rate which was set at the rate at which Slovenia entered the ERM II in 2004. The final phase of preparations followed in the second half of 2006. The BS ceased to independently implement monetary policy on 31 December 2006 and began implementing the single monetary policy of the euro system. Banks' balance sheets and all customer accounts were converted by the afternoon of 2 January 2007 as planned. The transition was smooth; the population and economy adjusted quickly to the new currency. As expected, there were some cases of prices being 'rounded up', particularly in the service and catering sectors.[8]

The third Banking Act was passed on 1 January 2007, when Slovenia was in the ERM II regime and preparing to enter the EMU. The major reason for the adoption of the new act was to comply with EU directives such as Directive 2006/48/EC and Directive 2006/49/EC, Council Directive 86/635/EEC, and Directive 94/19/EC. They brought new complex standards, the so-called Basel II. To transfer arrangements in the act called for extensive changes in key areas or amending legislation in almost all chapters. It was therefore considered more efficient and transparent, that, instead of a change in the *Banking Act 1999*, this was done with the new act. Article 2 explicitly transmitted provisions of Directive 2006/48/EC and Directive 2006/49/EC. The minimum amount of the share capital of a bank was put to €5 million. To curb excessive concentration of credit exposure to a single client and a group of connected clients in addition to large exposure limits of 25 per cent and 20 per cent the act introduced a 10 per cent limit in exposures to persons in a special relationship with a bank. Under the new deposit-guarantee scheme drafted in line with the EC Directive on Deposit-Guarantee Schemes 94/19/EC and determined by provisions of the Banking Act 1999 which became effective on 1 January 2001, the responsibility for repaying eligible funds to the public rests with banks and savings banks whose registered office is within Slovenia. Detailed standards were elaborated and prescribed by BS. Participation in the deposit-guarantee scheme was obligatory for all banks, savings banks and savings and loan undertakings authorized by the BS to provide banking services including accepting deposits, as well as for branches of banks with the registered office outside the territory of the Republic of Slovenia, which are partly or fully included in the host country deposit-guarantee scheme. Deposits in banks and saving banks with headquarters in Slovenia were covered up to €100,000. The calculation of the guaranteed deposit amount took into consideration the total balance of deposits of an individual depositor expressed in euros or foreign currency in a bank or savings bank on the commencement date of the bankruptcy procedure for that bank or savings bank.

One of the changes in the financial system was the migration of accounts of legal persons from the Agency for Payments to banks. That is, before transition, accounts of legal persons used to be with the Agency for Payments, which executed all payments between the legal persons within the country. The reform process began in 1994, when the foundations of the project were put in place and the project was taken over by the BS; strategic decisions were adopted in 1995 and the operational plan for the new payment system was drawn up in 1996. The institutions involved in the reform were the BS, the Ministry of Finance, the Agency for Payments, commercial banks, savings banks, the Banking Association, and the Statistical Office. To facilitate the migration, detailed guidelines for the migration of accounts of legal persons to the banking environment were drawn up. At the end of July 2000, the eligible banks obtained the special authorization granted by the BS and the Ministry of Finance, and on 11 September 2000 the migration of accounts commenced. The migration process was going on steadily and smoothly and the migration process was completed by the end of June 2002. The aim of the oversight of the payment system by the BS was first to protect the financial system from the consequences of the financial difficulties faced by participants, and second, to ensure safety and efficiency. In 2003, the BS commenced preparation for connection to the pan-European payment systems TARGET and STEP2. Activities related to ensuring and maintaining the operation of domestic payment systems took place in 2003. On joining the EU, Slovenian banks got the opportunity to join the STEP2 payment system, managed by the Euro Banking Association (EBA) for processing low-value cross-border payments in euros. The majority of banks were however in favour of joining STEP2 via the BS. On 8 November 2004 the BS became a direct participant in the STEP2 system, with banks participating via the BS having indirect participant status.

4 The crisis and the instability enhanced by regulation, 2007–2013

The financial turmoil, especially a lack of confidence and a considerable decrease in interbank lending badly affected Slovenian banks which had borrowed abroad extensively during the 'gambling period' preceding the crisis.[9] The effects were enhanced by high banking orientation of non-financial companies which financed themselves almost entirely via bank loans, while domestic savings of households only partly passed through to banks. Instead, a lot of domestic savings went through non-banking financial intermediaries abroad, and returned in the form of bank borrowing. Since October 2008, banks were unable to borrow abroad under the same conditions as they did before; the maturities and interest rates on loans deteriorated, resulting in a drop of loans to the corporations. By the crisis, the virtual wealth which had been created by credits ensured by collateral in shares of the so-called 'taikun' companies was devastated while credit obligations remained to be served. Due to the drop of economic activity, more and more non-financial companies became unable to serve their obligations, more and more loans turned to bad loans. Banks, open-handed and imprudent during the gambling period, became thrifty and prudent or could not provide credits because of their own indebtedness. The BS also, lenient before the crisis, became hard-hearted. The level of bad loans at home and non-performing investments in former Yugoslav republics began to increase. For a while, banks maintained their stock of lending enabled by the expanded ECB supply of liquidity at a fixed interest rate with full allotment and a maturity of up to one year, and the pool of securities eligible as collateral for loans. The government's borrowing abroad and depositing of the money in the banks was important for the maintenance of bank balance sheets. It did not suffice; the consequences of the recession were soon seen in the deterioration in the banking system's investment portfolio and in the need for loan reprogramming in the sectors which were hit hardest by the recession. Foreign banks began to squeeze crediting by reducing liabilities to their mother banks, while large domestic banks faced three problems: repayment of loans abroad, tougher rules on capital adequacy by the BS, and political demagogy against crediting 'taikuns' which frightened the bankers from restructuring credits and helping their clients.

The most notable feature of banks' operations in 2010 was the decline in total assets and overall operating loss. As the banks were repaying liabilities to banks abroad and to the ECB which had increased sharply in 2009, the government reduced its deposits, while only a modest increase in deposits of households was achieved. The banks adapted by reducing their investments in securities, and by curbing loans to non-financial corporations. The gap between credit demand and creditworthy demand widened, the arrears and non-settlement of liabilities increased. The deterioration in the quality of the credit portfolio and the resulting unavoidable increase in impairment and provisioning costs created the banks' losses. The downturn in economic activity in 2012 resulted in lower corporate and household demand for loans, in the tightening of the banks' loan collateral standards, and in an increase in funding costs which the banks passed through into higher loan costs. The main factor affecting the balance of financial account in 2012 were continuing repayments to the rest of the world. In a year, the banks' net repayments of liabilities on the wholesale financial markets amounted to 10 per cent of GDP. The banks compensated for the loss of international sources primarily by borrowing via the ECB's three-year long-term refinancing operations (LTROs). At the end of 2012, they amounted to €4 billion or 8.7 per cent of the banks' total liabilities, while deposits of non-financial companies and households with 51.7 per cent remained the most important source of funding.

The crisis revealed two weaknesses: the banks' overdependence on funding on the international financial markets, and high debt-to-equity ratios in non-financial corporations. The low level of equity implied a relatively low threshold for the coverage of business risks by the owners, and a large likelihood that risks would have to be assumed by creditors. Because domestic bank loans accounted for 59 per cent of corporate debt, they were heavily exposed to credit risk during a lengthy economic recession. Corporations faced the problem of how to reduce high indebtedness, illiquidity, and limited alternative financing. Some large corporations sought financing abroad, primarily in the form of trade credits and there were a few successful offerings of commercial papers by large corporations, while SMEs did not have any financing possibilities. Corporate leverage remained high, with a debt-to-equity ratio of 135 per cent. The banks were also forced to restructure their funding. Previous excessive funding on international financial markets and aggressive lending to increase or retain market share at home proved to be fatal. A contraction in their balance sheets and the tightening of credit standards was the result.

At the beginning of 2012, the proportion of the banking system's total classified claims that were in arrears more than 90 days reached 14.6 per cent, while exposures to corporations in bankruptcy accounted to 5.2 per cent of claims. With only 3.8 per cent of their classified claims more than 90 days in arrears, households remained relatively low-risk, partly due to very low general level of their indebtedness. Large domestic banks had the highest proportion of non-performing claims. The banks ended 2012 with the largest loss since the outbreak of the financial crisis. The main reasons of the pre-tax loss of €771 million were an increase of 32 per cent in impairment and provisioning costs and a decline of 13 per cent in net interest income. Given the deterioration in the quality of the credit portfolio and the contraction in credit activity, the banks' income risk was becoming increasingly important. Despite a fall in reference interest rates the banks' rising funding costs resulted in high lending rates for corporations, and declining net interest margins.

The BS, accepting the idea that in the adverse economic situation it is vital to maintain the capital adequacy of the banks, tried hard to achieve that by harsher capital requirements. A contraction in turnover was the unavoidable outcome. Although the banks improved their capital structure the shortfall on the capital adequacy increased; it was not the result of a decline in capital, but primarily of imposed differences in risk-weighted assets calculations.

Two fields of banking regulations faced the most frequent changes during the crisis period: regulation of deposit guarantee and regulation of capital adequacy. In the package of measures aimed at mitigating the effect of the financial turmoil, the new Banking Act ZBan-1B in November 2008, temporarily (until the end of 2010) introduced an unlimited deposit guarantee in the event of the bankruptcy of a bank or savings bank. The majority of changes to secondary legislation of deposit guarantee in 2010 were the results of amendments to the banking acts ZBan-1D, ZBan-1E and the Consumer Credit Act.

The period of crisis was also characterized by persistent changes in the capital adequacy regulation which increased uncertainty. In 2007, secondary legislation affecting banking supervision was issued primarily to continue harmonization with Directive 2006/48/EC. The emphasis in 2008 was on the examination and monitoring of the implementation of the new capital framework at banks and savings banks and the related calculation of capital requirements for credit and operational risk in the scope of Pillar 1 and the process of calculating the required level of internal capital in the scope of Pillar 2 of Basel II. Three directives were adopted in 2009 amending the banking Directive 2006/48/EC and the directive on the calculation of capital requirements for market risks. BS regulations required amending for the transposition of these regulations and the introduction of guidelines by the Committee of European Banking Supervisors. This brought about more significant changes with regard to the treatment of own fund instruments, large exposures and securitization, the calculation of the capital of banks and savings banks, regulation on large exposures of banks and savings banks, regulation on the calculation of capital requirements for credit risk in securitization, and the rules regarding the exposure of banks and savings banks to credit risk transfer. Most of the changes in banking regulations in 2011 were related to the transposition of Directive 2010/76/EU regarding capital requirements for the trading book and for resecuritizations, and the supervisory review of remuneration policies. Some of the provisions of this directive were transposed into the Slovenian legal system by the Amendment of the Banking Act ZBan-1G, while the remaining provisions were transposed in ZBan-1H. Two other regulations were issued in August 2011 on the calculation of capital requirements for credit risk under the standardized approach and under the internal ratings-based approach. A broad package of regulations was adopted on December 2011 to amend the calculation of capital requirements for position risk, currency risk and commodity risk. Banks had to comply with stricter quantitative and qualitative standards in the calculation of value-at-risk, and calculate additional capital requirements based on the calculation of value-at-risk for stress situations. In 2012 and 2013, a few key acts were adopted to facilitate the implementation of the measures for strengthening financial stability. The Measures of the Republic of Slovenia to Strengthen the Stability of Banks Act was adopted on 28 December 2012. It and the implementing regulations dealt with the management of non-performing loans and other risk-weighted asset items of a bank. The Bank Asset Management Company (BAMC) was established to ascertain efficient use and recovery of budget funds used for preventing the collapse of the banks, the stimulation of lending to the non-financial sector, and the establishment of conditions for the sell-off of the government's capital investments in banks.

The Act Amending the Banking Act ZBan-1J was also passed in December 2012. Its objective was to establish a special legal regime for resolving banking system issues resulting from limited possibilities for securing appropriate sources of funding to ensure capital adequacy. The act followed the principles emphasized by the EC in its draft directive establishing a framework for rescuing and restructuring credit institutions and investment firms. In accordance with the *ZBan-1J*, the BS may as a supervisor adopt measures against a specific bank which breaches risk management and capital requirement regulations or also in circumstances which might identify the likelihood of the occurrence of such breaches. In addition, the BS may act if it believes that the stability of the financial system is jeopardized.

The Act Amending the Banking Act ZBan-1L entered into force on 23 November 2013. The Act primarily relates to measures which the BS can impose on a bank, if increased risk arises and no circumstances are present which would indicate that the reasons for the increased risk will likely be eliminated in a reasonable period. Prior to the adoption of this act, four emergency measures were available to the BS: (a) appointment of an emergency administration for the bank, (b) sale of the bank's shares, (c) increase in the bank's share capital, and (d) transfer of the bank's assets. This act introduced a new emergency measure that may be used by the BS by reducing share capital, and the cancellation or conversion of the bank's hybrid financial instruments and subordinate debt into ordinary bank shares to ensure the coverage of its losses or to attain the required capital adequacy. The principle which should be followed is that an individual creditor cannot suffer losses greater than he would have suffered had the bank bankrupt. The new emergency measure complied with the Commission Communication on the Application of State Aid Rules to Support Measures in Favour of Banks in the Context of the Financial Crisis from 1 August 2013.

5 The breakdown and (the restoration?) of the banking system, 2013–2014[10]

Economic recession revealed deficiencies in the banks' risk management during the period of high economic growth which was enabled by credit addiction. When revenues of corporations declined and losses increased, the amount of non-performing loans began to rise. Loans to corporations (particularly in the construction sector and in holding companies) which increased enormously during the time of abundant credits, accounted for the largest proportion. As the recession persisted, the difficulties with the repayment of bank loans spread to other sectors, particularly to corporations depending on domestic demand, while risks in the households sector remained low. The proportion of non-performing claims more than 90 days in arrears or rated in the lowest categories (D and E) reached 20.9 per cent by October 2013, equivalent to €9.5 billion. The banks had to increase impairments and provisions which amounted to €5.1 billion at the end of October, or 11.2 per cent of the banks' total classified claims which were decisive in the banks' operating losses.

The Measures to Strengthen the Stability of Banks Act passed at the end of 2012 set out possible measures to strengthen the banks: capital increases, the purchase of claims and the transfer of claims to the Bank Asset Management Company (BAMC), guarantees by the Republic of Slovenia for liabilities of BAMC, and the special purpose vehicle (SPV) with a guarantee for needed liquidity to banks.

On the EU Council Recommendation of June 2013 the European Commission requested the execution of an independent asset quality review and stress tests (bottom-up and top-down) for a representative portion of the banking system as a prerequisite for the transfer of claims to the BAMC and the approval of state aid. Ten banks and banking groups which together constituted approximately 70 per cent of the banking system were involved in the review. To ensure the 'independence and credibility' of the review, the BS had to engage international consultants and real estate appraisers, who should conduct the reviews. The objective of the comprehensive review was to assess the ability of the Slovenian banking system to withstand sharp deterioration in macroeconomic and market conditions as projected for the future three-year period (2013–2015 inclusive) under the adverse scenario, and to determine the potential capital shortage in the case of its realization. The proclaimed reason for using an extreme scenario was to assess the robustness of the banking system in the most adverse hypothetical developments. The scope, conditions and contractors for the asset quality review and stress tests were determined by an inter-institutional committee after consultations with the European Commission (EC) and the European Central Bank (ECB).[11] The contracting authority for the asset quality review for seven banks and the stress tests for all included banks was the BS which also covered the costs while three banks included in the review (NLB, NKBM, Abanka) had to cover the costs of the review themselves. The review was coordinated and supervised by a Steering Committee comprising the BS, the Ministry of Finance, and observers from the EC, the ECB, and the European Banking Authority (EBA).

The aim of the asset quality review was the verification of data completeness and integrity, a review of individual loans and their rating classifications, a collateral valuation, and the identification of shortfalls in impairments and provisioning. The goal of the bottom-up stress tests was to determine the capital deficit/surplus of individual banks and the banking system under the conditions of the baseline and adverse macroeconomic scenarios for the three-year projection period (2013–2015), while the starting points were the balance sheet figures at the end of 2012. The bottom-up stress tests focused on the assessment of credit risk from performing, non-performing, and restructured loans, and risks from investments in securities. The credit portfolios assessed in these stress tests included lending to the domestic business sectors and claims from off-balance-sheet liabilities to these sectors. The securities portfolio included financial assets held for trading, financial assets available-for-sale, and financial assets held to maturity. The tests included three main elements of assessment: expected losses, a bank's loss absorption capacity, and capital shortfall/surplus resulting from the expected losses above expected available loss absorption capacity. The objective of the top-down stress tests was to provide a check against the results of the bottom-up stress. The underlying assumption was that using the same macroeconomic assumptions and the same starting point as the bottom-up stress testing can help to explain the bottom-up results by analysing and explaining the deviation between the two.

The macroeconomic scenarios for the stress tests were proposed by EC and ECB, while BS estimated the response of banking variables under the two scenarios. The baseline scenario was derived from the EC's spring forecast of macroeconomic developments and was revised downwards on the basis of macroeconomic figures for the first quarter of 2013. The scenario envisaged a further contraction in economic activity in 2013 and 2014 as a result of further decline in investment, and gradual rise of unemployment. In the low credit demand environment and with banks repaying their liabilities, lending to the private non-banking sector was expected to continue decreasing. Under the adverse scenario, Slovenia would undergo three years of severe economic recession. The drop in economic activity in this scenario was reinforced by structural weaknesses in EU member states and the need to reduce fiscal imbalances and to implement structural reforms. Because of that, investors would demand higher risk premiums for Slovenian government bonds, which would trigger a reassessment of the risk premium on other assets, for example, a drop in stock prices by 25 per cent and a drop in residential house prices by almost 27 per cent. The developments on the financial market would have an adverse impact on domestic and foreign demand; corporations would reduce their investment expenditure and cut employment, which would induce households to limit their consumption. A decline in credit demand, both from corporations for financing investments and from households for financing current consumption and residential expenditure, together with constraints on credit supply caused by the banks' difficulty in ensuring stable funding, would cause a further decline in lending to the private non-banking sector.

The adverse scenario was built upon very unlikely assumptions. It, for example, assumed an additional 9.5 per cent decline in GDP by the end of 2015, while the total decline since the outbreak of the crisis amounted to 10 per cent. The cumulative decline of 18 per cent in private consumption sharply exceeded the figure of 2.5 per cent recorded between 2009 and 2012. The downward exaggeration of not only adverse but also of baseline scenarios is well seen by comparing actual data with baseline scenario data; for example, the actual yield on a 10-year government bond at the end of June 2014 was 3.0 per cent, and at the beginning of February 2015, only 1.4 per cent, while the one used in baseline scenario for 2014 was put to 682 and for the adverse scenario 820 basic points. Thus, one could easily say that the very expensive operation was senseless and that the methodology was adapted to politically desired results of European authorities who have been trying to convince Slovenia to 'privatize', i.e. to sell the remaining state-owned companies to foreign companies. Thus, the airport of Ljubljana was sold to German Fraport, and Telekom is to be sold to German Telekom; both are predominantly state owned.

The calculations for needed capital were based on existing capital regulations. Accordingly, the banks have to meet a core tier-1 capital ratio (as defined by the EBA) of 9 per cent under the baseline scenario and 6 per cent

Table 9.1 Macroeconomic scenarios for the stress tests (yearly growth if not indicated)

	Baseline scenario			*Adverse scenario*			*Actual/ estimated*	
	2013	*2014*	*2015*	*2013*	*2014*	*2015*	*2013*	*2014*
GDP	–2.7	–1.5	0.1	–3.1	–3.8	–2.9	–1.0	2.0
Private consumption	–4.8	–3.5	–1.2	–5.3	–7.7	–6.5	–3.9	0.5
Gross fixed capital formation	–6.0	–2.7	1.9	–8.1	–13.1	–3.6	1.9	4.5
Net exports contribution	2.6	1.4	1.0	2.9	1.1	1.3	6.5	8.3
Employment	–2.6	–1.4	–0.3	–2.7	–2.5	–1.8	–2.2	0.6
Unemployment rate (% of labor force)	11.3	11.5	11.5	11.4	12.6	14.0	10.2	9.6
EURIBOR (3m, in bps)	25	50	79	58	156	222	25	33
10 year government bond yields (in bps)	602	682	702	638	820	845	680**	340***
HICP	1.9	1.4	1.5	1.8	1.5	1.9	1.9	0.6
Residential house price	–9.6	–4.3	–2.4	–11.0	–12.2	–7.1	–6.0	–5,2
Current account balance (% of GDP)	5.0	5.4	6.0	5.3	7.2	6.1	7.1	5.5
General government debt	64.1	66.2	69.6	64.7	71.5	84.0	70	84*
Credit volume	–7.2	–3.8	–1.9	–7.5	–6.5	–5.4	–8.4	–30.0*
Deposit volume	1.0	0.8	0.8	0.6	–0.5	–0.6	–0.5	5.4

*after transfer of bad loans to BAMC; ** yield on 10 year government bonds in June 2013; *** yield on 10 year government bonds in June 2014.

Source: BS, own calculations.

under the adverse scenario. The calculation of the stress test results was based on the EBA's definition of non-performing claims. All claims against customers rated D and E and classified claims against individual customers whose repayments were more than 90 days in arrears were classed as non-performing claims. The capital shortage was calculated under both approaches as the difference between the expected loss and the banks' loss-absorption capacity, i.e. the stock of impairments and provisions at the end of 2012, the estimated profit before impairments in the next three years, and the capital surplus over the minimum core tier-1 capital requirement. The potential capital shortfall in the banks at the end of the three-year period is shown in Table 9.2.

The differences between the capital deficits according to the two approaches are striking. Nevertheless, the extreme result of the bottom-up stress tests under the adverse scenario served as the starting point for the assessment of the required capital increases. The reviewed banks were classified into three groups. In the first, there are three large banks (NLB, NKBM, Abanka) in which teh BS required capital increase even before the beginning of the review and had state aid approved by the EC. Five banks in the second group might potentially have a capital shortfall by the end of 2015, two banks were liquidated. The restructuring plans of the first group were examined by the BS and EC together with the results of the stress tests and approval of state aid by the EC. The three banks also transferred the majority of their non-performing claims to the state-owned BAMC. The capital increases were provided in an amount derived from the capital shortfall identified under the adverse scenario by the government and with the state aid approval of the EC and with the rather problematic wipe out of qualified liabilities (shareholders and holders of hybrid and subordinated instruments). The banks in the second group had to draw up a capital strengthening plan that would demonstrate long-term viability, and to draw up measures to cover potential capital deficit by drawing fresh capital from existing or new owners. The BS was to ensure the solvency of banks facing temporary liquidity difficulties by acting as a lender of last resort in accordance with ECB rules. The ownership structure altered: the share of state-owned banks in capital increased from 22.9 per cent before the operation to 58.2 per cent after it.

Table 9.2 Results of stress tests for the banking system (in millions €)

		Projected loss	*Absorption capacity*	*Capital shortage*		
				Baseline	*Adverse*	*Difference*
Top down	Baseline	7,369	4,893	2,725	3,280	555
	Adverse	8,606	5,326			
Bottom up	Baseline	8,889	4,843	4,046	4,778	732
	Adverse	10,364	5,586			
Difference				1,321	1,498	

Source: BS Report.

At the end of 2012, the European Commission proposed banking union as a solution for the banking system in the EU. The accession of the member states to it would transfer decision-making on key banking policy to the supranational level. The four pillars of the system would be: (1) standard banking rules at EU level, (2) a single banking supervisor, (3) a single deposit guarantee scheme, and (4) common rules to avoid bankruptcy of banks and a shift from the bail-out to the bail-in solution if banks find themselves in financial difficulties. Planned improvements to the existing methodology primarily relate to the introduction of quantitative indicators and qualitative estimates in the assessment of the banks' risk profile. The system of micro-prudential risk indicators should be expanded and supplemented with macro-prudential risk indicators and should serve as the basis for monitoring the position of specific banks and the banking system as a whole, supervision, measures in line with legally defined powers, in terms of both micro-prudential and macro-prudential supervision, and potential decisions on the use of resolution mechanisms. It is hoped that banking union would ensure capital stability, dispersion of risks, stable structure of funding and increased profitability, which would allow the banks to generate internal capital via retained earnings, mitigate negative effects on lending activity, to enable banks to find it easier to access the wholesale funding market at acceptable prices. Lower funding costs would allow the banks to operate with a higher net interest margin, which would increase the profitability of the banks. The consolidation of the banking sector is also expected to bring synergies related to cost-efficiency through lower operating costs. It is uncertain whether the above hopes in the benefits of the new banking union are realistic. Will the banking union not face the fate of monetary and fiscal union? The former was a purely political undertaking with weak economic foundations encompassing countries which did not form optimal currency area and therefore turned to a burden when bad times arrived. The nearly forgotten fiscal union which does not encompass fiscal transfers turned to a meaningless fiscal pact. Will the new banking union not end as only an enormous administrative institution which will generate more and more meaningless rules?

Reformed banking supervision at the EU level affected supervision in Slovenia; the regulation on transition to the Single Supervisory Mechanism was adopted in November 2013. According to it, the ECB assumed banking supervision in November 2014. The comprehensive assessment comprised of three parts: an assessment of banking risks, an asset quality review, and stress tests for 130 credit institutions, including three Slovenian banks: NLB, NKBM and SID bank. The repeated tests showed negligible shortage of capital in two of them in the case of the highly unlikely adverse scenario.

The structure of bank funding, accumulated losses, continuous deterioration of the quality of the credit portfolio, and accelerated deleveraging by the banks raise the issue of a proper size of the Slovenian banking sector, both in terms of the number of banks and the size of assets. The consolidation of the banking sector and contraction of the banking system can be expected. A

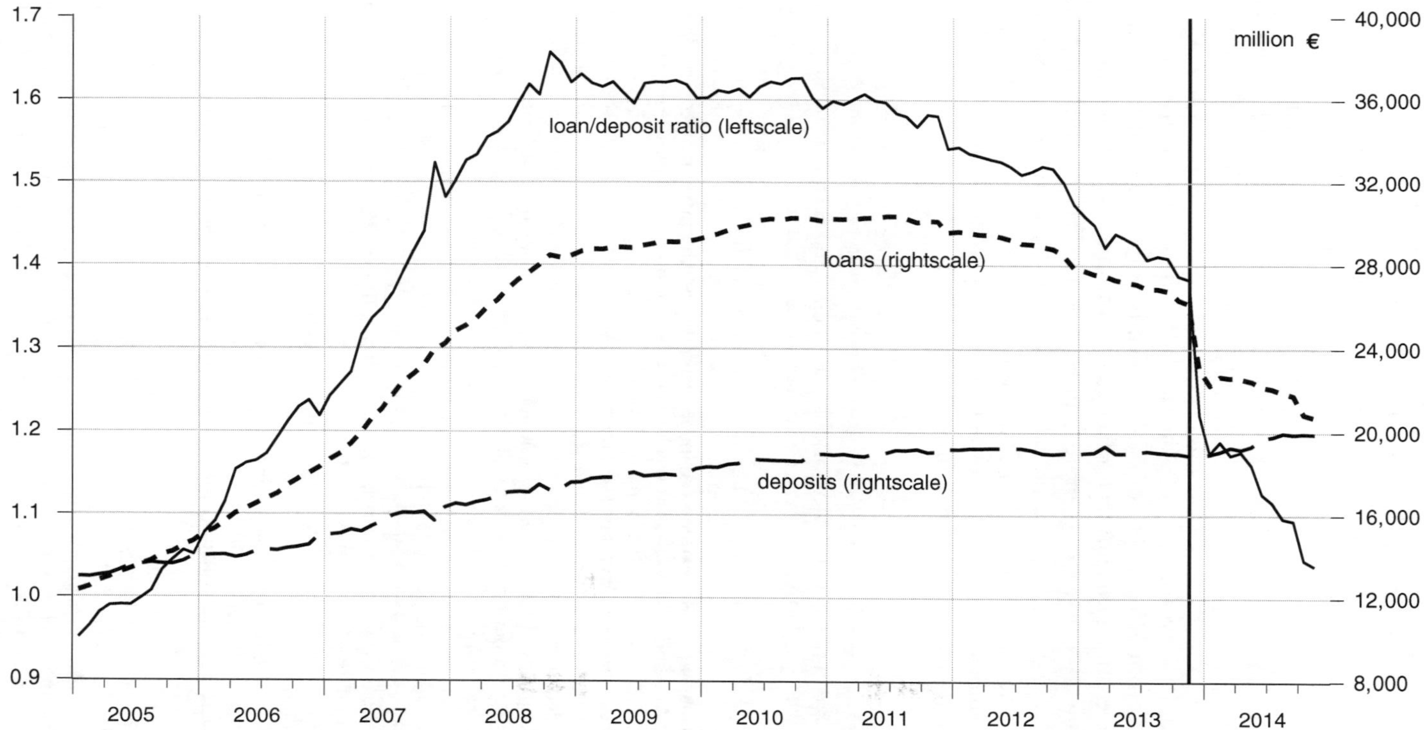

Figure 9.3 Loan/deposit ratio, loan and deposits

total of 21 banks (and three savings banks) were operating in Slovenia when the financial crisis broke at the end of 2008; the number of banks is expected to decline to 15 by the end of 2015. The enormous drop of claims by the banking system caused by the transfer of bad but also less 'bad' loans to BAMC indirectly affects all the indicators as shown in Figure 9.3. The amount of credits to the business sector which reached €21.3 billion in the middle of 2011, was until the transfer to BAMC gradually reduced to €17.2 billion and by transfer to less than €14 billion, the loan deposit ratio (including loans to households) decreased to 1.03, the size of the banking system in two years dropped from 140 per cent of GDP (which is only a 1.5 thousandth part of the euro banking system) to 126 per cent at the end of 2013, and the capital adequacy ratio increased to more than 15 per cent. The expectations that this will enhance credit activity and lead to economic recovery have proved to be wrong. The bankers have remained overly cautious which can be explained by the political and social atmosphere prevailing in the country. It is safer to do nothing than to take a risk of making a mistake.

Notes

1 For a comprehensive review of political, social, and economic development of Slovenia see 'Slovenia – From Yugoslavia to the European Union', The World Bank, 2004.

2 The predominant part of the systemic framework for an efficient market economy was created in 1990 and 1991, i.e. before political independence. The simple, transparent, and flexible system of direct taxes was introduced by the Income Tax Act and Profit Tax Act. The statutes regulating the monetary and financial system included the Bank of Slovenia Act, the Banks and Savings Banks Act and the Foreign Exchange Transactions Act, The Rehabilitation of the Banks and Savings Institutions Act were prepared in advance and passed together with the Declaration of Independence in June 1991. After independence, missing legal rules which guide economic conduct (company law) assured a predictable bargaining framework (codes regulating business transactions), enforced rules, and resolved disputes (bankruptcy, competition) were added.

3 For example, a document 'A Program for Economic Sovereignty and Restructuring of Slovenia' of March 21, 1991, proposed 10:1 conversion rate of the dinar to a new currency, its pegging to the Deutschmark, ECU or a basket, to assure a nominal anchor for a shock therapy stabilization programme. The government group changed their views in favour of unrestricted floating in a Memorandum on 8 October 1991, when the managed floating exchange rate system was already introduced.

4 In line with the Transformation of Authorized Investment Corporations Act, privatization funds established in 1992 as one of the pillars of privatization had to convert into investment companies and/or ordinary public limited companies by the end of 2003.

5 Banks should operate according to the principles of liquidity, safety and profitability (Article 4). The capital for establishment of a bank was set to at least 35 million tolars in cash. To keep the real value unaltered, the minimum amount of capital in the form of cash would be determined by the BS (Article 9). The BS determined the conditions for the operation of a bank and issued an unlimited or a limited operating licence. The guarantee capital should be of at least the

amount of the initial capital (Article 22). A more detailed definition of the different forms of guarantee capital was to be set by the BS (Article 23). The amount of total assets and off-balance sheet items of assets, weighted by the level of hazard, should not exceed 16 times the regulatory capital of the bank (Article 26). The bank's investments in land, buildings, business equipment holdings in other banks and non-banking organizations should not exceed the regulatory capital, while these investments, if obtained in realizing arrears should not be considered investment in land, buildings, business equipment holdings in other banks and non-banking organizations in the first three years after the acquisition (Article 28). To ensure safety a bank had to make provisions against potential losses arising from risky investments (Article 29). Banks, savings banks and savings cooperatives were obliged to operate so as to maintain their solvency; the detailed criteria for maintenance of liquidity were set by the BS (Article 38).

6 The Agency of the Republic of Slovenia to insure deposits in banks and savings banks was created by a special act adopted as a part of the financial package in June 1991. Agency was to be a specialized financial institution which was to be financed by the banks and state budget to ensure deposits in the banks in cases of bankruptcies. Banks and savings banks were required to pay an insurance premium in proportion of insured deposits while the size of the premium was to be determined by the agreement between the Ministry of Finance and the BS. However, the agency was never established and the provisional solution according to which the BS would play its role on behalf of the state was to be applied for such cases.

7 This is evident by, for example, comparing three consecutive acts on banking in a short period of 15 years; the Banks and Savings Banks Act 1991 had 5006 words, the Banking Act 1999 had 25,185 words, and the Banking Act 2006 had 47,532 words.

8 According to most estimates, the introduction of the euro contributed 0.3 percentage points to inflation, most in December 2006 and the remainder in subsequent months.

9 A favourable economic climate in Europe and the resulting high growth in foreign trade contributed to economic growth which exceeded the macroeconomic equilibrium output potentials. It was driven by high investment growth, particularly in construction works and financial deepening partly due to access to 'unlimited' amounts of money after entering the EU and EMU and the convergence of domestic interest rates with European interest rates.

10 This part of the paper is based on: Report on comprehensive review of the banking system and associated measures, BS, 2013.

11 Deloitte and Ernst & Young were selected to conduct the asset quality review, while several foreign real estate appraisers conducted the real estate valuations. The firms selected to conduct the stress tests were Oliver Wyman (bottom-up) and Roland Berger Strategy Consultants (top-down).

References

Legal Acts, Parliament of Slovenia

SLOVENIA, Banks and Savings Banks Act, Official Gazette (OG), No. 1/1991.

SLOVENIA, Foreign Exchange Transactions Act, OG, No.1/1991.

SLOVENIA, Foreign Countries Credit Relations Act, OG, No. 1/1991.

SLOVENIA, Bank of Slovenia Act, OG, No.1/1991.

SLOVENIA, Pre-rehabilitation, Rehabilitation, Bankruptcy and Liquidation of Banks and Savings Banks Act, OG, No.1/1991.

SLOVENIA, Constitutional Act on the Constitutional Act Implementing the Basic Constitutional Charter on the Independence of the Republic of Slovenia, OG, July 27, 1994.
SLOVENIA, Financial Conglomerate Act, OG, No. 43/2006.
SLOVENIA, Consumer Credit Act, OG, No. 59/10.
SLOVENIA, Banking Act, OG, No. 001-22-184/06.
SLOVENIA, Act Amending the Banking Act, ZBan-1B, OG, No. 109/08.
SLOVENIA, Act Amending the Banking Act, ZBan-1D, OG, No. 98/09.
SLOVENIA, Act Amending the Banking Act ZBan-1E, OG, No. 79/10.
SLOVENIA, Act Amending the Banking Act ZBan-1G, OG, No. 59/11.
SLOVENIA, Act Amending the Banking Act ZBan-1H, OG, No. 85/11.
SLOVENIA, Measures of the Republic of Slovenia to Strengthen the Stability of Banks Act, OG, No. 105/12.
SLOVENIA, Act Amending the Banking Act ZBan-1J, OG, No. 105/12.
SLOVENIA, Act Amending the Banking Act ZBan-1L, OG, No. 96/13.

EU Directives

Directive 2006/48/EC of the European Parliament and of the Council of 14 June 2006 relating to the taking up and pursuit of the business of credit institutions, OJ No L. 177 of 30. June 2006.
Directive 2006/49/EC of the European Parliament and of the Council of 14 June 2006 on the capital adequacy of investment firms and credit institutions, OJ No L. 177 of 30. June 2006.
Council Directive 86/635/EEC of 8 December 1986 on the annual accounts and consolidated accounts of banks and other financial institutions, OJ No L. 372 of 31 December 1986.
Directive 94/19/EC of the European Parliament and of the Council of 30 May 1994 on deposit-guarantee schemes, OJ No L. 135 of 31 May 1994.
Directive 2001/24/EC of the European Parliament and of the Council of 4 April 2001 on the reorganization and winding up of credit institutions, OJ No L. 125 of 5 May 2001.
Council Directive 89/117/EEC of 13 February 1989 on the obligations of branches established in a Member State of credit institutions and financial institutions having their head offices outside that Member State regarding the publication of annual accounts, OJ No L. 44 of 16 February 1989.
Directive of the European Parliament and of the Council 2002/87/EC of 16 December 2002 on the supplementary supervision of credit institutions, insurance undertakings and investment firms in a financial conglomerate, OJ No L. 35 of 11 February 2003.
Directive of the European Parliament and of the Council 2005/60/EC of 26 October 2005 on the prevention of money laundering and terrorist financing, OJ No L. 309 of 25 November 2005.
Directive 2007/64/EC of the European Parliament and of the Council on payment services in the internal market amending Directives 97/7/EC, 2002/65/EC, 2005/60/EC and 2006/48/EC and repealing Directive 97/5/EC, OJ No L. 319 of 12 May 2007.

Directive of the European Parliament and of the Council 2008/48/EC on credit agreements for consumers and repealing Council Directive 87/102/EEC, OJ No L. 133 on 22 May 2008.

Directive 94/19/ES of the European Parliament and of the Council on the system of assured deposits, OJ L No. 135, amended by Directive 2009/14/ES of the European Parliament and of the Council 94/19/ES on the system of deposit guarantees, OL L No. 68 of 13 March 2009.

Directive 2001/24/ES of the European Parliament and of the Council on reorganization and liquidation of credit institutions, OJ L No. 125 of 5 May 2001.

Other Sources

BANK OF SLOVENIA (1997, 1998, 1999, 2000, 2001, 2002, 2003, 2004, 2005, 2006, 2007, 2008, 2009, 2010, 2011, 2012, 2013) Annual report of the Bank of Slovenia. Ljubljana.

BANK OF SLOVENIA (2013) *Report on Comprehensive Review of the Banking System and Associated Measures.* BS, Ljubljana.

BANKE SLOVENIJE (1991, 1992, 1993, 1994, 1995, 1996) Letno poročilo [Annual report.]

MRAK, M., ROJEC, M. and SILVA-JAUREGUI, C. (eds) (2004): *Slovenia – From Yugoslavia to the European Union*, The World Bank, 2004.

10 Financial regulation in the United Kingdom from the Big Bang to post-crisis reforms

Elisabetta Montanaro

1 Introduction

Before the current financial crisis, the UK financial regulatory system had an extraordinarily high international reputation (IMF, 2003, p. 9–11). With such a reputation as this, the United Kingdom has exerted considerable influence on financial regulation over the years, both at global level and within the European Union. The participation of British supervisors in the work of the Basel Committee on Banking Supervision has indeed been particularly incisive from the very beginning (Bank of England, 1987a and 1987b; Hall, 1989; Kapstein, 1991; Hall, 1992). In Europe, important advances in the regulatory framework between 1999 and 2005, in the context of Financial Services Action Plan, had been broadly supported and encouraged by the UK (Quaglia, 2010; Ferran, 2012). The British antipathy to the expansion of EU law governing banks and financial markets only actually became an important characteristic of the UK regulatory policy after the crisis (Turner, 2009, p. 102; Great Britain. HM Government, 2013).

The factors that contributed to modifying the structural characteristics of the British banking system from the early 1980s onwards were also present in many EU countries. However, there can be no doubt that the transformation of the banking system due to the shift to market-based finance and the internationalization of financial markets were much more prominent in the UK than in other countries (Mullineux, 2012; Hardie and Maxfield, 2013).

With the establishment of the universal banking model after the 1986 Big Bang, the financial system in Britain assumed a countenance that was very different from the little community of bankers that made up the quintessentially British culture of the City of London. Interactions between the regulatory model and the financial structure assume a peculiar characteristic in the UK, due to the central importance always given to the target of promoting and consolidating London as a global financial centre. This important role has been – and in many ways continues to be (Carney, 2013) – the basis for many regulatory reforms introduced in the United Kingdom, especially from the 1980s onwards.

Even though the UK is referred to as a market-based system like the US (Allen and Gale, 2001), this classification does not fully explain the specifics of the British financial system, or the characteristics that led to its development. Banking is an extremely important segment of the British economy. As a proportion of the national economy, banking in Britain is second only to Switzerland among the G20 economies, and much more important than in the US (Bank of England, 2010; TheCityUK, 2012; Bank of England, 2014). With an intermediation on the wholesale markets between financial counterparties greater than intermediation between household savers and corporate borrowers, the British banking system has become the typical model for so-called market-based banking, the intrinsic fragility of which was bound to emerge during the crisis (Adrian and Shin, 2010; Hardie and Maxfield, 2013).

The British approach to financial regulation was an important driver of London's position as a global financial centre. Although the UK abandoned during the 1970s the self-regulation system in force before City globalization, the implementation of the later statutory regime retained many of the traditional characteristics of the old regime (Tomasic, 2010).

Until the financial crisis, the superiority of a light-touch, principles-based approach to financial regulation was claimed as the key factor in the success and international prestige of the British system (Davies, 1997; Furse, 2006). Many theoretical and empirical studies ascribe this greater efficiency to the collective benefits of market-friendly regulation (Llewellyn, 1999; Rajan and Zingales, 2001; Beck, Demirgüç-Kunt and Levine, 2003; Barth et al., 2004). It comes as no surprise that the principles-based approach to financial regulation was also considered by the banking industry as a model for 'better regulation' (IIF, 2006).

The effects of the crisis in Britain have shown the failure by the supervisory authority to enforce the broad discretionary powers allowed by principles-based regulation. The association between light- touch regulation and the vulnerabilities of financial systems has now been largely accepted, not only by comparative studies into which institutional factors contributed to the crisis (Dalla Pellegrina and Masciandaro, 2011), but by British regulators themselves. After the crisis, the view that focused on the economic benefices arising from the growth of the UK financial sector has been radically reconsidered (Haldane et al., 2010; Beck et al., 2014; Bank of England, 2014). As Turner clearly argues (2010), some of the activities performed by the UK financial sector do not provide any economic value and are not welfare enhancing. It is not clear, however, whether the broad UK regulatory reforms brought in to deal with the crisis can be seen as a radical departure from previous policies and practices.

The purpose of this chapter is to present the evolution of the UK financial regulatory system, starting in the 1980s and focusing mainly on banking regulation and supervision. The second section will illustrate the process of the deregulation during the 1980s, which culminate with the so-called Big Bang. The third section deals with the creation of a single regulator, a reform of the institutional architecture of financial supervision strictly related to the dramatic transformations of the UK financial system produced by the Big Bang. The fourth section discusses the regulatory reforms brought in after the crisis, which have been designed to introduce radical changes to both the financial landscape and the regulatory framework set up in the previous decades. The focus is on the theoretical debate about the ring fencing of retail banking, the peculiar British solution to solve the crucial issue of too-big-to-fail. Some conclusions are offered in section 5.

2 The Big Bang and financial deregulation

As Plender states (1986), the Big Bang is the best term to define two significant deregulation measures, the abolition of monopolized fixed commission on securities transactions and the removal of barriers to foreign entry into the Stock Exchange, which until then had been a sort a 'private club'. These reforms, according to their strongest critics and their most enthusiastic supporters, were considered as emblematic of Mrs Thatcher's Conservatism. According to Miller (1989), they contributed to turning London into one of the engines of financial globalization and, at the same time, they radically altered the financial landscape in the UK.

The removal of foreign exchange controls in October 1979, mostly undertaken to strengthen the role of the City in the world's financial markets, had exposed the domestic financial system to international competition. The Big Bang was the deliberate response of the government and the Bank of England to the competitive threat arising out of changes to the structure of the international securities market, and by the progressive lowering of home bias in the portfolio holdings of British residents.

Traditional segmentation in the British banking system in its three main sectors, commercial retail banks, investment (or merchant) banks and UK offices of foreign banks had already been in decline since the 1970s (Blair, 1994). This tendency – which was only emphasized by the Big Bang – did not actually start with deregulation, because in the UK there had never been any rules on allowable activities for banks. It was a spontaneous trend towards rationalizing and transforming management models, encouraged by the authorities and by the Bank of England in particular, especially directed to give a competitive advantage to the clearing banks. The financial deregulation brought in after the Big Bang arose out of the disappearance of market entry barriers deriving from the rulebook for the members of the Stock Exchange: fixed minimum commissions; the single capacity rule, which required a separation between brokers and the so-called jobbers (dealers and market-makers); the requirement that brokers and jobbers should be independent and not part of any financial group; and the exclusion of all foreign investors from Stock Exchange membership (Ingham and Thompson, 1993).

The City, thanks to the Euro-market, was still a major international centre, although it was split into two artificially divided segments: while large foreign institutions dominated major international business, undercapitalized British institutions were confined to the small domestic market. The weakness of the domestic financial services industry had made their reform inevitable, to avoid the risk that on the domestic securities market the City would become a sclerotic second-class financial centre, and that the most lucrative deals would be closed by foreign investors or tend towards other international financial centres (Bank of England, 1985; Gower, 1988; Lawson, 2006).

With the Big Bang, the ownership rules where amended to allow single non-member (national or foreign) to own 100 per cent of capital in a member firm; minimum commissions were abolished, and dual capacity was introduced.

Although the Big Bang deregulated the Stock Exchange, its impact on the structure of the British financial system was enormous and very rapid. By late 1986, half of the over 200 Stock Exchange member firms joined American, British, and European finance groups, banks, or investment companies. 'In one-step change banking and securities business was combined within newly established financial conglomerates and the separation of these activities which had characterized the UK financial services industry for three hundred years or more was abandoned' (Dale, 1992, p. 107).

The removal of barriers between business sectors, which in the past had been kept separate, meant that the entire regulatory structure needed to be reorganized. As stated by Gower (1988), the scholar who contributed most to the new system, the Financial Services Act (FSA) 1986, the second leg of Big Bang, came into force to deal with different objectives than Big Bang. The original purpose of the FSA was to draw up conduct-of-business regulation of the securities industry for the protection of investors. In 1981 a series of financial scandals showed that the existing regulations for fraud prevention and against conflicts of interests had become obsolete and more or less ineffective (Pimlott, 1985). In addition to fighting financial crime and protecting the reputation of the City, the intention was to adjust the legal regime of the investment industry to European law, designed to further the process of harmonization of company and securities law throughout the European area. The FSA was a classic example of prudential re-regulation following on from structural deregulation.

Blair (1994, pp. 95–96) highlights that the FSA was the result of a compromise between pressure from the industry, which was afraid of over-regulation due to setting up of a control body very like the American SEC on the one hand; and, on the other, pressure from both the general public and Parliament, who were afraid that industry interests would prevail over consumer protection by eliminating those rules which, in the past, had protected them against conflicts of interest.

The FSA 1986 brought in a prohibition on working in the investment business without prior authorization. Banking activity, or at least the taking of deposits and making credit, was subject to control by the Bank of England; its securities, underwriting, corporate finance, and investment management business were subject to the FSA. A new regulatory body was set up, the Securities and Investment Board (SIB), with chairman and board members jointly nominated by the Treasury and the Governor of the Bank of England, but incorporated as a private company. With such an ambiguous legal status, the SIB was conceived as the watchdog of the system rather than as the body that licensed and directly regulated the investment firms. The chain of public accountability of the SIB was limited by its nature as a private body, financed by levies on market participants. The Treasury was the Government Department with responsibility for regulating the financial services industry; however, it did not exert this control directly but by delegating powers to the SIB. In line with the principle of self-regulation, licensing functions were primarily assigned to the so-called 'Self-Regulatory Organisations' (SROs), trade organisations that had to be recognized by the SIB. These SROs, financed and managed by subsidiary companies, acted as second-level regulators of their shareholders, in line with their own rulebook, drawn up according to a set of model rules developed by the SIB. The regulatory style was therefore 'self-regulation within a statutory framework.' Moran (1988) states that, in spite of the government's declared intent to ensure higher levels of competitiveness, protect the industry from political control, and keep regulation simple and informal, this reform actually gave rise at the same time to powerful corporatist institutions (the SROs), a growth of political intervention in the industry, and more formality and complexity in regulation.

The prudential issues arising from the fusion of banking and securities business are the most critical aspects of the reform. The financial conglomeration deriving from changes to ownership rules brought about a real structural revolution, the threats of which the Bank of England understood perfectly well, partly because the change came about so rapidly (Bank of England, 1985).

The approach implemented by the UK with the Financial Services Act 1986 and the subsequent Banking Act 1987 can be defined as a sort of functional regulation. Under the functional approach, each type of business has its own functional regulator and supervisor. The division of responsibility of supervisory tasks between the Bank of England and the SIB depended upon group structure. A bank's securities business was supervised by the bank regulator if conducted by the bank itself, and by the securities regulator if conducted by a separately incorporated securities subsidiary. In the first case, the bank was subject to SIB regulation mainly in terms of the rule of conduct for investor protection, and the Bank of England became the 'lead regulator,' responsible for overall safety and soundness oversight. In the second case, the SIB was responsible for monitoring the solvency of the subsidiary, and the cooperation with the Bank of England, as the consolidated supervisor, came under 'supervisory colleges'.

Faced with the possibilities of contagion, a crucial policy issue was, as Dale (1992, p. 108) reminds us, whether to put in place strict firewalls of the kind imposed in the US by the Glass-Steagall Act. The criterion implemented by UK supervision of banks' securities business was actually based upon the assumption that risks were inseparable, and the policy should be that a parent bank had a moral obligation to stand behind its subsidiaries to cover losses, even beyond the requirements of their limited liability (Bank of England, 1985). The main rationale of this solution, as Gower (1988) explains, was that a single technically expert regulator would have applied consistent rules to the same activity, regardless of the entity in which it was conducted. Under this approach, at least in theory, regulatory arbitrage should have been avoided.

Discussions about the advantages and disadvantages of these separate supervisory approaches are still ongoing today (Group of Thirty, 2008). At the time, the UK regulatory arrangements after the Big Bang were judged by some as the best model to be implemented to deal with the challenges caused by increasing integration between different sectors in the financial industry. According to these arguments, the Big Bang was regarded as an example of 'financial modernisation', which significantly contributed to the decision by US regulators of repealing the Glass-Steagall Act (Schooner and Taylor, 2003). Others, though, considered this functional model as not consistent with a regulatory approach that allowed risks to flow freely between different parts of the group.

The more critical position is taken by Dale (1992, p. 111 ss.), who stresses a crucial problem with implementing functional regulation, i.e. the way the Bank of England supervised multifunction banking groups. Interpretation by the Bank of England of its requirement to provide consolidated supervision, as set out in European law with the Consolidated Supervision Directive of 1983, was actually very peculiar, even though this was due to the vagueness of the rules in the Directive itself (Hall, 1999, p. 101). According to the Bank, consolidated supervision did not require the consolidation of financial statements of different entities belonging to a group.

> The presumption must be that the supervisor of, for example, a securities company is the best judge of the adequacy of its capital. The Bank will not generally expect to have to make an independent quantitative assessment of the capital adequacy of group companies which are subject to detailed supervision by other UK supervisory.
>
> (Bank of England, 1986, p. 85)

The limits of such a lax approach to consolidated supervision would be seen in the years to come, especially after the collapse of Barings, and would be a powerful argument in favour of a single regulator as brought in by the Labour government in the late 1990s.

3 The single mega-regulator

Financial regulation in the UK during the 1980s and early 1990s is the story of a system seriously undermined by several episodes of banking crises and by financial scandals. After the BCCI collapse in 1991, the whole UK banking regulatory framework began to be disputed (Kinsella, 1992). Shortly afterwards came the near systemic crisis of the small banks (1991–1993), and, in 1995, the collapse of Barings, whose consolidate supervision was in charge of the Bank of England, as lead supervisor (Bank of England, 1995). Beyond these banking crises, there were numerous serious crimes or large-scale violations of conduct of business standards, including the most serious of all, the pension mis-selling scandal, which hit a vast number of retail clients. The need for enhanced protection of consumers of financial services in the UK, widely accepted by politicians of all colours, was actually, according to Black and Nobles (1998), one of the key factors in the reforms brought in by the New Labour government.

The financial scandals accentuated increasing dissatisfaction not only with banking supervision, but with the whole regulatory framework, considered excessively costly, inefficient and plagued by inconsistencies, with overlaps but also gaps (Briault, 1999). As predicted by Borio and Filosa (1994), the blurring of boundaries between banking, securities and the insurance industry, which arose from the conglomeration of financial institutions and the loosening of functional restrictions, had made the regime inadequate.

Lastra (2003) points out that the influence of European law, based upon the universal banking model, had an important role in the UK regulatory reforms of the late 1990s. In particular, the Capital Adequacy Directive set the minimal capital requirements for market risk using the same criteria for credit institutions and investment firms. In the UK, it posed the question of how a level playing field for banks and securities firms could be maintained if this Directive were to be implemented by different functional regulators.

No less important, as Jackson (2005) argues, were the concerns that financial development on the Continent, and especially the emergence of the eurozone, could marginalize the City. It is therefore unsurprising that the Labour reform particularly emphasized the efficiency gains of the new regime, not least in order to achieve industry consensus. Accordingly, clear provisions relating the proportionality principle of regulatory compliance costs were built into the legislative framework, reinforced by the other principle that requires the regulator to have regard to 'the international character of financial services and markets and the desirability of maintaining the competitive position of the United Kingdom' (Ferran, 2003).

Parallel to discussions about the Bank of England's performance as a banking regulator, consensus was being reached by politicians and economists about giving the central bank monetary policy independence, 'regarded as a practical consequence of new economic orthodoxy in which monetary policy is the main instrument for delivering price stability' (Ferran, 2003, p. 6; Martijn and Samiei, 1999).

The reform implemented by the Blair government gave the Bank of England monetary policy independence, but took away its banking supervisory and regulatory functions.

Responsibility for regulation and supervision of all parts of the finance industry were thus given to the SIB, which was now renamed the Financial Services Authority (FSA). The new single regulator took over the supervisory functions of the various self-regulatory organisations, but especially the Banking Supervision Division of the Bank of England. Unlike what one might have expected, after the adverse reputational effects of BCCI affair, the Bank of England accepted the devolution of its supervisory functions 'with some equanimity, or even relief' (Goodhart and Schoenmaker, 1993, p. 145).

The new arrangement substantially changed the institutional framework of banking regulation. Under a Memorandum of Understanding (MoU) signed in 1997 by the Treasury, the Bank of England and the FSA, the so-called tripartite system was approved, which laid down each authority's responsibilities, the chain of public accountability and what cooperation was required in emergency situations (Bank of England, 1998a and 1998b). According to the MoU, the primary responsibility of the Bank of England was summarized as contributing to 'the maintenance of the stability of the financial system as a whole'. The FSA had the responsibility for micro-prudential regulation of banks. The Treasury was to be politically responsible for regulation, and had to be informed of any emergencies that might cause wider economic disruption or when public support for specific operations might have been required. The Financial Services and Market Act 2000 (FSMA) legally defined the role and responsibilities of the FSA as the single financial regulator.

Inefficiencies in the UK functional supervision model were widely recognized, even before reforms were made. Much more controversial was the institutional structure implemented to overcome these inefficiencies. In the debate, the extraction of banking supervision from the central bank was generally considered as the inevitable consequence of the decision to create a unified supervisory agency (Taylor and Fleming, 1999). However, there were many arguments against and for the unification. Although, as Briault claims (1999), countries such as Norway, Denmark, Sweden, and Japan had already gone down this route before the UK, and other countries such as Australia were going to abandon older functional supervisory models, no country had such broad regulatory powers in terms of coverage, scope, and discretion as was seen with the Financial Services Authority (Llewellyn, 1999). When compared with the regulatory agencies of advanced countries, the FSA was an anomaly in business-regulated diversity terms and breadth of functions, which included both prudential and conduct-of-business regulation. No other integrated financial regulator had been set up in any country with a financial system as internationally important as the UK, and most of them had a predominantly prudential focus (Taylor and Fleming, 1999). In the following years, as Jackson (2005) states, the perceived successfulness of the UK model of consolidated supervision inspired many jurisdictions in the European Union and around the world to opt for this model.

Two alternatives have been at the centre of academic and policymaking attention. The first involved the alignment of regulatory responsibilities on an objective-based line, with the creation of two main cross-sector authorities, one responsible for prudential regulation of all financial institutions and the other in charge of conduct-of-business regulation. The second involved the creation of a single financial regulator with cross-sector jurisdiction and comprehensive objectives, the so-called 'mega-regulator'. Taylor (1995), probably the first supporter of the objective-based approach in financial regulation by means of the so-called 'Twin Peaks model', argues that a single regulator without a clear and well-defined mandate is in danger of becoming a bureaucratic monster. The institutional architecture of financial regulation ought to be objective-based: objectives and the culture of prudential regulation are different, and may be in conflict with the conduct of business. Goodhart (1996) too is in favour of regulating by objectives, due to the contrast between micro-prudential focusing on investor protection and macro-prudential focusing on systemic stability. Goodhart et al. (1998, p. 152 et seq.) state that the alleged economies of scale which are expected from a monopolist regulator would be difficult to achieve, and there is a risk that conflict between various regulatory cultures (systemic, prudential, and conduct-of-business) may be difficult to reconcile, or that one of them may be given undue powers. They also stress the problem of reputational contagion, i.e. the danger of regulatory failure compromising the reputation of an entire system and not just a part of it. They recommend the objective-based approach, where financial institutions are institutionally regulated for prudential purposes and functionally regulated for the purpose of business conduct. According to Abrams and Taylor (2000, p. 17), one disadvantage of the British mega-regulator is the number of targets, from systemic risks to fraud protection for individual advisers:

> Indeed, rather than improving accountability, the creation of a unified regulator might diminish it because of the difficulty of designing a single set of objectives for it. As a result, its statutory responsibilities may be vague and ill-defined which in turn give raise to problems of holding the regulatory agency to account for these activities.

Hadjiemmanuil (2000) stresses that not only has the UK brought in a single financial regulator, but also a single regulation. The FSA's public powers include authorization and the ongoing supervision of financial intermediaries, the investigation of suspected misconduct, the intervention in problem institutions, the imposition of administrative sanctions, and the prosecution of breaches of the regulatory regime where these constitute a criminal offence. Its powers extend to the vetting, regulation of conduct and sanctioning of misconduct of an individual carrying on certain key function within authorized financial institutions. In carrying out these functions, the powers of the FSA go well beyond the application of statutory norms in specific cases: they include very broad and mostly discretionary policy and rule-making powers. Procedural safeguards are envisaged as a counterbalance for these vast rule-making powers – i.e. a requirement to make open consultations and to carry out cost-benefit analyses when a certain rule may bring about a rise in regulatory costs. Nevertheless, as Hadjiemmanuil outlines, 'the bias of procedural constraints is in the direction of light, rather than intrusive regulation' (p. 184).

Dale and Wolfe (2003) maintain that the speciality of banks, in the sense of being uniquely exposed to systemic risks, has disappeared because their activities and risk exposures have become intermingled with non-banking activities. They give a positive assessment of the single regulator model, because it is the best way of applying prudential policy, i.e. 'the importance of aligning the remit of the regulation with the risk management function of regulated organisations, so that in the case of centralized risk management of diversified activities, the regulator perspective is the same as that of management.'(p. 208). Commenting on the early years of the FSA, Ferran (2003) stresses that the peculiarity of the UK single regulator approach can be seen in the fact that the UK associated an integrated legal framework with the institutional arrangement for financial regulation. The FSA tried to gain credit as a single regulator, not only in its appearance but also in its essence, by emphasizing its new integrated approach to regulation, the single risk-based approach to be used for all sectors, markets, and regulated firms. The risk-based approach to financial regulation means identifying hazards for the regulatory targets set by regulated firms, and dealing with such hazards by using the formal and informal tools placed at its disposal. In practical terms, these regulatory and supervisory measures are proportional to the hazards affecting both regulated institutions and regulatory objectives. Ferran then goes on, asserting that, because of this approach, the FSA gradually focused less on prudential supervision and more on the conduct of business. As Daripa, Kapur and Wright (2013) argue, the low cost approach, which was a deliberate feature of regulatory consolidation within the FSA, may have constrained its regulatory effectiveness and intensity, even if the main foundation of the light touch regime has been the then-popular reliance on self-correcting markets.

4 Responses to the financial debacle of 2007–2008: Institutional and structural reforms

The financial crisis, which hit the UK from 2007 with the collapse and nationalization of Northern Rock, demonstrated all the fragilities of the British financial system, characterized by an over-expansion of banking and leverage (Shin, 2009; Bank of England, 2014). The crisis also revealed the failures of the light touch supervisory approach, which, as the FSA pointed out (FSA, 2011, p. 261 ss.), arose from the political belief that the competitiveness of the UK financial services sector could have been damaged by an unnecessary restrictive and intrusive regulation. At the same time, the huge impact in the UK of the failures of Lehman and the Icelandic banks brought to light the contrast between keeping London as a world financial centre and the vulnerability to which the UK, as the host country of many branches and subsidiaries of global and European banks, was exposed (Turner Review, 2009).

Particularly the FSA was strongly criticized both inside and outside the UK for failing to assess the systemic risks of the business models used by British banks. However, it is true to say that in dealing with the Northern Rock crisis all the three Tripartite Authorities, and particularly the Bank of England, did not adequately fulfil their remit in ensuring financial stability (Campbell, 2008; Great Britain. House of Commons. Treasury Committee, 2008; Great Britain. House of Commons. Treasury Committee, 2009; IMF, 2011).

The prompt and comprehensive British banking rescue plan became a template for bank support in most of G20 countries (Quaglia, 2009). However, for the country the cost of the crisis was dramatic (Haldane, 2010; Cunliffe, 2014), and, as Woll argues (2014, p. 107), 'the British financial industry had lost not only its economic but also its political standing'. The nationalization or quasi-nationalization of two of the largest five UK banks clashed with the long UK tradition of a governmental hand-off approach.

The main UK regulatory responses to the crisis were the Banking Act 2009, the Financial Services Act 2012, and the Financial Services (Banking Reform) Act 2013. The three reforms are strictly connected by the common objective to find a solution to the 'too important to fail' problem, without which the size of the UK banking system would 'remain too large for the UK taxpayer credibly to support in future' (King, 2011, p. 5).

The Banking Act 2009 brought into the UK a Special Resolution Regime (SRR) for failing banks, and filled a legal gap, which became apparent with the difficulties encountered in finding an early resolution for the Northern Rock crisis in 2007 (Brierley, 2009). It provided a role for the prudential supervisor in triggering the resolution regime, and for the Treasury, mainly for its control powers on the possible use public funds. The role of lead resolution authority was however given to the Bank of England, as part of the new statutory objective to protect and enhance UK financial stability, consistently with the paradigm that a zero-failure regime would be neither feasible nor desirable. The financial stability objective was indeed not new for the Bank of England, but it was enlarged and redefined; in this new framework, the traditional Bank's oversight of interbank payment system was also put onto a statutory footing.

The Financial Services Act 2012, which came into force in April 2013, radically changed the institutional architecture brought in during the reforms of the late 1990s. The FSA was abolished and three new financial regulators created. The Bank of England returned to centre stage in financial regulation – the Governor's eyebrows are back – even if this has been balanced by the stronger role of the Treasury not only in crisis management, but also in providing macro-prudential authority with guidance and specific intervention tools. A 'Twin Peaks' model, amended by the insertion of the 'macro-prudential peak', has replaced the approach of the single regulator. The Bank of England retains its responsibility for financial stability (including powers as resolution authority and oversight of financial market infrastructures). In support of the objective to protect the financial stability, the Financial Policy Committee (FPC), a semi-independent committee inside the Bank of England, was formally established and was charged with macro-prudential supervision and regulation. Its function is identifying and monitoring systemic risks and taking actions to reduce them, including giving directions and making recommendations to the other supervisory authorities. The Prudential Regulation Authority (PRA), created as a subsidiary of the Bank of England, will be responsible for micro-prudential regulation and supervision of banks, insurers and investment firms considered 'systemically important.' The Financial Conduct Authority (FCA) is the organisation that has taken the legal status of the FSA and a significant portion of its previous functions as the regulator responsible for the conduct of business of all financial firms. The FCA will be also responsible for the micro-prudential regulation of financial services firms outside the PRA's supervision (Conway and Edmonds, 2012; Murphy and Senior, 2013).

The main reasons of the reform were, on the one hand, the asserted incompatibility between prudential regulation and consumer protection and market conduct, and on the other, the need to more closely integrate micro- and macro-prudential regulation and the resolution regime (King, 2011, p. 5). Theoretical and empirical analysis demonstrates, however, that these arguments are not conclusive. According to several authors, allocating macro- and micro-prudential supervision into the central bank could lead to less rules and more discretion, increasing the risk of regulator capture (Boyer and Ponce, 2010; Masciandaro et al., 2011). Black and Hopper (2012) outline that the reform risks introducing difficult coordination issues between the Bank of England, the Treasury and the micro-prudential regulators. As Ferran (2010) argues, the real basis for the reform was probably the wish of politicians to respond to public pressures, and the notion that inadequate supervision by the FSA had been the main cause for the collapse of Northern Rock.

The Financial Services (Banking Reform) Act 2013 was passed in December 2013; secondary legislation is expected to be completed by late 2015, and it will probably not come into force before 2019. With several non-marginal innovations, this Act implements the main recommendations of the UK Independent Commission on Banking (ICB), set up in 2010 to make recommendations for creating a more stable and competitive basis for UK banking in the longer term. The proposals drawn up by the Commission in its final report (ICB, 2011) are based upon the principle whereby the right policy approach for UK banking stability requires both structural reforms and greater loss-absorbing capacity. The structural reforms are intended to bring together two main targets: first, to solve the too-big-to-fail problem; second, to help insulate retail banking from external financial shocks, including by reducing resolvability problems arising from global interconnectedness.

The approach to the structural reform adopted by the ICB is retail ring fencing, which brings in the universal banking model, but places severe limits on the magnitude and the nature of the commingling of retail and investment banking within a single entity. In a long examination of the advantages of universal banking, the ICB says that retail ring fencing is better than any hypothetical full separation, because it is less costly for banks, allows customers to source banking services from a single provider, and, finally, because the benefits of diversification might allow the bank to still transfer capital between its different arms. According to the ICB recommendations, all core retail activities – taking of deposits from and providing lending to individuals and SMEs and associated payment services – the continuous provision of which is imperative and for which customers have no ready alternative, should be ring-fenced, i.e. should be placed in a legally, financially and operationally independent entity. Inside the ring-fenced body trading book activities (not only proprietary trading in the Volcker rule sense), any retail or wholesale services outside the European Economic Area cannot be carried out, as is the case with any services to financial counterparties, other than deposit taking and payment services.

In order of facilitate their resolvability, large UK ring-fenced banks should comply with capital requirements, leverage ratios and primary loss-absorbing capacity (i.e. long-term uninsured debt subject to bail-in powers) more stringent than those proposed by the international standards. As the ICB outlines, the reform is wholly consistent with maintaining the UK's strength as a global financial market, because operations of foreign subsidiaries of UK banks are outside the scope of ring fencing requirements, and ring fencing does not affect foreign banks' UK branches. In contrast, UK subsidiaries of foreign banks are subject to ring fencing requirements, if their retail activity inside the UK is significant in size. Explicitly, the scope of structural reform is nationally focused: it allows international standards to apply to the wholesale/investment banking business of the UK banks, where they tend to be global, while higher standards apply to UK retail banking, where markets tend to be national in scope (ICB, 2011, p. 28).

The Financial Services (Banking) Reform Act 2013 took on many recommendations made by the ICB, although there were many significant exceptions (Great Britain. HM Treasury, 2012). As John Vickers, Chair of the ICB, pointed out in his comments on the Bill (Vickers, 2012, p. 17), the Act leaves Government with too much scope to redefine the location and the height of the ring fence discretionally. For instance, the Government decided that ring-fenced banks could have counterparties and hold assets outside the EEA, if this did not create a barrier to resolution. An important concession was also made to UK-based G-SIBs, for which the government decided that, so long as such a bank can show that any non-UK operations do not pose a risk to UK financial stability, the higher requirements of primary loss-absorbing capacity would not apply to those non-UK operations. Nor has the government accepted the ICB recommendation that banks subject to enhanced capital requirements should have correspondingly enhanced leverage ratios (Vickers, 2013, p. 6, n. 7). Perhaps no less importantly, the government did not accept the Parliamentary recommendation on the so-called 'electrification' of ring fencing, which would define, in statute and from the start, what legal and operational links should be permitted between ring-fenced bank and its wider corporate group (Edmonds, 2013; Great Britain. House of Lords. House of Commons. Parliamentary Commission on Banking Standards, 2013).

According to Acharya (2011), ring fencing may be a useful way of insulating commercial banking against those risks, which have no real social use. Acharya also points out that retail ring fencing will not stop those risk-taking incentives inside the ring-fenced commercial banks, such as mortgage lending, corporate and personal loans, which have caused the greatest losses after the credit crunch. The higher capital requirements specified by the ICB are no guarantee of sufficient solvency, given that assets considered low-risk under prudential regulation (e.g. mortgages) may produce speculative bubbles and give rise to systemic hazards. Véron (2011) outlines that the tighter prudential regulation required by the ICB for retail banks ought to correct the previous 'financial mercantilism' by British supervisors, i.e. their tendency to encourage the global expansion of their big domestic retail banks by using only light-touch supervision. Chow and Surti (2011) argue that supervisory authorities will find it difficult to ensure institutional compliance on limits on market and counterparty risks and on intra-group credits, needed to ensure isolation and continuity of ring-fenced operations. It is easy to see that banks have many incentives to break these limits, because they reduce the allowed risk management strategies and increase the costs of providing banking services. Compared with the Volcker rule, retail ring fencing has the advantage of allowing diversification gains, albeit in a limited degree: the opinion of the authors is that this ought to reduce the risk that activities outside the ring fence move towards a shadow banking system. According to Haldane (2012), all proposals for structural reform – such as the Volcker rules, UK ring fencing, and the Liikanen Plan – could improve financial stability in two ways: during a crisis, by avoiding cross-contamination between the more hazardous investment banking and retail banking; in normal times, by allocating resources better from a social perspective. This allocation advantage, which can only come about at the cost of reducing the benefits of cross-subsidiarization, which universal banks now enjoy, might be compromised if there is no full separation of capital and cultures between commercial banking and investment banking. Viñals et al. (2013) compare the main structural measures proposed by the US, the UK, and the EU as part of their banking reforms. The nature and scope of the separation is significantly more severe under the Volcker rule. While US banks cannot run prohibited business lines anywhere in their global corporate structure, all European proposals permit banking groups to run business lines proscribed for depositor institutions within the group. Under either the UK or Liikanen proposals, activity restrictions are not imposed on the non-ring-fenced affiliates. The consequence is that the British ring-fencing model and the European model promote resolvability at the level of the retail bank, but not necessarily at a group level. Moreover, the UK approach is only nationally focused and does not compel the group to ring fence retail operations in other jurisdictions.

About the foreseeable effects of ring fencing on organizational models for cross-border banks, Tonveronachi (2013) outlines that UK ring fencing can be understood as a 'defensive strategy' to protect national deposit insurance. Reference to the trauma caused by the Icelandic banking crisis can be clearly understood, and this may bring about a deglobalization in banks and the abandonment of any regulatory playing field as set out by international prudential standards. In the same way, Gambacorta and Van Rixtel (2013) maintain that structural regulatory proposals aim at protecting depositors and cut the cost of the official safety net within home country jurisdiction. In particular, the Vickers solution seeks to restrict government support to retail banking and payment services within the European Economic Area. However, structural reforms may contribute to a fragmentation of banking markets along national lines, forcing multinational banks to operate in multiple jurisdictions with subsidiaries, possibly subject to a more restrictive regulation by the host country, in order to guarantee their orderly resolution in case of distress of the group or of a part of it (Bank of England. Prudential Regulatory Authority, 2014a; FSB, 2014).

5 Conclusions

The crisis has thrown doubt on several key aspects of the British regulatory paradigm, which, especially since the 1980s, had been seen at international level and in Europe as a successful model to be imitated. In the UK, as in other countries, a new direction has been sought for financial regulation. As the Turner Review (2009, p. 38–39) recognized, the global financial crisis challenged on both theoretical and empirical grounds the existing regulatory philosophy and the intellectual assumptions of efficient, rational, self-correcting markets on which it was based.

Until the financial crisis, the superiority of the light-touch, principles-based approach to financial regulation was claimed as the key factor in the success and international prestige of the British system. The association between light-touch regulation and the vulnerabilities of financial systems has now been largely accepted by the same British regulators. It is not clear, however, whether the broad UK regulatory reforms brought in to deal with the crisis can be seen, in this regard, as a radical departure from previous practice. After the crisis, the market-friendly approach, recognized as the main foundation of light touch supervision, has been replaced by an increased distrust on the skills, culture and ethics of the financial services industry (Black, 2010). However, the 'judgment-based supervision', which new UK regulators have pledged to adopt (Lastra, 2013; Bank of England. Prudential Regulatory Authority, 2014b) does not seem very different from the principles-based, risk-based approach, which has been a feature of the UK regulatory regime since 1990. 'The wisdom of hindsight, from which we benefit in considering the "light touch" approach, will not be available to us to evaluate the post-crash regulatory mantra of "intensive and intrusive" for some time yet' (Cohrs, 2012).

At the same time, perhaps paradoxically, the crisis has shown the difficulties that the British model has in reconciling itself with regulatory and institutional reforms in Europe. As Whyte (2011) argues, the common Continental narrative that the financial crisis would not have happened if 'Anglo-Saxons' had regulated financial system as strictly as Europeans is altogether misplaced. It is true however that the post-crisis EU regulatory approach to a maximum harmonization not only risks compromising the country's traditional ambition to shape European legislation in line with its own national interests, but also raises concerns about safeguarding London's ability to compete in global financial market (Great Britain. House of Lords. House of Commons. Parliamentary Commission on Banking Standards 2013, par. 36–37).

Significant contrasts between the UK and the EU originate in several rules brought into the EU after the crisis, considered as harmful to City interests. There are several examples: the proposed introduction of a financial transaction tax; the new regulation of hedge funds; the issue of the legality to empower the ESMA with discretion on banning short selling; the cap set by the CRD IV on bonus payment to bankers; the ECB location policy that euro-denominated instruments should be cleared only by a clearing house physically located in the euro area (Great Britain. HM Government, 2014).

The refusal of the UK to join the Banking Union is the latest proof of the dilemma that the British feel about the single market of financial services. The position taken by the Conservative party is that 'the challenges facing the euro area should be dealt primarily by the euro area itself' and 'UK taxpayers would not wish to accept liability for the resolution of a French or German bank based in London'. However, fear is widespread that non-involvement in the Banking Union risks marginalizing the UK in the EU, thus reducing the UK's ability to promote and shape the single market in financial services and the country's position within it (Great Britain. House of Lords. European Union Committee, 2014, p.60 ss.).

As things stand, it is difficult to tell whether the UK's official position will cause greater difficulties either for Europe, because effective financial integration without the City of London goes against its original plans for unity (Schoenmaker, 2012, p. 12; Barnier, 2013), or for the UK, which feels the need to protect itself against an increasing 'continental shift' in European financial regulation (Booth et al., 2011).

References

ABRAMS, R. and TAYLOR, M. (2000) *Issues in the Unification of Financial Sector Supervision*. Washington D.C.: IMF Working Paper WP/00/213.

ACHARYA, V. (2011) Ring-fencing is good, but no panacea. In: Beck, T. (ed.), *The Future of Banking*. [Online.] London: CEPR. Available from www.voxeu.org/epubs/cepr-reports/future-banking [Accessed: 3 April 2014.]

ADRIAN, T. and SHIN, H. (2010) The changing nature of financial intermediation and the financial crisis of 2007–09. *Federal Reserve Bank of New York Staff Reports*. 439 (March) (revised April 2010).

ALLEN, F. and GALE, D. (2001) *Comparative Financial Systems: A Survey*. [Online.] University of Pennsylvania. Wharton School Center for Financial Institutions Working Paper 01-15. Available from: http://econpapers.repec.org/scripts/redir.pf?u=http%3A%2F%2Ffic.wharton.upenn.edu%2Ffic%2Fpapers%2F01%2F0115.pdf;h=repec:wop:pennin:01-15 [Accessed: 14 March 2014]

BANK OF ENGLAND (1985) Changes in the structure of financial markets: A view from London – Speech by the Deputy Governor at the 'Euromoney' conference. *Quarterly Bulletin*, 1, 84–85.

BANK OF ENGLAND (1986) Consolidated supervision of institutions authorised under the Banking Act 1979. *Quarterly Bulletin*, 1, 85–90.

BANK OF ENGLAND (1987a) Convergence of capital adequacy in the UK and US – Notice issued by the bank's banking supervision Division 8 January 1987. *Quarterly Bulletin*, 1, 85–86.

BANK OF ENGLAND (1987b) Agreed proposal of the US Federal Banking Supervisory Authorities and the Bank of England on primary capital and capital adequacy assessment – Consultative paper issued by the BoE and the Federal Reserve System. *Quarterly Bulletin*, 1, 87–93.

BANK OF ENGLAND (1995) Report of the board of banking supervision inquiry into the circumstances of the collapse of barings. 18 July.

BANK OF ENGLAND (1998a) The Bank of England Act – Annex: Memorandum of understanding between HM Treasury, the Bank of England and the Financial Services Authority. *Quarterly Bulletin*, 2, 93–99.

BANK OF ENGLAND (1998b) The new lady of Threadneedle Street. *Quarterly Bulletin*, 2, 173–177.

BANK OF ENGLAND (2010) Evolution of the UK banking system. *Quarterly Bulletin*. 4, 321– 332.

BANK OF ENGLAND (2014) Why is the UK banking system so big and is that a problem? *Quarterly Bullettin*, 4, 385–395.

BANK OF ENGLAND. PRUDENTIAL REGULATION AUTHORITY (2014a) *Supervising International Banks: The Prudential Regulatory Authority's Approach to Branch Supervision*. [Online.] Available from: www.bankofengland.co.uk/pra/Documents/publications/ss/2014/ss1014.pdf. [Accessed: 3 February 2015.]

BANK OF ENGLAND. PRUDENTIAL REGULATION AUTHORITY (2014b) *The Prudential Regulation Authority's Approach to Banking Supervision*. [Online.] Available from: www.bankofengland.co.uk/publications/Documents/praapproach/bankingappr1406.pdf. [Accessed: 3 February 2015.]

BARNIER, M. (2013) The single market in financial services: We need the UK on board. [Online.] European Commission. Speech given at the Conference 'Britain, the EU and the Single Market in Financial Services'. London, 12 July 2013. Available from: http://europa.eu/rapid/press-release_SPEECH-13-636_en.htm. [Accessed: 26 June 2014.]

BARTH, J. R., CAPRIO, G. and LEVINE, R. (2004) Bank regulation and supervision: What works best? *Journal of Financial Intermediation*. 13 (2). p. 205–248.

BECK, T., DEGRYSE, H. and KNEER, C. (2014) Is more finance better? Disentangling intermediation and size effects of financial systems. *Journal of Financial Stability*, 10 (February), 50–64.

BECK, T., DEMIRGÜÇ-KUNT, A. and LEVINE, R. (2003) *Bank Supervision and Corporate Finance*. NBER Working Paper Series No. 9620.

BLACK, J. (2010) The rise, fall and fate of principles based regulation. [Online.] LSE Legal Studies Working Paper No. 17/2010. November. Available from: http://papers.ssrn.com/sol3/papers.cfm?abstract_id=1712862. [Accessed: 21 February 2014.]

BLACK, J. and NOBLES, R. (1998) Personal pensions misselling: The causes and lessons of regulatory failure. *Modern Law Review*, 61(6), 789–820.

BLACK, J. and HOPPER, M. (2012) Breaking up is hard to do: The next stage? [Online.] London: The London School of Economics and Political Science and Herbert Smith LLP. Available from: www.lse.ac.uk/collections/law/projects/lfm/9705_HS%20and%20LSE%20discussion%20paper%20third%20edition_d5.pdf. [Accessed: 5 January 2015.]

BLAIR, W. (1994) Liberalisation and the universal banking model: Regulation and deregulation in the United Kingdom. In: Norton, J. J., Cheng, C.-J. and Fletcher, I. (eds) *International Banking Regulation and Supervision: Change and Transformation in the 1990s*. International Banking and Finance Law, Vol. 1. London; Boston: Graham and Totman/M. Nijhoff; Norwell, MA: Kluwer Academic Publisher.

BOOTH, S., HOWARTH, C., PERSSON, M. and SCARPETTA, V. (2011) Continental shift: Safeguarding the UK's financial trade in a changing Europe. [Online.] Open Europe Report 12/2011. London: Open Europe. Available from: http://openeurope.org.uk/intelligence/economic-policy-and-trade/eu-financial-regulation/. [Accessed: 10 January 2015.]

BOYER, P. C. and PONCE, J. (2010) Central banks, regulatory capture and banking supervision reform. BCU Documento de Trabajo No. 003-2010 (September).

BRIERLEY, P. (2009) The UK special resolution regime for failing banks in an international context. Bank of England Financial Stability Paper No. 5 (July).

BORIO, C. and FILOSA, R. (1994) The changing borders of banking: Trends and implications. [Online.] BIS Working Paper no. 23 (October). Available from: www.bis.org/publ/work23.htm. [Accessed: 4 May 2014.]

BRIAULT, C. (1999) The rationale for a single national financial services regulator. FSA Occasional Paper Series, No. 2 (May).

CAMPBELL, A. (2008) The run on the Rock and its consequences. *Journal of Banking Regulation*, 9(2), 61–64.

CARNEY, M. (2013) *The UK at the heart of a renewed globalization*. [Online.] Bank of England. Speech given at an event to celebrate the 125th anniversary of the Financial Times. London (24 October). Available from: www.bankofengland.co.uk/publications/Documents/speeches/2013/speech690.pdf. [Accessed: 2 April 2014.]

CHOW, J. and SURTI, J. (2011) *Making banks safer? Can Volcker and Vickers do it?* IMF Working Paper WP/11/236 (November). Washington D.C.: International Monetary Fund.

COHRS, M. (2012) Crisis and crash: Lessons for regulation. [Online] Speech given at a gathering jointly hosted by the Bank's Agency for Scotland and Scottish Financial Enterprises 23 March. Available from: www.bankofengland.co.uk/publications/Documents/speeches/2012/speech558.pdf. [Accessed: 13 February 2015.]
CONWAY, L. and EDMONDS, T. (2012) Financial Services Bill. Bill 278 of 2010–12. [Online.] House of Commons Library. Research Paper 12/08. Available from: www.parliament.uk/business/publications/research/briefing-papers/RP12-8/financial-services-bill-bill-278-of-201012. [Accessed: 2 March 2014.]
CUNLIFFE, J. (2014) Ending too big to fail – Progress to date and remaining issues. [Online.] Bank of England. Speech given at The Barclays European Bank Capital Summit, London, 13 May 2014. Available from: www.bankofengland.co.uk/publications/Documents/speeches/2014/speech727.pdf. [Accessed: 3 January 2015.]
DALE, R. (1992) *International Banking Deregulation: The Great Banking Experiment*. Oxford: Blackwell Finance.
DALE, R. and WOLFE, S. (2003) The UK Financial Services Authority: Unified regulator in the new market environment. *Journal of Banking Regulation*, 4(3), 200–224.
DALLA PELLEGRINA, L. and MASCIANDARO, D. (2011) Good-bye light touch? Macroeconomic resilience, banking regulation and institutions. [Online.] Paolo Baffi Centre Research Paper Series No. 2011-109. Available from: http://ssrn.com/abstract=1958170. [Accessed: 20 May 2014.]
DARIPA, A., KAPUR, S. and WRIGHT, S. (2013) Labour's record on financial regulation. Birkbeck Working Papers on Economics and Finance. BWPEF 1301 (February). London: Birkbeck, University of London.
DAVIES, H. (1997) Financial regulation: Why, how and by whom? *Bank of England Quarterly Bulletin*, 1, 107–112.
EDMONDS, T. (2013) The Independent Commission on Banking: The Vickers report. [Online.] House of Commons Library. Available from: www.parliament.uk/briefing-papers/sn06171.pdf. [Accessed: 6 January 2015.]
FERRAN, E. (2003) Examining the UK's experience in adopting the single financial regulator model. [Online.] *Brooklyn Journal of International Law*, 28. Available from: www.law.yale.edu/documents/pdf/cbl/2-4Panel2Ferransingleregulator.pdf. [Accessed: 6 January 2015.]
FERRAN, E. (2010) The break-up of the Financial Services Authority. [Online.] University of Cambridge Faculty of Law. Legal Studies Research Paper Series No. 10/04. Available from http://papers.ssrn.com/sol3/papers.cfm?abstract_id=1690523. [Accessed: 2 February 2015.]
FERRAN, E. (2012) Crisis-driven eu financial regulatory reform. [Online.] University of Cambridge Faculty of Law. Legal Studies Research Paper No. 6/2012. Available from: http://ssrn.com/abstract=2028003. [Accessed: 18 March 2014.]
FINANCIAL STABILITY BOARD (FSB) (2014) Structural banking reforms. cross-border consistencies and global financial stability implications. [Online.] Report to G20 Leaders for the November 2014 Summit (27 October). Available from: www.financialstabilityboard.org/wp-content/uploads/r_141027.pdf?page_moved=1. [Accessed: 6 February 2015.]
FSA (2011) The failure of the Royal Bank of Scotland. FSA Board Report. London: Financial Services Authority.
FURSE, C. (2006) Sox is not to blame – London is just better as a market. *Financial Times*, 17 September.

GAMBACORTA, L. and VAN RIXTEL, A. (2013) Structural bank regulation initiatives: Approaches and implications. BIS Working Papers no. 412 (April).

GOODHART, C. A. E. and SCHOENMAKER D. (1993) Institutional separation between supervisory and monetary agencies. LSE Financial Markets Group. Special Paper Series. No. 52 (April).

GOODHART, C. A. E. (1996) Some regulatory concerns. *Swiss Journal of Economics and Statistics*, 132(4/2), 613–636.

GOODHART, C. A. E., HARTMANN, P., LLEWELLYN, D. T., ROJAS-SUAREZ, L. and WEISBROD, S. (1998) *Financial Regulation: Why, How and Where Now?* Abingdon, Oxon: Routledge.

GOWER, L. C. B. (1988) Big Bang and City revolution. *Modern Law Review*, 51 (January), 1–22.

GREAT BRITAIN. HOUSE OF COMMONS. TREASURY COMMITTEE (2008) The run on the Rock. Fifth report of session 2007–08. [Online.] London: Stationery Office. Available from: www.publications.parliament.uk/pa/cm200708/cmselect/cmtreasy/56/56ii.pdf. [Accessed: 4 February 2015.]

GREAT BRITAIN. HOUSE OF COMMONS. TREASURY COMMITTEE (2009) Banking crisis: dealing with the failure of the UK banks. Seventh report of session 2008–09. [Online.] London: Stationery Office. Available from: www.publications.parliament.uk/pa/cm200809/cmselect/cmtreasy/416/416.pdf. [Accessed: 15 April 2014.]

GREAT BRITAIN. HM TREASURY. DEPARTMENT FOR BUSINESS, INNOVATION and SKILLS (2012) *Banking Reform: Delivering Stability and Supporting a Sustainable Economy*. [Online.] London: Stationery Office. Available from: www.gov.uk/government/uploads/system/uploads/attachment_data/file/32556/whitepaper_banking_reform_140512.pdf. [Accessed: 7 January 2015.]

GREAT BRITAIN. HM GOVERNMENT. DEPARTMENT FOR BUSINESS, INNOVATION & SKILL (2013) *Guiding Principles for EU Legislation*. [Online.] London: Stationery Office. Available from: www.gov.uk/government/uploads/system/uploads/attachment_data/file/185626/bis-13-774-guiding-principles-for-eu-legislation.pdf. [Accessed: 15 April 2014.]

GREAT BRITAIN. HOUSE OF LORDS. HOUSE OF COMMONS. PARLIAMENTARY COMMISSION ON BANKING STANDARDS (2013) Changing banks for good. [Online.] First report of session 2013–14. Volume II. London: Stationery Office. Available from: www.parliament.uk/documents/banking-commission/Banking-final-report-vol-ii.pdf. [Accessed: 3 March 2014.]

GREAT BRITAIN. HM GOVERNMENT (2014) Review of the balance of competences between the United Kingdom and the European Union. The single market: Financial services and the free movement of capital. [Online.] London. Summer 2014. Available from: http://gcn.civilservice.gov.uk/. [Accessed: 15 April 2014.]

GREAT BRITAIN. HOUSE OF LORDS. EUROPEAN UNION COMMITTEE (2014) Genuine economic and monetary union and the implications for the UK. [Online.] 8th Report of Session 2013–14. HL Paper 134. London: Stationery Office. Available from: www.publications.parliament.uk/pa/ld201314/ldselect/ldeucom/134/134.pdf. [Accessed: 10 March 2014.]

GROUP OF THIRTY (2008) The structure of financial supervision. Approaches and challenges in a global marketplace. [Online.] Available from: www.group30.org/images/PDF/The%20Structure%20of%20Financial%20Supervision.pdf. [Accessed: 6 January 2015.]

HADJIEMMANUIL, C. (2000) Institutional structure of financial regulation: A trend towards 'megaregulators'? [Online.] 5 Y.B. Int'l Fin. & Econ. L. 127 2000–2001. Heini OnLine. [Accessed 11 June 2014.]

HALDANE, A. G. (2010) The $100 billion question. [Online.] Bank of England. Comments given at the Institute of Regulation and Risk, Hong Kong, 13 March. Available from: www.bankofengland.co.uk/archive/Documents/historicpubs/speeches/2010/speech433.pdf. [Accessed: 31 January 2015.]

HALDANE, A. G. (2012) On being the right size. [Online.] Bank of England. Speech given at the Institute of Economic Affairs 22nd Annual Series, The 2012 Beesly Lecture. At the Institute of Directors, Pall Mall (25 October). Available from: www.bankofengland.co.uk/publications/Documents/speeches/2012/speech615.pdf. [Accessed: 16 June 2014.]

HALDANE, A. G., SIMON, B. and MADOUROS, V. (2010) What is the contribution of the financial sector: Miracle or mirage? In: Turner, A. et al. *The Future of Finance: The LSE Report*. London: London School of Economics and Political Science.

HALL, M .J. B. (1989) The BIS capital adequacy 'rules'. A critique. *BNL Quarterly Review*, 169 (June), 207–227.

HALL, M. J. B. (1992) Implementation of the BIS 'rules' on capital adequacy assessment: A comparative study of the approaches adopted in the UK, the USA and Japan. *BNL Quarterly Review*, 180 (March), 35–45.

HALL, M. J. B. (1999) *Handbook of Banking Regulation and Supervision in the United Kingdom*. Cheltenham: Edward Elgar Publishing.

HARDIE, I. and MAXFIELD, S. (2013) Market-based banking as the worst of all worlds: Illustrations from the US and UK. In: Hardie, I. and Howard, D. (eds) *Market-Based Banking and the International Financial Crisis*. Oxford: Oxford University Press.

INDEPENDENT COMMISSION ON BANKING (ICB) (2011) Final report recommendations. September 2011. [Online.] London: Independent Commission on Banking. Available from: https://hmt-sanctions.s3.amazonaws.com/ICB%20final%20report/ICB%2520Final%2520Report%5B1%5D.pdf. [Accessed: 2 January 2015.]

INGHAM, H. and THOMPSON, S. (1993) Structural deregulation and market entry: The case of financial services. *Fiscal Studies*, 14(1), 15–41.

INSTITUTE OF INTERNATIONAL FINANCE (IIF) (2006) *Proposal for a Strategic Dialogue on Effective Regulation*. December. Washington D.C.: Institute of International Finance.

INTERNATIONAL MONETARY FUND (IMF) (2003) United Kingdom: Financial system stability assessment. IMF Country Report 03/46 (February).

INTERNATIONAL MONETARY FUND (IMF) (2011) United Kingdom: Financial system stability assessment. IMF Country Report 11/222 (July).

JACKSON, H. E. (2005) An American perspective on the U.K. financial services authority: Politics, goals and regulatory intensity. [Online.] Harvard Law and Economic Discussion Paper No. 522. Available from: http://papers.ssrn.com/sol3/papers.cfm?abstract-id=839284. [Accessed: 6 March 2014.]

KAPSTEIN, E. B. (1991) Supervising international banks: Origins and implications of the Basle accord. Essays in International Finance No. 185 (December). Princeton, NJ: Princeton University. Department of Economics. International Finance Section.

KING, M. (2011) Speech given at the Lord Mayor's Banquet for Bankers and Merchants of the City of London at the Mansion House. [Online.] *Bank of England Speeches*. Available from: www.bankofengland.co.uk/archive/Documents/historicpubs/speeches/2011/speech504.pdf. [Accessed: 5 February 2015.]

KINSELLA, R. P. (1992) *Some Regulatory and Supervisory Lessons of the BCCI Collapse*. Bangor: Institute of European Finance. University College of North Wales.

LASTRA, R. M. (2003) The governance structure for financial regulation and supervision in Europe. Financial Market Group Special Paper 149. London: London School of Economics.

LASTRA, R. M. (2013) Defining forward-looking, judgment-based supervision. *Journal of Banking Regulation*, 14 (July/November), 221–227.

LAWSON, N. (2006) Foreword. In: *Big Bang 20 Years On. New Challenges Facing the Financial Services Sector. Collected Essays.* London: Centre for Policy Studies.

LLEWELLYN, D. (1999) The economic rationale for financial regulation. FSA Occasional Paper 1 (April).

MARTIJN, J. K. and SAMIEI, H. (1999) Central bank independence and the conduct of monetary policy in the United Kingdom. IMF Working Paper WP/99/170 (December).

MASCIANDARO, D., VEGA PASINI, V. and QUINTYN M. (2011) The economic crisis. Did financial supervision matter? IMF Working Paper WP/11/26 (November).

MILLER, S. S. (1989) Regulating financial services in the United Kingdom: An American perspective. *Business Lawyer*, 44 (2/February), 323–364.

MORAN, M. (1988) Thatcherism and financial regulation. *Political Quarterly*, 59 (1/January), 20–27.

MULLINEUX, A. W. (2012) *U.K. Banking After the Deregulation*. Abingdon, Oxon and New York: Routledge Library Editions: Banking and Finance. Volume 23. (First published in 1987).

MURPHY, E. and SENIOR, S. (2013) Changes to the Bank of England. *Bank of England Quarterly Bulletin*, 1, 20–28.

PIMLOTT, G. F. (1985) The reform of investor protection in the U.K. – An examination of the proposals of the Gower Report and the U.K. government's white paper of January 1985. *Journal of Comparative Business and Capital Markets Law*, 7, 141–182

PLENDER, J. (1986) London's big bang in international context. *International Affairs*, 63 (1), 39–48.

QUAGLIA, L. (2009) The 'British plan' as a pace-setter: The Europeanization of banking rescue plans in the EU. *Journal of Common Market Studies*, 47 (5), 1063–1083.

QUAGLIA, L. (2010) Completing the single market in financial services: The politics of competing advocacy coalition. *Journal of European Public Policy*, 17(7), 1007–1023.

RAJAN, R. C. and ZINGALES, L. (2001) financial systems, industrial structure, and growth. *Oxford Review of Economic Policy*, 17 (4), 467–482.

SCHOENMAKER, D. (2012) Banking supervision and resolution: The European dimension. [Online.] DSF Policy Paper Series No. 19 (January). Available from: http://papers.ssrn.com/sol3/papers.cfm?abstract_id=1982168. [Accessed: 16 April 2014.]

SCHOONER, H. M. and TAYLOR, M. (2003) United Kingdom and United States responses to the regulatory challenges of modern financial markets. *Texas International Law Journal*, 38, 317–345.

SHIN, H. S. (2009) Reflections on Northern Rock: The bank run that heralded the global financial crisis. *Journal of Economic Perspectives*, 23(1), 101–119.

TAYLOR, M. (1995) *Twin Peaks: A Regulatory Structure for the New Century*. London: Center for the Study of Financial Innovation.

TAYLOR, M. and FLEMING, A. (1999) Integrated financial supervision: Lessons from Northern European countries. The World Bank Policy Research Working Paper no. 2223 (November). Washington D.C.: The World Bank.

THECITYUK (2012) Banking. [Online.] Finance Market Series (May). Available from: www.thecityuk.com/research/our-work/reports-list/banking-2012/. [Accessed: 8 April 2014.]

TOMASIC, R. (2010) Beyond 'Light Touch' Regulation of British banks after financial crisis. In: MacNeil, I. G. and O'Brien, J. (eds) *The Future of Financial Regulation*. Oxford: Hart Publishing.

TONVERONACHI, M. (2013) De-globalising bank regulation. *PSL Quarterly Review*, 66 (267), 371–385.

TURNER, A. (2009) *The Turner Review: A Regulatory Response to the Global Banking Crisis*. London: Financial Services Authority.

TURNER, A. (2010) What do banks do? Why do credit boom and burst occur and what can public policy do about it? In: Turner, A. et al. *The Future of Finance: The LSE Report*. London: London School of Economics and Political Science.

VÉRON, N. (2011) Some progress in the banking reform debate. [Online.] 18 April. Available from: www.bruegel.org/blog/author/9/sort/date/pp/10/page/4/. [Accessed: 8 March 2014.]

VICKERS, J. (2012) Some economics of banking reform. *Rivista di Politica Economica*, 4, 11–35.

VICKERS, J. (2013) Banking reform in Britain and Europe. [Online.] Paper presented at the Rethinking Macro Policy II: First Steps and Early Lessons Conference. Hosted by the International Monetary Fund. Washington D.C., April 16–17, 2013. Available at: www.imf.org/external/np/seminars/eng/2013/macro2/pdf/jv.pdf. [Accessed: 21 May 2014.]

VIÑALS, J., PAZARBASIOGLU, C., SURTI, J., NARAIN, A., ERBENOVA, M. and CHOW, J. (2013) Creating a safer financial system: Will the Volcker, Vickers, and Liikanen structural measures help? IMF Staff Discussion Note No. 13 (May).

WHYTE, P. (2011) Financial regulation: Britain the perennial outlier? [Online] 20 June 2011. London: Centre for European Reform (CER). Available from: www.cer.org.uk/insights/financial-regulation-britain-perennial-outlier. [Accessed: 10 January 2015.]

WOLL, C. (2014) *The Power of Inaction. Bank Bailouts in Comparison*. Ithaca and London: Cornell University Press.

11 Crisis management

The 1990s experience of the Nordic countries

Elisabetta Montanaro

1 Introduction

The Nordic financial crises began in the early 1980s, when financial deregulation and increased access to international markets activated a boom-bust cycle. As the theory predicts (Fisher, 1933; Minsky, 1977; Allen and Gale, 1999), and as the history of financial crises has shown (Kaminsky and Reinhart, 1999), many assets bubbles and bursts associated with banking and currency crises – as the Nordic crises were – are preceded by financial liberalization and over-indebtedness.

Macroeconomic external and internal shocks created the conditions for the burst and the emergence of the crisis (Drees and Pazarbaşioğlu, 1995).

According to Berg (1998, p. 206), the Nordic banking crises were due to 'bad banking, bad policies and bad luck'. Actually, given the inherent instability of financial systems, the recent crisis has shown that, in an environment of financial deregulation, it is very difficult for the various players, bankers, regulators and supervisors, borrowers and investors, to lean against the wind. The Nordic crises are a good illustration of such a view. For this reason, the conviction is growing today that, leaving market forces free to innovate, the management of financial crises is probably even more important than their prevention.

The main objective of crisis management policies is to re-establish the financial intermediation processes upon which the economy depends for an efficient allocation of capital, and to accomplish this objective at minimal costs. To limit the costs of banking crises, governments can use various mechanisms, mainly aimed at restoring banks' financial health and investors' confidence in the financial systems. These mechanisms reallocate wealth towards banks and away from taxpayers (Calomiris et al., 2004). The Nordic countries' successful experience in crisis management shows that several economic, regulatory and political prerequisites can help in different ways to minimize these distortions.

This chapter is organized as follows. The second section presents a brief description of the Nordic crises. The third section analyses the various solutions adopted to solve the crisis in the three countries, and the debate about their respective effectiveness. In the fourth, some brief conclusions are offered.

2 A stylized description of the Nordic crises

A systemic banking crisis hit Norway, Sweden and Finland in the period between 1988 and 1994. Reinhart and Rogoff (2008, p. 5) list the crises in Finland, Norway, and Sweden among the 'Big Five Crises' which came about after World War II. The three crises appear, to some extent, quite similar in their cause, timescale, and for the way they were managed. All three were twin crises, i.e. banking and currency crises, which, as Kaminsky and Reinhart (1999) show, are generally closely linked in the aftermath of financial liberalization. The rapid growth of bank lending, an increase of asset prices, poor risk analysis, weak control systems within the banks, and inadequate regulation and supervision were the main drivers which left the banking systems in these three Nordic countries structurally vulnerable to the macroeconomic shocks which came about in the period between the 1980s and the early 1990s (Llewellyn, 2002).

Up to the early 1980s, the banking systems in Finland, Norway, and Sweden were heavily regulated. According to Drees and Pazarbaşioğlu (1995), this regulation shared common principles and objectives: the priority was not ensuring financial stability, but rather maintaining low and stable interest rates and, especially in Norway and in Sweden (Englund, 1990; Berg and Eitrheim, 2009), channelling subsidized credit into housing and the government. Before liberalization, prudential regulation played a relatively minor role in the Nordic countries. With limits both on the amount of lending and on interest rates, banks had little incentive to take excessive risks. Banking was a protected industry whose profitability was in fact granted by regulation. There were capital adequacy requirements, at least for commercial banks, but they were not deemed to be important in this relatively safe environment. Both before and after liberalization banking supervision was also gradually given low priority in the Nordic countries.

Financial deregulation began in the Nordic countries between the late 1970s and the early 1980s, in line with the developments seen during those years in all advanced countries (Edey and Hviding, 1995). The impact of deregulation on the competitive conditions and the behavioural responses of banks produced the conditions of financial fragility that emerged with the crisis; regulation and the supervisory authorities were unable to provide a suitable response to the risks and the overvaluation of banks' performance that were already visible in the years immediately before the crises (Benink and Llewellyn, 1994).

Although they had many things in commons, the Nordic crises were three separate episodes, because in the early 1990s little cross-border banking took place between these Nordic countries (Borio et al., 2010).

Norway was the first in the sequence: the crisis began in 1988 and became systemic in 1991, several years after the peak of the business cycle. It was not as severe as those in Sweden and in Finland and, in comparison with these, had a more limited international dimension (BCBS, 2004; Vale, 2004;

Honkapohja, 2009; Stigum, 2009). In Norway, the abandonment of quantitative credit restrictions took place in 1984–1985. Deregulation produced an aggressive competition for market share in the credit market, mainly after the abolishment of the regulation on the establishment of new branches. The turn-around of the boom came in 1986 with the decline of oil prices. The Norwegian kroner was devalued, restrictive fiscal and monetary policies were introduced, and the economy went into recession during the first half of 1988. In 1988–1990, several small banks failed due to credit losses, and were merged with larger solvent banks. The severity of the crisis worsened in late 1990, when the rise in interest rates applied by Germany after reunification deepened the recession and worsened the weak condition of banks. In December 1990, the crisis began to strike the larger banks and the bank's own guarantee funds were effectively depleted. The situation continued to worsen, peaking in the autumn of 1991, when the second and the fourth largest banks lost their entire capital due to sustained huge credit losses. At this point, the crisis became systemic.

The Finnish and Swedish crises were much more serious than Norway's, and involved a greater international dimension (Kaminsky and Reinhart, 1999).

In Sweden, the globalization of Swedish industry, with large companies becoming increasingly active internationally, and banking deregulation promoted, mainly in the early 1980s, a large consolidation process, which included commercial and savings banks (Frisell and Noréus, 2002). In the early 1980s, the interbank market, the market for derivative instruments and forward markets in foreign currencies were rapidly taking hold. The money market facilitated circumventing the quantitative lending regulation, which was abandoned in the mid-1980s, in a period when Sweden experienced a protracted economic up-turn. Since nominal interest rates in Sweden were relatively high compared to other countries, when foreign exchange restrictions were lifted, the amount of loans granted in foreign currencies greatly increased (Englund, 1990). Banks funded these loans denominated in foreign currency mainly on the international interbank market. The period of strong economic growth ended around 1990. The impact of tighter monetary policy in Germany, associated with speculative attacks against the krona, and the recession in export contributed to Sweden's distress. The European ERM crisis in 1992 deepened the banking crisis. With the increase in interest rates set by the Riksbank to defend the krona, non-performing loans began to rise causing large bank losses. In November 1992, fixed parity with the ECU was abandoned and the krona fell more than 20 per cent. With the worsening of the crisis, access by domestic banks to international financial markets was cut back severely and the risk of foreign lenders refusing to roll over short-term credit lines became concrete (Englund and Vihriälä, 2009).

Finland experienced the most severe crisis and the most dramatic and lasting economic recession of the three Nordic countries. In Finland, deregulation of the financial markets started in the early 1980s, but already in 1980,

Finnish banks were allowed to cover commercial forward positions in the fast developing foreign currency market. The abolition of exchange controls in 1985–1986 allowed the private sector to borrow freely from overseas. This improved the availability of debt financing from sources other than domestic banks. From the mid-1980s onwards, also due to the exceptionally favourable macroeconomic conditions, overseas borrowing was widely used, with more than half of this financing intermediated by banks. As in Sweden, so also in Finland, the share of corporate debt denominated in foreign currency grew considerably and the banks became highly dependent on foreign money market funding. This was especially true for large savings banks and their commercial bank affiliates (Englund and Vihriälä, 2003, 2009). The end of the boom came in Finland in 1990. Real interest rates rose considerably, due to the tighter monetary policy in Germany and the defence of the Finnish markka against speculative attacks. The Finnish crisis precipitated in 1991 with the collapse of the Soviet Union, which brought about a quick, dramatic decrease in exports to Russia, previously a major importer of Finnish goods. From 1992, the banking crisis became systemic and several banks asked for public capital support.

Sandal (2004, p. 83–84) presents detailed data comparing the duration and the seriousness of the crisis in the three Nordic countries: cumulative fall in real GDP was 10.4 per cent in Finland (1990–93), 5.3 per cent in Sweden (1990–93), whereas in Norway GDP hardly fell at all. Finland had also the largest loan losses in the peak year of the crisis (4.4 per cent of GDP) and the largest cumulative fall in bank lending. The recovery of the banking sector took more time in Finland than in the other two countries: whereas the banking sector in Norway and in Sweden returned to profitability just two years after the peak of the crisis, it took four years in Finland.

3 Different models of crisis management and resolution in the Nordic countries

Although financial deregulation had been a radical change for the Nordic economies, no adequate preventive measures were implemented during the boom years to stabilize the financial system, maybe because they were considered politically unpopular. The fragility of banks had risen, due to the poor evaluation of borrowers, a weak capital base, and widespread access to foreign funding. From many points of view, the Nordic banking crises were thus 'accidents waiting to happen' (Sandal, 2004, p. 82).

Whereas in all three Nordic countries serious regulatory and supervisory failures were certainly the causes of the seriousness of the crisis, the solutions which they adopted for their resolution followed what would later be unanimously considered as best practices.

Following both the various crisis episodes, which arose in advanced and developing countries during the 1990s, and especially the current crisis, several studies have investigated the best practices for crisis resolution, in the light of the experience in the Nordic countries (Santomero and Hoffman, 1998; Calomiris et al., 2004; Borio et al., 2010). For systemic crises, private resolution methods, theoretically considered the best option because they minimize fiscal costs and moral hazard problems, are not feasible. Especially when the banks in distress are large, normal liquidation procedures may cause major disruptions to customers, fire-sale externalities, large direct losses to creditors, the loss of confidence in national and international investors, and enormous contagion phenomena. The use of public funds to bail out distressed banks always entails a trade-off between limiting the adverse impact on the real economy and creating distorted incentives, which may jeopardize financial stability in the future. Furthermore, as the recent sovereign crisis in the euro area shows, public bailouts may trigger a vicious loop between bank and sovereign crises. Strict conditions and restrictions imposed in exchange of public support, associated with a transparent and strict assessment of losses, can help to contain moral hazard, even if it is hard for them to eliminate the problem. With systemic crises, the objective of minimizing fiscal costs is not always easy to reach, especially if private insurance funds are not sufficient and there are no legal rules which allow the sharing of costs, not only among shareholders and managers but also uninsured creditors, or if these rules cannot be applied without triggering contagion (Honohan and Klingebiel, 2003).

The solutions adopted by the Nordic countries to manage and solve their systemic banking crisis involved many different types of public intervention. Indeed, one of the main characteristics of these Nordic crises was that so many of the largest banks incurred losses of such a dimension that they could not be covered without some large government intervention.

There is wide agreement that these interventions were successful in limiting both the costs and the duration of the crises (Drees and Pazarbaşioğlu, 1995; Berg, 1998; Allen and Gale, 1999; Hoggarth and Reidhill, 2004; Borio et al., 2010). In all three crises, problems were recognized early and the authorities swiftly intervened without exercising forbearance. Widespread political consensus supported the actions needed to restore confidence in the banking system. Only a few months after the crisis was recognized as systemic, a wide range of measures was announced and implemented. No Nordic country, with the partial exception of Norway, had already in place a legal framework to deal with failures of systemically important banks. However, specific new rules and institutions were quickly passed. In all three Nordic countries, the authorities considered as a priority to identify the losses quickly, and to allocate them to the previous shareholders. They showed particular commitment in ensuring that the losses were booked correctly and transparently. In all three countries, the *sine qua non* for government capital injection was that banks' equity be written down according to losses, determined by severe evaluations, also tightening accounting practices. Finally, as Borio et al. (2010) stress, in the Nordic countries the need to re-establish conditions for sustainable profitability in the long term, by reducing excess capacity and promoting operational efficiency, was also considered a priority. Conditions for public interventions therefore included balance-sheet contraction, disposal of branch network, and cost-cutting measures. In very few cases did the authorities in Nordic countries close problem banks and liquidate their assets. Generally, governments permitted banking operations to continue without interruptions. Avoiding any interruption in banking services was a major concern for governments. According to Berg (1998), they considered it essential to not only protect the payment system and limit a domestic credit crunch, but also to maintain the confidence of foreign banks in the national banking systems.

According to Claessen et al. (2004), the high quality of institutions of the three Nordic countries – measured in the six dimensions of democracy, political stability, rule of law, bureaucratic regulation, government effectiveness, and low corruption – contributed to reducing the fiscal outlay of crisis resolution and containing the economic costs of the crises. In general, fraud was a negligible issue in the three Nordic crises (Vale, 2004).

Although the three Nordic countries had in common the above features, the strategies used to handle the crises were different. The main divide runs, as several authors (Berg, 1998; Sandal, 2004; Mayes, 2009a) argue, between Norway, on the one hand, and Sweden and Finland on the other.

Table 11. 1 provides a synthetic comparison of crisis resolution models in the three Nordic countries.

Only in Norway were private solutions and private funding significant in solving the crisis, especially during the early stage (1988–1990) characterized by the failures of several small banks. Many ailing banks were saved by the intervention of bank-funded guarantee funds. These funds not only had the mandate of compensating depositors in the event of liquidation, but also of infusing capital and issuing guarantees against portfolio losses of a member bank, mainly in order to promote a merger with a safe bank (Vale, 2004).

Before the crisis, none of the three Nordic countries had a special legal framework to deal with a bank crisis. In both Norway (Vale, 2004) and in Sweden (Ingves and Lind, 1996; Jonung, 2009a), when the crisis struck the largest banks, and thus became systemic, all parties in Parliament quickly approved a special resolution regime. There were two main objectives in the legal framework for crisis resolution: allowing distressed banks to go on operating thanks to public intervention; allowing the cost of the crisis to be borne mainly by shareholders. The new resolution rules allowed for government intervention also before a bank's capital was depleted (Ingves et al., 2009), ensuring that public capital support could not delayed or obstructed by negotiations with existing shareholders. New regulations authorized public agencies for crisis management to write down existing shares against audited recorded losses, issue new shares and other capital instruments, to sell the bank or some activities to a third parties without the assent of existing shareholders; but also, to change the board of directors and management, to restrict dividend pay-outs, to impose operational restructuring, to make plans for reducing operating costs and disposing of branch network.

Table 11.1 A comparison of crisis resolution models in the three Nordic countries

Resolution methods and policies	*Norway 1988–1992*	*Sweden 1991–1994*	*Finland 1991–1994*
Public resolution agencies	Government Bank Insurance Fund (GIBF): resolution interventions in non-viable banks	Bank Support Authority (BSA) (Under control of Ministry of Finance)	Government Guarantee Fund (GGF) (Under control of Parliament)
	Government Bank Investment Fund (SBIF): recovery of viable banks together with private investors		
Special insolvency rules	YES Approved during the crisis	YES Approved during the crisis	NO Support measures were decided by the Government separately in each case
Safety nets during the crisis			
Emergency Liquidity support from Central Bank	YES – in the form of special lending no pledged by collaterals	YES – limited Only in the form of normal lending of last resort	YES – limited Only in the form of normal lending of last resort and short-term bridge loans to GGF
Private funded deposit insurance	YES	NO	YES – limited
More severe banking supervision and capital requirements	YES	NO	NO
Blanket guarantee of bank deposits and liabilities	NO	YES	YES

Continued

Table 11.1 Continued

Resolution methods and policies	*Norway 1988–1992*	*Sweden 1991–1994*	*Finland 1991–1994*
Resolution tools			
Private sector acquisitions	YES	NO	NO
Government take-over (nationalization)	YES	YES – limited, only of Nordbanken, in which the State was before the crisis the major owner	YES – limited, only of Skopbank acquired by Bank of Finland, which after few months sold its share to GGF
Government conditional capital support to undercapitalized banks	YES	YES – limited	YES Mainly in the form of preferred capital certificates designed for inclusion in bank's Tier 1
Transfer toxic assets to a public asset management company (Bad Bank)	NO	YES	YES
Forced write-down of shareholder equity	YES	YES – with exceptions	YES – with exceptions
Mandatory operational restructuring	YES	YES	YES
Mandatory mergers of weak banks	YES	YES	YES
Financing of resolution			
Bank funded guarantee funds	YES Relevant role	NO	YES Minor role
Public budget financing	YES	YES	YES
Reform of financial supervision	NO Since 1986, Kredittilsynet was the single financial supervisor independent form Norges Bank	YES (1991) Finans Inspektionen was created as a single financial supervisor independent from Sveriges Riksbank	YES (1993) Financial Supervisory Authority was created as an agency inside the Bank of Finland

The main differences between Norway and Sweden (and Finland) were the instruments used for crisis resolution. In Norway, when the crisis struck the largest banks, the government decided to act as the 'owner of last resort' (Vale, 2004, p. 14; Wilse, 2004). The public agency GBIF, created to manage public interventions in the distressed banks, received the mandate to buy shares and other equity capital instruments in Norwegian banks directly, when they were unable to raise capital in other ways. At the same time, supervisory authorities committed themselves to impose strict compliance with capital requirements upon banks, although this meant an increase and acceleration in required recapitalization interventions (BCBS, 2004). From 1995 onwards, the government progressively began selling nationalized bank shares by public issue. They were mostly acquired by foreign banks (Berg and Eitrheim, 2009; Steigum, 2009). Thanks to the increase in the market value of bank shares, which came about mainly in the late 1990s, net fiscal costs for Norway were absent or even negative according to the assessment criteria used (Hoggarth et al., 2002; Vale, 2004).

In Sweden and in Finland, bank nationalization was only considered feasible as a last resort and for short term (Nyberg and Vihriälä, 1994; Ergungor, 2007; Ingves et al., 2009; Honkapohja, 2009; Englund and Vihriälä, 2009). Unlike Norway, which used mostly traditional instruments of bank safety net, in Sweden and in Norway a generalized 'free' safety net was provided to all banks, by means of a blanket creditor guarantee issued by Parliament. This solution was considered necessary, mainly because both Sweden and Finland were much more dependent upon international credit than Norway. However, as several authors (Berg, 1998; Ergungor, 2007) outline, it generated an implicit subsidy, which largely benefited the shareholder of several undercapitalized banks that were allowed to continue operations, because of the blanket guarantee. The problems of moral hazard were in some way expanded by the large-scale concentration processes promoting during the crisis (IMF, 2002). At the same time, Sweden and Finland made widespread use, in the restructuring programmes of undercapitalized banks, of the solution of transferring most non-performing loans to a separate 'bad bank', or asset management company capitalized by the state. Government money was used to recapitalize the good part of the bank to make it saleable, and to provide capital to a 'bad bank'. The widespread recourse to asset management companies was one of the elements, which, according to many authors, contributed most to the success of the Swedish model (Calomiris et al., 2004; Ingves and Lind, 2008; Jonung, 2009b; Englund and Vihriälä, 2009). According to Borio et al. (2010), the purpose of the transfer of the troubled assets to the 'bad bank' was mostly to enable management of the healthy parts of the bank to focus primarily on restoring profitability, instead of having to also worry about managing and recovering non-performing loans. The main task of the asset management companies was to maximize the remaining economic value of the loan transferred, preventing fire-sales and their negative effects on the collateral's market prices (mainly properties) (Bergström, Englud and Thorell, 2003).

4 Conclusions

Right from the start of the current financial turmoil, experience of the Nordic crises has attracted much interest from politicians willing to learn lessons about the causes of systemic banking crises, how to deal with them, and how to manage them successfully.

The current global crisis has an international dimension, and has been made worse by the contamination between banks and financial markets; whereas the Nordic crises were 'pure credit' crises and their effects were only felt in those countries. Despite this, the same ingredients can still be seen: bad bank practices, weak banking regulation and supervision, inadequate market discipline, serious external imbalances, and inadequate macroeconomic policies related to financial liberalization.

Although the models of crisis management were different in each of the three Nordic countries, the policies implemented 'taught the world powerful lessons about the need for prominent state involvement in the resolution process' (Ingves and Lind, 2008, p. 21).

One must still wonder if experience of previous crises has left such long-lasting lessons to the Nordic countries, leaving them better equipped at a political and regulatory level to deal with financial crises of a systemic dimension. The fact that the three Nordic countries were hit relatively lightly during the recent crisis – especially Finland, which in the early 1990s saw a crisis much worse than the Great Recession of the 1930s (Mayes, 2009b) – would appear to prove that the crises in these countries had a positive learning effect, giving the lie to theories about some collective removal of those painful lessons of the past. Currently, the answer to such a question is still more or less open.

Generally speaking, as a consequence of the crises of the early 1990s, banking systems in the Nordic countries gradually became more concentrated and integrated, making the problem of dealing with cross-border banks' crises the principal – and yet unresolved – regulatory challenge for the Nordic countries. The ministries of finance, central banks, and financial supervisory authorities of the Nordic and Baltic countries have signed a Memorandum of Understanding on financial stability, crisis management and crisis resolution in August 2010 (Ingves, 2010). This is undoubtedly a big step forward, but experience shows that such non-binding agreements have only limited effects when an actual crisis comes about (Niepmann and Schmidt-Eisenlohr, 2010). This is especially true when the political approaches for crisis resolution remain, as they were during the 1990s, so widely different between the three Nordic countries. As a recent analysis by the IMF confirms:

> The authorities [have] different views on the relative merits of bailing-in and recapitalising banks and when and how to use taxpayers' funds. Some [stress] the flexibility associated with a bail-out approach, while others [point] to the importance of removing moral hazard through bail-ins.
>
> (IMF, 2013, p. 20)

A European solution, as part of the Banking Union, may be an opportunity, although it will not be easy, given that Finland's automatic membership of the Banking Union contrasts with Norway, which is precluded to join by its constitution, and Sweden that will probably remain outside it. New European financial regulation (the CRD/CRR and the Bank Recovery and Resolution Directive) and single banking supervision are destined to provide new and difficult challenges for Nordic regulatory coordination in financial crisis prevention and resolution.

References

ALLEN, F. and GALE, D. (1999) Bubbles, crises, and policy. *Oxford Review of Economic Policy*. 5(3), 9–18.

BASEL COMMITTEE ON BANKING SUPERVISION (BCBS) (2004) *Bank Failures in Mature Economies*. [Online.] Working paper No. 13. Available from: www.bis.org/publ/bcbs_wp13.pdf. [Accessed: 2 January 2015.]

BENINK, H. and LLEWELLYN, D. (1994) Deregulation and financial fragility: A case study of the UK and Scandinavia. In: Fair, E. and Raymond, R. (eds) *The Competitiveness of Financial Institutions and Centres in Europe*. Dordrecht, Boston, London: Kluwer Academic Publishers.

BERG, S. A. (1998) Bank failures in Scandinavia. In: Caprio, G et al. (eds). *Preventing Bank Crises: Lessons from Recent Global Bank Failures.* [Online.] World Bank Institute. Washington D.C.: The World Bank. Available from: http://documents.worldbank.org/curated/en/1998/09/442595/preventing-bank-crises-lessons-recent-global-bank-failures. [Accessed: 4 January 2015.]

BERG, S. A. and EITRHEIM, Ø. (2009) Bank regulation and Bank Crisis. The main developments in the Norwegian regulatory system before, during and after the banking crisis of 1988–92. [Online.] *Financial Market Regulation in the Wake of Financial Crisis: The Historical Experience Conference*, p. 169. Available from: http://ssrn.com/abstract=2101723. [Accessed: 30 December 2014.]

BERGSTRÖM C., ENGLUND P. AND THORELL P. (2003) Securum and the Way out of the Swedish banking crisis. [Online.] Summary of a report commissioned by SNS – Stockholm: Centre for Business and Policy Studies. Available from: www.sns.se/sites/default/files/securum_eng.pdf. [Accessed: 4 February 2014.]

BORIO, C., VALE, B. and VON PETER, G. (2010) Resolving the financial crisis: Are we heeding the lessons from the Nordic? [Online.] BIS Working Papers No. 311 (June). Available from: www.bis.org/publ/work311.htm. [Accessed: 17 April 2014.]

CALOMIRIS, C., KLINGEBIEL, D. and LAEVEN, L. (2004) A taxonomy of financial crisis resolution mechanism: Cross-country experience. World Bank Policy Research Working Paper 3379 (August).

CLAESSENS S., KLINGEBIEL D. AND LAEVEN L. (2004) Resolving systemic financial crises: policies and institutions, World Bank Policy Research Working Paper 3377, August.

DREES, B. and PAZARBASIOGLU, C. (1995) The Nordic Banking crises: Pitfalls in financial liberalisation? IMF Working Paper WP/95/61. (June). Washington D.C.: International Monetary Fund.

EDEY, M. and HVIDING, K. (1995) An Assessment of financial reform in OECD countries. *OECD Economic Studies*, 25(3), 7–33.
ENGLUND, P. (1990) Financial deregulation in Sweden. *European Economic Review*, 34 (May), 385–393.
ENGLUND, P. and VIHRIÄLÄ, V. (2003) Financial crises in developed economies: The case of Sweden and Finland. [Online.] Pellervo Economic Research Institute Working Papers. 63 (March). Available from: www.researchgate.net/researcher/7631526_Peter_Englund. [Accessed: 2 February 2014.]
ENGLUND, P. and VIHRIÄLÄ, V. (2009) Financial crisis in Finland and Sweden: Similar but not quite the same. In: Jonung, L., Kiander, J. and Vartia, P. (eds) *The Great Financial Crisis in Finland and Sweden. The Nordic Experience of Financial Liberalisation*. Cheltenham: Edward Elgar.
ERGUNGOR, O. (2007) On the resolution of financial crises: The Swedish experience. Federal Reserve Bank of Cleveland Policy Discussion Paper. 21 (June).
FISHER, I. (1933) The debt-deflation theory of great depression. *Econometrica*, 1, 337–357.
FRISELL, L. and NORÉUS, M. (2002) Consolidation process in the Swedish banking sector: A central bank perspective. *Sweriges Riksbank Economic Rewiew*, 3, 20–38.
HOGGARTH, G., REIS, R. and SAPORTA, V. (2002) Costs of banking system instability: Some empirical evidence. *Journal of Banking and Finance*, 25(5), 825–855.
HOGGARTH, G. and REIDHILL, J. (2004) Resolution of banking crisis: A review. *Bank of England Financial Stability Review* (December), 109–123.
HONKAPOHJA, S. (2009) The 1990's financial crisis in Nordic countries. Bank of Finland Research Discussion Papers 5/2009.
HONOHAN, P. and KLINGEBIEL, D. (2003) The fiscal costs implications of an accommodating approach to banking crises. *Journal of Banking and Finance*, 27, 1539–1560.
INGVES, S. (2010) The crisis of the Baltic – The Riksbank's measures, assessments and lessons learned. [Online.] Speech at Riksdag Committee on Finance. Stockholm: Sveriges Riksbank (2 February). Available from: www.riksbank.se/en/Press-and-published/Speeches/2010/Ingves-The-crisis-in-the-Baltic--the-Riksbanks-measures-assessments-and-lessons-learned-/. [Accessed: 21 May 2014.]
INGVES, S. and LIND, G. (1996) The management of bank crisis – In retrospect. *Sveriges Riksbank Quarterly Review*, 1, 5–18.
INGVES, S. and LIND, G. (2008) Stockholm solutions. *Finance and Development* (December), 21–28.
INGVES, S et al. (2009) Lesson learned from previous banking crises. Sweden, Japan, Spain and Mexico. Group of Thirty Occasional Paper 79 (April).
INTERNATIONAL MONETARY FUND (IMF) (2002) Sweden: Financial system stability assessment. IMF Country Report 02/161 (August).
INTERNATIONAL MONETARY FUND (IMF) (2013) Nordic regional report. IMF Country Report 13/274 (September).
JONUNG, L. (2009a) The Swedish model for resolving the banking crisis of 1991–1993. Seven reasons why it was successful. [Online] European Economy. Economic Papers 360. Brussels: European Commission. Directorate-General for Economic and Financial Affairs. Available from: http://ec.europa.eu/economy_finance/publications/publication14098_en.pdf. [Accessed: 19 March 2014.]

JONUNG, L. (2009b) Twelve lessons from the Nordic experience of financial liberalization. In: Jonung, L., Kiander, J. and Vartia, P. (2009) *The Great Financial Crisis in Finland and Sweden: The Nordic Experience of Financial Liberalisation*. Cheltenham: Edward Elgar.

KAMINSKY, G. and REINHART, C. (1999) The twin crises: The causes of banking and balance-of-payments problems. *American Economic Review*, 89 (June), 473–500.

LLEWELLYN, D. (2002) An analysis of the causes of recent banking crises. *The European Journal of Finance*, 8(2), 152–175.

MAYES, D. (2009a) Banking crisis resolution policy – Different country experiences. [Online] Norges Bank Staff Memo No. 10. Available from: www.norges-bank.no/Upload/77285/Staff_memo_09_10.pdf. [Accessed: 4 May 2014.]

MAYES, D. (2009b) Did recent experience of a financial crisis help in coping with the current financial turmoil? The case of the Nordic countries. *Journal of Common Market Studies*, 47(5), 97–105.

MINSKY, H. P. (1977) A theory of systematic financial instability. In: Altman, E. I. and Sametz, A. W. (eds) *Financial Crisis: Institutions and Markets in a Fragile Environment*. New York: Wiley.

NIEPMANN, F. and SCHMIDT-EISENLOHR, T. (2010) Bank bailouts, international linkages and cooperation. [Online.] Oxford University Centre for Business Taxation Working Paper No. 10/16. Available from: http://papers.ssrn.com/sol3/papers.cfm?abstract_id=1739132. [Accessed: 10 January 2015.]

NYBERG, P. and VIHRIÄLÄ, V. (1994) The Finnish banking crisis and its handling (An update of developments trough 1993). Bank of Finland Discussion Paper 7/94 (April 18).

REINHART, C. and ROGOFF, K. S. (2008) Is the 2007 U.S. sub-prime financial crisis so different? An international historical comparison. NBER Working Paper Series. Working Paper No. 13761 (January).

SANDAL, K. (2004) The Nordic banking crises in the early 1990s – Resolution methods and fiscal costs. In: Moe, T. G., Solheim, J. A. and Vale, B. (eds) *The Norwegian Banking Crisis*. Norges Bank Occasional Papers No. 33 (May). Oslo: Norges Bank.

SANTOMERO, A. and HOFFMAN, P. (1998) *Problem Bank Resolution: Evaluating the Options*. Philadelphia: University of Pennsylvania. Wharton Financial Institutions Center 98-05-B (October).

STEIGUM, E. (2009) The Boom and bust cycle in Norway. In: Jonung, L., Kiander, J. and Vartia, P. (2009) *The Great Financial Crisis in Finland and Sweden. The Nordic Experience of Financial Liberalisation*. Cheltenham: Edward Elgar.

VALE B. (2004) The Norwegian banking crisis, in Moe T.G., Solheim J.A. and Vale B. (eds), *The Norwegian Banking Crisis*, Norges Bank Occasional Papers No. 33, May, Chapter I, pp. 1–18.

WILSE, H. P. (2004) Management of the banking crisis and state ownership of commercial banks. In: Moe, T. G., Solheim, J. A. and Vale, B. (eds) *The Norwegian Banking Crisis*. Norges Bank Occasional Papers No. 33 (May). Oslo: Norges Bank.

12 Post-crisis international regulatory standards and their inclusion in the European framework

Mario Tonveronachi

1 Introduction

The political and social direness brought about by the crisis has led governments to take a more direct role in promoting and monitoring a comprehensive revision of the regulatory architecture, thus partly reverting their previous almost full delegation to independent regulatory authorities and standard setters (Backer, 2011, Bengtsson, 2011). The poor performance of regulators and supervisors before the recent crisis and the enlarged discretionary powers attributed to them by the post-crisis regulatory revisions, now also focusing on macro-prudential issues, are additional relevant reasons for explaining this shift. Consequently, the international, regional and national development of existing institutions or the building of new ones has come to characterize the regulatory response to the recent financial crisis.

At the international level, it was soon clear that the meetings of G20 second-tier government delegates and technical experts put up after the Asian crisis of the late 1990s had not enough political weight to face the new challenges. Starting from 2008, political leaders have assumed responsibility for the G20 meetings, now summits, and for delineating policy programmes. The Financial Stability Board (FSB), coming from the transformation of the preexisting ineffectual Financial Stability Forum, was designed as the operational arm of the G20 in the financial regulatory sphere. The qualifying presence of representatives of national finance ministries and treasury departments in the FSB constitutes further proof of the above-mentioned political shift (Gadinis, 2013). However, more than taking sole responsibility for regulation, public authorities have designed the FSB as a cooperative model.[1]

A similar evolution is visible in the European Union (EU). Because of the Lisbon Treaty, the European Parliament has acquired wider co-decision powers in the economic and financial field, while later reforms have enhanced the political standing of the European Commission. New institutions, such as the European Supervisory Authorities (ESAs) and the European Systemic Risk Board (ESRB), mark a shift towards more centralization, as in a higher degree does the newly created Banking Union for a subset of EU countries. For the financial sector, the goal was to adopt a single rulebook and a single supervisory handbook across all member countries. On the other hand, the crisis has also increased economic, financial and political fragmentation, producing in some member countries a rethinking on the transfer of national sovereignty due to the increased sensitivity to tailor rules and monitoring on local needs. In the financial sphere, this might mean that minimum international standards may acquire more relevance for the EU than their questioned homogeneous implementation inside the area.

The enhanced political drive has relevant implications. Social and political reactions to the recent crisis have widened the range of objectives and the potential for trade-offs. For instance, the goal to keep the financial system global and managed by systemically important financial institutions (SIFIs) may in a significant measure conflict with the goal of national stability and the sustainability of government finance (Persaud, 2010, Pistor, 2010). We will argue that the recent regulatory developments configure the search for a new political balance between global finance and national interests, posing new problems of coherence at the international level. In addition, political cycles and the fading memory of the recent crisis may in the future redirect or weaken the thrust for reforms. With respect to the past, this may introduce a larger dose of time inconsistency, i.e. higher regulatory uncertainty.

A further implication concerns the relation between politics and supervision. The recent reforms have created new authorities or strengthened old ones to deal with the enlarged scope of regulation. Being the current approach to regulation based more on principles than on rules, the effect is to increase further the discretionary powers of supervisors, whose practices result difficult to discipline inside clear and effective guidelines. We already have clear signs that politics does not intend to leave sensitive issues in the sole hands of independent authorities. For example, this is the case for the US Financial Stability Oversight Council, where the Treasury secretary has the last word on matters related to systemic firms. For the UK, the government and the Parliament have the power to decide where to put the division in their ring fencing scheme, and the Treasury to approve the authority's proposals extending or restricting the general rules for individual firms. This on top of frequent political practices, such as the spoil system and the control of the authorities' funding, which often render the autonomy of such agencies at least dubious. Enhanced supervisory powers with a heavier political presence and attention make the new political balance more difficult to design and more unstable, both at the national and international level.

Given the above premises, we analyse in Section 2 the main features of the G20 approach to financial reforms, which constitute the basis of its mandate to the FSB. We argue that the goal to preserve and deepen financial globalization is encountering obstacles due to the defensive reactions by some national authorities, to the lack of coincidence in national interests, to strengthened differences in regulatory approaches, and to the difficult task of homogenizing rules and practices when the scope of regulation widens and trade-offs multiply. The difficulty encountered in giving substance to the G20's general principles is a necessary premise for the analysis that we offer in Section 3 on the work done by the FSB and several international standard setters, the Basel Committee on Banking Supervision (BCBS) in particular, up to the recent Brisbane G20 Summit. The results and proposals presented at that meeting are supposed to end the first phase of the FSB's work, which has mainly focused on the production of new standards and the revision of old ones related to resilience and to crisis resolution processes, especially for global systemic banks (G-SIBs). Given our focus on the banking industry, we discuss the activity of the BCBS on and around the new Basel III standard, its cooperation with the FSB on matters such as compliance with the new standard and principles on bank risk management, and the initiatives by the FSB on crisis resolution and G-SIBs. We then analyse in Section 4 the wide range of reforms adopted and proposed by the EU for the banking sector, including those related to the new institutional setup. The European experience is particularly revealing of the difficulties of adopting common global rules due to the heterogeneities that characterize even an area supposed to possess a single financial market. Section 5 offers some conclusions and perspectives.

2 The global market and international standards

Stripping its declarations from abundant rhetoric, the G20 action was and continues to be not very effective for enhancing policy cooperation to deal with the economic and fiscal aspects of the recent crisis.[2] Counting on the FSB, better results were obtained for financial reforms, where the focus has been on safeguarding the global nature of finance by means of a stronger assertion of the common adherence to strengthened international regulatory standards and codes. Given the negative cross-border financial and economic externalities produced by the crisis, the absence of effective coordination even where supranational institutions existed, as in the European Union, has produced national ring-fencing reactions, with the possibility of their de-facto transformation into deglobalization strategies. A coordinated response was then put high in the G20/FSB agenda.

Absent a single international supervisor capable of enforcing common standards, the chosen goal to preserve and deepen global finance did not leave much room for a radical rethinking of the pre-existing regulatory framework, if such rethinking was ever taken into consideration. The passage from the G8 to the G20, incorporating the more relevant emerging economies, has not up to now introduced relevant changes in the former agenda. Some excerpts help to clarify the continuity in the general approach to regulation.

The G20:

> We pledge to strengthen our regulatory regimes, prudential oversight, and risk management, and ensure that all financial markets, products and participants are regulated or subject to oversight, as appropriate to their

> circumstances. [...] We will also make regulatory regimes more effective over the economic cycle, while ensuring that regulation is efficient, does not stifle innovation, and encourages expanded trade in financial products and services.
>
> (G20, 2008, p. 3)

The President of the (then) FSF:

> The goal will be to strengthen the resilience of the system without hindering the process of market discipline and innovation that are essential to the financial sector's contribution to economic growth.
>
> (Draghi, 2008, p. 7)

The G20:

> Financial markets will remain global and interconnected, while financial innovation will continue to play an important role to foster economic efficiency.
>
> (G20, 2009, p. V)

The US Treasury Secretary:

> [T]he central objective of reform is to establish a safer, more stable financial system that can deliver the benefits of market-driven financial innovation even as it guards against the dangers of market-driven excess.
>
> (Geithner, 2009, p. 2)

The G20 2009 London Summit agreed to transform the Financial Stability Forum into the FSB, with the following mandate:

- assess vulnerabilities affecting the financial system and identify and oversee action needed to address them;
- promote coordination and information exchange among authorities responsible for financial stability;
- monitor and advise on market developments and their implications for regulatory policy;
- advise on and monitor best practice in meeting regulatory standards;
- undertake joint strategic reviews of the policy development work of the international standard setting bodies to ensure their work is timely, coordinated, focused on priorities, and addressing gaps;
- set guidelines for and support the establishment of supervisory colleges;
- manage contingency planning for cross-border crisis management, particularly with respect to systemically important firms; and
- collaborate with the IMF to conduct Early Warning Exercises.

In the FSB website we also read:

> As obligations of membership, members of the FSB commit to pursue the maintenance of financial stability, maintain the openness and transparency of the financial sector, implement international financial standards (including the 12 Key International Standards and Codes[3]), and agree to undergo periodic peer reviews, using among other evidence IMF/World Bank public Financial Sector Assessment Program reports. The FSB, working through its members, seeks to give momentum to a broad-based multilateral agenda for strengthening financial systems and the stability of international financial markets. The necessary changes are enacted by the relevant national financial authorities.

Following the Action Plan established at the London Summit, the 2010 G20 Seoul Summit endorsed the framework proposed by the FSB for addressing the too-big-to-fail (TBTF) issue, which included the methodology for singling out systemically important institutions (SIFIs) and the need to subject them to additional loss absorbency capacity, increased supervision and effective resolution mechanisms. In other words, SIFIs are not to be dismantled, but they should bear the weight of stricter rules and more intense supervision.

Summing up, the system should remain global; private financial innovation in products and institutions remains at the heart of financial dynamics and must not be stifled by regulation (confirming that the morphology of the financial system remains substantially market driven); operational efficiency maintains their central role, so that, for instance, SIFIs are a physiological presence in the framework; and regulatory reforms must mend the previous system only as far as the latter had permitted 'excesses'.

Let us briefly linger on some problems connected with the above position.

Global finance requires free movement of capital and intermediaries. For financial contracts, this poses the problem to elect a jurisdiction for eventual disputes; for cross-border financial firms the issue is under which national rules they must operate and be supervised. Cross-border banks conduct their foreign operations by means of branches or subsidiaries. While foreign branches are not separate legal entities from their parent firm and, as a rule, are subject to the home country control, subsidiaries are legally independent local companies owned by foreign capital and, to a certain extent, are regulated and supervised by the authorities of the host country. Another relevant difference is that, contrary to branches, subsidiaries are normally subject to limits for intra-group funds transfers.

However, the impulse given in the 1970s to global banking by the end of the Bretton Woods agreement and the two petrol crises began to present an increasingly complex scenario. Some crises of cross-border banks, such as the one of Banco Ambrosiano, showed the necessity of consolidated regulation and supervision and of cooperation between home and host authorities, especially on how to share the burden of crisis resolution.

Starting from the 1975 Basel Concordat, which began to outline the principles of consolidated supervision and of the home country control, international standard setters have identified two related fronts. First, minimum international regulatory and supervisory standards in order to easy the process of mutual recognition. Second, crisis resolution procedures in order to safeguard the interests of both home and host investors. Actually, although resolution problems were in fact what promoted the entire process, as we shall see in the following sections only recently it was possible to obtain some significant results, but due to a different goal, that of safeguarding a 'hidden' investor, the government as rescuer of last resort. In any case, sustainable global banking requires finding appropriate solutions on the two fronts.

International common minimum standards have been identified as the way to put global players on a level playing field and consequently to weaken barriers against foreign operations. In the absence of 'hard laws' coming from a supranational regulatory authority with enforcement powers, two problems arise: the enforceability of agreements reached at the level of the international standard setters, the so-called soft laws, and the appropriateness of common rules for different jurisdictions.

Regarding the enforceability of soft laws, experience shows that relying on voluntary international cooperation is not an effective solution (Brummer, 2010), hence the attempt of building international institutions that might acquire some features of hard law producers. The discussions about FSB's powers, on which more in the next section, concern whether some of its outputs, such as peer reviews and public disclosures, may *de facto* force, at least FSB's members, to effective compliance of its deliberations.

The limit to the enforceability of soft law would not produce serious consequences if the various jurisdictions were homogeneous enough to make it easy to design a commonly accepted framework. To a certain degree, the principle of the regulatory playing field assumes that the same rules are applicable to different jurisdictions, their heterogeneities mainly seen as possessing quantitative not qualitative dimensions. A bank is a bank; a capital market is a capital market, independently of where they operate.

If we descend from the paradise of formal models to the purgatory of reality, a more nuanced approach seems preferable, where qualitative legal, political and social differences are relevant. In these conditions, a possible international hard law could only resemble a sort of constitution, stating very general principle and leaving each jurisdiction to adapt them to local circumstances. But this means that only general objectives should inform the constitution, such as a stable contribution of finance to growth and development, not the level playing field defined as the homogenization of rules. When heterogeneous jurisdictions prevail, the necessity to reach widely accepted agreements obliges the pole of minimum standards to be set low and leaves agreements open to national discretion, thus contradicting the objective of the level playing field. It is not by chance that the deliberations of international standard setters are mainly based on principles and that large doses of discretion are present also in their rules (Jordan and Majoni, 2002).

In the present and foreseeable conditions, an international authority with effective enforcement power is out of question since critical non-coincident national interests or fiscal implications are involved. Facilitating cooperation among jurisdictions and reporting on the adoption of international standards is as far as any international agreement, and presently the FSB, can go. However, given the above scenario, judging on compliance is not a clear-cut affair, leaving room for asymmetric exertion of influence.

These are enough reasons for complicating the FSB's mission because of the difficulties to find an equilibrium between the necessity for a wide, global acceptance of a large set of standards and their homogeneous implementation. A task made more difficult by the post-crisis proliferation and tightening of standards and rules.

Despite the neoliberal agenda that characterizes the FSB's mandate, the lesson of the recent crisis has led even the mayor global financial jurisdictions (such as those of the UK and the USA) to search for a political compromise between the interests of their financial global players, domestic stability and the involvement of government as rescuer of last resort. Critical components of this rebalancing are structural reforms and resolution procedures for tackling the crises of systemically important banks. Moreover, the asymmetry of power between unleashed global finance and most jurisdictions has increasingly dented the full acceptance of the free movement principle.[4]

Worthy of note is that the most powerful financial jurisdictions have also felt the need to adopt structural measures for shielding their domestic financial systems from fragilities coming from foreign activities. Although the USA and UK are trying to preserve their dominance in shaping international regulation, also following the principle that who comes first dictates the agenda, they are moving on two slightly different planes. The disproportion between the City of London and UK's domestic market favours discretional mutual recognition, based on the principle of equivalence of results, not on the formal compliance of specific rules, to ensure free movement for wholesale banking. At the same time, the domestic economy should be shielded by ring fencing retail banking. This means that the UK approach prefers international regulation based more on general principles than on detailed rules, hence leaving supervisors to evaluate discretionally the equivalence with other jurisdictions.[5] Counting on a deep domestic financial market, the USA now seem, on the contrary, wanting to assert their central international role by imposing to large banks stricter specific standards, via the Volcker rule, higher capital requirements, stronger stress tests, resolution requirements and obliging relevant foreign institutions to the same treatment as domestic ones.[6]

In addition, although urged by the defence of the internationalization of finance, the recent focus on the resolution of international banks might come to introduce some limits to global banking. For banking groups, two resolution methods are available. The bottom-up or multiple points of entry method, where the parent company and its subsidiaries comply separately with the conditions of resolvability dictated by local regulation, thus fragmenting the regulatory requirements and intra-group activities of the bank. The top-down or single point of entry method, which requires that the resolvability conditions are satisfied by the parent company for the entire group but also that the host authorities are satisfied by the formal commitments given by both the parent company and its resolution authority. Especially when local branches or subsidiaries are domestically relevant, host authorities could prefer the bottom-up solution or could dictate strict conditions for accepting the top-down approach (Herring, 2007).

The idea that ex ante common stricter stability requirements will not impede the repetition of banking crises is gaining traction even among regulators and supervisors. This may open more space for tailoring rules on local conditions, thus putting the onus on national supervisors of proving to their international peers the effectiveness of their domestic regulatory framework. However, the acceptability of global banking increasingly depends on the belief that G-SIBs can fail without endangering home and host countries. Reliable supervisory practices completed by effective resolution regimes are expected to put a brake to the deglobalization of financial systems.

In any case, it is clear that any form of subsidiarization, whether concerning retail banking or systemic institutions, leads to a certain degree of fragmentation in global banking and widens the field for relevant country regulatory differences.

We have argued elsewhere (Tonveronachi, 2010) that the post-crisis reforms have dangerously enhanced the discretionary power of supervisors without intervening in the causes that made supervisory practices procyclical in the past. Besides, given the increased attention by politicians to finance, supervisors should be now even more conscious of how difficult is leaning against the wind (and the lobbies) and that the dynamic complexity of both finance and regulation leaves ample room for mistakes and loss of reputation. These problems reach their apex for banks that are too big to fail, to manage and to supervise, or that are simply too big. Banks reaching ten thousand between subsidiaries and branches, with complex international operations and relations may present unsurmountable problems to be swiftly resolved. Recently the FDIC, now the agency also in charge of the resolution of large US banks, rejected the living wills of the 11 biggest US banks because they could not permit to manage their resolution without creating large externalities. If the resubmission would fail again, a formal interpretation of the Dodd-Frank could trigger the provision that banks that cannot be properly managed, supervised and resolved should be dismembered.[7] Since we do not believe that the political context will allow for this solution, we are back to the problems that prompted the first Basel Concordat, with the aggravating factor that now banks are larger and more global than in the 1970s.

The scenario offered by the adopted and ongoing reforms is therefore one in which the quest for a new political balance where national stability and the defence of government finance weight more with respect to the previous scenario that was substantially directed at creating the conditions for the international expansion of finance. Although the fundamentals of regulation have not changed, the recent crisis has convinced national and international authorities to introduce some doses of realism into the former ideologically dominated approach, with some timid form of structural regulation entering an otherwise pure prudential framework. Obviously, the reform agenda continues to be dictated by the problems posed by large international intermediaries. In the banking industry, on which our focus is directed, the new equilibrium is based, for ex ante resilience, on stricter Basel standards and on new outlines of banks' risk management for realigning incentives. Ex post, recovery and resolution procedures for systemic intermediaries should avoid both the recourse to public funds, when their failure might endanger the basic functions of the financial system, and pre-emptive national defensive strategies that would fragment international finance. As we shall see, *obtorto collo* also small doses of ring fencing and structural regulation come to be tolerated as minor evils with respect to the renationalization of finance. These are the new equilibrium's ingredients that will be discussed in the following sections.

3 Banking regulatory reforms up to the G20 Brisbane summit

After its constitution, discussions have arisen on whether the FSB would be able to overcome two pre-crisis limits that have characterized the adoption of international standards.

The first was the uneven adoption and enforcement of international standards and codes, also considering that the task of making them more even has been made more difficult and more necessary because of the widening and strengthening of regulation and supervision.

We have already argued that, having to take into account the heterogeneities of different jurisdictions, standards are primarily based on principles and anyhow the rules too are drafted to allow for national specificities. If supervision is a field where principles and discretion prevail, regulation too is open to heterogeneous implementation, as crucially has been the case for the definition of the components of the different tiers of the banks' regulatory capital. A country may also decide for a partial adoption of the standards, or for inserting changes in relevant aspects.[8] The international playing field may be rendered further uneven by some countries introducing stricter standards, which, if coherent with the principle of minimum harmonization, may pose problems for the recognition of cross-border activities. Some commentators single out the FSB's periodic peer reviews as the instrument that can tight the discipline of, at least, the G20 member countries.[9] Under this respect, the G20's 2009 London Summit had also asked to strengthen the role of the

Financial Stability Assessment Programme conducted by the IMF and World Bank.[10] Other commentators (e.g. Eichengreen, 2010) would have preferred a WTO type of solution, where outlier behaviour by some jurisdictions could allow retaliatory measures.

The FSB is also called to tackle another problem inherited from the pre-crisis period, i.e. the uncoordinated production of standards and codes by specialized international institutions, each looking at its own piece of garden. Some of the causes leading to the recent crisis can be ascribed not only to faulty domestic supervisors but also to the piecemeal approach to regulation and supervision by both domestic and international regulators. Requirements with different severity applied to different parts of the financial system, incoherent overlapping and unregulated institutions produced an increasingly fragile framework, of which the violent growth of the so-called shadow banking sector is just an example. It is unlikely that this lack of strict cooperation may be satisfactory solved at the supervisory level. The present effort by the FSB and international standard setters is to redesign consistently the various pieces composing the regulatory framework under the general umbrella that we have outlined in the previous sections.

Consequently, the FSB has identified six 'priority areas' (Basel III, compensation practices, resolution regimes, SIFIs, OTC derivatives markets, shadow banking) on which to focus its progress reports and peer reviews, and eleven 'other areas' (regulatory perimeter, hedge funds, securitization, enhancing supervision, macro-prudential frameworks and tools, oversight of CRAs, accounting standards, enhancing risk management, deposit insurance, integrity and efficiency of financial markets, financial consumer protection).

We may judge the work done so far from the vantage point of the progress report and the new proposals submitted by the FSB and other standard setters to the G20 Brisbane Summit of November 2014.

Significantly, the FSB considers as substantially completed the first phase of its mission, which was to fix the 'fault lines that caused the crisis' (FSB, 2014a). This means moving 'away from the design of standards [...] towards new and constantly evolving risks and vulnerabilities' (ibid). In the new phase, the Board will continue monitoring on standard compliance and cooperation among jurisdictions. Noteworthy is the call for support from the G20 to maintain for the future 'the FSB's effectiveness as a decision-making body' (ibid).

In the paragraph dedicated by the Brisbane G20 communiqué (G20, 2014) to financial reforms we read:

> Our reforms to improve banks' capital and liquidity positions and to make derivatives markets safer will reduce risks in the financial system. We welcome the Financial Stability Board (FSB) proposal [...] requiring global systemically important banks to hold additional loss absorbing capacity that would further protect taxpayers if these banks fail. Progress has been made in delivering the shadow banking framework

> and we endorse an updated roadmap for further work. We have agreed to measures to dampen risk channels between banks and non-banks. But critical work remains to build a stronger, more resilient financial system. The task now is to finalise remaining elements of our policy framework and fully implement agreed financial regulatory reforms, while remaining alert to new risks. [...] We welcome the FSB's plans to report on the implementation and effects of these reforms, and the FSB's future priorities.

The communiqué refers to the progress made in the six priority areas singled out by the FSB and to the proposed future priorities. The FSB's general report to the G20 (FSB, 2014b) summarizes the state of the art on reforms as it can be derived by a series of documents produced by the same board and by other standard setters. We will examine those regarding the banking industry, beginning with the work done by the BCBS.

3.1 Basel III and surroundings

The Basel Committee has presented to the G20 Brisbane Summit three reports, on the implementation of Basel standards (BCBS, 2014a), on national discretions in applying the capital framework (BCBS, 2014b), and on the excessive variability in banks' regulatory capital ratios (BCBS, 2014c).

To a large extent, the end of the first phase of the post-crisis agenda declared by the FSB is due to the BCBS having substantially completed its work on Basel III, including the capital frameworks for global and domestic SIBs and the final standards for the leverage ratio and the two liquidity ratios (LCR and NSFR). Most of the BCBS 27 member jurisdictions being well on track for the adoption of Basel standards, the Committee is also strengthening its Regulatory Consistency Assessment Programme (RCAP), which includes monitoring the progress in adopting Basel III, assessing consistency of national or regional regulations, and analysing their prudential outcomes.[11] Although many of the largest banks are already satisfying most of the requirements due for 2019, the feedbacks from the RCAP show that some problems that were already afflicting the Basel II release have not disappeared. The specific reports, on national discretions and excessive variability of risk weights, points to two relevant factors capable of weakening comparability, hence the regulatory level playing field.

The first report shows the use of a very different mix of the many discretions left by the Basel standards, also by the EU legislation and across the EU member countries when they are allowed by European directives and regulations. The Committee will begin in 2015 to consider which discretions should be eliminated or redrafted to increase the comparability of implementation.

However, this is not the entire story because national supervisors may apply the same principle or rule with different vigour. For instance, regulatory bank capitalization, the core of the Basel standard, depends not only on the definition of the components allowed to form the different tiers of regulatory capital, but also, given the same mix of risks, on differences in banking and supervisory practices as especially reflected in the output of internal risk models in terms of risk weighted assets. It is well known that the 'philosophy' of the BCBS is making capitalization sensitive to risks. If local supervisors and banking practices may twist the computation of risks, the entire Basel edifice goes in disrepute. Three studies conducted by the Committee for the banking and trading books show a variability in the risk weights that cannot be explained by different mix of risks.[12] The introduction of the unweighted leverage ratio into the Basel III framework testifies to the necessity to put at least a floor to the undervaluation of risks. However, the second specific report also contains some proposals directed at strengthening the standardized approaches, to use them as floor and benchmarks for the internal model approaches, to review modelling practices, and review the calibration of the leverage ratio. The experience gained since Basel I.5 (that introduced for the first time internal modelling for the trading book, later extended to the banking book by Basel II) has seriously shattered the confidence in internal modelling to the point of forcing the introduction of unsophisticated and unweighted risk floors.[13]

Although clearly in a defensive position, the BCBS sticks to the comparability–level playing field paradigm, proposing to limit both national discretion and the variability of risk weights.[14] The fact is that the very philosophy of basing prudential regulation on risk sensitive measures is at risk. Strengthening floors ultimately means to subtract credibility and effectiveness to risk modelling. It was explicitly a goal of the Committee to allow internal modelling to make regulatory capital converge to economic capital, i.e. the one freely computed by banks. The expected result was a diminution of regulatory capital, as the transitory floors adopted in Basel II with reference to Basel I also testify. As expected, but with the bad timing of happening at the outset of the recent crisis, the adoption of the internal rating based approach (IRB) led to lower capital requirements, and many banks were allowed to shift to the advanced IRB approach in order to further save capital (Haldane, 2011; Le Leslé and Avramova, 2012; Vallascas and Haggendorff, 2013). Basel II.5 and Basel III have in some instances increased risk weights, especially for the trading book, showing that the calibration of the different components of the regulatory framework becomes crucial. If the new floors proposed by the Committee will result high enough, they may easily render the capital requirements coming from the IRB approach ineffective.[15] In other words, the higher the evaluation of model risk, the stronger the case for abandoning costly modelling methods.

This is fundamentally the position taken by Tarullo (2014a), the Fed official responsible for regulation, when proposing to adopt only standardized methods and the leverage ratio and to add, only for systemic banks, stress-test exercises.[16] Such a change could even prefigure just adding stress tests on top of an unweighted leverage. This would be a fatal stroke for the Basel approach, which was dreaming with Basel II for all banks, small and large, to migrate to IRB methods. Proposals such as that of Tarullo in reality mean to switch to a different concept of risk sensitivity, one where the relevant supervisory focus is on systemic risks evaluated for systemic banks through stress tests. The regulatory and supervisory framework that is being adopted by the US authorities also prefigure a different approach with respect to the Basel one. Instead of treating all banks alike and imposing to everyone the methods calibrated for the large ones, the distinction is made between local banks that base their operation on lending customer relationships and large banks operating at arm's length (Tarullo, 2014b).

Apart from adjustments and simplifications also coming from the dialectic working of the RCAP, for the time being the essentials of Basel III will remain the reference standard, at least for large banks. However, as the above discussion and the EU implementation, which will be discussed in the next section, show, some relevant fissures begin to appear in the very fabric of the level playing field paradigm.

In the last years, a significant part of the activity of the FSB and BCBS was also devoted to produce the outlines for banks' corporate governance and risk management. Since we are rather sceptical on the 'didactic' activity by regulators and supervisors, we refer the interested reader to section 2.2 of FSB (2014b), where reference may be found to the numerous publications by the BCBS and FSB. More relevant is the issue of incentives related to compensation practices on which regulators are legislating, or may do in the future.

Distorted incentives coming from compensation practices are considered as having played a relevant role in the recent crisis. Apart from ethical and distributive aspects, the argument is that remunerations are weighting excessively on banks' non-interest costs, thus depriving banks of a precious internal source of capital, and that their structure, with a high share of bonuses linked to short-term results, produced incentives leading to excessive risk taking. For the first point, Basel III's rules on the conservation buffer include provisions for supervisors to limit bonus payments when Core tier-1 capital becomes lower than 7 per cent. The FSB principles and standards for sound compensation practices (FSB, 2009a, 2009b) explicitly abstain from dictating specific rules while providing some general principles that include:

- independent and effective board oversight of compensation policies and practices;
- linkages of the total variable compensation pool to the overall performance of the firm and the need to maintain a sound capital base;
- compensation structure and risk alignment, including deferral, vesting and clawback arrangements;
- limitations on guaranteed bonuses;
- enhanced public disclosure and transparency of compensation; and
- enhanced supervisory oversight of compensation, including corrective measures if necessary.

One crucial element is the definition of material risk-takers (MRTs), i.e. of the part of the bank's staff to which the remuneration policies apply. As the FSB recognizes, now that the implementation of the above principles 'by FSB jurisdictions is essentially completed ... there remain significant differences among jurisdictions in the approach to, and implications of, identifying the MRTs ... these can lead to potential level playing field issues' (FSB, 2014b, p. 6). We have a further example of how, having to face heterogeneous realities, the widening and deepening of international standards produces more the appearance than the substance of the level playing field, as we shall see in section 4.1 for the EU.

3.2 Too big to fail and crisis resolution

The second element of what we have defined the new regulatory balance is the too big to fail issue. As we have already stated, the chosen approach is to let systemic banks survive. Enlarging the risk-sensitive framework from idiosyncratic to systemic risks, G-SIBs are to be subject to higher capital and liquidity requirements, more intense supervision, including more robust stress testing, and an effective resolution regime.

Following the mandate by the G20, Basel III contains an additional core tier 1 capital requirement for G-SIBs, going from 1 per cent to 2.5 per cent according to their systemic footprint.[17] This measure marks a further step in the no confidence towards, and departure from, risk-sensitive IRB modelling. Moreover, enhancing the Pillar 2 activity of Basel III, more intense supervision gives further room to national discretion and weakens comparability and time consistency. As the recent experience of EU and US stress testing shows, we are far away from deriving from them useful comparative judgments (Montesi, 2014, Steffen 2014).

The weakening of confidence both on ex ante prudential measures to sustain bank resilience, and on spontaneous loss sharing related to international banking failures, has led to work actively for the first time on the resolution of systemic financial institutions. In 2011 the FSB published its Key Attributes of Effective Resolution Regimes (KA).[18] We read in its preamble that an effective resolution regime should

> make feasible the resolution of financial institutions without severe systemic disruptions and without exposing taxpayers to loss, while protecting vital economic functions through mechanisms which make it possible for shareholders and unsecured and uninsured creditors to absorb losses in a manner that respects the hierarchy of claims in liquidation [bail-in].
>
> (FSB, 2011, p. 3)

This means that the resolution regime should be applied only when such dangers exist, i.e. only to systemic banks, in order to protect the economy from systemic externalities and public debt from bail-out interventions. To exclude the latter requires resolution authorities having the power to impose bail-in with legal certainty. Furthermore,

> Jurisdictions should have in place a resolution regime that provides the resolution authority with a broad range of powers and options to resolve a firm that is no longer viable and has no reasonable prospect of becoming so. The resolution regime should include:
>
> (i) stabilisation options that achieve continuity of systemically important functions by way of a sale or transfer of the shares in the firm or of all or parts of the firm's business to a third party, either directly or through a bridge institution, and/or an officially mandated creditor-financed recapitalisation of the entity that continues providing the critical functions; and
>
> (ii) liquidation options that provide for the orderly closure and wind-down of all or parts of the firm's business in a manner that protects insured depositors, insurance policy holders and other retail customers.
>
> In order to facilitate the coordinated resolution of firms active in multiple countries, jurisdictions should seek convergence of their resolution regimes through the legislative changes needed to incorporate the tools and powers set out in these *Key Attributes* into their national regimes.
>
> (Ibid)

G-SIBs are required to

> have in place a recovery and resolution plan ... are subject to regular resolvability assessment ... and are subject of institution-specific cross border cooperation agreements [crisis management groups].
>
> (FSB, 2011, p. 5).

Because orderly resolution may require temporary funding, resolution authorities

> should make provision to recover any losses incurred (i) from shareholders and unsecured creditors subject to the 'no creditor worse off than in liquidation' safeguard; or (ii) if necessary, from the financial system more widely. Jurisdictions should have in place privately-financed deposit insurance or resolution funds, or a funding mechanism with *ex post* recovery from the industry.
>
> (FSB, 2011, p. 12)

Although stating the need for cooperation inside the crisis management groups, the document seems to express a preference for the single point of entry approach to resolution (see previous section 2). The resolution authority of the home country should be in command of all the resources of the firm, provisional to the equal treatment of domestic and foreign creditors.

The KA document makes it clear that cross-border recognition of resolution actions is necessary to dispel legal uncertainties and thus make the resolution regime effective. This issue is also the object of a more recent consultative document, which focuses on three points (FSB, 2014c).

Critical for the effective resolution of international banks is that

> entry into resolution … should not trigger statutory or contractual set-off rights, or constitute an event that entitles any counterparty of the firm in resolution to exercise contractual acceleration or early termination rights … the resolution authority should have the power to stay temporarily such rights.
>
> (FSB, 2011, p. 10)

The Lehman failure has shown that without stay agreements the firm's counterparties may ask a foreign court for the immediate execution of the contracts irrespective of the resolution going on in the home country. Recently, 18 G-SIBs and other large dealer banks have voluntarily signed a protocol under which counterparties agree to the cross-border enforceability of temporary stays on early termination and cross-default rights in over-the-counter bilateral derivative contracts (ISDA, 2014). An international private agreement that overcomes the difficulty of inserting comparable legislation in many jurisdictions may be read both as a confirmation of the necessity of private-public cooperation and as a pre-emptive private move for the protocol to be taken as model by national jurisdictions. The FSB (2014c) suggests that its members should adopt the above protocol model as uniformly as possible, viewing the private agreement as a valuable addition for reinforcing 'the legal certainty and predictability of recognition under the statutory framework once adopted' (FSB, 2014c, p. iii).

The second critical prerequisite concerns the transfer of assets and liabilities required by the resolution process. Legally empowering and assisting foreign resolution authorities to dispose of assets and liabilities, also regarding local branches and subsidiaries, is part of the general recognition framework.

The third prerequisite concerns the write-down and conversion of debt (bail-in) because also in this case the action of the resolution authority may not be recognized and enforced by courts outside the issuer's home jurisdiction. As we have seen for the first point, the FSB favours a private contractual solution as filling the gap until jurisdictions will adopt a statutory framework according to which 'prudential or resolution authorities should require entities issuing debt governed by the law of a foreign jurisdiction to include recognition clauses for statutory bail-in in those debt instruments' (FSB, 2014c, p. 15).

Because the above documents lack a specific proposal on loss-absorbing capacity of G-SIBs, which is required to align the resolution authorities to a common minimum standard thus facilitating cross-border recognition, the

FSB has presented to the G20 Brisbane Summit a consultative document, developed in consultation with the BCBS, on total loss-absorbing capacity of banks (TLAC) (FSB, 2014d). In it we read that '

> for home and host authorities and markets to have confidence that systemically important banks are truly no longer 'too big to fail' and are resolvable without the use of public funds, they must have confidence that these firms have sufficient capacity to absorb losses, both before and during resolution.
>
> (FSB, 2014d, p. 4)

To note that according to the FSB, completing the reform package with this proposal would meet the G20 mandate to end the too big to fail problem (FSB, 2014a).

The TLAC proposal is composed of two pillars. As we shall see below, the first pillar contains specific requirements for resolvability. The second pillar may add further requirements according to the evaluation by the resolution authorities of the systemic footprint of the G-SIB or its components.

The proposal for pillar 1 sets a minimum TLAC between 16 per cent and 20 per cent of the risk-weighted assets, being satisfied by the instruments included in the Basel III minimum capital requirements and by additional debt instruments that contractually can bear losses or be transformed into equities with legal certainty. As in Basel III, a leverage ratio, defined as the minimum TLAC/exposures and not lower than 6 per cent, acts as a floor.[19] In addition, to ensure an early resolution entry of the G-SIB and thus the loss-absorbency capacity required by resolution, it is proposed that debt instruments should not be lower than 33 per cent of the minimum TLAC requirement.

Another relevant feature of the proposal is the definition of the resolution entity to which the TLAC applies.

> A G-SIB may consist of one or more resolution groups. It may form a single resolution group with the parent company, which may be a holding company or an operating entity, as the sole resolution entity or, alternatively, consist of two or more resolution groups with a corresponding number of resolution entities. Under this proposal, a Minimum TLAC requirement will apply to each resolution entity within each G-SIB and will be set in relation to the consolidated balance sheet of each resolution group. When a resolution entity enters resolution, TLAC issued by the resolution entity and held by external creditors would be written down and/or converted into the equity of the (re-capitalised) resolution entity (or a newly established bridge entity). Losses would be absorbed in the first instance by the shareholders and thereafter by the external creditors of the resolution entity according to the applicable creditor hierarchy.
>
> (FSB, 2104d, p. 7)

The next point is one that we have often raised before, that the resolution regime must strike a balance between the global activity of a G-SIB and the defence of national interests.

> A key objective of the new TLAC standard is to provide home and host authorities with confidence that G-SIBs can be resolved in an orderly manner and thereby diminish any incentives to ring-fence assets domestically. A resolution entity should generally act as a source of loss absorbing capacity for its subsidiaries where those subsidiaries are not themselves resolution entities. The FSB proposes that subsidiaries located outside of their resolution entity's home jurisdiction that are identified as material and that are not themselves resolution entities are subject to an internal TLAC requirement in proportion to the size and risk of the material subsidiaries' exposures... The FSB proposes a quantum of internal TLAC for review in the QIS that must be pre-positioned at material subsidiaries be equivalent to 75–90% of the TLAC requirement that would apply to a material subsidiary on a stand-alone basis, but that the specific internal TLAC requirement is defined by the relevant host authority in consultation with the home authority and validated through the RAP. This quantum of pre-positioned internal TLAC is intended to provide sufficient comfort for host authorities that sufficient resources are available to absorb losses in local material subsidiaries but provide some flexibility to deploy non-pre-positioned internal TLAC as necessary across the group in resolution.
>
> (FSB, 2014d, pp. 7–8)

Because the debt share of the TLAC can be as low as 33 per cent, 66 per cent of TLAC may be made up of common equities (CET1 in the Basel parlance). With a TLAC of 16 per cent of RWA, this means that CET1 may reach 10.56 per cent of RWA. If we take the minimum local TLAC of a subsidiary at 75 per cent of its stand-alone level, the prepositioned (local) TLAC may require CET1 as 7.9 per cent of RWA, i.e. a level that is a bit higher than the minimum 7 per cent Basel common equity requirement. The result is, for material subsidiaries, a subsidiarization of G-SIBs to 'provide sufficient comfort for host authorities'. Obviously, the announced future calibration, on whose methodology we are not given any hint, may change these percentages and therefore the previous result. Anyway, evident in the proposal is the weight of the US intermediate holding approach to foreign relevant intermediaries.

3.3 Structural reforms

In collaboration with the OECD and IMF, the FSB (2014e) has recently produced a report to the G20 on the cross-border consistencies and global financial stability implications of structural banking reforms, an issue that constitutes the third and final element of what we have defined the new regulatory equilibrium.

A long citation from the report well clarifies the issue.

> Structural banking reforms have recently been implemented or proposed in a number of jurisdictions, which account for a material share of global banking assets. The most far-reaching reforms are in jurisdictions that are home to global systemically important banks (G-SIBs), as well as host to substantial operations of G-SIBs. The recent financial crisis highlighted concerns around the complexity and resilience of banking group structures. A broad aim of many structural banking reforms is therefore to introduce a separation between certain 'core' banking activities – such as payments and retail deposit-taking – and the risks emanating from investment banking and capital market activities. The reforms are designed to reduce risks to banking groups stemming from trading activities, limit the range of activities covered by the public safety net, and more generally to simplify legal and operational structures of complex banking groups, in order to enhance their supervisability and resolvability with a view to reducing systemic risk, enhancing depositor protection and limiting fiscal exposures. The reforms have mostly taken the form either of functional separation of types of financial activities through outright prohibitions, 'ring-fencing' or subsidiarisation; or of geographical separation via local subsidiarisation requirements for domestic operations of foreign banks.
>
> (FSB, 2014e, p. 1)

Among the jurisdictions that have adopted, or are in the way of adopting, structural measures, the most relevant are the USA, the UK and the EU.[20] The report offers a comprehensive summary and assessment of what are up to now are not quite finished designs. A brief analysis of these schemes is useful for our discourse.

The USA have introduced two measures.[21] The Volcker rule, which vetoes proprietary trading and relevant connections with hedge and private property funds; the rule is not intended to exclude from banks with insured deposits the most risky activities, but only those that are not useful from a social perspective. The foreign banking organisations rule, which obliges relevant foreign subsidiaries to organise as intermediate holding companies (IHC), subjects them to the regulatory and supervisory requirements applied to similar US bank holdings. Since, contrary to the original proposal, foreign branches and agencies are not included in the IHC rule, the result is in fact a process of enhanced subsidiarization, linked mainly to entities with relevant retail activities, which weakens the principle of the home country control. With IHCs obliged to satisfy regulatory and supervisory requirements locally, a certain degree of fragmentation in international banking derives, coherent with what we have already seen for the TLAC proposal.

Less definite is the picture coming from the Act with which the UK has adopted part of the proposals contained in the Vickers' Report on ring fencing.[22] The legislated rules are full of exemptions that also apply to individual entities and that are dealt with in the secondary legislation. Since the latter is yet in progress and, being subject to the political orientation of the government and parliament might change in the course of time, the discussion of the rules must take into account this type of flexibility. The purpose is to ring fence retail activities, the definition of whose perimeter is subject to general and individual specifications, from the more risky investment ones. The legislation applies to UK-incorporated entities with more than £25bn of core deposits, including subsidiaries of foreign banks, but excluding branches of foreign banks and overseas subsidiaries of UK banks. As far as possible, the ring-fenced body should be legally, financially and operationally independent from the rest of the corporate group. Proprietary trading, market making and commodity trading are prohibited in principle, but are allowed to be performed by other entities inside the same group. Branches of banks incorporated outside the European Economic Area are subject to recognition by the relevant UK supervisory authority following the equivalence principle and on the guarantee by the foreign authority on equal treatment and on the effectiveness of the resolution framework. As for the USA, international wholesale banking is not subject to specific rules and it is thus open to the recognition judgment of the supervisory authorities. With respect to the USA legislation, in principle the ring-fenced body is allowed a more restricted range of activities, but the separation is weaker remaining the forbidden activities inside the same group.

The EU Commission has prepared a draft proposal for a Regulation based on the Liikanen Report, which has to be discussed and approved by the Council and the European Parliament. The proposal, which is a sort of mix of the US and UK schemes, applies to parent EU banks and subsidiaries and branches of EU and non-EU banks, exceeding certain dimensional thresholds, and bans proprietary trading also inside the group. The possible ring fence of other activities, notably market making, from deposit taking is left to be decided by supervisors. The scheme also allows supervisors to pose limits to intra-group and external connections. Recognition of similar schemes adopted by other jurisdictions is based on the principle of equivalence.[23]

Worthy of note are the more open regime reserved to wholesale banking (except for the EU draft), the 'unstable' powers given to politicians or to supervisors in shaping a new sort of limited specialization, and the potential relevance of international agreements. For the latter, the principle of equivalence stems from the new version of the BCBS Core Principles (BCBS, 2012b), being a restatement of the home-host relationship. Overall, the aim is to defend deposit insurance and the public purse from (unnecessary) risky activities and at the same time to simplify the process of crisis resolution. Although the schemes have different implications for international banking, some degree of fragmentation is an intended consequence (FSB, 2014e, p. 14).

4 European institutional and regulatory reforms

We have recalled in the introduction of this chapter the set of institutional reforms introduced in the EU in order to decrease differences in financial rules and supervisory practices, with the goal of arriving at a single rulebook and single supervisory handbook that were thought to be necessary conditions for the effective attainment of the single European financial market and to avoid the adoption of laxer supervisory practices by some EU member countries. In fact, one of the lessons derived from the recent financial crisis was that with highly interconnected national markets the weaker regulatory and supervisory components are liable to produce strong negative externalities in other parts of the Union.

The European Banking Authority became operational in 2011, empowered both with the production of the common technical standards necessary to make EU Directives and Regulations related to the banking industry enforceable and with overseeing their homogeneous application. According to the initial intent, this and focusing the financial legislation more on regulations than directives should have marked a trend towards maximum harmonization, departing from the traditional policy of dictating minimum standards and leaving ample room for national discretion.

However, different national causes and consequences of the financial and economic crisis, and different political evaluations derived from them, boosted the institutional fragmentation already existing inside the EU. On the one side, the countries pertaining to the euro area decided to jump to a near-maximum harmonization model through the creation of the Banking Union (BU), while the adoption of the euro by other member countries was put on hold.[24] On the other side, some member states, notably but not only the UK, are reconsidering the opportunity to follow that trend, and are on the contrary pursuing the renationalization of some of the powers previously transferred to EU institutions. The wider scope and the deepening of regulation and supervision discussed in the previous sections have also represented a relevant centrifugal factor. A confused variable institutional geometry results, where in the land between the two polarized sides stand countries that might enter into the BU without belonging to the euro area and countries that are variously attracted by the UK model of Europe à la carte.

According to the EU treaties, institutional subsets like the BU cannot adopt measures that are inconsistent with those applied to the Union in general. Because the Single Supervisory Mechanism (SSM), the first pillar of the BU, must follow the rulebook produced by directives, regulations and EBA's technical standards regarding the entire Union, its harmonization activity should be primarily felt for the supervisory practices adopted by its members. Given the ample discretionary powers given to supervisors, this might count more than the maximum harmonization of rules, thus deepening the differences with the rest of the Union.[25] A second implication is that the institutional and political fragmentation might be felt in the production of primary and secondary EU legislation because directives, regulations and technical standards have to allow for greater national freedom than the one envisaged when the new institutional architecture was designed. How much that design was realistic is, however, matter for discussion. Even inside the more demanding euro area, historical, legal and procedural differences still count for the admissibility of maximum harmonization, potentially obliging to transfer to the general EU legislation wider casuistic or weaker requirements than otherwise necessary. As we will see, this may affect the way in which international standards are converted into EU legislation.

In what follows, we shall analyse how the Basel III framework and the FSB's Key Attributes for resolution has been translated into EU legislation.[26]

4.1 Compliance with Basel III

The Basel III framework has been translated into EU legislation in 2013 through the Fourth Capital Requirements Directive (CRD IV) and the Capital Requirements Regulation (CRR) that came into force on January 1, 2014. Consistently with the effort to homogenize regulations across member states, the substantive part of standards (Pillar 1 and 3) is contained in the CRR, which applies directly, differently from the implementation of previous Basel releases that were made by means of directives. However, given that the legislation applies to all EU banks, irrespective of their magnitude and legal form, and given the heterogeneous financial morphology and development of EU member countries, the CRR contains significant doses of national discretion and much of what is related to supervision (Pillar 2) is left to the national implementations of the CRD IV.

The BCBS has recently produced a report assessing the implementation of the Basel capital framework in the nine EU member states that are members of the Basel Committee (BCBS, 2014d).[27]

> The assessment focused primarily on a detailed review of the CRD IV/CRR package along with its accompanying European Banking Authority (EBA) standards and guidelines as of 30 June 2014. The review also examined Member State-level requirements under CRD IV/CRR. The approach was to ascertain whether the EU banking prudential framework incorporates Basel minimum standards in both letter and spirit and that it is clearly specified, transparent and consistently adopted so as to promote confidence in prudential outcomes in the nine Member States. Where EU-wide capital regulations or Member State regulations and provisions were identified as deviating from the Basel framework, they were evaluated for their impact on the capital ratios of a set of internationally active banks in the nine Member States.
>
> (BCBS, 2014d, p. 2)

An interesting feature of the document is that it assesses compliance both at the EU level, for primary and secondary legislation, and at a country level. As a recognition of the attempt to provide for a single rulebook, the RCAP notes that many technical standards produced by the EBA, and endorsed by the Commission, 'will go beyond what is described in the Basel framework, for instance by specifying harmonized rules for the entire EU in areas where the Basel framework allows national discretion' (BCBS, 2014d, p. 11). Of note is that the materiality of eventual deviations from Basel III is evaluated with reference to significant internationally active banks. In other words, although recognizing that the Basel framework is applied to all EU banks, the RCAP focuses on whether deviations from Basel may give to SIBs unfair international competitive advantages and is particularly sensitive on compliance for the innovations introduced since Basel II.5 on risk weighting and the quantity and quality of capital.

The latter qualification is relevant when reading Table 12.1, taken from the report (BCBS, 2014d, p. 15). The table summarizes as materially non-compliant the results of the EU assessment. Many deviations that are not considered material for the 20 large banks in the sample, but that could be so for national banking industries, do not affect the result. A relevant instance are deviations from standardized or IRB approaches. Since large banks mainly use the IRB approach, significant deviations from the Basel standardized approach do not qualify as material.

Many deviations singled out by the RCAP come de facto from EU legislation accommodating specific interests coming from individual or groups of member countries. Examples are capital deductions for investments in capital instruments of insurance subsidiaries; capital instruments issued by mutually owned institutions; discounted risk-weights for exposures to SMEs; and preferential treatment for covered bonds.

Specific interests also play a significant role for the key components where the document places emphasis, first of all the extent to which large banks may cherry pick between standardized or IRB approaches, as best suited to save capital. According to Basel, a bank using the IRB approach is allowed to

> permanently apply the standardized approach for non-significant units and asset classes that are immaterial in terms of size and perceived risk profile. By contrast, the scope allowed under the CRR extends well beyond that envisaged under the Basel framework. It covers a variety of exposures including sovereigns, Member States central banks and regional governments, local authorities, administrative bodies, public sector entities, institutions and intragroup exposures, and equity exposures incurred under legislative programmes to promote specified sectors of the economy.
>
> (BCBS, 2014d, p. 20)

Table 12.1 Summary assessment grading

Key components of the Basel capital framework	*Grade*
Overall grade:	MNC
Scope of application	C
Transitional arrangements	C
Pillar 1: Minimum capital requirements	
Definition of capital and calculation of minimum capital requirements	LC
Capital buffers (conservation and countercyclical)	C
Credit risk: Standardised Approach	LC
Credit risk: Internal Ratings-Based Approach	MNC
Credit risk: Securitisation framework	LC
Counterparty credit risk framework	NC
Market risk: Standardised measurement method	LC
Market risk: Internal models approach	C
Operational risk: Basic indicator approach and standardized approach	C
Operational risk: Advance measurement approaches	C
Pillar 2: Supervisory review process	
Legal and regulatory framework for the Supervisory review process and for taking supervisory actions	C
Pillar 3: Market discipline	
Disclosure requirements	C

Source: BCBS 2014d, p.15

Definition of the grades: C (compliant), LC (largely compliant), MNC (materially non-compliant) and NC (non-compliant). Compliant: if all minimum Basel provisions have been satisfied and if no material differences have been found that would give rise to prudential concerns or provide a competitive advantage to internationally active banks; Largely compliant with the Basel framework if only minor provisions have not been satisfied and only if differences that have a limited impact on financial stability or the international level playing field have been identified; Materially non-compliant with the Basel framework if key provisions of the framework have not been satisfied or if differences that could materially impact capital ratios and Non-compliant with the Basel framework if the regulation has not been adopted or if differences that could severely impact capital ratios and financial stability or international level playing field have been identified.

For instance, the fact the IRB approach may variously produce higher or lower risk weights for sovereigns than the standardized approach may lead a bank to select the more favourable approach in a point of time and afterwards, if obliged to stick to it, to 'distort' its portfolio to save capital. If on the contrary supervisors were flexible, they would allow for regulatory arbitrage. According to the report, at present the result is an overstatement of CET1 ratios.

In the same vein, the report judges the EU as non-compliant for the counterparty credit risk framework, which represents a key innovation of the later versions of Basel. This negative judgment crucially affects the EU's overall grade. The counterparty valuation adjustment (CVA) represents an adjustment of the nominal exposure coming from the evaluation of the counterparty risk, and thus introduces a further risk capital charge. According to the report, the CRR is non-compliant because of the exemptions allowed for

> transactions between EU banks and 'CVA-exempted entities'. Banks subject to the CRR can exclude exposures to pension funds, Member States central governments, regional governments and local bodies wherever they qualify for a 0% risk weight under the Standardised Approach for credit risk, as well as qualifying non-financial end-users. This constitutes a material department from the Basel framework in that it materially boosts bank capital ratios.
>
> (BCBS, 2014d, p. 21)

We leave the reader to give name and address to the jurisdictions that may have pushed for introducing into the CRR the above 'deviations' from the Basel standard. More interesting is a general point that we have already addressed in section 2, whether legitimate local differences and policy priorities should be allowed by international standards. The report does not and cannot address the problem whether the 'exemptions' of the CRR come from legitimate interests. The problem lies with Basel III, in the scope of allowed national discretions that, as we have seen in 3.1, are under review for further tightening.

Once again, we are facing the difficulty in striking a balance between the international level playing field and national or regional interests. In this perspective, it is instructive to read the part of the RCAP document reporting the counter-deductions offered by the relevant EU authorities (BCBS, 2014d, pp.6–7). Without going into the specific points, two aspects are worth mentioning. First, the conflicting interpretations advanced on key aspects of Basel III come from the vagueness proper of a standard based on principles. Second, the ability of strong jurisdictions to put the case for significant revisions. We have already seen that, according to our interpretation, the new BCBS proposal on external ratings may derive from the necessity to accommodate its framework with the mandate of the US Dodd-Frank. Here, the EU authorities make explicit reference to new discussions inside the BCBS that might render some of the contrasted points minor or null deviations. According to the BCBS, the RCAP should serve to discipline its member jurisdictions. The reality shows that, at least in part, the opposite may be true.

Building on the CRD III, which had broadly incorporated the FSB's principles and standards for sound compensation practices (see before, section 3.1), the CRD IV, and the technical standards delegated to the EBA, introduces new provisions directed at reducing the variability of rules across

EU member countries.[28] The production of more homogeneous standards necessarily requires including provisions that are more specific and go beyond those produced by the FSB. In particular, the CRD IV introduces the so-called 100/200 per cent rule (according to which bonuses cannot be higher than 100 per cent of fixed remuneration, a percentage that can reach 200 per cent if approved by shareholders with a qualified majority), and quantitative and qualitative criteria for the identification of material risk-takers. Notwithstanding stricter rules, the FSB reports that several EU countries are introducing additional rules on top of those provided for by the CRD IV (FSB, 2014f). Other member countries, the UK in particular, substantially object to the design and to adopting the EU subsidiarity principle in this matter. This is a further case of national reactions related to extending the scope of regulation while keeping, or deepening, the level playing field at the international or regional level.

4.2 The EU on bank resolution

The directive on bank recovery and resolution (BRRD), agreed in April 2014 and to be implemented by EU member states by end 2014,[29] broadly complies with the FSB Key Attributes discussed above, section 3.2 (FSB, 2014g, BCBS, 2014d).

Along with the objectives stated in the FSB's KA, – preserving essential operations and minimizing exposure of government finance to losses -, the BRRD also seeks to prevent domino effects in an increasingly integrated area. Specific attention is then paid to cooperation and agreements between home and host authorities inside the EU.

The BRRD seeks 'to tackle potential bank crises at three stages: preparatory and preventative, early intervention, and resolution.' (Council of the European Union, 2014, p. 1) For every stage, the proportionality principle should apply, which means that this special regime should replace ordinary liquidation procedures only when systemic effects are expected by a bank's failure.

The first stage deals with banks having to draw up recovery and resolution plans that must be approved by the relevant authorities. Differently from the KA, the BRRD also includes provisions for recovery powers, i.e. for preventive action exercised by the supervisory authority. A bank must draw up a recovery plan that should include all possible measures that could be taken by the management of the troubled institution when the conditions for early interventions are met. For both recovery and resolution plans, the directive expresses a strong preference for adopting the top-down approach, although for relevant branches and subsidiaries of foreign groups the host authority may reasonably argue for these plans being drafted and approved on a local individual basis.

Although being reframed in the context of recovery planning, the early intervention framework builds on the experience of the US FDIC and of some EU countries, and is consistent with the prerogatives of the supervisory review process as laid down in the second pillar of Basel III. The early intervention powers should include all circumstances considered necessary to restore the financial soundness of an institution, including the power to appoint a temporary administrator for replacing or temporarily collaborating with the management of an institution (BRRD, Whereas 40). Early intervention is also a prerequisite for spotting at an early stage if the institution must promptly enter the resolution procedure when its resources still permit an orderly and less costly resolution.[30]

The third stage, concerning resolution, does not present relevant differences with respect to the FSB's key attributes, although on several aspects it is necessarily more specific. For instance, on the institutional side the EBA's governance must make room for national resolution authorities' membership. The directive also dictates specific quantitative standards for the resolution fund. At the end of the transition period, it must be at least equal to 1 per cent of secured deposits, coming from the contributions of banks, and the resolution authority may make recourse to it only after equities and debt subject to bail-in have covered losses for at least the 8 per cent of total liabilities; since the latter include own funds, this means the 8 per cent of total assets. If we take as reference an average risk-weight of 50 per cent, which as we have seen is the implicit reference of the Basel III leverage ratio floor, perhaps not by chance this amounts to the 16 per cent minimum TLAC ratio proposed by the FSB (on this more below). The result is that the resolution fund should intervene only after the TLAC buffer is exhausted. Moreover, the contribution by the fund 'is limited to the lower of 5% of total liabilities including own funds or the means available to the resolution funds and the amount that can be raised through *ex-post* contributions within three years' (BRRD, Whereas 73).

The directive includes the mandate to the EBA for producing technical standards directed at homogenizing its implementation across EU member countries. The EBA has recently produced a proposal for technical standards related to minimum requirement for own funds and eligible liabilities (MREL). In the proposal we read,

> The EBA expects these RTS to be compatible with the proposed FSB term sheet for Total Loss Absorbing Capacity (TLAC) for Globally Systemically Important Banks (G-SIBs). Where there are differences resulting from the nature of the EBA's mandate under the BRRD, as well as the fact that the BRRD MREL requirement applies to banks which are not G-SIBs, these differences do not prevent resolution authorities from implementing the MREL for G-SIBs consistently with the international framework.
>
> (EBA, 2014, p. 5)

As for the TLAC, the MREL must be coherent with the capital requirements proposed by Basel III, in this case as implemented by the CRD IV/CRR.

The EBA proposal consistently extends the proportionality principle utilized in the BRRD for recovery and resolution plans to the resolvability criteria. In Box 1, p. 10, it presents stylized examples of how to treat differently banks that are small, medium-sized or SIBs.[31] If the small bank may be liquidated without entering the resolution process, its MREL is derived directly from the Basel minimum capital requirement. Larger banks, whose entering into resolution is required to protect critical functions, must be subject to a MREL higher than the Basel minimum requirement given the necessity to recapitalize the part of activity that survives.[32] On this account, the EBA correctly deals with the problem whether the limit posed on the use of the resolution fund permits resolution without recourse to public funds. It then adds the condition that the MREL must be set at a level consistent with these two constraints.

The differences between the FSB proposal and the BRRD and the EBA's proposed technical standards come from some requirements included in the directive and the need to take also into account non-SIBs. The MREL is set on a case-by-case basis and does not consequently fix a common minimum standard. The requirements for liabilities to be eligible for MREL differs in some respect to those included in the FSB proposal. The metrics of the TLAC is based on risk-weighted assets, while the MREL is based on total liabilities (after full recognition of counterparty netting rights), even if risk-sensitive capital ratios must be considered. The MREL does not include the condition that a minimum percentage of the MREL must consist of non-capital instruments. Considering that the TLAC also includes a discretionary pillar 2 and the MREL is based on judgmental evaluations of the resolution authority, a quantitative comparative analysis is practically impossible.

A critical component of the banking union is its second pillar, the single resolution mechanism (SRM). As required by the EU treaties, its framework is fully consistent with the BRRD and the EBA technical standards. The differences lie in the creation of a single resolution authority and a single resolution fund, and in the recourse of last instance to the European stability mechanism (ESM).[33]

5 Conclusions

The recent crisis produced a significant degree of fragmentation in international finance, especially in the wholesale segment. The leading international political actors soon realized that to reaffirm the global nature of finance a new balance had to be struck, where a thorough revision and hardening of regulatory standards had to go hand in hand with new mechanisms capable of soothing national fears.

Acting as the operational arm of the G20, the Financial Stability Board have coordinated the activities of the international standard bodies, helped to focus on priority areas, contributed with the new resolution regime, and cooperated in supervising the implementation of the new or revised standards.

At the November 2014 G20 Brisbane Summit, the FSB reported on the work done so far, declaring as substantially completed the first phase of its mission based on the design of standards, having thus fixed the 'fault lines that caused the crisis'.

In the banking industry, the new balance is founded on three elements: a revision of the Basel framework, a novel mechanism of crisis resolution for SIBs and the introduction of some structural measures.

Our analysis of the above three elements has singled out the tension between fully restoring global finance and erecting national safeguards. To a certain extent, the tendency is to allow for some national ring fence for retail banking and to protect the global nature of wholesale banking. This implies a redraft to the axiom of the level playing field, previously based on the homogenization of rules. National rules are becoming less homogeneous for the retail segment and the internationalization of wholesale banking is increasingly entrusted to the recognition of equivalent results. The principle of the home country control is thus weakened, especially where some sort of subsidiarization gets a foothold. Moreover, the wider scope given to supervisors' discretionary power increases the weight of principles with respect to rules.

As far as the above tendency goes, the production of international standards traditionally anchored to homogeneous rules is increasingly assuming the role of regulatory floors, so that the variability of their implementation increases and compliance is more difficult to assess by means of international peer reviews.

Similar arguments apply to the implementation of the new resolution framework, which should help to solve the too big to fail problem. To follow its general principles might appear to be a relatively easy exercise, but the tension between global business and national interests resurfaces again when we look at the international cooperation that they require. When we go into the details of the resolution plans of such large, complex and interconnected banks and on the specific resolvability conditions that they should satisfy, the fears of host countries strongly reappear, so much that even the FSB proposal implies *de facto* a new sort of subsidiarization.

The first response to the crisis by the authorities of the European Union was to build new institutions with the explicit mandate to increase the harmonization of rules and supervisory practices among its member countries. The goal to build a single financial market was seen as requiring a highly levelled playing field and it was considered as a priority for opposing the fragmentation caused by the crisis acting on markers that had previously undergone a process of convergence not one of integration. Harder hit by the crisis due to its incomplete institutional design, the euro area has made a further step towards centralization with the creation of the Banking Union. For the EU implementation of Basel III and of the resolution framework, the push towards greater harmonization has meant to avoid some of the national discretion left by the two international standards and to introduce regional specificities; the banking union will further rein in, although not completely, national discretion.

However, the Union has also been interested by centrifugal reactions to the crisis. Without coordination, several countries have legislated on some issues before and independently from the EU; structural reforms are a clear example. To a certain extent, these were strong signals sent to the central authorities on where not to go. In addition, different national lessons learnt from the crisis and the widening and deepening of regulation have sharpened national sensitivities, which have pushed in the opposite direction to enhanced harmonization. As a result, the compromise between different views and interests have left the CRD IV and CRR with significant margins of national discretion. The directive on bank recovery and resolution is by definition a minimum standard, and variously customized national implementation will confront the more homogeneous block of the countries adhering to the banking union. The future outcome may be an increased polarization between countries pertaining or not to the banking union and the continued use of intergovernmental agreements concerning a restricted number of EU countries instead of treaty reforms directed at higher political, economic and financial harmonization for all. The increased harmonization of some countries will probably confront a higher overall variability. In other terms, presently the EU is not capable of escaping from the regulatory fragmentation interesting the international arena. Whether or not this represents a positive development is a matter for further discussion. However, uncertainty remains and might increase over the identity of the European Union.

Notes

1 According to Backer (2011, p. 752):

> The FSB template points to the organization of governance as a collegial enterprise in which states and traditional law-based systems interact with nonstate actors and their norm-based systems to develop integrated governance with global reach.

2 The G20 declarations, starting from the 2008 Washington meeting, may be found in the G20 website. For a review of the first shaping steps taken by the G20 see Wouters et al. (2010) and the literature cited there. To maintain the momentum of its legitimacy, the G20 has afterwards broadened its agenda to matters such as development, energy and climate change, corruption, tax and international trade. See also Rottier and Véron (2010) and Lanoo (2014).

3 The standards and codes relating to the financial sector concern banking supervision; securities regulation; insurance supervision; crisis resolution and deposit insurance; insolvency; corporate governance; accounting and auditing; payment, clearing and settlement; market integrity.

4 Besides some national defensive measures against the swings of international funds, the IMF has made a timid reflection on the subject (Kregel, 2009; IMF, 2012; UNCTAD, 2013).

5 See for example the recent report by HM Government (2014) on the financial services and the free movement of capital in the EU single market. For the ring fencing of domestic retail banks, see the Vickers Report and its partial implementation into law (ICB, 2011, UK Parliament, 2013). Worth to remember is that the UK law on ring fencing leaves the government and supervisors the

power to decide where to put the fence, in general and for single intermediaries. Significantly, banks were recently asked to inform their supervisor on how they intend to ring fence their retail activities.

6 The requirement for relevant foreign intermediaries to assume the structure of intermediate holding companies is presented and discussed in Tarullo (2013, 2014b).

7 To make things a bit confused, all these 11 banks had passed the Fed stress test exercise. As we will discuss in section 3.2, the attempt is to make the resolvability issue, of which the living wills are part, and the supervisory prudential issue running in coherent directions.

8 For the banking sector, this is also because the Basel regulation was born to deal only with internationally active banks. Presumably as a consequence of many jurisdictions, the EU in particular, having adopted Basel for every type of banks, its later releases have become less clear on their perimeter, often only distinguishing a different treatment for internationally systemic banks. Differently from the EU, starting from Basel I the USA have tended to tailor regulation for its small communities banks on their unsophisticated operations. This approach has been recently reaffirmed and strengthened by Tarullo (2014c) when discussing the adoption of Basel III inside the Dodd-Frank frame. As we shall discuss below, he argues that their lending practices based on customer relationship need a significant flexibility that is not consistent with the schematized Basel rules designed for arm's length operations.

9 See for example the contributions contained in Griffith-Jones et al. (2010).

10 Of note, a fundamental, although optional, component of the FSAPs are the reports on the observance of standards and codes (ROSCs). Cfr. IMF and WB (2011).

11 One of the critical points mandated by the G20 is to exclude or mitigate the reliance of risk-weight computations on external ratings. The US Dodd-Frank law includes a similar provision. Basel III contains, on the contrary and especially for the standardized methods, reference to external ratings, so that the BCBS's recent evaluation of the US adoption of Basel III, although founding it largely compliant, lamented their absence in the securitization framework. As an example of the dialectic function of the RCAP, the BCBS has afterward produced a proposal intended to reduce reliance on external ratings for securitization exposures. www.bis.org/bcbs/publ/d303.pdf.

12 These studies are available at www.bis.org/bcbs/implementation.htm. In several cases, the responsibility of national supervisors comes from permitting banks not to adhere to a single method for every counterparty and every risk, but to cherry pick for different assets or risk categories the method leading to the lowest risk weight.

13 The Chairman of the BCBS, Stefan Ingves, alerts that 'if we don't … succeed in properly restoring the credibility of risk-weighted capital ratios, a more important role have to be played by other parts of the regulatory system, such as the leverage ratio' (Ingves, 2014).

14 The Committee acknowledges that the complexity coming from the pursuit of increased risk sensitivity, which should remain at the core of the regulatory framework for banks, 'may not always strike an appropriate balance between the complementary goals of risk sensitivity, simplicity and comparability' (BCBS, 2013, p. 1). Worthy of note also is the absence in the above reports of the problem affecting comparability due to the adoption of different accounting standards and to the discretion that these standards allow to banks.

15 To have an idea of the calibration problems posed by the different parts of the Basel framework let us make a simple exercise. According to Basel III, ordinary banks must keep the minimum tier-1 capital ratio (T1C/risk-weighted assets) at

6 per cent and the minimum leverage ratio (L), defined as T1C/Total exposure, at 3 per cent. Because RW (average risk-weight ratio) is equal to L/T1C, the minimum RW should be equal to 50 per cent. The function of L should be to impose higher levels of T1C if RW goes below the RW threshold. But according to Basel III's capital requirements, the banks should add to T1C the conservation buffer (2.5 per cent). Maintaining RW at 50 per cent, the minimum L would be 4.25 per cent, not 3 per cent. In other words, L = 3 per cent is not calibrated on the physiology of capital requirements, which would require an addition of the conservation buffer to the numerator of L. Adding the buffer, the minimum physiological RW would decrease to 35.3 per cent. Furthermore, G-SIBS with the highest systemic footprint must add a further 2.5 per cent to capitalization, which means raising T1C from 8 per cent to 11 per cent and constraining RW to be not lower than 27.3 per cent, eight points less than for smaller banks. Leaving the leverage floor at 3 per cent for all banks means that if a non-SIB computes an RW of 27.3 per cent it must raise its T1C at 11 per cent, the same as a G-SIB. In other words, being the floor for T1C equal to Leverage ratio/RW, the homogeneous leverage floor does not discriminate between systemic and non-systemic banks. Having the US proposed to increase the leverage ratio to 6 per cent for its larger banks, if the latter respect the 11 per cent T1C ratio their RW cannot fall under 54.5 per cent; otherwise they must increase T1C. The systemic nature of the G-SIBs is thus recognized and IRB calculations are potentially rendered ineffective. We can then understand why there so much debate over the definition and calibration of the leverage ratio.

16 At present, the Basel standardized methods heavily rely on external ratings. The G20, the US Dodd Frank and the EU authorities have variously requested to avoid or weaken the use of external ratings in risk-weighted regulatory capital requirements. The ongoing work in the USA and EU shows the difficulty of designing alternative methods while maintaining risk sensitivity without leaving banks excessive discretion. When regulation wants to rein in the measure of risks for level playing field reasons such problems resurface in every part of the regulatory framework.

17 The Committee has also dealt with the issue of domestic systemically important banks (D-SIBs), stating principles akin to those for G-SIBs, but refraining from the prescriptive approach adopted for the G-SIBs framework. Discretion is left to national jurisdictions on D-SIBs' assessment and additional loss absorbency requirements (BCBS, 2012a).

18 The document refers generically to financial institutions. The FSB published in October 2014 a revised version of the document that differs from the previous one only for containing in Appendix II a sector-specific guidance. We will only refer to banks.

19 Following the exercise made in the previous footnote 15, the two constraints are now the TLAC not lower than two times the T1C and the leverage ratio not lower than 6 per cent. The implicit RW is 50 per cent. However, the first constraint implies a TLAC ratio of 12 per cent, lower than the 16 per cent minimum with which the bank must comply. Anyway, this leverage ratio is more binding than the Basel one because it becomes effective when RW becomes lower than 37.5 per cent.

20 For the risks associated to the divergences in the above structural reforms, see Viñals (2013).

21 The Dodd-Frank Act had also introduced a third measure, the push out rule intended to oblige to discontinue or segregate certain swap activities. This rule has been recently cancelled on pressure exercised by the financial industry.

22 The Act has crucially not adopted the recommendations on the overseas activities of large UK banks.

23 France and Germany have already introduced legislation on this matter. Proprietary trading and relations with hedge and private property funds must either be discontinued, or transferred to a ring-fenced entity inside the group. Market making is permitted in order to preserve the universal banking model.

24 We may envisage a legal breach in this attitude because the EU treaties oblige member countries, excluding the opt-out given to the UK and Denmark, to pursue active convergence policies and adopt the euro once having satisfied the criteria for admission.

25 However, the centralization of supervision on the ECB is limited to large banking groups, while national authorities remain in charge for smaller banks under a single supervisory handbook produced by the SSM.

26 The third aspect of the new regulatory balance, structural reforms also for Europe has been dealt previously in section 3.3.

27 The nine countries are Belgium, France, Germany, Italy, Luxembourg, the Netherlands, Spain, Sweden and the United Kingdom. The BCBS assessment does not consider compliance with liquidity and leverage ratios and with the treatment of SIBs since they are yet to come into force. Since work on technical standards on these matters is still going on, we will broadly follow the Committee on limiting the analysis to capital standards.

28 Pushed by the popular outrage produced by asymmetric structures of remuneration and by the CRD III, many EU countries had produced uncoordinated legislation. For a summary, see FSB (2014f).

29 Exceptions are bail-in powers that must apply from end 2015 at the latest.

30 We have seen in section 3.2 that the FSB proposal stresses the importance that enough debt instruments are included in the TLAC in order to ring fence enough resources for the bail-in that can only be triggered by resolution.

31 The examples are not well calibrated. Having chosen in the three exercises an average risk weight of 35 per cent, it is always the leverage ratio and not the risk-sensitive capital ratio that determines the level of MREL. The result is that the computed MREL is always lower than the 16 per cent minimum of the TLAC.

32 As in the TLAC, if the resolution authority consider that some liabilities that formally meet the conditions for inclusion in the MREL cannot contribute to loss absorption or recapitalisation, the MREL needs to be increased to account for their exclusion.

33 On 8 December 2014 the Board of Governors of the European stability mechanism adopted the ESM direct recapitalization instrument that permits the ESM to recapitalize a systemic and viable euro area financial institutions directly as a last resort measure, i.e. only after private investors have been bailed-in and the resolution fund has contributed. The resources devoted to this instrument are limited to €60 billion. http://esm.europa.eu/press/releases/esm-direct-bank-recapitalisation-instrument-adopted.htm.

References

BACKER, C. (2011) Private actors and public governance beyond the state: The multinational corporation, the financial stability board and the global governance order. Penn State Dickinson School of Law, *Scholarly Works*. Paper 8. http://elibrary.law.psu.edu/fac_works/8.

BASEL COMMITTEE ON BANKING SUPERVISION (BCBS) (2012a) A framework for dealing with domestic systemically important banks. October.

BASEL COMMITTEE ON BANKING SUPERVISION (BCBS) (2012b) Core principles for effective banking supervision. September.

BASEL COMMITTEE ON BANKING SUPERVISION (BCBS) (2013) The regulatory framework: balancing risk sensitivity, simplicity and comparability. Discussion Paper, July.

BASEL COMMITTEE ON BANKING SUPERVISION (BCBS) (2014a) Implementation of Basel standards. November.

BASEL COMMITTEE ON BANKING SUPERVISION (BCBS) (2014b) Basel capital framework national discretions. November.

BASEL COMMITTEE ON BANKING SUPERVISION (BCBS) (2014c) Reducing excessive variability in banks' regulatory capital ratios. November.

BASEL COMMITTEE ON BANKING SUPERVISION (BCBS) (2014d) Assessment of Basel II regulations – European Union. December.

BENGTSSON, E. (2011) Repoliticalization of accounting standard setting: The IASB, the EU and global financial crisis. *Critical Perspectives on Accounting*, 22, 567–580.

BRUMMER, C. (2010) Why soft law dominates international finance – not trade. *Journal of International Finance Law*, 13(3), 623–643.

COUNCIL OF THE EUROPEAN UNION (2014) Council adopts rules on bank recovery and resolution. 6 May.

DIRECTIVE 2014/59/EU (2014) Establishing a framework for recovery and resolution of credit institutions and investment firms. Available at http://eur-lex.europa.eu/legal-content/EN/TXT/PDF/?uri=CELEX:32014L0059&rid=1.

DRAGHI, M. (2008) How to restore financial stability. *Bundesbank Lecture Series*, September 16.

EICHENGREEN, B. (2010) International financial regulation after the crisis. *Daedalus*, Fall.

EUROPEAN BANKING AUTHORITY (EBA) (2014) Draft regulatory technical standards on criteria determining the minimum requirements for own funds and eligible liabilities under Directive 2014/59/EU. Consultation Paper, 28 November.

FINANCIAL STABILITY BOARD (FSB) (2009a) Principles for sound compensation practices. April.

FINANCIAL STABILITY BOARD (FSB) (2009b) Principles for sound compensation practices. Implementation standards. September.

FINANCIAL STABILITY BOARD (FSB) (2011) Key attributes of effective resolution regimes for financial institutions. October.

FINANCIAL STABILITY BOARD (FSB) (2014a) Financial reforms – Completing the job and looking ahead. letter to G20 Finance Ministers and Central Bank Governors. September 15.

FINANCIAL STABILITY BOARD (FSB) (2014b) Overview of progress in the implementation of the G20 recommendations for strengthening financial stability. November 14.

FINANCIAL STABILITY BOARD (FSB) (2014c) Cross-border recognition of resolution action. September 29.

FINANCIAL STABILITY BOARD (FSB) (2014d) Adequacy of loss-absorbing capacity of global systemically important banks in resolution. Consultative document, November 10.

FINANCIAL STABILITY BOARD (FSB) (2014e) Structural banking reforms. Cross-border consistencies and global financial stability implications. Report to the G20 leaders for the November 2014 summit, 27 October.

FINANCIAL STABILITY BOARD (FSB) (2014f) Implementing the FSB principles for sound compensation practices and their implementation standards. Third progress report, November.

FINANCIAL STABILITY BOARD (FSB) (2014g) Towards full implementation of the FSB key attributes of effective resolution regimes for financial institutions. November.

G20 (2008) Declaration following the Washington meeting. November 15.

G20 (2009) Enhancing sound regulation and strengthening transparency. Working group 1, Final report, March 25.

G20 (2014) Leaders' communiqué. Brisbane summit, 15–16 November.

GADINIS, S. (2013) The Financial Stability Board: The new politics of international financial regulation. *Texas International Law Journal*, 48(2), 157–176.

GEITHNER, T. (2009) Written testimony of the secretary of the treasury before the joint economic committee, financial regulatory reform. November 19.

GRIFFITH-JONES, S., HELLEINER, E. and WOODS, N. (eds) (2010) *The Financial Stability Board: An Effective Fourth Pillar of Global Economic Governance?*, Special Report, The Center for International Governance Innovation, Waterloo, Ontario, Canada.

HALDANE, A. (2011) Capital discipline. Speech given at the American Economic Association, Denver, Colorado, 9 January. www.bankofengland.co.uk/publications/Documents/speeches/2011/speech484.pdf.

HERRING, R. (2007) Conflicts between home and host country prudential supervisors. Wharton Financial Institution Center, Working Paper No. 07-33.

HM GOVERNMENT (2014) Review of the balance of competences between the United Kingdom and the European Union. The single market: Financial services and the free movement of capital. Available at https://gcn.civilservice.gov.uk/.

INDEPENDENT COMMISSION ON BANKING (ICB) (2011) Final Report. Recommendations. September, at http://bankingcommission.independent.gov.uk/.

INGVES, S. (2014) Implementing the regulatory reform agenda – the pitfall of myopia. 6 November, at www.bis.org/speeches/sp141118.htm.

INTERNATIONAL MONETARY FUND (IMF) (2012) The liberalization and management of capital flows: an institutional view. November. At www.imf.org/external/np/pp/eng/2012/111412.pdf.

INTERNATIONAL MONETARY FUND and WORLD BANK (IMF and WB) (2011) Review of the standard and codes initiative, www.imf.org/external/np/pp/eng/2011/021611.pdf.

INTERNATIONAL SWAPS AND DERIVATIVE ASSOCIATION (ISDA) (2014) ISDA 2014 resolution stay protocol. 4 November.

JORDAN, C. and MAJONI, G. (2002) Financial regulatory harmonization and the globalization of finance. The Worlds Bank, Policy Research Working Paper No. 2919, October.

KREGEL, J. (2009) Managing the impact of volatility in international capital markets in an uncertain world. April, Working Paper No. 558, Levy Economics Institute of Bard College.

LANNOO, K. (2014) The G20, five years on. CEPS Essay No. 9, March.

LE LESLÉ, V. and AVRAMOVA, S. (2012) Revisiting risk-weighted assets. Why do RWAs differ across countries and what can be done about it. IMF, WP/12/90, March.

MONTESI, G. (2014) Banche sotto stress. La Voce.info, at www.lavoce.info/wp-content/uploads/2014/11/Dossierstress1.pdf.

PERSAUD, A. (2010) The locus of financial regulation: Home versus host. *International Affairs*, 86(3), 637–646.

PISTOR, K. (2010) Host's dilemma: Rethinking EU banking regulation in the light of the global crisis. Columbia University Law School, Law and Economics Paper No. 378, June.

ROTTIER, S. and VÉRON, N. (2010) An assessment of G20's initial action items. Bruegel Policy Contribution, Issue 2010/08, September.

STEFFEN, S. (2014) Robustness, validity and significance of the ECB's Asset Quality Review and Strewss Test Exercise. European Parliament, Directorate General for Internal Policy – Economic Governance Support Unit, October.

TARULLO, D. (2013) International cooperation in financial regulation. Cornell International Law Journal Symposium: The Changing Politics of Central Banks, February 22. At www.federalreserve.gov/newsevents/speech/tarullo20130222a.htm.

TARULLO, D. (2014a) Rethinking the aims of prudential regulation. Remarks at the Federal Reserve Bank of Chicago Bank Structure Conference, May.

TARULLO, D. (2014b) Statement before the Commission on Banking, Housing and Urban Affairs. U.S. Senate, Washington, D.C., September 9.

TARULLO, D. (2014c) A tiered approach to regulation and supervision of community banks. Community Bankers Symposium, Chicago. At www.federalreserve.gov/newsevents/speech/tarullo20141107a.pdf.

TONVERONACHI, M. (2010) Empowering supervisors with more principles and discretion to implement them will not reduce the dangers of the prudential approach to financial regulation. *PSL Quarterly Review*, 63(255), 363–378.

UK PARLIAMENT (2013) Financial Services (Banking Reform) Act. At http://services.parliament.uk/bills/2013-14/financialservicesbankingreform.html

UNCTAD (2013) Capital account regulations and global governance: the need for policy space. Policy Brief, No. 28.

VALLASCAS, F. and HAGGENDORFF, J. (2013) The risk sensitivity of capital requirements: Evidence from an international sample of large banks. *Review of Finance*, January, 1–42.

VIÑALS, J. (2013) Creating a safer financial system: will the Volcker, Vickers , and Liikanen structural measures help?, IMF Staff Discussion Note, May.

WOUTERS, J., STERKX S. and CORTHAUT T. (2010) The international financial crisis, global financial governance and the European Union. Working Paper N. 52, Leuven Centre for Global Governance Studies.

Index